VASILII TREDIAKOVSKY

Studies of the Harriman Institute, Columbia University

VASILII TREDIAKOVSKY

The Fool of the 'New' Russian Literature

Irina Reyfman

STANFORD UNIVERSITY PRESS, *Stanford, California*

Stanford University Press
Stanford, California
© 1990 by the Board of Trustees of the
Leland Stanford Junior University
Printed in the United States of America

CIP data appear at the end of the book

Published with the assistance of a special grant from
the Stanford University Faculty Publication Fund to
help support nonfaculty work originating at Stanford.

To Simon

Acknowledgments

I wish to record my intellectual indebtedness to Iurii Mikhailovich Lotman, under whose guidance this project was conceived many years ago, and to whom I no doubt owe much of my identity as a scholar. I am also extremely grateful to William Mills Todd III, who generously offered his expert help and kind support during my years at Stanford University.

I acknowledge the generosity of The Council for Research in the Humanities at Columbia University, whose Summer Fellowships (1987 and 1988) expedited the completion of this project. I want to thank the Department of Slavic Languages at Columbia University for helping to finance the typesetting of the Russian text.

I am pleased to express my deep gratitude to Mark Altshuller, Robert Belknap, Gregory Freidin, Boris Gasparov, Monika Frenkel Greenleaf, Hugh McLean, Cathy Popkin, James L. Rice, and Ilya Serman for reading drafts of this book and providing me with their invaluable advice. I extend my thanks to my teachers, colleagues, students, and friends for their intellectual generosity and support.

I am indebted to Nancy Workman, who ably edited the manuscript, and I am grateful to Helen Tartar, Mary Pasti, and Julia Johnson Zafferano of Stanford University Press for their expert help in the final stages of the effort.

Finally, I want to thank my family, both near and far. I am especially grateful to my husband, Simon, for his unfailing support and encouragement throughout the project and his inestimable technical help. I thank my son Alexander for his help with translations, and Paul, for his patience.

I.R.

Contents

A Note on Transliteration

I have used the Library of Congress system of transliteration with the following exceptions: For surnames ending in *skii* and *oi* I use the *sky* and *oy* endings more traditional in English usage; for the surnames Herzen and Kuechelbecker I retain the original German spelling.

Variations in the spelling of the name Trediakovsky (spelled also Tred'iakovsky, Trediiakovsky, and Tret'iakovsky) are disregarded in translations but kept if quoted in the original. The same rule applies to the title *Tilemakhida*, which contemporaries also spelled variously as *Tilimakhida* and *Telimakhida*.

Vowels with umlauts in German quotations and proper names are rendered *ae*, *oe*, and *ue*.

VASILII TREDIAKOVSKY

Introduction: Myths and Literary History

Historians of literature face essentially the same task all historians do: the task of reconstructing the past from traces of past events contained in the present, that is, from the end products of past events and accounts of these events presented by contemporaries. In trying to deduce the past from these traces, historians cannot escape evaluating how adequately their sources reflect the reality they are attempting to reconstruct. Accounts of events tend to be less impartial than end products of the same events: They are by nature interpretations of the occurrences to which their authors were witnesses and therefore are apt to be reflective and judgmental. These accounts convey what their authors thought about themselves and about their epoch, which does not necessarily coincide with the opinions of other contemporaries, or with what later epochs think about them, or with the factual picture that can be reconstructed through the scholarly analysis of end products of the epoch or other accounts of the same events.

Some authorial reflections are unique; others echo majority opinions and set forth prevalent beliefs. It is possible, I think, to speak of a certain collective self-image of a particular epoch as it can be deduced from generally accepted opinions. At least as helpful in reconstructing an epoch's self-image are conscious deviations from common views, inasmuch as dissenters cannot avoid rehearsing widely held views in order to deny them. A self-image is certainly an abstraction, a mental construct formulated by a researcher dealing with a multitude of its manifestations. It is also a reality shared by the exponents of a particular self-image.

The existence of the self-image of a particular epoch presents researchers with the serious problem of the image's accuracy. We are forced to deal with a vicious circle: To construct a picture of the past, we inevitably rely upon contemporary testimonies about events. The consistency of these testimonies seems to ensure the accuracy of our perception. But the consistency of generally accepted opinions is precisely what lures us into mistaking false common beliefs for an accurate picture of the past. Some traps are obvious and therefore not dangerous: One would hardly fall victim to the common medieval Russian belief that all of Russia's neighbors were pagans (or Moslems, *busurmany*, which amounted to the same thing for the exponents of this view). Other traps are much less evident and can easily catch even a seasoned researcher.

Students of general opinions need to distinguish false communal memories from accurate accounts of events. One of the most common and least conscious properties of communal memories is selectivity: What an epoch chooses to remember and what it chooses to forget reflect its conceptions of itself. Of course, every memoirist has to select his or her material, but when a majority forget one and the same thing or remember and exaggerate another, we deal not with individual forgetfulness or personal decisions to falsify history but with a certain aspect of the epoch's self-image.

Another important signal of the possible inaccuracy of communal memories is the presence of motifs, patterns, and structures that cannot be found in raw historical material but are characteristic of the texts generated by what Ernst Cassirer calls the mythological mode of thought, such as myths, epics, and folktales. The story of George Washington and the cherry tree might very well be true: Children make mistakes, are caught, and learn their lesson. Some of them are even as truthful as little George. But consider an incident that, according to popular belief, happened to little Volodia Ul'ianov (Lenin).

Little Volodia was happily playing with his siblings and cousins when he accidentally bumped into a small table and knocked over a carafe. The carafe broke into pieces, and his aunt came to investigate the accident. She wanted to know who was at fault, but all the children denied their involvement. Little Volodia, the youngest, also said: "Not me." One night two months later Volodia's mother came to wish him good night and found him in tears. "What's wrong?" she asked and heard the terrible confession. The boy fell asleep only after his mother had promised to write his aunt, reveal his secret, and convey his apologies. That, the story concludes, was the last time Lenin ever lied.[1]

As soon as we compare the stories, we see an unmistakable pattern: A young boy with a great future displays extraordinary qualities—in this case, amazing, almost heroic honesty. We recognize the mythological nature of the stories and easily identify the myth: the myth of a hero. A hero is distinguished by exceptional qualities from early childhood. The young Hercules demonstrates amazing strength while still in his cradle, the precocious Till Eulenspiegel displays an astonishing propensity for obscene and indecent jokes at a very tender age, and the young Washington and Lenin show an honesty unusual for small boys.

Mythological motifs and patterns in communal views of past events allow the student of history to detect systematic unintentional distortions of factual reality by the exponents of these views. The study of these patterns is therefore extremely important and fruitful. However, they are frequently either considered trivial and unworthy of scholarly attention and weeded out from the historical picture of the past or are not recognized for what they are—a superimposition upon historical material by the "collective consciousness" (to use a parallel to the Jungian "collective unconscious"). In either instance the self-image of an epoch is ignored, and the important consequences of its existence both for contemporary events and for the formation of historical accounts of the epoch go unappreciated.

The impact of the epoch's self-image upon contemporary events is essentially the problem of feedback. Does this self-image influence the development of events and, if yes, in what way? In other words, was it important that Peter the Great's contemporaries perceived him as a mythological figure, either divine or satanic, and how did their perception affect the reception of his reforms, their effectiveness, and even their essence? Or how did the fact that participants in the French Revolution perceived it in mythological terms, as the beginning of a new historical era (the best evidence of which was the introduction of the new calendar), shape the development and the consequences of this social cataclysm?

Another problem concerns the influence of the epoch's self-image upon the perception of that epoch in the future, that is, how the image affects the selection of "facts" to remember and include in future historical accounts, as well as their interpretation and evaluation. We must ask, in other words, how historiography is shaped by the prevalent views of the participants in the historical events under consideration. Ultimately we need to consider what impact those collective views have on researchers' perceptions of their material: To what degree are researchers free from the commonly accepted picture of the past and able to evaluate this picture impartially? The self-image of the epoch is powerful in that it is usually not fully conscious and therefore is accepted uncritically by the people who generate it, as well as by future generations brought up in the same tradition. Thus, despite their efforts to evaluate sources, historians still might be affected by the self-image of the past transmitted by tradition.

Historians of literature face additional difficulties in that their task, as it is defined by many literary scholars, includes not only the description of past events but, in respect to literary works, their evaluation as well. As René Wellek states, "History cannot be divorced from criticism."[2] Although not every scholar, including myself, will subscribe to this requirement without reservations, the problem exists, and ignoring it is difficult. Historians of literature cannot escape addressing such questions as why certain works are popular and others are not, and why some of those popular (and even not so popular) works retain their aesthetic appeal through centuries, whereas others die almost immediately despite their contemporaries' vociferous praise. Why too are some works more influential than others, and why does their impact on the development of literature not always correspond to their alleged aesthetic value? Attempting to answer these questions forces scholars to confront the question of whether a literary work has an eternal aesthetic value or whether all evaluation has to be done, of necessity, in a historical context.

While I am not a hard-core relativist regarding questions of aesthetic value and do not endorse some of the populist implications of this school of thought, I appreciate the interest of Stanley Fish, Barbara Herrnstein Smith, and Jane Tompkins in what they call the institutionalization of literary value, and especially their probes into the ways the status of a work of art is established.[3] Indeed, taste, status, and aesthetic value seem to be largely subjective categories that the literary establishment tries to impose upon the general public. Questions remain, however: How does the literary establishment reach its verdict? What influences its decisions? What makes the general public accept (or, in some cases, reject) these decisions? How free is whoever decides the fate of a work in making decisions?

What I believe is worth exploring in this cluster of problems is the degree to which the subjective self-image of the epoch affects value judgments, both contemporary and retrospective. In literary history, the focus is on the self-perceptions of a literary milieu, that is, the prevalent reputations of writers, the agreed-upon evaluations of works, the commonly accepted picture of the literary past and present and so forth. The role of the subjective element needs to be examined.

The self-image manifests itself in two major forms: (1) in polemical exchanges, critical essays, historical surveys, and other formal reflections upon past and present literature that are made by the participants in the literary process and (2) in their less formal and sometimes even unformulated opinions of themselves, contemporaries, and literary predecessors. The first are conscious efforts to shape literary process. Historians of literature pay due attention to these texts, and their influence upon literature is recognized and studied. Informal opinions, the second type of manifestation, tend either to circulate as "common knowledge" or to take the form of such products of the collective consciousness as anecdotes, legends, and rumors. Historians of literature are tempted to view common knowledge (e.g., "Driven by a passion for education, Mikhailo Lomonosov came to Moscow on foot for schooling" or "The Germans in the Academy of Sciences interfered with Lomonosov's effort to promote native Russian science") as established facts (the more so in that such notions permeate the conventional critical genres) and include it in histories of literature without further critical evaluation. The anecdotes, legends, and rumors, on the contrary, are considered unreliable sources, peripheral to the mainstream literary process, and therefore are largely disregarded by serious historians of literature. What remains unnoticed in this approach is that common knowledge is frequently interdependent with anecdotes, legends, and rumors and therefore has to be considered among the phenomena of the collective consciousness.

The products of the collective consciousness deserve the close attention of historians of literature, inasmuch as, tacit and unconventional as they are, they have a powerful impact on the reception of literary works, on the way reputations are established, and consequently on the shaping of cultural memories, including the history of literature. Cultural memories, in turn, affect the transmission of ideas and influence the direction and pace of literary change.

The Russian literary situation of the eighteenth century and the first third of the nineteenth century allows literary historians a convenient look at the general mechanisms involved in creating the history of a literature. It allows them to assess the importance of different factors—the quality of a literary work, the circumstances of a writer's life, and the writer's aesthetic views, on the one hand, and the interference of the phenomena of the collective consciousness, on the other—in the formation of general opinions about literature and in the eventual creation of the history of a literature. Analyzing the ways in which accounts of the literary past are formed adds in turn to the comprehension of the literary process itself—to the understanding of the ways in which literary tradition is transmitted and continuity established, as well as to the better exposition of the factors involved in literary change.

The Russian literary situation is particularly useful for my purposes because memories of eighteenth-century literary life, brought to us by tradition and incorporated into histories of literature, contain obvious discrepancies with what we know to be established facts. The distortions in the accounts form a pattern that permits us to identify the mythological nature of these distortions and to recognize in them features of the creation myth. Given the particular circumstances of eighteenth-century cultural and literary life in Russia, accounts of mid-eighteenth-century Russian literature took the shape of the myth of the beginning of the "new" Russian literature, with Mikhailo Lomonosov cast in the role of culture hero and Vasilii Trediakovsky in the role of fool. The details of the myth and its contents (the distribution of roles, in the first place) were determined by the peculiarities of the literary life of the mid-eighteenth century, by the literary views of its participants, and by features of their personal and social lives. The myth was assimilated by subsequent generations of Russian writers and remained active until the middle of the nineteenth century. Vestiges of the myth can still be found in modern historical accounts of mid-eighteenth-century Russian literature.

The inaccurate accounts of the historical past that circulated in Russia in the late eighteenth and early nineteenth centuries mostly concerned the appraisal of the three major writers of the period: Vasilii Trediakovsky, Mikhailo Lomonosov, and Aleksandr Sumarokov. In Trediakovsky's case, the reality and the accounts of this reality are especially discrepant: A prominent and productive writer, he was practically excluded by critics and historians from the literary process of his time. Contrary to many documentary indications, his contemporaries and descendants presented him, not as a respectable poet and scholar, but as a miserable fool, an ignoramus, and the laughingstock of his colleagues and readers. Trediakovsky's reputation as a failed writer overshadowed his early fame, his significant success among contemporaries, and his contributions to poetry, versification, literary theory, criticism, linguistics, and the development of the Russian literary language. Moreover, Trediakovsky's contemporaries and literary descendants frequently reassigned his accomplishments, such as the introduction of syllabo-tonics or the development of Russian hexameter, to Lomonosov. As a result, Trediakovsky went down in history as a paragon of talentlessness, a barren pedant, the author of worthless poems written in ludicrous language and meter. His name became a swear word used to condemn literary rivals.

Lomonosov, on the contrary, was given the title of first and best Russian poet. He was credited with all the achievements of modern Russian literature: the reform of versification; the creation of the lyric, historical prose, and even dramaturgy; and the codification of the Russian literary language. In 1765, right after Lomonosov's death, Count Andrei Shuvalov, a minor poet and a patron of the arts, wrote about Lomonosov in the introduction to his "Ode sur la mort de Mr. Lomonosof": "It is true that before Mr. Lomonosov we had several rhymesters, such as Prince Kantemir, Trediakovsky, and others, but in comparison to him they were like troubadours to Malherbe."[4] Several years later, in 1774, the same enthusiastic attitude inspired Mikhail Murav'ev's "Eulogy to Mikhailo Vasil'evich Lomonosov." The author calls Lomonosov "the Russian Homer, the Russian Pindar, or, to say it better and more justly, the creator of the Russian Parnassus" and proclaims him "the most eloquent among mortals."[5] There were even favorable opinions about Lomonosov's excellence as a historical writer and playwright, although as a dilettante historian and the author of two tragedies written to order, he certainly did not deserve to be credited with priority or with eminence in these genres.[6] Nevertheless, in the epitaph on his tomb Lomonosov was called "teacher of eloquence, poetry, and the history of his fatherland. Originator of Russian meter, author of tragedies in his native language."[7] Similarly, Jacob von Staehlin, Lomonosov's colleague at the Academy and one of his first biographers, observed in his "Traits and Anecdotes for Lomonosov's Biography Taken from His Own Words" (1783): "Which tragedies he was the first to write in the Russian language and what he published about ancient Russian history, etc.—all of this can be seen in minute detail in his works, which he published consecutively, as well as in the protocols of the Academy Chancellery and Conference."[8] Ivan Elagin, in his *An Attempt at a Narration About Russia* (1789–93), compared Lomonosov the historian simultaneously to Livy, Tacitus, and Sallust—as well as to Thucydides.[9]

Even more important than the exaggerated praise for Lomonosov's tragedies and historical writings was the fact that the manifestations of admiration for him came from all literary groups, regardless of their programs. Thus, among Lomonosov's laudators quoted above, Shuvalov was an ardent proponent of Lomonosov's poetry who devotedly translated the poet's complete works into French. Murav'ev's poetic style, on the other hand, showed the strong influence of Sumarokov's poetic principles, which did not, however, interfere with Murav'ev's admiration for Lomonosov. Elagin was an even more devoted supporter of Sumarokov and a fierce literary enemy of Lomonosov, whom, in the 1750's, he vilified in many sarcastic parodies and epigrams. In extolling Lomonosov's abilities as a historical writer, Elagin, in his treatise on Russian history, did not refrain from sharp criticism of Lomonosov's poetry and the very historical works that he extolled. However, by the turn of the century literary convention demanded that Lomonosov be praised, and Elagin could not help but do so. Similarly, Nikolai Karamzin, who did not approve of Lomonosov's linguistic position, felt obliged to call him "the father of Russian eloquence and inspired poetry."[10]

Sumarokov, who in the 1750's and 1760's had enjoyed the role of recognized head of the leading poetic school, began in the 1770's to be frequently assigned the place of Lomonosov's disciple. He tried in vain to refute these assertions:

I am already tired of hearing the usual discussion of Mr. Lomonosov and me. . . . Finally, in Mr. Lomonosov's epitaph it is indicated that he was a teacher of poetry and eloquence: but he did not teach anybody and did not succeed in teaching anybody. . . . Posterity can or must think that I too, according to this epitaph, was his disciple, yet I was already writing poetry before the public had even heard the name of Mr. Lomonosov. Indeed, he began to write in Germany, whereas I began in Russia, without having received any instruction from him or even having heard of him. Mr. Lomonosov was a few years older than I; but it does not follow from this that I am his disciple, of which fact, without diminishing in the least the honor of this poet, I notify posterity.[11]

We know that Sumarokov was right, that his first poetic experiments preceded Lomonosov's entrance into the Russian literary arena. But public opinion about the secondary nature of his poetry was so strong that eventually, for his insistence that he was an original poet, independent of Lomonosov, Sumarokov received a reputation as an ungrateful "usurper" of Lomonosov's fame, particularly Lomonosov's fame for introducing syllabo-tonics—an honor that Sumarokov never claimed. Thus, Staehlin wrote in "Traits and Anecdotes for Lomonosov's Biography": "At that time [in 1739, when Lomonosov sent his 'Ode on the Taking of Khotin' to the Academy of Sciences] Sumarokov had not yet even thought of writing poetry, much less in this meter; nevertheless later, in the reign of Empress Elizabeth, he wanted to arrogate to himself the name and honor of [being] the first author to introduce this meter into Russian versification."[12]

Sumarokov was not alone in his protests against what he thought was a distorted picture of the literary past. The journalist and publisher Nikolai Novikov, in his journal *Drone* (1769–70) and in his *A Historical Dictionary of Russian Writers* (1772), more than once objected to the contemptuous attitude toward Trediakovsky and his works, as well as to the idea of Sumarokov's inferiority vis-à-vis Lomonosov. The latter issue found its way into Fedor Emin's magazine *The Infernal Mail* (1769), which featured "correspondence" between demons on topical issues of the time. In one letter the One-Eyed Demon related to his friend the Lame Demon the outcome of a literary argument he had witnessed. One participant in the argument, M., a connoisseur of literature, "mathematically" proved the superiority of Mr. S. (Sumarokov) over Mr. L. (Lomonosov). The audience, however, reacted unexpectedly: "What came, friend demon, of M.'s words?—that everybody said: Viva the Lyricist! He is the best poet in the whole world, and S. is a man of mediocre rank [*chelovek posredstvennogo zvaniia*]."[13]

The above example does not simply suggest the existence of different points of view on this or that literary matter. It demonstrates to what extent this complex of established ideas was stable, closed to reason, and difficult to alter. This extraordinary stability, felt even by contemporaries, attests that the stereotypic view of the literary figures under consideration was not merely a result of obliviousness or ignorance: In that case it could easily have been corrected. A distortion of the facts that shows both consistency and a resistance to logical argument conceals a different type of reasoning. Certain features of this inaccurate account of the literary past testify to the mythological character of the reasoning that governed its emergence, development, and functioning. Memories of the literary past indeed formed a myth—the myth of the beginning of the "new" Russian literature.

A creation myth tells about the forging of primordial chaos into order and about the first arrangements and regulations given to the inhabitants of the new world. Here we are dealing with the myth of the creation of a "new" Russian literature. The main character in a creation myth, a demiurge or a culture hero, gives things their proper disposition and sets rules for future generations.[14] The hero frequently leaves his home territory to fetch a boon or gift—fire, knowledge, or any other material or spiritual value from which his community would benefit and which signifies the beginning of a new era for it. The hero is thus in a sense the ancestor of the present community.

Ancient notions about poets and their functions in the community that survive in the modern cultural consciousness facilitate and promote the investment of a poet with heroic qualities and with an ancestral role. In primitive societies, where poetry is intermixed with magic, a poet combines the functions of a singer with those of a shaman and a prophet. Like a culture hero and a shaman, an ancient poet, at some point in life, is called from oblivion and passivity and endowed with powers to influence and lead the community. In modern literatures the vestiges of the poet's ancient faculties survive as a belief in the poet's prophetic gift and ability to create with words.[15]

In the myth under consideration the role of culture hero was given to Lomonosov. He was proclaimed the father of Russian literature, who, by introducing European literary ideas into Russia, started an epoch and established models for future generations of Russian writers to follow. In the eyes of Aleksandr Radishchev, Aleksandr Pushkin, Vissarion Belinsky, and many others he was "the cultivator of the Russian word," "the father of Russian poetry," and the "first" Russian poet.[16]

The creation myth may have another important character: the antihero, who represents defeated chaos and sets antirules in the newly created world. This character has a close association with the culture hero and to a great extent constitutes the embodiment of latent unheroic traits in the hero's nature. Indeed, the mythological culture hero often has a double nature:

heroic and foolish. Being capable of guile and comical actions as well as great deeds identifies the hero as a trickster: "They [tricksters] are beings of the beginning, working in some complex relationship with the High God; transformers, helping to bring the present human world into being; performers of heroic acts on behalf of men, yet in their original form, or in some later form, foolish, obscene, laughable, yet indomitable."[17] The trickster's unseemly behavior constantly recalls the chthonic side of this character's nature, and his intermediary position between cosmos and chaos.

Sometimes, however, the comical side of the culture hero's nature is represented by a different personage—a foolish twin or a dumb demonic creature.[18] In this case creative functions are distributed between them: The hero creates all the good and useful things, the twin, all the bad and harmful things, and the relations between them are conflictual. In the myth of the "new" Russian literature the role of antihero was given to Trediakovsky.

It is extremely difficult to deal with the foolish counterpart of the culture hero. The comical nature of this character eludes unambiguous definition: "All tricksters are foolers and fools, but their foolishness varies; sometimes it is destructive, sometimes creative, sometimes scatological, sometimes satiric, sometimes playful."[19] Therefore, the boundaries between such antiheroic figures as the trickster, the fool, and the scapegoat are unclear, nor can these figures always be classified unequivocally. The three to a certain extent constitute one personage (and therefore share and exchange characteristics), since they all represent the opposite of the hero, the antihero. In different circumstances different features become dominant. As Dorothy Norman puts it: "At times, the 'fool' as a symbol of innocence can have great power. At others, in being unaware of, or miscalculating, what is required of him, he can be a negative character, harmful both to himself and the social order." The author hints at the explanation for this phenomenon: "When the jester is free to attack the hero, this may, of course, suggest that a given society is stable, and that those in power feel secure."[20] Extrapolating, one can say that when a society does not feel secure and is not sure of its own norms and regulations (as was indeed the case with eighteenth-century Russian literature), it can regard the culture hero's enemies as villains and attempt to crush them to protect the unstable order.

In different cultural traditions the figure of the fool splits into various personages, producing such seemingly unrelated characters as saintly fools, satanic figures of Manichaean or Christian extraction, jesters or clowns, folktale fools, comical folk-theater personages (Pierrot, Hans Wurst, Harlequin, pedants, et al.), and the modern literary antiheroes. Their mythological nature is not always obvious, but they retain their primary characteristics as mythological antiheroes: their ambivalent creativity, their affinity to chaos and death, and their close association with the realm of laughter. I will attempt to demonstrate that Trediakovsky's comical image, as it emerged in the literary polemics of the mid-eighteenth century and developed in the literary consciousness of the late eighteenth and the first half of the nineteenth centuries, was shaped by the needs of the myth of the beginning of the "new" Russian literature and that this image was indeed endowed with the characteristics of a mythological fool, in accordance with both ancient and more recent traditions.

What were the circumstances that brought about this distortion of the historical picture? Two kinds of phenomena contributed to the formation of the myth: the mythogenic spirit of the epoch in general and the peculiarities of the literary life of that time. The sense of beginnings, of a new era, permeated all levels of eighteenth-century Russian culture, especially literature. This mythogenic spirit, which met with the principles of normative aesthetics characteristic of the literary consciousness of that time, and with the peculiar forms of literary polemics that these aesthetics generated, was responsible for the rise of the myth about the beginning of the "new" Russian literature.

In surveys of Russian literature, the literature that emerged in the early eighteenth century is called "modern." In Russian the term used is "new," *novaia russkaia literatura*. Unlike the word *modern*, *new*, *novyi*, connotes renovation, renewal, the idea that the new is different in quality from the old. *Modern* defines a phenomenon in time, whereas *new* has to do with its changed essence. In other words, *new* suggests that a mythological spirit of rebirth permeates the "new" literature.

This linguistic fact might, at least to a certain degree, reflect the way Russians view historical change. Indeed, Russians have had a tendency to comprehend cultural and political changes, especially those on a large scale, in eschatological terms. Russian accounts of their conversion to Christianity, the schism of the Russian Church, and Peter the Great's reforms, for example, are couched in terms of the total destruction of the existing social and cultural order brought about by the struggle between the "old" and the "new." As Iurii Lotman and Boris Uspensky state: "One of the most stable oppositions that organized Russian culture for the span between the Christianization of Russ and Peter I's reforms was the opposition 'oldness/novelty' [*starina/novizna*]." Similarly, Nikolai Berdiaev in his *Russian Idea* (1946) stresses the "catastrophic" development of Russian history.[21] Depending on the ideological position of the exponent, this attitude toward change could lead either to the rejection of the new situation and the anticipation of the Apocalypse (as was, for example, the case with the Old Believers and with the opponents of Peter's reforms) or to an enthusiastic acceptance of the new and to an involvement in the construction of the resulting "new" world.[22]

Russia's break with the Middle Ages, accelerated by Peter's reforms, was one of those events that had for Russians a clear eschatological significance. I do not plan to discuss here either the actual impact of the Petrine reforms on Russia's cultural development or the question of when and in what manner— gradually or abruptly—the so-called westernization of Russia occurred.[23] I am interested instead in how the reforms were perceived by contemporary Russians and their immediate descendants and, even more specifically, by supporters of the change. Peter's supporters rejected their own past, seeing it not as a different type of culture but, in J. G. Garrard's words, as "a cultural wasteland." They saw the essence of the Petrine reforms as the replacement of the chaos of preceding times with the well-proportioned edifice of true culture. This notion of a complete break with the past and of the entrance into a totally new stage of historical development acquired in the cultural consciousness of the epoch the distinct features of a creation myth, with Peter the Great in the role of the father, creator of the new Russia.[24]

The mythological spirit of the time manifested itself in contemporary appraisals of Peter the Great. In his "Oration on Peter the Great's Burial," Feofan Prokopovich, Archbishop of Novgorod and an ardent supporter of the reforms, claimed that Peter "resurrected Russia," or even "gave birth to her." In Feofan's words, Peter was Russia's "father," her creator: "As he has made his Russia, so shall she remain." Trediakovsky, in his "Elegy on Peter the Great's Death" (1725; revised in his *Compositions and Translations in Verse and Prose*, 1752), called Peter "the new creator of his state." Antiokh Kantemir, the first Russian satirist and an admirer of Peter, expressed the spirit of the epoch in the following lines:

> Мудры не спускает с рук указы Петровы,
> Коими стали мы вдруг народ уже новый.

The wise do not let go from their hands Peter's decrees, which have suddenly transformed us into a new nation.

Lomonosov, in his ode "On the Name Day of Grand Duke Petr Fedorovich" (1743), expresses the idea of Peter's divine nature even more straightforwardly: "Russia, he was your God, your God."[25]

This notion was passed down to subsequent generations. Aleksandr Radishchev presented Peter as the Maker who "was the first to give impetus to this vast mass [i.e., Russia], which, like the primordial element, was motionless." Karamzin compared Peter to "a radiant god of light" who "appeared at humanity's horizon and illuminated the deep darkness around himself." The image was canonized in Pushkin's poem *Poltava* (1829), in which Peter is given certain attributes of Zeus, the god of thunder:

> Из шатра,
> Толпой любимцев окруженный
> Выходит Петр. Его глаза
> Сияют. Лик его ужасен.
> Движенья быстры. Он прекрасен.
> Он весь, как Божия гроза.[26]

From the tent, surrounded by a crowd of his favorites, Peter comes. His eyes shine. His face is terrible. His movements are swift. He is beautiful. He is like a divine thunderstorm.

Literary figures of the first post-Petrine generation absorbed the mythological spirit of Peter's reforms. They felt a responsibility to live up to Peter's colossal plans and to create a new literature worthy of the new and magnificent Russia.[27] This intention is evident in Trediakovsky's poem "Epistle from Russian Poetry to Apollo" (1735), in which he announces the birth of Russian literature and invites Apollo to come to Russia:

> Девяти парнасских сестр, купно Геликона,
> О начальник Аполлин, и пермесска звона!
>
> . . .
>
> Нову вещь тебе хочу сею объявити,
> И с Парнаса тя сюда самого просити.[28]

O Apollo, head of the nine Parnassian sisters, and likewise of Helicon, and of the Permessian sound! . . . With this I want to announce to you a new phenomenon, and ask you to come here yourself from Parnassus.

The same spirit guided the writer in his translation, in 1730, of Paul Tallemant's novel *Voyage à l'île d'Amour* (1663). In the introduction he presented the book as "new" to Russian society (*novaia Rossiiskomu svetu*). In his speech to the Russian Assembly about the Russian language (1735), he repeatedly stressed the fact that Russian was entering a new stage of its development and that the primary duty of writers and translators was to form and "purify" the new language according to the example of modern European languages such as Italian and French.[29] He called his treatise on versification *A New and Brief Method for Composing Russian Verse* (1735), implying that the treatise was to open a new era in Russian poetry.

This same concept, that Russian literature was beginning, can be traced in Lomonosov's works. He wrote in his "Letter on the Rules of Russian Versification" (1739): "Our poetry is just beginning." Similarly, he concluded his "Preface on the Usefulness of Church Books in the Russian Tongue" (1758?) with a passage about "Great Moscow," which was "encouraged by the sounds of a new Parnassus." Lomonosov's belief in his own leading role in this process is evident in his report on the scientific and literary works he wrote for the Academy of Sciences in 1764: "While I was still in Germany, I sent to Russia rules of versification according to which even now all Russian poets act with good results, and Russian poetry entered a good state."[30]

Sumarokov's "Epistle on Poetry" and "Epistle on the Russian Language" (both 1747) were inspired by the same desire to provide proper poetic rules to the newly emerging Russian literature. In the essay "To Inane Rhymesters" (1759) Sumarokov characterizes his own pioneering efforts in the following terms:

We did not have poets yet, and there was nobody from whom one could learn. I went as if without a guide through a thick forest that concealed from my eyes the dwelling of the Muses, and although much indebted to Racine, I caught sight of him only when I had come out of this forest, and when Mount Parnassus had already appeared before my eyes. But Racine was a Frenchman and could not give me instruction in the Russian language. For the Russian language and purity of style, in either poetry or prose, I am not indebted to anybody except myself.

In addition, Sumarokov viewed himself as the father of Russian theater: "I introduced Racine's theater to you, Russians," he wrote in 1762 in the elegy "To Mr. Dmitrevsky upon the Death of Mr. Volkov."[31]

This strong belief in the exemplary value of their own works, shared by the writers of the mid-eighteenth century and their heirs, was a manifestation of the general mythological spirit of the epoch. It was a crucial precondition to the formation of the myth of the beginning of the "new" Russian literature, since it shaped the writers' view of themselves and their literary rivals. The task of creating the "new" Russian literature burdened eighteenth-century Russian authors with an enormous responsibility. They believed everything they created had the status of a model and thus would determine the future of Russian literature. Their rivals, on the contrary, interfered with the creation of prototypes and produced bad examples to corrupt and spoil the emerging literature. The normative aesthetic mentality, with its firm belief in the existence of only one possible artistic decision (one's own), characteristic of mid-eighteenth-century Russian literature, strongly contributed to the sense of literary self-righteousness.

The exciting feeling of novelty and one's ability—and responsibility—to give shape to Russian literature was not confined to the first post-Petrine generation of writers. It survived for at least another hundred years. The young Karamzin still felt that he was molding the new Russian literature when, in 1787, in his poem "Poetry," he again announced the birth of Russian literature:

> О россы! век грядет, в который и у вас
> Поэзия начнет сиять, как солнце в полдень.[32]

> O Russians! the time is coming when in your country too poetry will shine like the sun at noon.

Apparently Karamzin's effort did not satisfy his literary descendants, because half a century later the future Decembrist Aleksandr Bestuzhev opened his programmatic essay "A View on Russian Literature in the Course of 1824 and the Beginning of 1825" with a paradox: "We have criticism but no literature." In 1828 Nikolai Nadezhdin, beginning his career as a critic, proclaimed the helpless state of contemporary Russian literature. "Woe, woe is our poor literature," he wrote in his very first essay, "Literary Apprehensions for the Future Year," and called it a "barren wasteland." The following year yet another young critic, the Slavophile-to-be Ivan Kireevsky, concluded his essay "A Survey of Russian Literature for the Year 1829" with a bitter passage:

> But if we examine our literature in comparison with the literatures of other countries, if an enlightened European, upon unfolding before us all the mental treasures of his country, asks us, "Where is your literature? of what works can you be proud before Europe?" what will we answer him? . . .
> Let us be impartial and admit that we still do not have the full reflection of our people's mental life, that we still do not have a literature.

Two years later still, Vissarion Belinsky opened his career with the same declaration: "What are the reasons for such emptiness in our literature? Or *do we in fact have no literature*? . . . *Yes—we have no literature.*"[33]

This lasting sense of beginnings, characteristic of the first 100 years of modern Russian literary development, supported the myth of the "new" Russian literature and ensured its survival. It preserved the myth's relevance in changing literary contexts and made it useful in polemical conflicts up to the mid-nineteenth century. Different—and often opposing—literary groups raised the name of Lomonosov like a banner in their struggle with their rivals. The fact that he was their alleged literary forebear served as evidence of the validity of their artistic principles. Trediakovsky, on the contrary, was a bogey to scare the public away from unconventional artistic decisions. His name was used to tease and enrage literary enemies. Opponents were condemned as Trediakovsky's progeny: He was proclaimed their father or, more frequently, grandfather or uncle.

History related in terms of kinship is a myth: "Abraham begat Isaac; and Isaac begat Jacob; and Jacob begat Judas and his brethren." Connections to ancestors determine the present state of a community. A good, righteous forebear ensures a community's prosperity; an evil and stupid one explains its failures. A connection with one's grandfather rather than one's father may suggest an association with primeval chaos and destructive chthonic forces. An indirect ancestor, an uncle, say, may represent the mythological father's double, a pseudofather, a substitute. In folk epics, a young fatherless hero is frequently brought up by his uncle, who, in some instances, turns out to be a wrecker, the hero's secret enemy and rival.[34] In the Russian tradition, the uncle's secondary, substitutionary nature is vividly reflected in the fact that the word *diad'ka* (a diminutive of *diadia*, "uncle," with a suffix that gives the word a shade of disrespect) was frequently used for substitute figures, such as a bridegroom's surrogate father at weddings, a servant who looked after a young gentleman and often was his first tutor, or an older soldier who helped to train a young draftee. Radischev, who introduced the name *diad'ka* for Trediakovsky, was fully aware of this tradition and exploited it to stress Trediakovsky's role as an indirect ancestor, a surrogate father, of Russian literature. If Lomonosov was the real father of the "new" Russian literature, Trediakovsky was its *diad'ka*. This kinship compromised Trediakovsky's alleged followers and presented their path in literature as a back road leading nowhere and harmful to Russian literature.

In the late eighteenth and early nineteenth centuries, the myth of the "new" Russian literature was a prevalent picture of the past, but this picture was by no means absolutely dominant.

Along with rapturous praises to Lomonosov we find critical remarks about him and his artistic principles or particular works. Trediakovsky drew not only derision and scorn but also pity, recognition of his contributions, and, in rare cases, even admiration. These discrepancies can be explained to some extent by the fact that opinions shift and frequently do not entail total commitment on the part of their exponents. However, deviations from the myth did not result solely from human inconsistency; they were meaningful in more than one way. A shade of ambivalence in mythological personages is necessary for their survival in cultural memory. Recollections of the foolish side of Lomonosov's image as the father of Russian literature, as well as of the heroic side of Trediakovsky's image as a fool, preserved the creative powers inherent in the myth and thus perpetuated the mythological picture of the literary past in the consciousness of their literary descendants. At the same time, some deviations from the myth certainly represented conscious attempts at its deconstruction, which led to the challenging of dominant artistic principles, to the introduction of once-forbidden innovations, and, eventually, to the revision of the mythological picture of the past.

The story of the injustice done to Trediakovsky can help to answer some of the questions proposed in the opening pages of this chapter. It seems that the self-image of an epoch can indeed influence the development of contemporary events, as well as affect the future. The myth of the beginning of the "new" Russian literature clearly had an impact upon its development. This myth determined the dominance of Lomonosov's artistic principles and doomed Trediakovsky's quest for diverse poetic forms to long-term failure: The forms he introduced would remain at the periphery of literary tradition. More specifically, the myth gave Russian poetry such features as the predominance of iambs, particularly iambic tetrameter; the overwhelming prevalence of rhyme; and the relatively late introduction and restricted usage of tonic meters. As far as poetic style goes, the myth probably promoted the preference for metaphors, favored by Lomonosov as the chief means of achieving poetic effect, as opposed to Trediakovsky's stylistic ornateness.

The myth certainly was not neutral in its evaluation of the artistic merit of its main characters' works. It gave a clear advantage to Lomonosov, whereas Trediakovsky had little hope of a sympathetic or even unprejudiced evaluation of his legacy. Even more important, the myth alienated Trediakovsky's poetic principles, made them aesthetically foreign to the Russian reader brought up on the iambic tetrameter, stylistic moderation, carefully balanced syntax, and metaphoricalness bequeathed to Russian literature by Lomonosov. Trediakovsky's attempts to create a specific language of literature by introducing contrasting stylistic elements and syntactical inversions, as well as his passion for experimental forms and meters, lay outside the Lomonosovian tradition. The myth has made it virtually impossible for later generations of Russian readers to take pleasure in reading Trediakovsky or even to analyze his works in an impartial scholarly way.

Finally, it seems evident that the self-image of the mid-eighteenth century helped shape historical accounts of this epoch. The myth determined to a large extent the choice of facts to include in histories of eighteenth-century Russian literature. It modified and sometimes significantly distorted contemporary reports of events, as well as their interpretation by subsequent generations. Vestiges of the myth are still present in scholarship today.

The myth of the "new" Russian literature serves as a reminder that the sources traditionally considered reliable by historiographers, because they are genuine and because the opinions they express were accepted by the majority of their contemporaries, might not in fact be impartial and therefore are not always trustworthy. These sources might have been affected by the need of the collective consciousness of the epoch to make sense of seemingly haphazard historical events by organizing them in familiar patterns, preserved since prehistoric times in the cultural memory of humankind. An analysis of the myth of the "new" Russian literature exposes the ancient mythogenic forces that are still at work today.

Chapter 1

Vasilii Trediakovsky:
Man and Myth

Trediakovsky's reputation, ruined in the mid-eighteenth century in the heated polemics with his literary rivals, seems to have been improving ever since. Nikolai Novikov, a journalist, publisher, and philanthropist, was the first to undertake, in the 1770's, the thankless task of the poet's rehabilitation. His attempts were continued in the early 1800's by Radishchev and in the 1830's by Pushkin. Russian literary scholars of the nineteenth century treated Trediakovsky fairly in the main, and after the extensive twentieth-century studies of the eighteenth century in general and of Trediakovsky's works in particular one would expect that the poet's reputation as an ungifted versifier and ridiculous pedant would have disappeared.[1] This is not the case, however, and one continues to encounter, in articles, dissertations, and textbooks, characterizations of Trediakovsky's theories as "scholastic" and "eclectic," of his style as "somewhat barbaric" (*dikovatyi*), of his stylistic ideas as "perverse," of his poetry as grotesque, tasteless, and clumsy. Dmitrij Čiževskij, for example, finds "the elegance of a dancing hippopotamus" in Trediakovsky's early poetry. In a recent article even Trediakovsky's "type of personality" (*sklad lichnosti*) is called "somewhat barbaric."[2] Those authors who try to avoid disparaging Trediakovsky still seem to experience certain difficulties in evaluating his works and assigning him a place in the history of Russian literature. They face annoying questions: How did it happen that despite his obvious services to Russian literature, Trediakovsky was scorned and rejected by his contemporaries and literary descendants? How could a distinguished writer and scholar gain a reputation as the most ungifted and wretched poet of all time? Why has this reputation endured for two centuries and withstood the scrutiny of intensive scholarly investigation? Was there something in his life or works that destined him to become a model failure for generations to come?

Vasilii Kirillovich Trediakovsky, the oldest of the three founders of the "new" Russian literature, was born in 1703 in the southern city of Astrakhan, on the Volga River Delta near the Caspian Sea. He was the son of a poor provincial priest. His education, curiously enough, commenced in a school run by Italian Capuchins, who in the early eighteenth century had established a Catholic mission in Astrakhan. To this school Trediakovsky was indebted for the basics of Greek, Latin, and Italian, as well as for his first exposure to Western culture. In 1723, having completed his education at the school, he left Astrakhan for Moscow. The circumstances of his departure remain unclear. Trediakovsky himself cited his "desire for education" (*okhota k ucheniiu*) as a driving force behind his flight. In Moscow he entered the Slavo-Greco-Latin Academy, recently converted by Peter the Great into an institution of higher education. After two years at the Academy, Trediakovsky fled again, this time to Europe, to continue his education. In the beginning of 1726 he arrived at The Hague penniless, spent about two years there studying French, and then proceeded on foot to Paris, where he remained until 1730, attending classes in theology, mathematics, philosophy, history, and philology at the University of Paris.[3]

The years spent abroad were crucial in the formation of Trediakovsky as a philologist and as a writer. He was able to obtain firsthand knowledge of the French literary life of the late 1720's and, moreover, to partake in it. He wrote French poetry in the libertine tradition characteristic of the Regency period, poetry sophisticated enough to attract the attention, some 200 years later, of the Symbolist Mikhail Kuzmin, who translated Tredia-

Vasilii Trediakovsky. Engraving by A. Kolpashnikov, included in the 1775 edition of *Deidamia*. The inscription quotes an anonymous laudatory poem to Trediakovsky (1776); for the text and translation see pp. 92–93. (Trediakovsky, *Izbrannye proizvedeniia*, between pp. 320 and 321) kovsky's French poems (as well as one poem in Latin) into Russian in 1932. Trediakovsky's interest during the early years of his career in the *vers de société* and the theme of love (which was still a novelty in early eighteenth-century Russia), his detailed knowledge of European literary life, as well as his lifelong devotion to the ideas of "enlightened despotism," can be traced to his years in The Hague and Paris. He was also indebted to the French literary milieu for many of his linguistic views—first of all, for his interest, in the 1730's and 1740's, in the idea of usage as the main criterion of language standards.[4]

In 1730 Trediakovsky returned via Germany to Russia. For the next fifteen years he was certainly a leading figure in Russian literary and scholarly circles. He worked hard as a writer, translator, and linguist, opening his career in 1730 with the publication of a translation of Paul Tallemant's allegorical novel *Voyage à l'île d'Amour*. In his introduction to the book he set forth his linguistic views; in the appendix to the translation he published his own original poems in Russian, French, and Latin. Despite displeasure with its frivolous contents on the part of the conservative public and some church officials, the book was an enormous success in educated Russian circles and was regarded as an important step toward the enlightenment of Russians. Johann Daniel Schumacher, at that time the librarian and from 1737 the all-powerful chancellor of the Academy of Sciences in Saint Petersburg, wrote to him on February 1, 1731: "I rejoice at the good success that your book has had among educated people, not only because of my love for you but also for our sake. Rulers, knowing well that once poetry and music begin to soften the mores of a nation, however barbaric the nation may be, will in the end benefit."[5]

After Tallemant's novel, Trediakovsky planned to translate either Molière's *Le bourgeois gentilhomme* (1670) or *Le voyage de Cyrus* (1727) by André Michel de Ramsay, but the former, in his words, "does not flow well in our language" and the latter did not satisfy the taste of his patron, Prince Aleksandr Kurakin.[6] Trediakovsky translated an excerpt from *The Spectator* but did not publish it.

In 1732 the Academy of Sciences contracted with Trediakovsky to edit the translation of *Mémoires d'artillerie* by Surrirey de

Saint-Remy, thus commencing Trediakovsky's 25 years of affiliation with the Academy. This affiliation became official in 1733,
when he became acting secretary of the Academy, with a salary
of 360 rubles a year. His duties, as they were described in the
contract, included the following: "(2) To perfect the Russian language, in accordance with my modest abilities, in prose, as well
as in verse. . . . (4) To finish the Russian grammar that I have
begun and to work with others on a Russian dictionary. (5) To
translate from French and Latin into Russian all that is given to
me."[7] In other words, Trediakovsky was to perform duties as a
linguist, poet, and translator, and accordingly in the coming
years he wrote official odes and other poetry to order, translated
German, French, and Italian poetry and prose, and regularly rendered into Russian the plays that, in the 1730's, were performed
by Italian troupes at Empress Anna's court in Saint Petersburg.
Later, in 1743, Trediakovsky called the performance of these duties "gross [*valovaia*] and very difficult work."[8]

Trediakovsky combined his labors as an Academy translator
and an official poet with work on literary theory, in particular on
the principles of Russian versification. He published the results,
A New and Brief Method for Composing Russian Verse, in 1735. This
book initiated a sweeping reform of Russian versification and
became Trediakovsky's most influential work in the field of literary theory. The writer aspired to fulfill his obligation to beautify
and "perfect" the Russian language as well. In 1735 the Russian
Assembly was established at the Academy of Sciences, apparently by Trediakovsky's efforts. Trediakovsky envisioned it as
an imitation of the Académie française. At the opening meeting,
Trediakovsky delivered his "Speech to the Russian Assembly,"
in which he expounded his linguistic views and proposed mea-
sures to ensure the flourishing of the Russian language.

In 1736 Trediakovsky's possessions were destroyed in a fire,
the first calamity of this sort that fate had in store for him. Unable to pay his creditors, Trediakovsky left Saint Petersburg in
1738 and spent a year in the provinces. While in retreat, he commenced the translation of the first volumes of Charles Rollin's
histories—the work he would continue until his death.[9]

In February 1740 Trediakovsky lived through a bitter experience that became one of the best remembered episodes of his

life: He was assaulted by Cabinet Minister Artemii Volynsky.
The conflict occurred in connection with the wedding of jesters
organized for Empress Anna's amusement in early 1740. Volynsky, who was responsible for the empress's entertainment, sum-
moned Trediakovsky and commanded him to write a poem for
this occasion. Following a disagreement, Volynsky ordered that
the poet be severely beaten and himself joined in the beatings.
Exactly what provoked the minister's anger is not quite clear. It
could have been a poem that Trediakovsky allegedly had written
about him or the poet's association with Prince Aleksandr Kurakin, Volynsky's enemy. At any rate, the minister's ire was so severe that Trediakovsky was beaten again and again, jailed in the
guardhouse (where the notorious poem "The Salutation Said
During the Jesters' Wedding" was finally written), and sent
home in such poor health that, prepared to die, he bequeathed
his books to the Academy library and his belongings to his con-
fessor. Trediakovsky survived and eventually even received
monetary compensation for his sufferings, but not until Volynsky himself had fallen victim to political intrigues and had been
arrested and executed.[10]

In 1742 Trediakovsky married his second wife, Mar'ia Sibi-
leva. (His first wife, Fedos'ia Fadeeva, whom Trediakovsky abandoned when he fled Astrakhan, died in 1728 of cholera.) They
had one son, Lev. The marriage made Trediakovsky's financial
circumstances, already overburdened by his obligations to support his sister and nephew in Astrakhan, even more difficult.
Trediakovsky's career ambitions thus were nourished not only
by the desire for recognition but also by the persistent poverty in
which his family lived.

One did not get a promotion easily in the Saint Petersburg
Academy of Sciences at that time: The Academy was bureaucratic, inert, and deeply troubled by an internal lack of order. In
addition, the Academy Conference was overwhelmingly German and therefore apparently not zealous in promoting Russian
scholars. Thus it is not surprising that Trediakovsky took special
pride in the fact that in 1745, after much trouble and many peti-
tions, he became the first Russian to be appointed a professor at
the Academy. He received the title Professor of Latin and Russian Eloquence and an annual salary of 660 rubles.[11]

By the end of the 1740's Trediakovsky's position as the first writer of his time and a leading linguist was undermined by the increasing prominence of Lomonosov on the literary scene. Their personal relations began in 1741, when Lomonosov returned to Russia from Germany, where he had been sent for schooling. Despite Lomonosov's criticism of Trediakovsky's reform of versification, their relations were at first friendly and cooperative, but toward the end of the 1740's they became more and more inimical. In addition, Sumarokov, who in the late 1730's was an admirer of Trediakovsky's poetic innovations, had first become a follower of Lomonosov and then declared his artistic independence. Amicable theoretical disputes among the three writers evolved into a bitter personal conflict that continued through the 1750's and 1760's, terminating only when all the participants had died.[12]

The infighting had a profound negative impact on Trediakovsky's academic career, as well as on his success as a writer. Lomonosov and Sumarokov, together with their supporters, vigorously denied Trediakovsky's claim to be the reformer of Russian syllabo-tonics. They questioned his literary ability and suspected his scholarly competence. As a result, many of his works in the late 1740's and 1750's in literary theory and linguistics went unappreciated. From the early 1750's on, he began to experience difficulties in publishing his works. Finally, in the late 1750's, his conflict with the academicians, Lomonosov in particular, made his position in the Academy intolerable. In August 1757 Trediakovsky ceased to attend the Academy. A year later, the Academy president ordered his salary stopped and asked for an explanation. Trediakovsky, citing insults to his scholarly and literary honor, as well as illness and depression ("hemoptysis and hypochondria"), refused to return to the Academy. He emphasized, however, that his bad health did not preclude his performing his academic duties at home. Nevertheless, he was dismissed in 1759.

Even after his dismissal, Trediakovsky persevered in his lifelong labor of love. He continued to work on Rollin's and Jean Baptiste Louis Crévier's histories. In addition, he translated a compendium of Francis Bacon's philosophy by Alexander Deleyre (together with the philosopher's biography, written by David

Mallet and adapted into French by Deleyre), as well as Voltaire's "Essai historique et critique sur les dissensions des Eglises de Pologne." In the 1760's the poet also completed his most famous (or notorious) work, the poem *Tilemakhida* (published in 1766), a paraphrase in verse of the political novel *Télémaque* (1699) by François Fénelon. Trediakovsky's accomplishments were not recognized, however, and he died in poverty and disgrace in 1769.

Trediakovsky's misfortunes during his life and the prolonged lack of appreciation after his death no longer obscure the outstanding part he played in the introduction and cultivation of a variety of European literary principles in eighteenth-century Russia. It is difficult to pinpoint a field to which Trediakovsky did not contribute; literary theory, rhetoric, the theory of versification, linguistics, the art of translation, history, poetry—all these were enriched by his tireless exertions. He was both a theorist and a practitioner: He presented new ideas in a systematic way, provided models, and experimented with different approaches. In many respects he was a trailblazer, a pioneer, who mapped out for Russians vast new fields of knowledge and made these fields ready for further cultivation. There is no doubt that Trediakovsky's contemporaries, who later despised and ridiculed him, were frequently indebted to him for their introduction to the ideas that they subsequently developed so successfully and whose source they did not care (or, sometimes, dare) to acknowledge.

Trediakovsky's most widely recognized contribution is the reform of Russian versification, which he initiated with his treatise *A New and Brief Method for Composing Russian Verse*. In this work Trediakovsky questioned the syllabic system of versification that had been dominant in Russia since the 1660's. He considered syllabic verse in the Russian language "inadequate" (*nedostatochny*), lacking "measure and cadence" (*mera i padenie*), and therefore deserving to be called mere prose.[13] In his view, a new rhythmical principle—regular alternation of stressed and unstressed syllables—was necessary to create a verse appropriate for the Russian language. Trediakovsky suggested measuring verse by feet, rather than by syllables, and proposed to keep the same foot (preferably the trochee) throughout the line in eleven- and thirteen-syllable lines. These innovations produced a kind of verse that Trediakovsky called "tonic" (*tónicheskii*) and that served as a starting point for the further revision of syllabics undertaken in 1739 by Lomonosov in his "Letter on the Rules of Russian Versification." Trediakovsky's and Lomonosov's combined efforts resulted in the syllabo-tonic (or, as it is sometimes called, syllabo-accentual) verse that predominates in Russian poetry to this day.

Interpretations of the reform and of Trediakovsky's role in it differ. Some authors consider the reform the result of a spontaneous "tonization"—an increase in the regular distribution of stresses—arising at that time in Russian syllabic verse. Trediakovsky's part (if any) lay, then, in recognizing and sanctioning this trend. Others see the reform as a drastic break with the existing system and an introduction of revolutionary principles and accordingly regard Trediakovsky as an ingenious and bold innovator. Finally, both parties can assert either Trediakovsky's or Lomonosov's leading role in the reform. Lomonosov's advocates usually contrast Trediakovsky's timidity and indecisiveness with Lomonosov's radical approach.[14]

Today, regardless of emphasis, Trediakovsky's leading, or at least ground-breaking, role in the reform is generally acknowledged by the majority of specialists in Russian metrics. It is agreed that he not only introduced the principles of Russian syllabo-tonic verse but also successfully experimented with various tonic and syllabo-tonic meters, stanzas, and unrhymed verse. Although these experiments were not always appreciated in Trediakovsky's lifetime, they played an important role in the development of new poetic forms throughout the eighteenth century and especially in the beginning of the nineteenth century. Finally, it was Trediakovsky who, in his revised *Method for Composing Russian Verse* (1752), gave a theoretical summary of the reform, taking into account Lomonosov's, Sumarokov's, and his own achievements in the field and thus providing Russian poets with a comprehensive theory of syllabo-tonics.[15]

Another field to which Trediakovsky made significant contributions was the development of the literary language. This task was felt to be especially urgent in post-Petrine Russia, inasmuch as Church Slavonic was losing its function as a language of literature and culture and vernacular Russian was in disarray, struggling to absorb the influx of foreign words and adapt itself to the needs of the emerging high society and the growing bureaucracy, of science and literature.

As a young man, in the introduction to his translation of Paul Tallemant's novel and later in his "Speech to the Russian Assembly," Trediakovsky advocated the predominant use of secular language, rather than Church Slavonic, in the new Russian literature. His effort was directed to the consolidation and codification of vernacular Russian and the development of linguistic means for expressing mundane themes, such as sexual love and courtship—themes that the Russian literary tradition before the eighteenth century had all but avoided. However, as he matured as a writer, Trediakovsky revised his views on Church Slavonic and rediscovered its value as a source of poetic elements in the high style. His linguistic experiments, frequently derided by his contemporaries, anticipated the heated debates on the nature of the literary Russian language in the first quarter of the nineteenth century between the so-called Archaists, who appreciated the domestic tradition, and the Innovators, who looked to the West for linguistic models—debates that played a crucial role in the formation of contemporary standard Russian.

Feeling himself responsible for the enrichment and systematization of the Russian language, Trediakovsky also worked to resolve a number of specific linguistic problems, such as the composition of the Russian alphabet, principles of spelling, questions of grammar and etymology, and the development of vocabulary. His ideas, always provocative and stimulating, gave rise to many productive discussions and significantly influenced the shape of the modern Russian language despite the ridicule of contemporaries and later generations. Trediakovsky's effort to develop Russian philosophic terminology in the "Oration on Wisdom, Prudence, and Virtue" (1752) was particularly valuable: Many of the terms he suggested in this work permanently entered the Russian language.[16]

Finally, Trediakovsky was the first to transplant, consciously and systematically, the European generic system to Russian soil. Through his efforts, Russians became acquainted with many secular genres that until then they had been barely familiar with:

the *précieux* romance, ode, sonnet, rondo, and elegy, among others. Especially important was Trediakovsky's endeavor to give not just a comprehensive theory of genres but also examples of various poetic forms, often for the first time in the Russian language.[17]

This list of Trediakovsky's achievements as a scholar and a writer, which are now rarely disputed, makes the question Why was he denied recognition for so long? even more urgent. Why, one cannot help but wonder, was he scorned and ridiculed by his contemporaries and literary descendants? And why is the effect of this old attitude still felt today? The list of available explanations is neither long, nor very convincing: theoretical and poetic timidity, which resulted in an inability to break completely with the syllabic tradition and Baroque aesthetics; self-contradictions and eclecticism; an unpleasant disposition and a predilection for political and religious denunciations; and, finally, lack of talent.

Arguments that the obsoleteness of Trediakovsky's literary principles is a source of his reputation as a total failure are not satisfactory. First of all, there is no evidence that an adherence to syllabics or Baroque aesthetics was enough to provoke universal ridicule and hatred. Antiokh Kantemir, Trediakovsky's contemporary, never abandoned syllabics, but his attachment to traditional versification did not prevent future generations from acknowledging, in historical perspective, his achievements as a prominent satirist. Baroque features in the works of Lomonosov and Gavrila Derzhavin never hurt their reputations. Furthermore, in my opinion, Trediakovsky's break, in the 1730's, with the Old Russian tradition was not particularly timid. On the contrary, it was bold, even insolent at times, and the tradition-loving critics of Trediakovsky's translation of *Voyage à l'île d'Amour* obviously saw it this way when they accused him "of impiousness, of godlessness, of deism, of atheism, and of all manner of heresies."[18]

As for the references to contradictions and eclecticism, it is important to remember that such references are often convenient excuses for our inability to understand the inner logic of an artistic system that is removed in time. Change does not necessarily mean incongruity, and the evolution of Trediakovsky's

literary and linguistic views, despite two distinct and even di-
ametrically opposed stages in his development, was in fact intrinsically logical and consistent. If there was a contradiction in
Trediakovsky's position, it was between the objective meaning
of his ideas and his works on the one hand and his own interpretation of them on the other. But this contradiction was a
product of a normative aesthetic mentality and was shared by all
eighteenth-century Russian writers.[19]

The poet's alleged bad temper and love for denunciation
were by no means his sole prerogative. Rudeness and personal
animosity were peculiar to mid-eighteenth-century literary polemics, and not one of the three main participants was overnice
in his expressions or too noble in his choice of methods.[20] Moreover, the correlation between an artist's everyday behavior and
his or her artistic reputation is by no means straightforward.
Rude and arrogant conduct in certain circumstances may be perceived as heroic and add to the artist's positive image. Nobody
reproaches Lomonosov for his rows in the Academy Conference
or for the beatings he administered to an innocent Academy gardener and the gardener's pregnant wife. On the contrary, for
some of his admirers these episodes illustrate his heroic struggle
against German domination in the Academy and were the manifestation of his indomitable Russian spirit. At the same time, the
fact that the generally humble Trediakovsky was not always fair
to his literary rivals somehow still seems sufficient to justify the
general two-century-long contempt for the poet.

Finally, according to the most frequent explanation of his
bad reputation, Trediakovsky lacked talent and was therefore
unable to embody his interesting and potentially fruitful ideas in
his works, thus discrediting them in the eyes of his colleagues
and generations of Russian readers, critics, and writers to come.
Radishchev was the first to introduce this viewpoint in his interpretation of Trediakovsky's works in the chapter entitled "Tver"
in *A Journey from Petersburg to Moscow* (1790). He revised and developed it in his apology for Trediakovsky, *Memorial for a Dactylo-
Trochaic Knight*. Nikolai Karamzin spelled out this opinion in the
entry on Trediakovsky in his *Pantheon of Russian Authors* (1802):

If desire and diligence could replace talent, whom would Trediakovsky
not surpass in poetry and eloquence?

But stubborn Apollo always hides behind a cloud for feigned poets and pours his rays solely upon those who have been born with his stamp.

Neither talent nor taste itself can be acquired: Taste itself is talent. Education shapes, but does not create, the author.

Ever since then, this opinion has been virtually indispensable to any discussion of Trediakovsky's works. The difference is in tone: It can be jeering and contemptuous, or mild and regretful, depending on an author's general attitude toward Trediakovsky. Many modern works on Trediakovsky still cite talentlessness as a cause of his failure.[21]

This argument deserves to be discussed more thoroughly. It forces one to examine the concept of talent and its usefulness for resolving the enigma of Trediakovsky's fate.

As has been mentioned, the notion of Trediakovsky's lack of talent goes back to the late eighteenth century, the time when the Romantic idea of talent as a divine gift of creativity began to take shape in Russia. This idea replaced the preceding one—that knowledge and education ought to be the main properties of a poet. Accordingly, the reason for censuring Trediakovsky's works changed: Among his contemporaries Trediakovsky was notorious for the absence of these essential artistic qualities, but in the Romantic epoch he became known as a learned but worthless versifier.

The Baroque idea of the divine origin of poetry and the analogy between poet and Creator was already known to Russian seventeenth-century syllabicists—as well as to Lomonosov, who, as Ilya Serman points out, borrowed it from Leibniz.[22] However, the Russian Baroque was devoid of the exaltation of the European Baroque and promoted a much more moderate and rational variant of the style. The idea of creativity as obsession or Pythian enthusiasm, like the later Romantic idea of frenzied genius, would have been totally foreign both to Russian syllabicists and to the mid-eighteenth-century Russian poets who espoused normative aesthetics.[23]

In the eighteenth-century theory of literature, the notion of talent was a rational notion, subject to sober analysis. In this manner it is discussed in Lomonosov's *Brief Handbook of Eloquence* (1747). Lomonosov asserted that the art of eloquence required "natural ability" (*prirodnoe darovanie*) in addition to four other "means" (*sredstvii*). For Lomonosov, natural ability consisted of "spiritual and corporeal" (*dushevnye i telesnye*) elements. The former included wit and memory, the latter "a loud and pleasant voice, a sound wind [*dolgii dukh*], and a strong chest," as well as "stoutness and a stately appearance." He described the state of inspiration—in the Romantic consciousness, an indispensable sign of an artist's contact with the divine—as a rhetorical figure rather than as a state of frenzied enthusiasm: "Rapture [*voskhishchenie*] is when a composer [*sochinitel'*] presents himself as if his mind were lost in a fantasy [*predstavliaet sebia kak izumlenna v mechtanii*] that has originated in extremely great, unexpected, or frightful and supernatural circumstances. This figure is almost always combined with invention and is prevalent mostly among poets."[24]

This state of rapture was to be governed by rules, to be rational and orderly: eighteenth-century Russian poets fully shared Nicolas Boileau's notion of "beautiful disorder" (*beau désordre*). Trediakovsky gave a very close equivalent of this oxymoron in his translation of Boileau's *L'art poétique*, rendering it *krasnyi besporiadok* (beautiful disorder). Sumarokov, in his "Epistle on Poetry," warned aspiring writers of epics that the genre required self-discipline, and epic "noise" was supposed to be "orderly" (*V epicheskikh stikakh poriadochen est' shum*). Without such self-control on the author's part the poetic rapture became, in the eyes of the adherents of normative poetics, pure inanity, and poetic discourse began to resemble the movements of "a mad cat" (*ugorelaia koshka*). An unrestrained rapture was not a figure, legitimate in high genres, but an "intoxicated enthusiasm" or, rather, "a confused confusion in which round is mixed up with rectangular."[25] Absence of talent was thus understood as absence of knowledge, absence of true understanding of the rules, absence of reasoning ability, or absence of self-control.

Discussing Trediakovsky's alleged talentlessness, we are invited to accept a concept of a certain historical period as an absolute category and to apply it to phenomena that were governed by different aesthetic norms. But even if we accept talent as an absolute property that was first fully recognized by the Romantics but could nevertheless be found in earlier historical periods, we have no working procedure for distinguishing talented writers from talentless ones.

Indeed, the question of talent is closely intertwined with the even more controversial question of aesthetic value. It can probably be stated that a talented artist usually produces aesthetically valuable works, and vice versa, it can be assumed that the author of aesthetically valuable works is a person of talent. In other words, "the criterion of talent is the creation of original artistic values." [26] The correlation is not absolute, since a great artist could produce an occasional unfortunate work and a humble author could achieve an unexpected success. [27]

If we accept the ability to create works of aesthetic value as a criterion of talent, we still need the means to determine whether a particular work is aesthetically valuable. Unfortunately, the modern theory of literature does not provide an easy solution to this problem. Although in the last decades the relativistic approach to the problem of aesthetic value has become unpopular and it is generally agreed that a literary scholar should attempt to determine the aesthetic value of a work (whether understood as intrinsic or relational value) through an objective process of evaluation, any reliable criteria for making the determination are lacking. Intuitively every reader tends to believe that the category of literary value exists, but the arguments for and against a particular work remain largely subjective. The category that is most traditional and most frequently used in aesthetic evaluation, taste, is problematic itself, inasmuch as its content has been constantly changing over the course of literary history. [28] Attempts to develop formal evaluative procedures and to establish them experimentally, although they have produced valuable insights into the theoretical aspects of the problem, have so far failed to yield any practical results.

Since formal procedures for aesthetic evaluation are not available, we are still obliged to rely on our subjective impressions of a literary work, opinions of contemporary readers, and the work's influence upon subsequent literary developments. The case of Trediakovsky is very complicated in this respect. On the one hand, for the modern reader, even a qualified one, any immediate aesthetic response to the works of Russian poets of the mid-eighteenth century is questionable. The works of Trediakovsky, as well as, to a lesser extent, those of Lomonosov and Sumarokov, can hardly be considered fully alive as aesthetic entities. They are old-fashioned and difficult to read and retain a largely historical interest.

In general Lomonosov's and Sumarokov's poetry seems to be slightly more readable than Trediakovsky's (but still, I repeat, one rarely reads their works for pleasure). There are several possible explanations, which have to do with the intrinsic qualities of their poetry and the prevailing tradition. Trediakovsky was an author who went through distinct stages of development and who experimented with unfamiliar forms boldly and even recklessly. Moreover, he focused his attention upon the aspects of poetic language that most easily become obsolete. To create a language of literature distinct from the everyday parlance, he employed unusual and often contrasting stylistic elements, experimenting with word order and intonation. The result was what he called in his introduction to *Tilemakhida* a "fabulous flow of discourse" (*bakharskoe techenie slova*)—an idiosyncratic style, intense and embellished.[29] This approach was alien to Lomonosov, who was more interested in imagery and who practiced a temperate approach to stylistics, and to Sumarokov, who valued clarity and moderation both in style and in imagery.

But even more important for the understanding of Trediakovsky's apparent obsoleteness is that, for the reasons I plan to discuss in the present work, Russian literature largely followed the path suggested by Lomonosov. Lomonosov and his tradition (a tradition so powerful that it has absorbed his moderate rival, Sumarokov) stands between us and Trediakovsky and interferes with our perception of his works. Readers raised in the Lomonosovian tradition are not equipped to appreciate Trediakovsky's poetics. Modern Russian readers see Trediakovsky, unlike Simeon Polotsky or Antiokh Kantemir, as part of Lomonosov's generation and tend to judge Trediakovsky by the rules left to them by Lomonosov. The rules do not apply, but not necessarily because Trediakovsky was less talented than Lomonosov. The principles that he introduced now seem strange and archaic, but in their time they were not archaic but revolutionary, even if in a different way from those of Lomonosov. To judge

Trediakovsky by his own rules, we have to remember that Lomonosovian poetic principles are not absolute, that although they might seem universal to a person who belongs to the nineteenth- and twentieth-century Russian literary tradition, they are no less conventional and temporal than Trediakovsky's alleged barbarisms.

Inasmuch as the subjective approach has failed, we are obliged to take a historical stance and to examine Trediakovsky's influence upon the development of Russian literature. The impact of his ideas and works was undisputably strong and positive. Trediakovsky was an active member of the literary community, and his opinions were valued and his ideas absorbed. His reform of versification directly affected the Russian poetry of his time. A number of poets in the capital, as well as in the provinces, readily accepted his new system of versification and started to write poetry according to syllabo-tonic principles. Trediakovsky's future enemies, the students of the Cadet School (*Sukhoputnyi shliakhetnyi korpus*) in Saint Petersburg, including Sumarokov, were among his followers. As P. N. Berkov puts it, "Sumarokov was at this time not an ordinary follower of Trediakovsky, but his vigorous champion." Lomonosov too, despite his caustic criticism of Trediakovsky's reform of versification, strongly depended on it in his own development as a poet. Even the subsequent feud among the three writers could not completely erase Trediakovsky's authority: Both Sumarokov and Lomonosov, however reluctantly, acknowledged Trediakovsky's competence even during the most bitter polemics. Despite the widespread ridicule and scorn, Trediakovsky's theoretical ideas continued to be valued up to the end of the eighteenth and the beginning of the nineteenth century. Gavrila Derzhavin named Trediakovsky his first teacher in versification: "The rules of poetry I derived from Trediakovsky's works." Trediakovsky's *A New and Brief Method for Composing Russian Verse*, one of the works to which Derzhavin refers here, was virtually the only manual on poetics at that time, and Derzhavin depended on it out of necessity. However, Derzhavin's colleagues at the end of the eighteenth century avoided openly admitting their knowledge of Trediakovsky's works, whereas Derzhavin chose to re-

veal his. Derzhavin's acknowledgment was the more valuable in
that the poet was well aware of the myth about Trediakovsky the
fool and even contributed to its formation with his parodies of
Trediakovsky's poetry.[30]

Trediakovsky's works not only significantly influenced the
development of literary theory but were also well received by
the reading public. Contrary to popular belief, his readers did
not start laughing their heads off the minute he entered the literary arena. Trediakovsky's debut was most happy and successful, and he continued to enjoy considerable popularity well into
his mature years. Existing data convincingly show that despite
the controversy surrounding Trediakovsky's name, his works attracted readers throughout his career.

The 1730's were the happiest years in Trediakovsky's life as a
writer. Upon his return from France he enjoyed tremendous
success in all his areas of activity. His translation of Tallemant's
novel was met with enthusiasm and secured him a reputation as
a leading translator. His poems found praise, which prompted
Trediakovsky to publish them in the supplement to his translation of *Voyage à l'île d'Amour*. His ideas about language and literature were absorbed and implemented by his colleagues and
followers. Trediakovsky's brilliant debut brought him an audience with Empress Anna and employment in the Academy of
Sciences.

His fame did not disappear with time. Largely ignoring Trediakovsky's emerging reputation as a laughable failure of a
writer, the public continued to read and enjoy his works. Contemporaries continued to appreciate him as a translator. They
avidly read his 30-volume translation of the histories by Rollin
and Crévier. I. F. Martynov, upon examining the Rare Books
Collection in the Library of the Academy of Sciences in Leningrad, concluded that these translations were in all major private
book collections of the eighteenth century. The popularity of
Trediakovsky's translations of Rollin long outlived the translator
himself. Karamzin testified in his *Pantheon of Russian Authors*
that Trediakovsky's translation of *Histoire ancienne* was still read
by the provincial gentry at the beginning of the nineteenth century. The journalist Nikolai Grech confirmed this testimony: He
recalled that as a fourteen-year-old boy he himself "knew almost

by heart Rollin's ancient and Roman histories in Trediakovsky's translation."[31]

Other translations by Trediakovsky were also widely read. His translation of the anonymous moral code of a young noble-man, *La véritable politique des personnes de qualité* (the book had been ascribed to N. Rémond de Cours or Cherbonnière, whereas Trediakovsky attributed it to François Fénelon) went through four editions: It was printed in 1737, 1745, 1765, and 1787. For the eighteenth century, this was a good indication of success. Andrei Bolotov, the author of famous memoirs about the life of the eighteenth-century provincial gentry, provides another ex-ample of readers' interest in Trediakovsky's translations. His memoirs preserve an enthusiastic opinion of Trediakovsky's translation of John Barclay's *Argenis* (1621; Trediakovsky's trans-lation, *Argenida*, was published in 1751): "He [Bolotov's acquain-tance] praised this book to the skies and said that it was possible to find everything in it—politics, morality, pleasure, etc., etc." Bolotov subsequently bought and read the book, which he in turn liked very much.[32] Even *A Voyage to the Isle of Love*, a book that Trediakovsky himself grew to hate and copies of which, ac-cording to the testimony of his colleague at the Academy, G. F. Mueller, he tried to buy and destroy, did not completely fall out of favor with readers and was republished in 1778.

Eighteenth-century readers continued to appreciate Tredia-kovsky not only as a translator but as a literary scholar and poet as well. *A New and Brief Method for Composing Russian Verse*, the two volumes of *Compositions and Translations*, *Tilemakhida*, and other works are found in the libraries of eighteenth-century statesmen, scholars, and poets, and the condition of the books indicates that the volumes were frequently read by the owners.[33] The interest in Trediakovsky's works did not disappear after his death: In 1773 his work *Three Discourses on Three Most Important Russian Antiquities* (1755) appeared in print, and in 1775 an anony-mous admirer published his tragedy, *Deidamia*. *Deidamia* was even honored by plagiarism: In 1769, soon after Trediakovsky's death, the novelist Mikhail Chulkov retold it in prose and pub-lished it under his own name.[34]

Trediakovsky was by no means known only in exclusive lit-erary circles. He enjoyed considerable popularity among the general reading public. His poems, especially love songs from *A Voyage to the Isle of Love*, can be found in eighteenth-century collections of poetry. Trediakovsky essentially brought this genre into the Russian canon, and the popularity of his often sensual and even erotic songs continued in lower cultural circles long after Sumarokov had replaced him as the leading songwriter among the educated public.[35]

Trediakovsky's poetry and prose had their readers, then, and served as a source of political, philosophical, and historical knowledge, as well as aesthetic delight. However, the tradition has preserved for us an overwhelming quantity of totally different opinions about the poet: opinions that picture him as a worthless scribbler, a malicious envier, and an incompetent and tasteless pedant. These opinions emerged in works written during the polemical exchanges of the mid-eighteenth century, in which Trediakovsky was one of the main participants and a frequent target. The passage of time did not soften the opinions, as usually happens, but, on the contrary, reinforced and developed them. Laughing at Trediakovsky, criticizing and parodying his works, the poet's critics consistently interpreted the idiosyncrasies of his aesthetic position as clumsiness, inability, and downright stupidity. Gradually, Trediakovsky's image as an inept versifier started to overshadow his real personality and his real artistic views. In the eyes of subsequent literary generations, Trediakovsky lost all integrity as a poet and became an ungifted poetaster, a despicable "professor of eloquence," and the father of the laughable *Tilemakhida*. Trediakovsky's biographies became strings of anecdotes stressing his pedantry, stupidity, and talentlessness. The fantastic accounts of the poet's life included the story about his meeting with Peter the Great, who allegedly said about him: "A toiler forever, he will never become a master."[36] "The most benevolent box on the ear" (*vsemilostiveishaia opleukha*) that he allegedly received from Empress Anna and the beatings inflicted by Artemii Volynsky (a true and sad story circulated as a hilarious joke) gave biographies of Trediakovsky a touch of commedia dell'arte.[37] Trediakovsky's alleged meanness and wretchedness were stressed by undocumented accounts of his kneeling before Empress Anna while reading his odes.[38]

The last example conveniently demonstrates how pseudo-historical evidence formed the image of Trediakovsky as an incompetent and abject scribbler. Ivan Lazhechnikov, in his 1856 memoir on Pushkin, claimed that this episode, sketched in his own historical novel, *The Ice House* (1835), in which Trediakovsky figures as a character, was backed by an eyewitness report:

Here are the words of Iv[an] Vas[il'evich] Stupishin (a person quite remarkable in his time and quite significant), who died, if I am not mistaken, in 1820 as a ninety-year-old man: "When Trediakovsky appeared with his odes, he always, on Biron's order, crept on his knees from the very vestibule through all the rooms, holding his poems on his head with both hands; having crept in this way to the persons before whom he had to read his works, he bowed low to them. Biron always made a fool of him and laughed his head off.[39]

Lazhechnikov's source was I. V. Stupishin, a statesman of Catherine the Great's time (in 1793 he was the governor of Moscow). Simple calculations show that this information could not have been more than a rumor: Even if Lazhechnikov's recollections were correct and Stupishin was in fact ninety in the year of his death, he would have been only ten at the time of Empress Anna's death in 1740; it is thus highly unlikely that he would have been admitted to court and would have witnessed the events that he described in such detail. Lazhechnikov's informant had obviously presented hearsay evidence as if it were historical.

Eventually Trediakovsky's image as a wretched versifier acquired such authenticity in the eyes of later generations that it fully replaced his real identity. As Aleksandr Morozov wrote in his introduction to a collection of Russian parodies: "There are people who, having no real idea about Trediakovsky's true character and historical significance, ascribe to him verses that have stuck in their memory, not even suspecting that these verses are the latest parody: 'The Empress Catherine, oh! / Went to Tsarskoe Selo.'"[40] The illusion was so complete that this image served as a prototype for literary characters named Trediakovsky in Lazhechnikov's novel, in Nikolai Polevoy's comedy *The First Performance of "A Miller Who Is a Wizard, a Quack, and a Matchmaker"* (1839), in Polevoy's "dramatic tale" *Lomonosov; or, Life and Poetry*

(1843), and in Nikolai Khmel'nitsky's "historical comedy" *Russian Faust* (between 1843 and 1845). In Lazhechnikov's depiction of Trediakovsky the distortion is especially impressive. The novel collected all the rumors and biased opinions about the poet, ridiculous as they were, into one convenient cluster.

From the moment in Lazhechnikov's novel that Trediakovsky makes his first entrance, he elicits nothing but laughter and disgust:

The round face, like a map of hemispheres, bluish, squeezed by a greasy tie, on which rested a plump, double chin; a wart on the left cheek, an ingratiatingly pompous physiognomy, a steep shining forehead, inserted into a floury tallowy setting with two floury toupées on the sides and a black snood behind—in a word, this was Vasilii Kirillovich Trediakovsky *himself*. (p. 41)

Trediakovsky's appearance corresponds to his inner portrait, the main features of which are pedantry and smugness:

Oh! by the self-satisfaction that had deeply inscribed on his face the word *pedant*—by this banderole that flutters on the forehead of every ungifted toiler of erudition—by the wart on the cheek, you would guess immediately the future professor of eloquence Vasilii Kirillovich Trediakovsky. (p. 55; cf. p. 255)

Although *Tilemakhida* was written almost 30 years later, in 1766, Lazhechnikov presents Trediakovsky with the notorious poem already under his arm. Historical truth is less important here than this token, by which the reader easily recognizes the unfortunate poet:

He carried a huge folio under his arm. And here it is not hard to guess what he was carrying . . . his name, his glory, which rustles over you with its owl's wings as soon as you pronounce this name, the hair shirt of talentlessness, the chains of patience, the tool of mockery for all ages [*vozrastov*], for the fool and the man of sense. In a word, he carried *Tilemakhida*, that lofty creation which for almost a century . . . had no equal. (p. 55)[41]

Further mockeries of the poem follow. Thus, the main character of the novel, Artemii Volynsky, gives "the monstrous book a look as if it were a stone brought to kill him with its weight" (p. 55). Later it is sarcastically called "a notorious booklet" (*zna-*

menitaia knizhitsa; p. 57). Quotations from the poem are meant to make the reader (as well as the characters in the novel) laugh. On the whole, it is agreed between the author and the reader that *Tilemakhida* is the most hilarious book in the world.

Trediakovsky's style is another target for the author's sarcasm. Its parody in the novel is rather clumsy, but several key words, allegedly typical of Trediakovsky, are introduced to make the parody plausible. Latinisms (such as *entusiasmus*), Slavonicisms, inappropriate vulgar expressions (such as "the lad of love," *parenek liubvi*, for Cupid), inversions, and frequent exclamations were apparently sufficient to meet the reader's expectations.

Lazhechnikov does not forget another indispensable feature of Trediakovsky's legendary biography, his hatred of Lomonosov. He makes Trediakovsky deliver a comical philippic:

Let bugs, clinging to blades of grass, hurry [literally, "bristle," *toporshchatsia*] to Parnassus; let the pitiful fisherman [*rybachishka*] from Kholmogory [i.e., Lomonosov] in the German land squeak and screech on a *pipe* [*sopelka*] his despicable ode [*odishka*] on the taking of Khotin, which inane judges praise to the skies. My trumpet sounds to all the ends of the earth and drowns it out; this song [i.e., Lomonosov's ode] will sink in 22,205 verses of my poem! 22,205 by the most accurate count! (p. 59)

Popular anecdotes about Trediakovsky's life (related, for the sake of comical effect, by the poet himself) complete the image. With comical delight Trediakovsky tells Volynsky about the box on the ear that he received from Empress Anna: "Her Majesty herself deigned to rise from her seat, came up to me, and from her generous hand granted me the most benevolent box on the ear" (p. 56). In the same naive manner Trediakovsky relates the story of his (purely legendary) meeting with Peter the Great (p. 66). It is noteworthy that the author, not very familiar with the facts of Trediakovsky's life, transfers the meeting to Arkhangelsk, instead of Astrakhan, where Trediakovsky was born and where the meeting could at least theoretically have taken place (Peter was in Astrakhan in 1722).[42]

Polevoy, in his plays, offers similar, if less elaborate, images of Trediakovsky: Smugness, stupidity, servility, and, above all, exaggerated literary pretensions are the basic characteristics of Trediakovsky's namesakes in both *The First Performance* and *Lomonosov*. The Trediakovsky in Polevoy's plays recites his *Tilemakhida* and *Deidamia*, praises hexameters and unrhymed verse, and mixes Latin with Church Slavonic and low-style, colloquial Russian. He is smug and pitiful, annoying and laughable.

These fictional images of Trediakovsky were approved by critics, among them, Vissarion Belinsky, one of the most influential Russian literary reviewers. Belinsky wrote favorable reviews of Lazhechnikov's novel and Polevoy's plays. The critic's minor disagreements with their interpretations—Belinsky thought that for the sake of fairness Lazhechnikov should have concealed his contempt for Trediakovsky, and he cleverly advised Polevoy not to rely unconditionally on the eighteenth-century reports about Trediakovsky, since they were frequently inspired by polemical considerations—did not change his basic negative opinion of the poet. Belinsky's approval reinforced the image of Trediakovsky the wretched "professor of eloquence and most of all of poetical ingenuities," as Belinsky on many occasions disdainfully called him.[43] By the end of the 1840's this image of Trediakovsky the poetaster was all but generally accepted. As Petr Perevlessky, the editor of one of the two nineteenth-century collections of Trediakovsky's works, wrote in the introduction to his 1849 edition: "To the idea of him [Trediakovsky] is always attached the idea of model talentlessness and unprecedented banality; he has become a universal laughingstock; his name was made into a swear word. In our time, to call somebody a Trediakovsky means to insult him deeply and to make a lifelong enemy of the most vicious and intolerant kind."[44]

This image of Trediakovsky as a ludicrously incompetent but eager writer still stands between us and the historical Trediakovsky. We, who to a large extent have lost the immediate perception of eighteenth-century literature and have to rely upon the opinions of contemporaries for value judgments, are forced to deal more with a legend about Trediakovsky, brought to us by tradition, than with a historically adequate characterization of the poet and his works. As Iurii Tynianov formulates it in his essay "On Parody" (1929): "And a folkloric Trediakovsky is a phenomenon that has taken root remarkably firmly and has almost fully overshadowed concrete literary facts."[45]

The existence of the unfavorable "folkloric" image of Trediakovsky evokes a question: How has this image influenced judgments about Trediakovsky's works? What impact has the writer's reputation as an utterly worthless versifier had upon the evaluation of his legacy? Which came first, the harsh judgment of his works or his reputation as a wretched poetaster? Trediakovsky himself was inclined to think that his reputation affected readers' reaction to his poetry. In 1756, when his poor reputation had already established itself in the literary circles hostile toward Trediakovsky, he conducted an experiment, publishing his ode "Spring Warmth" ("Veshnee teplo"; the first letters of the title, *V* and *T*, indicated the initials of the real author) under the name of his colleague at the Academy, Andrei Konstantinovich Nartov. The result was astonishing and distressing for the author: "This ode was showered with praise and printed in books. Although I was successful in the substitution of a different author, nevertheless this very success plunged me almost into despair, for I saw that the disdain was really directed only at me and not at my works."[46]

It could be argued that every failure complains of injustice. However, as I have tried to show, in the case of Trediakovsky the discrepancy between what he had accomplished and how he was judged was truly striking. Even if we concede that Trediakovsky was not especially talented as a poet, this fact hardly justifies the cruelty and malignancy of the attacks against him during his lifetime or after his death. The injustice and ingratitude surely went far beyond the usual polemical exaggerations that eventually fade and sink into oblivion. On the contrary, the image of Trediakovsky as a pitiful poetaster has shown extraordinary stability and perseverance, and these features certainly cannot be explained away merely as poor judgment or ignorance on the part of his contemporaries and literary descendants. Such an explanation would not account for the durability of this image and its resistance to reason. Rather, these features suggest that a different type of reasoning underlay the formation and the circulation of this image. A close examination of Trediakovsky's parodical portrait reveals certain features that make it recognizably mythological in nature. Trediakovsky's image, which circulated in place of historically correct accounts of the poet, displays the characteristics of a mythological fool, one of the two main characters in the myth of creation.

Chapter 2

The "New" Russian Literature

The self-image of the eighteenth century as an epoch of mythological beginnings was to a certain extent justified by reality, in
no small part by the rapid development of literature throughout
the century. Indeed, this period was a momentous one in Russian literary history: Russian literature was secularized, and it
started to develop into an art and a profession; printing became
commonplace, and the Russian mass reader was born; the system of versification underwent a radical reform; Russian journalism and Russian criticism were born; the first novel in Russian
translation was published, and the first original Russian novel
was written. In a word, it was an age of change and transformation. At the end of the seventeenth century the reading public
still enjoyed folk interpretations of out-of-date European chivalric romances, such as *Bova the King's Son* (*Bouve de Haumtone*,
Bevis of Hampton, Bovo d'Antona). A hundred years later *Bova* was
left to the lower social circles, and the refined Russian public, in
perfect tune with European literary movements, was reading Voltaire and Abbé Prévost. Radishchev's attention to *Bova*, like Karamzin's authorship of the "heroic tale" *Ilia Muromets*, reflected
a new Pre-Romantic interest in antiquity and folk literature, an
echo of the fashionable Ossianism.[1] The age that began with a
literature still firmly rooted in medieval aesthetics ended with
Gavrila Derzhavin, a Pre-Romantic, who, according to wide-

spread contemporary opinion, "passed his lyre" directly to Pushkin himself.

After the initial fermentation and restructuring in literature during the Petrine epoch—of which the two most prominent syllabic poets of the eighteenth century, Feofan Prokopovich and Antiokh Kantemir, were representative—came the most important step toward the assimilation of European literary ideas, when, in the 1730's, first Trediakovsky, then Sumarokov, and finally Lomonosov entered upon their literary careers. The three of them were the most prominent and, as the literary circle was not populous, the most influential literary figures of their time. They came from different backgrounds, received different training, and held different views on literary matters, but they shared an important trait inspired by the ideology of the Petrine reforms: a desire to work for their fatherland, which was bolstered by a firm belief in their mission as the initiators of the "new" Russian literature and in the correctness of their own prescriptions for its development.

Trediakovsky, the oldest of the three writers, started his career at the Academy of Sciences in Saint Petersburg when Lomonosov and Sumarokov were still students. He received better training as a philologist than his rivals and was the only professional literary scholar among the three. He was also the only one to come into direct personal contact with European literary circles and to have firsthand experience writing poetry according to contemporary European standards. Destined by birth to become a cleric, this able and energetic man instead found his way to the Sorbonne and the libertine literary salons of Paris, then became a professor in the young Russian Academy of Sciences and introduced Russians to a spectrum of European knowledge.

Like Trediakovsky, Lomonosov made his own destiny. He came from the cultural and geographical periphery of the Russian state and eventually emerged as a leading figure of Russian science and literature, the first genuine Russian scientist and the organizer of scientific research and education in Russia. A peasant by birth, he became a renowned chemist and physicist, a linguist, and a poet; he was elected an honorary member of the Swedish Academy and the Academy in Bologna; before he died, he attained the high rank of state councilor.

Mikhailo Lomonosov. Artist unknown. (Lomonosov, *Sochineniia*, frontispiece)

Lomonosov was born in 1711 to a fisherman's (officially, "peasant") family in a northern village near Arkhangelsk.[2] Despite his low social station, Lomonosov did not grow up in poverty and ignorance. His father was a prosperous shipowner who sailed the White and Barents seas catching fish and delivering goods to the Solovetski Islands and the Kola Peninsula. As a young boy, Lomonosov joined his father on these expeditions, which broadened his horizons and enriched his knowledge of the world. Literacy was common among the sophisticated sailors of Arkhangelsk and its vicinity, and the young Lomonosov learned to read and write Church Slavonic from a fellow villager and from a deacon in a local church. Soon he became locally famous for his expressive recitations of the Holy Scriptures. Later he got hold of three secular books—Meletii Smotritsky's *Grammar*, Leontii Magnitsky's *Arithmetic*, and a translation of the Psalter in verse by Simeon Polotsky—and learned them practically by heart. He recalled these books as "the gateway to his education." Driven by a desire for knowledge, and probably also by his father and stepmother's lack of support for his ambitions, Lomonosov left home for Moscow and in January 1731, like Trediakovsky eight years earlier, entered the Slavo-Greco-Latin Academy. To be admitted, he had to lie about his origins and claimed that he was the son of a nobleman. (Several years later he was forced to change his story and said that his father was a priest. Eventually, he admitted his peasant origin.) At the Academy Lomonosov learned classical languages, studied poetics and rhetoric, and read Latin authors. He apparently also read books in philosophy, physics, and mathematics on his own in the Academy library. Placed initially with younger students because he did not know Latin, the language of instruction at the Academy, Lomonosov took only two years to complete three grades and be placed in the poetics class. When he was attending the philosophy class in 1736, he, as one of the most gifted students, was selected to continue his education in the newly organized gymnasium at the Academy of Sciences in Saint Petersburg. From there he was soon sent to Germany with three other students to study mining. He spent almost three years in Marburg, studying with Christian Wolff, a philosopher and mathematician. In 1739 he went to Freiberg to study chemistry and metallurgy with Johann Friedrich Henckel. Lomonosov's means in Germany were meager, the more so in that he and his Russian companions quickly learned the merry ways of German students and took to drinking and womanizing. They left debts and unpleasant memories of their brawls behind them after their departure from Marburg. Henckel was instructed by the Academy officials to be strict with the students. Lomonosov soon started to quarrel with him over money, as well as his teaching methods, and eventually left Freiberg without his instructor's consent—or even knowledge. After traveling around Europe in an attempt to get help from Russian diplomats in returning to Russia, he went back to Marburg, where, in 1741, he eventually received permission from the Academy of Sciences to go home and the money for the trip. In June 1741 Lomonosov arrived in Saint Petersburg, having left his wife behind; he had secretly married her a year before, and she joined him later, in 1743.

Upon his return to Russia, Lomonosov started his career at the Academy of Sciences, which lasted for almost 25 years, until his death in 1765. His knowledge was encyclopedic and his interests amazingly varied. He worked as a chemist, physicist, geologist, astronomer, historian, literary theoretician, and linguist. In 1745 he became a professor of chemistry at the Academy. He organized the first chemistry laboratory in Russia and started to train students there. He introduced mosaic art to Russia, published the first Russian grammar written in Russian, and was instrumental in organizing Moscow University in 1755.[3]

His years at the Academy, although productive for Lomonosov as a scientist and a scholar and very fruitful for Russian science in general, were not easy and left him frustrated. Lomonosov perceived the academic environment to be hostile toward him, a Russian genius, and accused the German professors, who were in the majority at the Academy, of being unfair to him and of harboring anti-Russian sentiments. He remained as quick-tempered as he had been during his student days in Germany and not infrequently tried to resolve academic arguments by not-so-academic means.

Lomonosov never considered writing poetry his primary occupation, but it was poetry that secured him his prominent place in the history of Russian culture. He started to write poems while in the Slavo-Greco-Latin Academy, as was required of all students, but not until he went to Germany did he take to it seriously. In January 1736 he bought Trediakovsky's *A New and Brief Method for Composing Russian Verse* and studied it thoroughly, leaving numerous comments in Russian, Latin, German, and French in the margins of the book. He took the book to Marburg with him. In Germany Lomonosov read Johann Christian Guenther and Johann Christoph Gottsched, as well as other German, French, and Italian authors. At the same time, he attempted to compose poetry according to European standards. He translated an Anacreontic ode that he found in one of Gottsched's essays, and Fénelon's ode "Montagnes de qui l'audace" (1681). In 1739 Lomonosov wrote his famous "Ode on the Taking of Khotin," which he sent, together with his "Letter on the Rules of Russian Versification," to the Academy of Sciences. Upon his return to Russia he began regularly to write solemn odes in honor of various ceremonial occasions. He was the one who developed the canon of the Russian solemn ode, a leading poetic genre up to the end of the eighteenth century. Lomonosov advocated high civil purpose in poetry and left few intimate lyrics, although his paraphrases of the Psalms and spiritual odes sometimes sound very personal. As far as imagery is concerned, Lomonosov's poetry is remarkable for its high metaphorism and cosmic passion, though he preferred a more moderate approach in language and phraseology and, unlike Trediakovsky, was interested neither in modernisms nor in extreme archaisms as a means of poetic expression.

Sumarokov, the third of the literary leaders, was the only one of noble birth. His father started military service during Peter's reign and, having switched to a civilian career, eventually rose to the rank of real privy councilor. Sumarokov's first education was at home, under the supervision of his father and a tutor. In 1732, when Sumarokov was fourteen or fifteen years old (he was born on November 25, 1717 or 1718), he entered the newly established Cadet School in Saint Petersburg, an institution of higher learning for the children of the nobility. The school, which offered a diverse but shallow curriculum, encouraged literary interests among its charges. Apart from Sumarokov, a number of writers graduated from the school in the first twenty years

Aleksandr Sumarokov. An eighteenth-century engraving. (Sumarokov, *Stikhotvoreniia*, frontispiece)

of its existence. The school exposed Sumarokov to the theater, inasmuch as the cadets took part in the performances of various troupes that appeared at Empress Anna's court. While still at school, he wrote his first poems, congratulatory odes to Anna, in which he showed himself to be a follower of Trediakovsky's reform of versification. Sumarokov graduated in 1740, and after more than fifteen years in the military service, which was service in name only, he became, in 1756, the director of the first permanent theater in Russia, established by Empress Elizabeth in Saint Petersburg. He occupied this position until 1761, when he was dismissed. He never returned to service and devoted the last sixteen years of his life to full-time writing. Sumarokov supported Catherine II in her coup d'état in 1762 and apparently expected to be included in the empress's inner circle as a poet and adviser, but his devotion (compromised by his quick temper, which he did not check even for the empress) was not appreciated, and he soon fell out of favor. Sumarokov was unfortunate in his personal life as well: His first marriage disintegrated, and his second marriage, to a serf, made him a social outcast. He was probably married a third time, again to a serf. In the last years of his life he suffered from extreme poverty and severe alcoholism. His son Pavel testified in his biography of his father that when Sumarokov died in 1777 there was not enough money in the house to bury him, and his friends, the actors of the Moscow theater, contributed to his funeral.

Sumarokov's services to Russian literature were almost as varied as Trediakovsky's. He was a lyricist, a satirist, a fabulist, and a caustic parodist, but above all a writer of love songs and a playwright. He could indeed be called the father of modern Russian dramaturgy and, in his capacity as manager of the first permanent troupe in Saint Petersburg, of Russian theater. Sumarokov made contributions to the theory of literature and to the formation of the Russian literary language. He edited one of the two first Russian private journals, *The Diligent Bee* (1759). Sumarokov also succeeded in bringing together what might be called the first literary association in Russia: a group of younger poets (Ivan Elagin, Mikhail Kheraskov, Aleksei Rzhevsky, Vasilii Maikov, among others) who considered him their teacher, thought of themselves as allies, and supported and developed their teacher's artistic principles. The group disliked Lomonosov's high metaphoric style, preferring the clarity of Sumarokov's diction.

Sumarokov was the first member of the nobility in Russia to become a full-time writer. Even before his retirement, during his years in the military and as director of the theater, literature was his main occupation. Pushkin called Sumarokov a man "passionate about his art," interpreting his devotion to literature as a sign of true professionalism, which Lomonosov, interested more in science than poetry, lacked, in Pushkin's opinion.[4] Trediakovsky was even more of a professional in this respect, but he belonged by birth and occupation to the species of learned philologists, which was about to become all but extinct or at least pushed to the background in Russia for the next 100 years or so. Sumarokov, on the other hand, was the first in a long chain of noblemen who would usurp the Russian cultural scene in the late eighteenth and early nineteenth centuries—a chain in which Pushkin was the most brilliant link.

Trediakovsky, Lomonosov, and Sumarokov knew each other well and enjoyed, at some stages of their association, if not friendship, then certainly mutual respect. They worked together on various aspects of literary theory and competed, peacefully and productively, in testing the theory in their works. In later years, however, their relations grew stormy, and any collaboration other than rivalry became impossible. They continued fighting to the end of their lives; Sumarokov, who survived the other two, kept the polemics alive well after his rivals were themselves dead. In these fights, as in the earlier cooperative effort, new aesthetic principles—that is, new for eighteenth-century Russia—continued to be put forth and assimilated into Russian literature.

Fighting and arguing, the three poets formed different alliances at different points of their relationship. In the 1730's and early 1740's, Sumarokov was a supporter of Trediakovsky's. The mid-1740's were relatively peaceful, but by the end of the 1740's Sumarokov had broken off with Trediakovsky and sided with Lomonosov, only to quarrel with Lomonosov passionately in the early 1750's. In the late 1750's Lomonosov thought that his rivals had united against him and commemorated this event in his epigram "The Malicious Reconciliation of Mr. Sumarokov with Mr. Trediakovsky" (1759). His supposition was hardly true, and the three poets never really reconciled their differences.[5]

Lomonosov's criticism of Trediakovsky's *A New and Brief Method for Composing Russian Verse*, which he wrote in the margins of the book in 1736–37, is a monument to the first disagreements. Lomonosov accepted Trediakovsky's reform in general, disputing only two points: Trediakovsky's preference of trochees to iambs and his prohibition on alternating feminine and masculine rhymes. Nevertheless, Lomonosov's overall appraisal of the treatise and the poems included with it was so negative and rude that an eighteenth-century reader who had the chance to read Lomonosov's copy of Trediakovsky's book commented on the back cover: "He is as fierce as the hound of hell [i.e., Cerberus]" (*Uzh tak on zol, kak pes byl adskii*). Most of all, Lomonosov disapproved of Trediakovsky's style and in fact rejected the very fundamentals of Trediakovsky's approach to the language of literature. He consistently condemned the elements of Trediakovsky's style that he considered excessive—inversions, archaisms, and colloquialisms—as well as all unusual or, from his point of view, unseemly words and expressions. This criticism says more about Lomonosov's stylistic moderation than about Trediakovsky's alleged intemperance. The rest of the remarks for the most part criticized what Lomonosov saw as imperfections, such as unsophisticated rhymes, faulty imagery, supposed plagiarism—criticisms usual for the eighteenth-century normative aesthetic mentality. The leitmotif of the future attacks on Trediakovsky—criticism of his style—was already present in this very first disagreement between the two rivals.[6]

Despite Lomonosov's arrogance, Trediakovsky's book definitely helped him to formulate his own views on syllabo-tonics, to which he had been exposed in Germany, in the "Letter on the Rules of Russian Versification." Apparently, both Sumarokov and Trediakovsky disagreed with the principles proposed in this essay. Sumarokov, as Lomonosov claimed in 1760, wrote a "reviling epigram," and Trediakovsky, a letter, but we do not know what sort of disagreement theirs was, since neither the epigram nor the letter have survived. Trediakovsky's letter never even reached Lomonosov, for the Academy decided, "in order to stop further useless and vain arguments, not to send this letter, full of learned quarrels, and not to spend the postage in vain."[7]

The disagreement did not prevent the three writers from becoming collaborators upon Lomonosov's return to Saint Petersburg in 1741. Thirty years later Sumarokov wrote that at that time he and Lomonosov were "friends and conversed every day and took sound advice from each other."[8] Trediakovsky apparently joined them in their discussions, which resulted, in 1744, in a joint venture: the three poets published a booklet containing three anonymous translations of the 143rd Psalm with an introduction by Trediakovsky. The publication was designed to resolve a theoretical dispute concerning the semantics of meter. Trediakovsky, who by this time had abandoned his initial preference for the trochee, asserted that meters did not have internal qualities that made them more suitable for particular genres or topics and, therefore, could be used equally in all genres. Lomonosov and Sumarokov held that the iamb, being an "ascending" meter (i.e., having the first syllable unstressed and second stressed), was intrinsically "noble" and therefore proper for heroic verse, whereas the trochee, being a "descending" meter, was "tender" by nature and therefore suitable for elegiac poetry. To resolve the argument, Lomonosov and Sumarokov used iambs in their translations, and Trediakovsky employed trochees. The authors appealed to the readers for the resolution of this dispute.[9]

The harmony began to disintegrate soon after this joint enterprise. As Academy professors, Lomonosov and Trediakovsky were required to evaluate literary works and translations published at the Academy. In 1747 they reviewed Sumarokov's first tragedy, *Khorev*, and in 1748, *Hamlet*. Trediakovsky's reviews were negative. He criticized *Khorev* for an "important error": The instructive power of the tragedy was undermined, he said, by the fact that "vice prevailed and virtue perished." Trediakovsky thought this fault was corrected in *Hamlet*, but the "erratic style" and grammatical mistakes remained. He did not find all that to be an obstacle to the publication of the tragedies, for their author, in Trediakovsky's view, certainly deserved clemency.[10] The offended Sumarokov retaliated. In his "Epistle on the Russian Language" he alluded to Trediakovsky's "foul [*gnusnyi*] style." To make matters worse, in the "Epistle on Poetry" he wrote of Lomonosov that "he is the Malherbe of our lands, he is akin to Pindar," and contrasted him to Trediakovsky: "But you, Shtivelius, can only talk nonsense." Sumarokov continued his attacks on his rival in the comedy *Tresotinius* (1750), in which the main character was a transparent parody of Trediakovsky. Trediakovsky immediately answered with an essay, "A Letter Containing a Discussion of a Poem That Has Now Been Published by the Author of Two Odes, Two Tragedies, and Two Epistles, Written from a Friend to a Friend."[11] In this essay, Trediakovsky criticized Sumarokov's paraphrase of the 143rd Psalm, which he had praised six years before in his introduction to their collective translation. He also found many faults in all of Sumarokov's other works to date: his ode to Empress Elizabeth (1743), both of his tragedies, and the comedy *Tresotinius*. He accused Sumarokov of incompetence, especially in regard to Church Slavonic and classical languages, and extreme conceit. Sumarokov retorted with an essay, "Response to Criticism" (1750), and another comedy, *The Monsters* (1750; the initial title of the comedy was *The Court of Arbitration*), in which Trediakovsky was parodied in the person of the pedant Krititsiondius.

Relations between Sumarokov and Lomonosov in the late 1740's and the early 1750's were not entirely unclouded either, despite Sumarokov's enthusiastic words for Lomonosov in the "Epistle on Poetry." Like Trediakovsky, Lomonosov apparently did not approve of Sumarokov's first tragedy, even if his criticism was milder and was probably not made public. In response Sumarokov wrote an essay, "Critique of the Ode," in which he criticized Lomonosov's ode "On the Anniversary of Empress Elizabeth's Ascending the Throne" (both 1747) and defended his tragedy. Although the essay was not finished and remained unpublished until after Sumarokov's death, Lomonosov was probably familiar with at least some of Sumarokov's criticisms at the time.[12] Nevertheless, these disagreements did not ruin their alliance, and in the confrontation between Sumarokov and Trediakovsky, Lomonosov cautiously but firmly supported the former. This quickly led to open hostility between Lomonosov and Trediakovsky. The writers exchanged epigrams and satires. Lomonosov interfered with the publication of Trediakovsky's translation of John Barclay's *Argenis*, objecting, among other things, to the preface to the translation where Trediakovsky discussed the reform of versification and affirmed his having first introduced syllabo-tonics to Russia. Trediakovsky responded with criticism of Lomonosov's works and insisted that Lomonosov should be barred from evaluating *Compositions and Translations in Verse and Prose*, the two-volume edition of Trediakovsky's works published in 1752.

Sumarokov supported Lomonosov in his attacks on Trediakovsky. In 1751, as he remembered later, they both still "cursed the inane writers . . . and the translation of *Argenida*." [13] But in the meanwhile, he had apparently become irritated by Lomonosov's intrusion into the realm of dramaturgy, however involuntary, with the tragedies *Tamira and Selim* and *Demofont*, written in 1750–51 by order of Elizabeth. By that time Sumarokov was already surrounded by supporters, and his camp launched an attack against the transgressor. Sumarokov himself, as Ilya Serman argues, assaulted the style of Lomonosov's tragedies in the series of parodies *Nonsense Odes*. [14] His disciple Ivan Elagin wrote a parodical playbill in which Lomonosov was labeled "Racine in spite of himself" (*Racine malgré lui*) and his tragedy *Tamira and Selim*, as well as his poetics in general and his main interest at that time, mosaic art, was ridiculed. Soon after that, in 1753, Elagin wrote his "Epistle from Mr. Elagin to Mr. Sumarokov," better known as the "Satire on a Fop and Coquettes," a conscious imitation of Boileau's second satire, in which Elagin extolled Sumarokov and criticized Lomonosov. The satire evoked stormy polemics in which a great number of the literati of that time took part. [15]

The polemical clashes continued on and off until 1757, when Lomonosov provoked a new turmoil with his anticlerical and obscene "Hymn to the Beard." The poem was a caustic criticism of the Synod for the prohibition of Alexander Pope's "Essay on Man," which had been translated by Lomonosov's disciple Nikolai Popovsky. This phase of the polemics was marred by mutual accusations of being atheists, slanderers, and informers. Among other things, Lomonosov mistakenly thought that Trediakovsky was the author of a number of denunciatory letters signed "Khristofor Zubnitsky," which, together with the parodical "The Disguised Beard, or Hymn to a Drunken Head," were disseminated in Saint Petersburg. The enraged Lomonosov wrote a poem, "To Zubnitsky," in which he, in turn, called Trediakovsky "an atheist and a hypocrite, a fabricator of anonymous letters."[16]

In 1759 Lomonosov was angered by Sumarokov's journal, *The Diligent Bee*. The poet became somewhat paranoid and suspected virtually all materials in the journal of being directed against him personally. Trediakovsky's critical essay "On Mosaic" infuriated him. Lomonosov used his influence to stop Sumarokov's *Nonsense Odes*, which parodied Lomonosov's poetical principles and style, from being published in the journal. Eventually he succeeded in getting the journal closed.

The next year Lomonosov defeated Sumarokov again. A certain Abbé Etienne Lefevre, a clergyman at the French embassy in Saint Petersburg, spoke at the literary salon of Baron Aleksandr Stroganov, the president of the Academy of Arts, and Count Andrei Shuvalov, a poet and a patron of the arts. In his (mostly political) speech "Discours sur le progrés des beaux arts en Russie," Lefevre gave a brief outline of Russian literature and praised Sumarokov and Lomonosov, rather clumsily comparing them to Racine, Horace, and Corneille and naming them both "creative geniuses" (*génie créateurs*). The "Discours" was to have been published by the Academy of Sciences. However, Lomonosov could not tolerate being praised together with his rival, and even less was he able to allow that Sumarokov was also a creative genius. Through his efforts the first printing of the "Discours" was destroyed. The "Discours" was edited and eventually published anew without the ill-fated words. Moreover, Andrei Shuvalov in his own speech at the same salon in May 1760, in an apparent attempt to soothe Lomonosov's ire, presented Lomonosov as a creative genius and the father of Russian poetry and Sumarokov as only a skillful playwright lacking true creativity. The speech was published in France in the journal *L'année littéraire*. Ten years later Sumarokov still remembered this insult, complaining that "Andrei Petrovich [Shuvalov] abused me in front of all Europe."[17]

By this time Trediakovsky had completely withdrawn from the literary disputes, worn out by the infighting. Soon after the Lefevre episode Lomonosov and Sumarokov, too, exchanged their last thrusts. Sumarokov published a fable, "An Ass in a Lion's Skin," in which he rudely alluded to Lomonosov's low origin. Lomonosov answered with the fable "A Pig in a Fox's Skin." With this fable, unpublished in Lomonosov's lifetime, his participation in the polemics ended. Sumarokov alone continued to fight his now unresponsive rival. He ridiculed Lomonosov's attempt at an epic, the "heroic poem" *Peter the Great* (canto 1 was published in 1760, and canto 2, in 1761). He called Lomonosov "Firs Firsovich Gomer" and "Monkey the Poet," implying that the poet's effort to imitate Homer was absolutely ridiculous. After Lomonosov's death, Sumarokov tried to explain and clarify the past clashes—for contemporaries and, especially, for literary descendants—in a series of critical essays.

The polemical fray had no apparent winner. All three participants felt defeated. As early as 1755 Trediakovsky wrote in his essay on Sapphic and Horatian strophes, addressed to Sumarokov:

I became tired of retorting to your charges. . . . I beg you, forget about me; let a man who has fallen in love with solitude, calm, and peace of mind alone. . . . Let me spend my remaining days in serenity and benefit society in some way with my rank and with the work entrusted to me by my superiors. . . . Take pity on me, feel affection toward me, eject me from your thoughts.[18]

Lomonosov, frustrated, also vowed to ignore Sumarokov's attacks. He wrote—humbly, but evidently not quite sincerely—in his letter to Ivan Shuvalov of January 19, 1761: "I forget all his [Sumarokov's] animosities and do not want to take revenge on him in any way, and God did not give me a malicious heart. . . . I wish him no evil. I do not even think of avenging the insults. And I only ask my Lord that I not have to associate with him."[19] Even allowing for some theatricality, we can feel the writers' despair. Sumarokov, in the last years of his life, thought in turn that public opinion was grossly unfair to him in undeservedly elevating Lomonosov, and wrote bitterly: "I do not ask the public to prefer me, for solicited praises are disgusting; and if Mr. Lomonosov is given a preference in odes as well, I will not grieve over it; I only wish that the analysis and the praises were well founded."[20]

Later historical accounts, however, began to ascribe the victory to Lomonosov. Staehlin wrote about the poets' relations in his "Traits and Anecdotes for Lomonosov's Biography": "Lomonosov scared him so much that Sumarokov did not dare to open his mouth in his presence."[21] Biographers started to depict Lomonosov as a proud and aloof genius who did not stoop to answer his despicable rivals: "When complaining to his patron of his enviers, Lomonosov did not engage in battle with them, being aware of his superiority; he said of them that *they praised him with their abuse*; only once, urged by his friends, did he write an epigram on Sumarokov." In the interpretation of a later generation, the polemics became a series of shameless attacks by the two giftless poetasters Trediakovsky and Sumarokov on the great and reserved Lomonosov: "How could such a pitiful rhymester [Trediakovsky] upset our immortal Pindar with his critiques? Sumarokov loved Trediakovsky and published the scurrilous escapades of the creator of *Tilemakhida* in his journal."[22]

The polemics between Lomonosov, Sumarokov, and Trediakovsky displayed a feature that has puzzled its students ever since the scholarly evaluation of the literary life of the eighteenth century began in the middle of the last century: It was extraordinarily rude and personal. The participants routinely called each other pigs, bats, asses, owls, or simply animals (*skot* and *skotina*), laughed at their rivals' physical handicaps, and used coarse language in characterizing their enemies. At the same time they viewed literary accusations as personal affronts and were easily insulted by even the slightest criticism of their aesthetic positions. Their touchiness certainly exceeded the usual authorial sensitivity, and their nastiness matched their touchiness. The scholars who have studied the polemics have generally attributed this feature to extraliterary causes, such as the bad temper of the participants, the epoch's underdeveloped literary and social consciousness, or the sharpness of contemporary social conflicts.[23]

The origins of the rudeness and the personal complexion of the polemics had to do, however, with the essence of the literary life of the mid-eighteenth century. This was well understood by Grigorii Gukovsky, who convincingly interprets the polemics in his essay "On Russian Classicism" (1929). He associates the bit-

terness and personal nature of the infighting with the aesthetic
mentality of the period. Gukovsky argues that a belief in one
and only one true artistic ideal, existing outside time and space,
was typical of the Russian eighteenth-century literary consciousness, which rapidly assimilated the aesthetic ideas of European
Classicism. The creative act was understood to be rational and to
be governed by a set of rules. Every artistic goal, therefore, had
in principle only one solution. Since the means of achieving the
literary ideal were held to be rationally determined, writers of
alien schools were regarded as villains or (at best) as blockheads
and ignoramuses. Thus, literary arguments took on moral significance and became bitter and personal.[24]

Gukovsky's explanation of the peculiarities of the polemics
was part of his general conception of eighteenth-century Russian literature. Even now this crucial period of Russian literary
development does not enjoy a commonly accepted interpretation. As a modern scholar laments: "Probably there is no other
period in the history of Russian literature for which so many
terms have been proposed, from the simple 'literature of the transitional epoch' to False [*lozhnyi*] Classicism, Pseudo-Classicism,
School [*shkol'nyi*] Classicism, Classicism, Baroque, Enlightenment, etc."[25] The term "literature of the transitional epoch,"
sometimes applied to the literature of Peter's reign, most vividly
reflects the uncertainty with regard to the status of eighteenth-
century Russian literature as an intermediary between medieval
and modern Russian literature. The terms of the "Pseudo-
Classicism" cluster, the products of Romantic aesthetic consciousness critical of Classicism, reinforce the long-standing
reputation of eighteenth-century Russian literature as secondary
and unoriginal. They present the Russian literature of that time
as doubly imitative, trying to catch up with Europe by slavishly
imitating seventeenth-century French literature, which was itself no more than a "Pseudo-Classical" attempt to imitate the
great Greek and Latin authors. Both approaches treat eighteenth-
century Russian literature, or at least some stages of it, as auxili-
ary, preparatory for the triumphs of Russian literature in the
Golden Age, and devoid of independent significance and aesthetic value.

In the twentieth century the particle *pseudo* has been all but dropped from definitions of the predominant eighteenth-century Russian style. This operation promoted the works of that period to the rank of "real" Classicism and began the systematic study of eighteenth-century literature as an original period. The Classicism model, whose most prominent proponent was Gukovsky, views post-Petrine Russian literature as a local, but nevertheless original, outgrowth of European, especially French, Classicism. Rationalism served as its philosophical foundation, which fact determined the peculiarities of the aesthetics of that time: the rational approach to the creative process and to evaluation, the idea of imitating models, and the hierarchy of genres, as well as the rationalistic concept of language and its poetic usage.[26]

The Classicism model has been prevalent since Gukovsky's studies of eighteenth-century literature. However, there is no agreement about the usage of the term, and it can be applied narrowly—only to the literature of the 1750's or only to Sumarokov and his immediate associates—or broadly, including among Russian Classicists both Kantemir, whose literary activities were largely confined to the 1730's, and Derzhavin, who continued writing well into the nineteenth century. Another drawback of this term is that it was employed in the literary polemics of the first quarter of the nineteenth century between the so-called Archaists and the Innovators, or Classics and Romantics, and thus bears negative connotations. The proposed alternative and complementary terms include *Renaissance, Baroque, Enlightenment, Sentimentalism,* and even *early Realism.* Of these, *Baroque* is generally accepted as meaningful for late seventeenth- and early eighteenth-century Russian literature, but its application to later eighteenth-century works—for example, those of Lomonosov and even Derzhavin—although it has some proponents, is somewhat of a scholarly extravagance. *Renaissance* was in fact never meant to have a serious scholarly application; it was used by Gukovsky to characterize Lomonosov's versatility and love for the grandiose. *Enlightenment* (*Prosveshchenie*) adds to the terminological confusion, for capitalized, it mixes literary history with the history of philosophy, and lowercased, it confounds simple love for education with the problems of aesthetics. *Sentimentalism* is useful when applied to the Russian literature of the late eighteenth century but loses its meaning when applied to earlier decades. The attempts to find samples of Realism before the second third of the nineteenth century endorse an eclectic approach to literary history.

Instead of continuing a terminological battle, it is more productive, I believe, to concentrate on the fact, emphasized by Gukovsky, that eighteenth-century Russian writers of different and even feuding schools seem to have one important feature in common: a normative approach to aesthetics. They believed in one true artistic ideal and understood the creative act as rational; that is, they held that the creation of a work of art could be accomplished only by adhering to the rules that would ensure the conformation of the work to the ideal.

Trediakovsky's, Lomonosov's, and Sumarokov's artistic views can serve as an example. Their literary beliefs were different (in exactly what way they differed is beyond the scope of the present work) but had a very important feature in common: They were normative, and the norm was understood as rationally determined.[27] Moreover, by the end of the 1740's some vague, but to a certain extent agreed-upon, idea of the literary norm had been worked out. For example, as Ilya Serman observes, an "aesthetics of rational clarity" was accepted at that time, "regardless of fierce personal animosity, by Sumarokov and Trediakovsky, and partly even by Lomonosov."[28] Likewise, the concepts held by the active participants in the literary process of that time—concepts of the artistic ideal, the system of genres, literary authority, language, and so forth—were similar enough to provide mutual understanding and to ensure fruitful interaction. Indeed, disagreements in the field of theory did not as a rule lead to quarrels and personal animosity, but rather were resolved in literary competitions—which would be impossible without a common ground.[29] The works (i.e., the realizations of the theoretical views), not theory, caused the trouble, because there was always a possibility that from somebody's point of view a work would not adhere to the norm and therefore would not have the right to exist. But even as targets of criticism, the assaulted authors, angry as they may have been, frequently responded to criticism in a positive way and obediently corrected their alleged mistakes, accepting the authority of the norm. Both Sumarokov and Lomonosov, however reluctantly, took into account Trediakovsky's criticism of *Khorev* in his "Letter from Friend to Friend" and incorporated the suggestions into their subsequent tragedies. Similarly, Lomonosov edited his *Demofont* in response to Sumarokov's *Nonsense Odes*, eliminating those expressions that Sumarokov derided as inadmissible according to the stylistic norm. As Serman argues, Sumarokov's rational understanding of poetic semantics influenced Lomonosov's notion of tropes in general and persuaded him to moderate his high-flown imagery.[30]

The eighteenth-century approach to tropes demonstrates clearly the similarity of the theoretical views of the writers of that time. The ways in which they criticized one another's imagery were strikingly alike. Guided in their statements by the normative literary theory, they claimed to know exactly which metaphors or similes could be allowed and which were forbidden. Accusations of illogicality, ignorance of the laws of nature, and illiteracy migrated from one critical essay to another. One writer's accusations were virtually indistinguishable from another's: "Whiteness is not a color," "A sword cannot be in hands, but in a hand," "The author's logic in this case is similar to the following conclusion: *Today a stick stands in the corner, therefore tomorrow it will rain*," "In this stanza, sir, you have sinned not only against grammar but against a general philosophical truth as well."[31] Such accusations could easily be readdressed to the accusers themselves. Thus, in his answer to Trediakovsky's "Letter from Friend to Friend," Sumarokov protests against Trediakovsky's readdressing to him Sumarokov's own criticism of incompetent writers, given in his "Epistle on Poetry," and readdresses the passage back to Trediakovsky: "I do not know to whom these lines are more becoming, to me or him."[32]

Critics considered their own understanding of language and the world to be not just impeccable but exclusively possible and did not allow for any individual interpretation of linguistic norms and the laws of nature. As with infractions of poetic rules, the critics saw individual variations in imagery as blunders, grave mistakes, or ill will and held the author of the work under analysis responsible for such transgressions. The critics implied that the transgressing author was not only incompetent as a poet but was also incapable of logical thinking. This notion of personal responsibility and the habit of harsh castigation for seemingly minor mistakes (or what the critics thought to be mistakes), coupled with the firm belief on the part of eighteenth-century writers in the correctness of their own views of language and nature, produced the painfully personal tone in the polemics between Trediakovsky, Lomonosov, and Sumarokov, which was responsible for the abuses of civility. This feature was not an accidental and superficial detail of the polemics but a fundamental trait of eighteenth-century literary life in Russia. It had very important consequences, which I will examine in the following chapter.

Chapter 3

Criticism, Parody, and Myth

Two forces produced a distorted picture of literary life in the middle of the eighteenth century: the mythogenic spirit that underlay the cultural self-conceptions of the epoch, and the passion with which the participants in the literary process asserted their individual artistic principles as exclusively correct and therefore universal. The details of this distorted picture were worked out in fierce literary clashes over normative aesthetic principles. The myth of a new Russia, transfigured by Peter, provided the pattern for the formation of the distorted historical picture and ensured the survival of the distortion beyond the initial polemical heat.

Gukovsky's idea that the concept of the rationally determined aesthetic norm governed Russian literary life in the mid-eighteenth century explains the nature of the literary polemics to a considerable extent. However, his approach does not address the specifics of the critical methods employed by the eighteenth-century Russian writers. An analysis of these methods enables us to draw important conclusions about the ways in which the artistic principles of the period influenced the formation of the literary reputations of the participants in the polemics and, eventually, the formation of historical accounts of mid-eighteenth-century literary life.

The goal of an eternal and absolute artistic ideal denied a

writer the right to artistic individuality. A tendency to judge a work of art according to a normative set of rules and to reject those works that did not follow the rules elicited very specific critical methods. It is possible to say that parody was the main critical method of the epoch.

The Russian eighteenth century was amazingly prolific in parodies, nor did parody occupy its usual marginal position. It was among the leading polemical genres and was the main weapon in every round of the literary polemics between Trediakovsky, Lomonosov, Sumarokov, and their allies. Every issue elicited scores of parodies. Sumarokov's school first attacked Lomonosov in the early 1750's with a parody of Lomonosov's tragedy in a humorous playbill, "From Russian Theater." When Elagin's "Satire on a Fop and Coquettes," directed against Lomonosov's group, intensified the polemical exchanges, four pieces in these exchanges were written as parodies. In another round of polemics, Lomonosov's "Hymn to the Beard" was parodied at least twice. In the 1760's Lomonosov parodied Sumarokov's fable "An Ass in a Lion's Skin" in his piece "A Pig in Fox's Skin." In the 1750's and 1760's Sumarokov in turn parodied Lomonosov's and Vasilii Petrov's poetic principles in his *Nonsense Odes* and Trediakovsky's in his "Little Song," "Song," and "Sonnet Composed on Purpose in Bad Style." The parodies of Trediakovsky's works also included Andrei Andreevich Nartov's "An Announcement" and the anonymous "Epitaph" (possibly written by Ivan Barkov).

In addition, eighteenth-century parody was aggressive and frequently intruded into other polemical genres, especially the epigram. For example, Trediakovsky's argument, in his *A New and Brief Method for Composing Russian Verse*, in favor of a rule that prohibited the alternation of masculine and feminine rhymes—

Such a mixing of verses would be as disgusting and hideous for us as if someone were to give in marriage the most admirable, the most tender European beauty, shining with the very bloom of youth, to a decrepit, black, ninety-year-old Arab

—was mocked in Lomonosov's epigram on behalf of Russian poetry, "On the Mixing of [masculine and feminine] Russian Verses" (1751–53?):

Штивелий уверял, что муж мой худ и слаб,
Бессилен, подл и стар, и дряхлой был арап;
Сказал, что у меня кривясь трясутся ноги
И нет мне никакой к супружеству дороги.[1]

Shtivelii insisted that my husband was thin and weak, impo-
tent, mean, and old and that he was a decrepit Arab; he said
that my legs were bending and trembling and that there was
no way for me to enjoy conjugal life.

Similarly, Lomonosov's epigram "Artful singers . . ." (1753) includes a parody of Trediakovsky's grammar and spelling, and
the "Epigram on El[agin]" (1753; probably by Mikhail Sobakin)
contains a parody of Elagin's "Satire on a Fop and Coquettes."[2]
The list of examples could be continued, but these suffice to illustrate my point.

Features of parody can also be found in comedy. Sumarokov, in *Tresotinius*, parodies Trediakovsky's linguistic theories
and his style. He puts into Tresotinius's lips a parodical song
written in "trochaic feet" (*khoreicheskimi stopami*)—a clear hint at
Trediakovsky's metrical preferences. Another parodical character in this comedy, Bobembius, represents Lomonosov. The
speech and views of Krititsiondius, a character in Sumarokov's
comedy *The Monsters*, also parody Trediakovsky's aesthetic and
linguistic conceptions.

Finally, parody regularly appeared in critical essays and
theoretical statements. A. A. Morozov, in his introduction to a
collection of Russian parodies, discusses some instances: a parody of Lomonosov's odes in "Conversations of the Dead" published in the May 1759 issue of *The Diligent Bee* and a parody of
his tragedy *Tamira and Selim* in the essay "A Journey of Reason,"
published in the magazine *Useful Amusement* (1760, part 1).[3]
Similarly, Lomonosov's criticism of Elagin's "Satire on a Fop and
Coquettes" in his letter to Ivan Shuvalov of October 1753 was in
fact a parody. Lomonosov pretended that he did not understand
Elagin's metaphors:

I do not think that A[leksandr] P[etrovich] could possibly wish to be
called "a son born from the goddess [who was born] of the brain," that
is, the grandchild of a brain, especially as there is no way such a thing
could happen. . . . To call A. P. "Boileau's bosom companion" is un-

just. If somebody had called Racine Boileau's bosom companion, he would hardly have tolerated it; it is amazing that A. P. can bear it.[4]

Taking the metaphors out of context, Lomonosov laid the device bare, thus demonstrating its absurdity and creating a parodical effect.

Prose paraphrases of poetic works—a critical method that was quite widespread in the middle of the eighteenth century—were also frequently done with a parodical effect in mind: "So here are all its [the ode's] bare contents: You have fought enough, we already have peace; and you, neighbors, surrender and rely on this hand that will overcome all enemies, as many as there may be. But why am I so daring as to want to glorify *Elizabeth*: She is incomparably glorified without my intervention."[5] Removed from the poetic structure, imagery and tropes displayed their conventional character and thus their ludicrousness in the eyes of the critic.

Finally, the criticism of the mid-eighteenth century was parodical in its frequent mockery of grammatical inaccuracies and individual spelling, its quibbles at misprints and other minor features of a work. All these can be found in Trediakovsky's criticism of Sumarokov's works in "Letter from Friend to Friend," as well as in essays Sumarokov wrote throughout his life—"Critique of the Ode" (1747), "Response to Criticism" (1750), "On Orthography" (1771–73), "On Versification" (the 1770's), and many others.[6]

However, much more important than the inclusion of parodies in critical essays or the superficial similarities in modes was the fact that the criticism in the mid-eighteenth century had the same attitude toward the artistic text as parody had. Parody has no respect for authorial individuality; it does not hesitate to show a work's incongruity in comparison with its implied abstract ideal. Parody accomplishes this end by taking the most distinctive features of a work out of context and hyperbolizing them, thus creating a deliberately chaotic text. The same disregard for the author's individuality can be observed in eighteenth-century criticism. Eighteenth-century critics applied the norms as they understood them to the given work and rejected anything that went beyond those norms, no matter how appropriate it might be within the artistic system under analysis. In critical essays, however, the incongruity of a given work with the ideal was not demonstrated by creating a parallel parodical text, but was proved logically.

Thus, in his *Nonsense Odes*, Sumarokov parodied the highly metaphorical style of Lomonosov's odes. In his critical essays, he demonstrated the incongruity between Lomonosov's metaphorical usage and the norms of the language, common sense, and the laws of nature. Sumarokov took Lomonosov's images out of context, treated them as linguistic mistakes, explained what was wrong with Lomonosov's innovative usage, and reduced his imagery to pure logical absurdity. Trediakovsky employed a similar critical method. In discussing Sumarokov's version of the 143rd Psalm in his "Letter from Friend to Friend," he logically proved that Sumarokov's metaphors were unacceptable from the point of view of linguistics and common sense.

The similarity between criticism and parody is especially striking when they turn upon the same phenomenon. For instance, in Gertrude's monologue in *Hamlet*, Sumarokov used a gallicism, *ne tronuta* (untouched, not affected): "And looked untouched upon my husband's death."[7] This neologism elicited objections from both Lomonosov and Trediakovsky. Lomonosov parodied it in the last line of an epigram:

> Женился Стил, старик без мочи,
> На Стелле, что в пятнадцать лет,
> И не дождавшись первой ночи
> Закашлявшись, оставил свет.
> Тут Стелла бедная вздыхала,
> Что на супружню смерть нетронута взирала.[8]

Stil, an old man without any strength, married Stella, who was fifteen, and having a fit of coughing, he left this world, unable to wait until the first night. Then poor Stella sighed, looking untouched upon her husband's death.

Trediakovsky analyzed this line from the normative linguistic point of view:

This *touch* of his, instead of *move to pity*, for the French *toucher* is so strange and ridiculous that it is impossible to express it in words. You can immediately feel the indecency of this word in our language because of the euphemism. In the tragedy *Hamlet* the author makes the woman named Gertrude say that she "looked untouched upon her husband's death." Who among us will not understand this line in the following sense, namely, that Gertrude's husband died never knowing her in respect of marital right and conjugal duty? However, the author did not mean this: He wanted to show that she did not grieve a bit over his death.[9]

Sumarokov had in fact made a conscious attempt to introduce one of the meanings of the French verb *toucher* into the Russian language. He replaced "pitilessly" (*bezzhalostno*) with "untouched" in the fair copy of his tragedy just before sending it to the Academy of Sciences for publishing. He never corrected the usage despite Lomonosov's and Trediakovsky's mockery. Trediakovsky and Lomonosov chose to ignore his stand and saw in the usage only the author's sloppiness and inaccuracy. Nevertheless, by the beginning of the nineteenth century, the Russian language had accepted the new meaning.[10]

Another common critical method in the middle of the eighteenth century was to rewrite—totally or partially—a criticized text. The original text was rejected for failing to meet the norm, and a new one, written in accordance with the rules, was suggested. Most frequently only one "wrong" line was replaced. For example, in "Critique of the Ode" Sumarokov proposed the elimination of the inversion in the line "The hunter where did not aim his bow" (*Okhotnik gde ne metil lukom*): "*Where*, according to grammatical rules, has to be put before *the hunter*, and thus we have to say: 'Where did the hunter not aim his bow.' But this is spoiled for the sake of meter alone." In the same work he also suggested a change in another line of Lomonosov's ode. Instead of "Or have I now forgotten myself / And deviated from the way / that I had followed earlier?" he proposed: "Or, having now forgotten myself, / Have I deviated . . ."[11] When criticizing Sumarokov's ode in "Letter from Friend to Friend," Trediakovsky likewise substituted his own lines, "Deeds that penetrate into the sky, / Into forests, and into proud waves," for Sumarokov's, "Deeds that pierce the skies, / Forests, and proud waves." In the same work he suggested two replacements for Sumarokov's line "Increase the age of this damsel," which contained a metrical irregularity.[12]

Sometimes critics did not confine themselves to minor changes in an analyzed work and proposed new versions of whole stanzas. Trediakovsky suggested changes in emphasis and punctuation in the fifth stanza of Sumarokov's paraphrase of the 143rd Psalm. The critic concluded the alteration with a comment that is characteristic of his normative aesthetics: "Please judge now with all impartial fairness whose stanza is more grandiloquent." Trediakovsky does not even attempt an investigation into the peculiarities of Sumarokov's artistic task (such as, in this case, the intonation, indicated by punctuation). Instead he judges the poem according to the vague and subjective notion of "grandiloquence," which, nevertheless, he presents as a universally accepted criterion.[13]

The same lack of interest in artistic individuality underlay the literary competitions in which the writers frequently engaged. In these competitions, authors translating the same work or developing the same theme offered their "correct" versions in place of the less perfect artistic productions of their rivals. Criticism and artistic exploration overlapped. The authors did not simply put forth a new version but implied that all other versions were inferior. In the essay "Some Stanzas by Two Authors" (the 1770's), Sumarokov placed his stanzas beside Lomonosov's, not to allow the readers to enjoy different poetic approaches, but to enable them to see with their own eyes the superiority of his own artistic method. Similarly, Sumarokov, following Trediakovsky, attempted to translate Fénelon's *Télémaque* to assert his own excellence and thus discredit Trediakovsky's work. Sumarokov neither finished his translation nor published it. Apparently, the small fragment was sufficient to assure him of the superiority of his approach over Trediakovsky's.

Even the most peaceful of these competitions, the translation of the 143rd Psalm by Trediakovsky, Sumarokov, and Lomonosov—which, as Trediakovsky explained in the introduction to the publication of the three translations, was designed not as a contest but as a search for the correct theoretical decision—was based on the same rejection of the very idea of individuality. All three poems were good, Trediakovsky claimed, because they coincided in their treatment of the chosen theme: "Their only appreciable difference is in ardor and representation, but an amazing agreement in meaning is offered here, and from that it could be concluded that all good poets, no matter how differently they present their individual keenness and power of thought, however, arrive at one common point, and, thanks to that, do not depart from due center." The good poet is the one who approaches the ideal ("point, center"); bad poets do not know "where their immobile point is, or the target at which they should aim." The good poets reach similar decisions, and the bad ones "are further from each other in their difference than is proper." [14]

As we see, the criticism of the mid-eighteenth century was mainly concerned with the fidelity of the criticized text to abstract aesthetic norms. Critics focused mostly on the analysis of artistic decisions that were unsuccessful from their point of view. When approaching a work, they admitted neither the existence of artistic norms different from their own nor the possibility of mistakes in their views on literature, language, and the universe.

The three critical methods discussed above—parody, criticism proper, and the replacement of the original text with a new one—were similar in their attitude toward an author's text. Ignoring its individuality and imposing on it the critic's own artistic criteria, they revealed the conventionality of the poetical devices of the criticized piece and thus destroyed it as an artistic unity. That is precisely what parody does to the parodied text. As Tuvia Shlonsky puts it, "The method of parody is to disrealize the norms which the original tries to realize, that is to say to reduce what is of normative status in the original to a convention or a mere device." [15] This end is achieved, as Tynianov points out, by "alteration of a literary work . . . as a *system*, [that is, by] transferring [it] into another system." [16] In other words, parody interprets the individual features of a parodied work according to artistic rules suggested by the parodist. Pretending not to understand this contradiction, the parodist attains a comical effect.

Eighteenth-century parodists applied this method with a vengeance. Fully confident that their rivals' artistic decisions could not be correct, they were straightforward in their disregard of the individuality of a parodied work (even perceiving this individuality as a negative feature) and in their desire to demonstrate the work's absurdity. So too with the critics of this period. Because they appraised a criticized work according to an abstract norm, critics could not comprehend it as an artistic unity. Therefore they considered it an absurdity, a violation of good taste, and a "confusion deserving of laughter and contempt." [17] A distortion of the artistic system of a criticized work produced a parodical effect.

To be sure, features of parody can be found in the criticism of all epochs, but only a strictly normative aesthetic mentality could generate criticism that was so close to parody in its approach and results. Lidiia Ginzburg, in her book *On the Lyric*, points out the methods in nineteenth-century criticism that were similar to those of eighteenth-century Classicism. Specifically, metaphors were frequently judged by normative principles—linguistic usage, logic, and common sense.[18] There was, however, an important difference: The idea of one and only one perfect artistic decision had disappeared, and criticized authors could and frequently did use in their defense an argument about the "individuality" of their works. Thus, in the episode, analyzed by Ginzburg, P. A. Viazemsky, having exhausted all possible responses to Pushkin's criticism of one of his poems, finally retreated to this argument: "Get it into your head that this waterfall is nothing but a man churned up by a sudden passion. From this point of view, it seems that all the parts agree and all the expressions receive *une arrière-pensée*, which echoes everywhere." [19] Eighteenth-century writers never appealed to the special, individual point of view that would justify their artistic decisions, because only one possible point of view—that of reason—could be implied. Offended and enraged by their peers' criticism though they might be, eighteenth-century writers felt compelled to correct their alleged violations of the rules. The authority of the norm was above personal feelings and even authorial pride.[20]

The same disregard for individuality can be detected in the critics' desire to rewrite an "incorrect" text. They saw such a text as a piece of nonsense, created out of stupidity or ignorance, which could be rearranged according to the rules and thus brought closer to the ideal. The author's plans and intentions were not taken into account. However, unlike criticism and parody, which preserved both conflicting artistic systems (the author's as well as the critic's or parodist's) for the reader, rewriting cast a criticized text aside and replaced it with a new one. The distortion of the criticized text did not occur before the reader's eyes, and a parodical effect was therefore lacking. Hereafter I will be interested in parodies and critical essays as texts that preserve the author's, albeit distorted, voice.

The exposition in parody of the conventional character of an individual artistic system turns the author's conventional style into his or her individual voice. As Tynianov says, "Instead of an author's persona [*avtorskoe litso*], an author's personality [*avtorskaia lichnost'*], with its everyday gestures, appears."[21] For eighteenth-century Russian literature this had enormous consequences. The literature of Russian Classicism was impersonal in principle. In an ode, tragedy, or fable the author was totally irrelevant. The author spoke on behalf of eternal truths, and no one was interested in an author's artistic and human individuality. The only relevant consideration was the work's conformity with the ideal. Criticism and parody eroded the abstract, supraindividual existence of a literary work. In the hands of the critic, a given work revealed a connection with a particular author's personality. It was always a negative personality, because the critic or parodist made an author responsible only for bad works: Good works belonged to eternity.

This phenomenon resulted in the appearance, in criticism and parodies, of certain images of literary opponents. Although some personal features allowed the reader to relate these images to particular people, they were in fact very far from lifelike. They were grotesque, parodical characters that critics offered as realistic portraits of their rivals. The symbolic names affixed to these images emphasized their grotesqueness. Thus, in parodies and satires Ivan Elagin was presented as Balaban (fool, blockhead) or Afrosin (from the Greek for "stupidity"). Trediakovsky appeared as Tresotinius (from the French *très sot*, "very stupid, foolish"), Tresotin, or simply Sotin. Sumarokov received the name Akolast (from the Greek for "wild, insolent"), and Lomonosov was known as Teleliui (fool, goof). The names all alluded to the stupidity, ignorance, and bad temper of their owners. Abstract as they were, these images gave the polemics of the mid-eighteenth century its well-known personal character.

The images of the three main participants in the literary po-

lemics, Lomonosov, Sumarokov, and Trediakovsky, were naturally the most established and complete. However, each was developed to a different degree. Trediakovsky's parodical image
was the most elaborate. It was first introduced by Sumarokov in
his "Epistle on Poetry": "And you, Shtivelius, can only talk nonsense." Then the characters Tresotinius and Krititsiondius, two
ridiculous pedants who held some of Trediakovsky's most cherished views, appeared in 1750, in Sumarokov's comedies *Tresotinius* and *The Monsters*. By the middle of the 1750's Trediakovsky was universally known as Shtivelius (or Shtivelii), Tresotinius (or Tresotin), and Sotin.

Trediakovsky's three hypostases shared certain comical features. They all adhered to idiosyncratic ("bad") style, promoted
unusual letters and odd spellings, and championed unpopular
meters, first trochees and later the notorious "dactylo-trochees"
(hexameters). All these traits can easily be traced to Trediakovsky's works. Parodists and critics picked them to represent Trediakovsky's literary position, exaggerated them, and included
them in his parodical image.

Trediakovsky's allegedly bad style was the most ridiculed
feature of his comical persona. As Lomonosov lamented in 1757,
"For a long time your disgusting style has been a cause of laughter and grief for us." [22] More specifically, the poet was reproached
for stylistic excesses, either frivolous colloquialisms or grave
Slavonicisms. Sumarokov, in his essay "On Orthography," provided a formula that, despite its obvious straightforwardness
and polemical spirit, is still the most frequently quoted characterization of Trediakovsky's linguistic position: "Mr. Trediakovsky in his youth tried to spoil our orthography with the diction
of the common people, according to which he arranged his
orthography; and in old age [he tried to spoil it] with extreme
Slavonicisms, which he made even more extreme." In this passage Sumarokov quite correctly presents Trediakovsky's linguistic views diachronically: first "diction of the common people,"
then "extreme Slavonicisms" (*glubochaishaia Slavenshchizna*). Popular belief, however, ascribed both views to Trediakovsky simultaneously, thus adding another flaw—namely, "mixing of
styles," or indiscriminate employment of conflicting stylistic elements—to the list of his stylistic failures. His usage, of course,

was far from indiscriminate: In his choice of stylistic elements Trediakovsky followed well-defined principles, although the principles were different in the early and later years of his literary career. It is noteworthy that the young Trediakovsky actually promoted not common but "foppish" talk. Sumarokov refused to distinguish between the two: It was important for him that in the 1730's Trediakovsky's style was too colloquial for his taste and in the 1750's and 1760's, far too bookish.[23]

Along with ridiculing Trediakovsky's colloquialisms and Slavonicisms, his contemporaries reproached the writer for the abuse of inversions. Trediakovsky's parodical doubles—Tresotinius of *Tresotinius*, Krititsiondius of *The Monsters*, and others—employed peculiar syntax in their poems: the word order was completely scrambled and the flow of phrases was frequently interrupted by sudden exclamations such as "oh!" and "ah!" Sumarokov's "Song," a parody of Trediakovsky's poetry, is a good example:

> Прочь от мя ушла свобода,
> Мой сбег с ней прочь, о! и нрав.
> Прочь любовная невзгода,
> О любезный будь мой здрав.[24]

Freedom has abandoned me, and oh! my temper has fled with it too. Go away, love misfortune, O my dear, be well.

The second line is jumbled in the Russian original: The possessive pronoun *moi* (my) is separated from its noun, *nrav* (temper), by six words, the exclamation "oh!" and the conjunction "and" among others. In the fourth line the pronoun is not only in postposition but is also separated, by a verb, from the word that it defines.[25] Inversions and exclamations can both be found in abundance in Trediakovsky's works. In fact, especially in the 1750's, the poet used inversions even more intensively and elaborately than his parodists would reproduce. What was a carefully calculated device aimed at the creation of a high poetic style suitable, in Trediakovsky's opinion, for certain genres, Trediakovsky's critics tried to present as the uncontrolled interference of Latin syntax.

Trediakovsky's interest in questions of orthography and his advocacy of unusual spellings, which he introduced in his treatise *Conversation on Orthography* (1748), provided the scoffers with a wealth of material for mockery. The pedant Tresotinius, in Sumarokov's comedy, hilariously quarrels with everybody about the choice of letters for the Russian alphabet. Like Trediakovsky in his treatise on orthography, he insists that the letter *s*, *zelo*, is more suitable for the Russian alphabet than з, *zemlia*:

Tresotinius. Zapis'—here put an *s*.
A Solicitor. My good sir, those of us in offices do not use the *s*; now even in ABC books there is no *s*.
Tresotinius. I want, and I really want, to put an *s* and not a з.

In his work on orthography, Trediakovsky defends *s* because of its Latinized form and cites the fact that Peter the Great preferred it to з. Sumarokov, however, calls it by its Church Slavonic name, *zelo*, thus emphasizing its alleged archaic origin.[26]

Lomonosov, in turn, made fun of Trediakovsky's orthography in epigrams. In "Artful singers . . . ," for example, he parodied Trediakovsky's spelling of masculine adjectives in the plural by Church Slavonic rules. To achieve a comical effect, Lomonosov applied these rules to everyday words:

> На что же, Трисотин, к нам тянешь *И* некстати?
> Напрасно злобный сей ты предприял совет,
> Чтоб, льстя тебе, когда российский принял свет
> *Свиныи визги вси и дикии, и злыи,*
> *И истиныи ти, и лживы, и кривыи.*

Wherefore, Trisotin, are you imposing [the ending] и on us inappropriately? You should not have taken that malicious advice, so that, flattering you, Russians accepted *all pig squealings, both the wild and the vicious, and the true ones, and the false, and the wry.*

Lomonosov presents the two last lines of the passage as a quotation from Trediakovsky. Traditional archaic spelling in this pseudoquotation comically contrasts with the vulgar and absurd contents, reinforcing the image of Trediakovsky as a bad stylist.[27]

Another prominent feature of Trediakovsky's parodical image was a fondness for trochees. This detail reflected Trediakovsky's early views on syllabo-tonics: When he proposed his first syllabo-tonic verses in *A New and Brief Method for Composing Rus-*

sian Verse in 1735, certain theoretical premises of his reform moved him to proclaim the superiority of the trochee over other feet.[28] In the early 1740's he changed his view and acknowledged the equality of all meters, but his reputation as the proponent of trochees had taken root. It was reinforced by his 1743 dispute with Lomonosov and Sumarokov about iambs and trochees. Trediakovsky's goal in this dispute was to assert the equality of the trochee, not its superiority, but the stereotype was set, and Trediakovsky came down in history as a poet with an unreasonable weakness for trochees.

In the late 1760's Trediakovsky's supposed love for trochees was overshadowed by another idiosyncrasy ascribed to him—a fondness for hexameters, or, as Trediakovsky himself called them, dactylo-trochees. This predilection was part of Trediakovsky's image as the creator of the unfortunate *Tilemakhida*. To restore the epic spirit of the classic plot, Trediakovsky rendered Fénelon's political novel into verse. He introduced a meter that he suggested was a Russian equivalent of the classical model and that he described as a combination of six trochaic and dactylic feet, with an occasional spondee. Later the meter proved to be an apt imitation of the original and was used, along with a similarly constructed pentameter, by Nikolai Gnedich and Vasilii Zhukovsky in their respective translations of the *Iliad* and the *Odyssey*, as well as in numerous nineteenth-century imitations of other classical forms. However, Trediakovsky was hardly ever commended for the development of this meter. On the contrary, it was generally acknowledged that the use of hexameters contributed to the spectacular failure of his attempt at an epic poem. Mockeries of the verse in *Tilemakhida*, together with mockeries of the poem's supposed soporific qualities and its gigantic size, became indispensable whenever Trediakovsky's name was mentioned. His skillful attempt to create a national equivalent of classical meter was perceived as a clumsy blunder, worthy only of laughter and sneering.[29]

The name "pedant" consolidated all the details of Trediakovsky's comical image as it emerged in the literary polemics of the mid-eighteenth century. The notion of pedantry was a basic element of Trediakovsky's image at the very beginning of its formation. Shtivelius, the nickname Sumarokov suggested for Trediakovsky in his "Epistle on Poetry," was borrowed from a German translation of L. H. Holberg's comedy *Jacob von Tyboe eller den stortalende soldat* (1725), in which it belonged to the ridiculous magister who unsuccessfully courted the young heroine. The pedant's name in the original was Magister Stygotius, but in German translation he was renamed Magister Stifelius, after the mathematician Michael Stifel (Stifelius), who had a reputation as a pedant because of his love for complicated operations with numbers and his unsuccessful prediction that the world would end in 1533.[30] In 1750 Sumarokov endowed another pedantic character with Trediakovsky's features. This was Tresotinius, in the comedy of the same name. Soon after that, Sumarokov wrote another comedy, *The Monsters*, in which Trediakovsky was impersonated by the pedant Krititsiondius.

Trediakovsky, in his criticism of *Tresotinius* in "Letter from Friend to Friend," correctly pointed out that Sumarokov's first comedy borrowed certain features and situations from Molière's comedy *Les femmes savantes* (1672).[31] The name Tresotinius itself was coined after the name of Trissotin, a character in the play. Like Molière's character, Tresotinius wants to marry the young heroine, but does not succeed. He writes poetry and reads his ridiculous creations to the ladies. The squabble between Sumarokov's Tresotinius and Bobembius resembles the quarrel between Molière's Trissotin and Vadius. The main plot of *The Monsters* follows *Les femmes savantes* even more closely. The relations between the young heroine's parents are similar. Her mother has the upper hand in the house, and the father is henpecked and even beaten by his wife. Like Molière's characters, they have chosen different bridegrooms for their daughter. Unlike Molière's Trissotin, Krititsiondius is not the main candidate for the heroine's hand in this play, but he intends to marry her nevertheless.

The plots were certainly not unique in European comedy. Trediakovsky himself named yet another play to which Sumarokov was indebted: Holberg's *Jacob von Tyboe*. In this play there is also a pedant among the heroine's unsuccessful suitors. The main dramatic situation in *Tresotinius* also resembles the one in *Tartuffe*. As in Molière's play, the conflict in *Tresotinius* revolves around the infatuation of the heroine's father with a pedant and hypocrite who wants to marry the reluctant heroine. Sumarokov, then, attempted to introduce into Russia a comedic plot that was widespread in Europe and that included a pedant among its popular characters. The comparisons to Molière or Holberg would not be particularly significant if Sumarokov had confined himself to the imitation of plots, which were archetypal.[32]

However, Sumarokov not only imitated general situations popular in European comedy but tried to transplant onto Russian soil the forms and principles of literary infighting reflected in Molière's comedies. It is well known that Molière pictured two of his literary enemies in the characters Trissotin and Vadius: the poet Abbé Charles Cotin and the poet and scholar Gilles Ménage. Sumarokov reproduced this pair as Tresotinius and the rhetorician Bobembius, who corresponded to Sumarokov's literary opponents Trediakovsky and Lomonosov.[33] Trissotin's and Vadius's quarrel served as a model for Tresotinius's and Bobembius's heated dispute about whether the letter т should have one or three "legs." Still, the subject of the dispute was taken from a Russian situation and reflected Lomonosov's and Trediakovsky's linguistic arguments.[34]

Certain details facilitated the use of Trissotin's image to ridicule Trediakovsky. Thus, like Trediakovsky in his youth, Molière's character is a proponent of the linguistic theories of Claude Favre de Vaugelas, the "purifier" of the French language.[35] Like Trissotin, who writes poems that he himself considers specimens of elegant love poetry, Trediakovsky entered Russian literature as a proponent of the love theme. The pronounced eroticism of Tresotinius's song in Sumarokov's comedy ("Seeing your beauty, / I have become aroused") refers both to Trediakovsky's sensual early poetry and Trissotin's dubious sonnet (Molière used an actual poem by Cotin). Trissotin's attempts at the role of ladies' man are reflected in Tresotinius's awkward efforts to talk gallantly to the young heroine, Klarisa. The reference here is also to Trediakovsky's linguistic views in the 1730's: Sumarokov's character, like the young Trediakovsky in his translation of *Voyage à l'île d'Amour*, uses elements of foppish talk, such as the overuse of the epithets *sladkii* and *priiatnyi* ("sweet" and "pleasant") and the polite *vy* (plural "you") instead of *ty* (singular "you").

In *The Monsters* Sumarokov connected Trediakovsky with

another notorious figure in French seventeenth-century literary history—Jean Chapelain. Poet, linguist, and founder of the Académie française, Chapelain was a highly esteemed figure of his time, but by the end of the seventeenth century, thanks to Boileau's severe criticism of his poem *La Pucelle* (1656), he became known as a paragon of pedantry and talentlessness.[36] In this capacity he appears in the opening lines of Sumarokov's "Epistle on Poetry." In *The Monsters*, Chapelain's name serves to mock Krititsiondius, Trediakovsky's double. Sumarokov almost directly calls Trediakovsky "Chapelain": Krititsiondius reproaches the author of *Khorev* and *Tresotinius* for calling "the wisest Mr. Chapelain . . . by the fictitious name Tresotinius." This is a clear mockery of Trediakovsky's "Letter from Friend to Friend," in which he states several times that by Tresotinius Sumarokov meant "our mutual friend [i.e., Trediakovsky himself], indicating him, however, by an inexact name."[37] Krititsiondius's eulogy of Chapelain actually makes fun of Trediakovsky: Krititsiondius praises Chapelain for his translation of Herodotus, which is an obvious substitution for Rollin's *Histoire ancienne*, translated by Trediakovsky. Finally, Sumarokov depicts Krititsiondius as a ridiculous epigone of Chapelain: "I made an addition to the book that Mr. Chapelain composed about the letter *i*, which, perhaps, is ridiculed by everyone; but posterity will have something else to say about it and will not believe that I was considered by my contemporaries to be a madman."[38] The book attributed to Chapelain is, of course, Trediakovsky's *Conversation on Orthography*, in which, among other things, he discussed which letter was more suitable for the Russian alphabet, *i* or *и*.

Sumarokov had good grounds for endowing Trediakovsky with the name "the Russian Chapelain." Upon his arrival in Russia from Paris, Trediakovsky obviously tried to play the same role as organizer of cultural life for which Chapelain was famous. He proposed the establishment of the Russian Assembly, a replica of the Académie française, which Chapelain had started with Cardinal Richelieu's patronage. In his contract with the Academy of Sciences and in his "Speech to the Russian Assembly," Trediakovsky took upon himself the creation of a grammar and a dictionary, which were supposed to purify the Russian language exactly as Chapelain's grammar and dictionary had purified the French language. Finally, like Chapelain, who formulated the canon of the unities in "Les sentiments de l'Académie française sur 'le Cid'" (1632), Trediakovsky took upon himself the introduction of classical literary rules into Russia. He attempted to fulfill these intentions in *A New and Brief Method for Composing Russian Verse* and in the translations of Horace's *De arte poetica* and Boileau's *L'art poétique*. Trediakovsky's efforts in this direction, like Chapelain's, were not appreciated, bringing him yet more mockery as a pedant. Except in Sumarokov's comedy, the name of Chapelain was not used for Trediakovsky in the eighteenth century. The comparison resurfaced, however, in the nineteenth century, when the Innovators used it in their polemics with the Archaists and when Lazhechnikov included it into his ironic characterization of Trediakovsky in the novel *The Ice House*.[39]

The images of the pedants Shtivelius and Tresotinius took better root, and these nicknames became Trediakovsky's usual appellations. They forced his contemporaries and his literary heirs to forget the young and enthusiastic Trediakovsky who had arrived in Russia from Paris eager to introduce new literary notions and genres to his compatriots: the *précieux* romance, love poetry in the libertine tradition, and a style modeled after the speech of "the most distinguished and skillful noble estate" (*znatneishee i iskusneishee blagorodnykh soslovie*).[40] Ironically, Trediakovsky's libertinism, his interest in the linguistic theories of Vaugelas, and his attempts to introduce *vers de société* were precisely what contributed, as an analysis of Sumarokov's Tresotinius suggests, to the identification of Trediakovsky with Trissotin and thus to the establishment of his image as a pedant.

Lomonosov's and Sumarokov's comical images never developed to such an extent. However, parodical characters in which contemporaries saw allusions to Lomonosov and Sumarokov can easily be found in the literary criticism and polemics of the middle of the eighteenth century.

Lomonosov was known for his high-flown, inflated, and obscure style, which Sumarokov parodied in his *Nonsense Odes*:

> Превыше звезд, луны и солнца
> В восторге возлетаю нынь,
> Из горних областей взираю
> На полуночный океан.[41]

Above the stars, the moon, and the sun, in raptures, now I ascend; from the celestial provinces I look down upon the northern ocean.

The turgidity of Lomonosov's style, as well as his other deficiencies, was often attributed to his inclination to strong drink. Thus, in the anonymous "Epistle from Vodka and Moonshine to L[omonosov]," the drinks complain that they are held responsible for the poet's high-flown style:

> А ныне пухлые стихи твои читая,
> Ни рифм, ни смыслу в них нигде не обретая
> И разбирая вздор твоих сумбурных од,
> Кричит всяк, что то наш—не твой сей тухлый
>   плод,
> Что будто мы—не ты стихи слагаешь,
> Которых ты и сам совсем не понимаешь,
> Что не пермесский жар в тебе уже горит,
> Но водка и вино сим вздором говорит,
> Что только ты тогда и бредишь лишь стихами,
> Как хватишь полный штоф нас полными устами.

And now, reading your inflated poetry, not finding either rhymes or sense anywhere, and going over the nonsense of your muddled odes, everybody cries that this is our, not your, rotten fruit, that we, not you, write the poetry that you yourself do not understand at all, that it is not a Permessian fever that burns in you, but vodka and wine that speak through this nonsense, that you produce your delirious poetry only when you drink a whole bottle of us in great gulps.

Another sarcastic attack on this unfortunate habit was a poem by Trediakovsky written in the late 1750's: "Tsyganosov, when he sleeps off the Castilian waters . . . ." The poem alluded to a mistake (rather, a misprint) in the epithet "Castalian dew" in Lomonosov's *Collection of Various Compositions in Verse and in Prose* (1751) and attributed the mistake to the author's alcoholic intoxication.[42]

The comical drunkard is portrayed as rude and arrogant:

> Он, знатно, что тогда шумен был от вина;
> Бросаться ж на людей—страсть пьяницы всегда.

He was then apparently drunk with wine; it is always the passion of a drunkard to attack people.

He is pictured as an upstart and braggart:

> Дел славою своих он похвалялся больно,
> И так уж говорил, что не нашлось ему
> Подобного во всем, ни ровни по всему.

He greatly boasted about the glory of his deeds, and it appeared from his talk that there was nobody who could be compared to him or who could be his equal.

Ignorant and stupid, he cannot be considered an original poet:

> Такого в наши дни мы видим Телелюя,
> Огромного враля и глупого холуя,
> Который Гинтера и многих обокрал
> И, мысли их писав, народ наш удивлял.

Such is the Teleliui that we see in our days, an enormous liar and a stupid flunky, who robbed Guenther and many others and, copying their thoughts, amazed our people.[43]

References to Lomonosov's low origin, called "meanness" with all the insulting nuances of the word, completed Teleliui's portrait. Sumarokov described him as

> в чину урода
> Из сама подла рода,
> Которого пахать произвела природа.

a high-ranking freak of the meanest origin who was created by nature to plow.

In a word, Lomonosov was "Parnassian mud, a scribbler, and not a creator."[44]

Sumarokov appeared in the polemics as a malicious envier and boaster. Here is Lomonosov's scornful opinion of him, expressed in his letter to Ivan Shuvalov of January 19, 1761: "How you can deal with such a man, who speaks only in order to scold everyone, praises himself, and considers his poor rhyming more important than all human knowledge!"[45] Trediakovsky also found Sumarokov's alleged pretensions unjustified. Sumarokov, in his opinion, was nothing but a poor ignoramus: "I cannot refrain from offering you now, dear sir, irrefutable proof that the author's knowledge is so small that it could not be smaller."[46] Rivals attributed Sumarokov's envy and malice to his evil nature,

of which his physical defects (stuttering and a tic) were the clear-
est indications:

> Кто рыж, плешив, мигун, заика и картав,
> Не может быти в том никак хороший нрав.[47]

A redhead, a baldhead, a blinker, a stutterer, and a triller of *r*'s
simply cannot be of good disposition.

The verdict was a familiar one: Sumarokov was a plagiarist
and a worthless versifier. Such was Lomonosov's passionate accusation, uttered in response to the praise (*"génie créateur"*) given
to Sumarokov by Abbé Lefevre in his "Discours sur le progrés
de beaux arts en Russie." Lomonosov wrote with spite and indignation: "The *génie créateur* used all the best pieces from the
French poets in his tragedies, but with lots of awful offenses
against the Russian language, and disgustingly integrated them
with his own thoughts."[48]

These rude and often unjust characterizations made up the
collective image of the "inane rhymester" (*nesmyslennyi rifmot-
vorets,* in Sumarokov's words), which is how the literary opponents of the mid-eighteenth century saw one another. Such a
stereotypic image was attached to a concrete literary figure by
means of a few individual traits, such as Lomonosov's actual
weakness for alcohol, Sumarokov's tic and stutter, and Trediakovsky's interest in trochees. The majority of the characteristics,
however, recurred: boasting, plagiarism, stupidity, ignorance,
lack of taste and talent.

The boundaries between conventional and individual traits
were not fixed. For example, Lomonosov made an attempt to
convert alcoholism, his own real-life trait, into a conventional
trait in a literary rival's comical portrait. He tried to ascribe it to
Trediakovsky in his poem "To Zubnitsky":

> Никто не поминай нам подлости *ходуль*
> И к пьянству твоему потребных *красоуль.*

No one should remind us of the mean *stilts* and the *bowls* that
are needed for your drinking.

The stilts and bowls were mentioned in Trediakovsky's epigram published in his *A New and Brief Method for Composing
Russian Verse,* but in real life Trediakovsky was no drunkard.[49]

Nevertheless, Lomonosov at least partly succeeded, and accusations of drunkenness can be found in later portrayals of Trediakovsky. Lazhechnikov mentions it on several occasions in his novel (pp. 68, 73, 256). The legend of Trediakovsky's alcoholism was undoubtedly promoted by his daring translation of Boileau's *"docte et sainte ivresse"* (in his "Ode sur la prise de Namur," 1694) as "sober intoxication," *trezvoe pianstvo*, in his "Ode on the Surrender of the City of Gdansk" (1734; in the 1752 version Trediakovsky changed it to "strange intoxication," *strannoe pianstvo*).

The value of these comical characterizations was not absolute, and a negative trait in such an image could be understood in a different context as a positive one, and vice versa. Thus, theory and practice did not agree on the question of imitations. Theory permitted and encouraged them, but as soon as criticism revealed an author's personal responsibility for "bad" work, imitation began to be seen as plagiarism—the attitude that prevails in literatures with a firm notion of authorship. Likewise, what literary opponents saw as shameless boasting could be, in the author's view, a sincere assertion of the objective value of an artistic position. In the context of normative aesthetics, straightforward positive self-appraisals were justified and even necessary to promote correct artistic principles.

These self-appraisals, as well as dithyrambs by supporters, present another, contrasting outlook upon the literary activities of Trediakovsky, Sumarokov, and Lomonosov. They preserve the writers' lofty images, developed in the context of the same polemics. Instead of Balabans and Teleliuis (which had at least some individual features), these highly conventional images presented ideal Russian Pindars and Northern Racines. The names of outstanding ancient and modern writers were used in appellations, not for individual human beings, but for types. Even the difference between common nouns and proper names faded, and a surname became a title, designating not an individual but a class.[50]

Of this nature was Sumarokov's praise for Lomonosov in his "Epistle on Poetry," in which he compared him to Malherbe and Pindar. The poet was even more highly extolled in the poem by Nikolai Popovsky that accompanied Lomonosov's portrait in the first volume of his *Collection of Various Compositions in Verse and in Prose* (2nd ed., 1757–59):

> Московский здесь Парнас изобразил витию,
> Что чистый слог стихов и прозы ввел в Россию.
> Что в Риме Цицерон и что Вергилий был,
> То он один в своем понятии вместил,—
> Открыл натуры храм богатым словом россов
> Пример их остроты в науках Ломоносов.[51]

The Moscow Parnassus has depicted here an orator, who introduced to Russia a pure style of poetry and prose. What Cicero and Virgil were for Rome, that he alone encompasses in himself. He opened the temple of Nature with the rich language of the Russians, Lomonosov is an example of their sharpness of mind in sciences.

Sumarokov also received his share of exaggerated praise. Thus, Elagin wrote to him in the "Satire on a Fop and Coquettes":

> Открытель таинства любовныя нам лиры,
> Творец преславныя и пышныя "Семиры,"
> Из мозгу рождшейся богини мудрой сын,
> Наперстник Боалов, российский наш Расин,
> Защитник истины, гонитель злых пороков,
> Благий учитель мой, скажи, о Сумароков!
> Где рифмы ты берешь?[52]

He who discovered for us the mysteries of the love lyre, creator of the famous and splendid *Semira*, son of the wise goddess who was born from the brain, Boileau's bosom companion, our Russian Racine, proponent of truth, persecutor of vicious faults, my good teacher, tell me, O Sumarokov, where do you find your rhymes?

Trediakovsky's lofty image was subtle, but it did exist even after his early fame seemed to have betrayed him. In 1766 an anonymous supporter wrote a poem on Trediakovsky's portrait, which contained the following lines:

> Стих начавшего стопой прежде всех в России,
> Взор художеством черты представляют сии:
> Он есть Тредиаковский, трудолюбный филолог,
> Как то уверяет с мерой и без меры слог.
> Почести лишить его страсть коль ни кипела,
> Но воздать ему венок правда предуспела.[53]

The features of the person who was the first in Russia to begin to use feet in poetry are presented for view through art: He is

Trediakovsky, a diligent philologist, as is confirmed by measured and unmeasured styles [i.e., poetry and prose]. No matter how there seethed a desire to deprive him of the honor, the
truth succeeded in rendering a crown to him.

The image of Trediakovsky the pioneer did not take root and
was soon totally replaced in the literary consciousness of the
epoch by Trediakovsky's parodical image. Moreover, Trediakovsky's positive qualities, such as diligence, and his achievements,
such as the fact that he was (with Lomonosov) the first Russian
professor to be appointed to the Academy of Sciences, were re-
classified as comical and included in his parodical image. Radishchev called him "the indefatigable toiler Trediakovsky," and
Karamzin wrote with irony: "Trediakovsky's name will be known
to our most remote descendants. Let us preserve his image and
respect in him—diligence, learning, and nature's ill fortune." [54]
These features reinforced the central idea in Trediakovsky's
comical portrait: pedantry.

For a long time both Lomonosov and Sumarokov had two
contrasting images, one pejorative and one laudatory. Sometimes laudatory characteristics were applied to both, but the do-
mains of priority were divided: Lyrics were considered Lomonosov's realm and dramaturgy Sumarokov's. But overall Sumarokov
seemed to be the natural victor. Indeed, in the 1750's and 1760's,
he was the recognized leader of a whole group of young poets,
whereas Lomonosov was alone and, after his disciple and pro-
tégé Popovsky died in 1760, did not have followers. When Catherine the Great ascended the throne in 1762, Sumarokov, who
had political ties with the empress's supporters, could expect—
and initially received—her endorsement. Lomonosov, a recognized extoller of Elizabeth, fell into disfavor. His death went almost unnoticed. Semen Poroshin, the tutor of the young Grand
Duke Paul, wrote down the boy's reaction to the news of Lomonosov's death in his diary: "I told him about Lomonosov's death.
He said: 'Why should we pity the fool, he only squandered government funds and accomplished nothing.'" [55] The boy's opinion
apparently reflected the way Lomonosov was treated at Catherine the Great's court—despite her well-publicized visit to him in
June 1764.

In the beginning of the 1770's, however, the situation began
to change. Over Sumarokov's vigorous objections, an idealized

image of Lomonosov swiftly replaced the previous parodical one. From this point on, virtually all the achievements of eighteenth-century Russian literature began to be attributed to Lomonosov. At the same time, certain undesirable features of his image were reinterpreted as favorable. Lomonosov's notorious rudeness became heroic strength, and his low origin was now cited to his advantage. Overshadowed by admiration, the parodical image of Lomonosov, formed in the polemics with his literary rivals, was practically forgotten.

The metamorphosis of Lomonosov's image was especially amazing given the atmosphere of sharp ideological disagreement within the literary circles of the last third of the eighteenth century. Politically independent men of letters who belonged to the nobility and gentry (Fonvizin, Novikov, and Radishchev, among others) disapproved of what they perceived to be the flattery of despots in Lomonosov's odes, whereas writers of lower social status (Vasilii Petrov or even, for that matter, Derzhavin), who tended to cooperate with the government, continued the Lomonosovian tradition of the laudatory ode. The ideological infighting failed to interfere with the canonization of Lomonosov's name. The independents eventually had to accept the high literary appraisals of Lomonosov.

Sumarokov's prestige, accordingly, began to diminish. Opinions about him in the late eighteenth and early nineteenth centuries were in general favorable, but reserved. His name, unlike Lomonosov's, rarely appeared with the epithet "great" and even less often with "divine" or "inimitable." His position as the first Russian dramatist was generally recognized, although his abilities in this field were not always praised. Moreover, he was no longer given the first place in literature in general. Indeed, by the end of the eighteenth century even some of his admirers considered him Lomonosov's disciple. Radishchev wrote in his *A Journey from Petersburg to Moscow*: "A great man can give rise to a great man; and this is your triumphant crown. O Lomonosov, you brought forth Sumarokov." Sumarokov's disciple Kheraskov expressed the same opinion, so insulting for Sumarokov: "At the time when this great man [Lomonosov] outlined the path to the dwelling of the muses and laid the cornerstone of our Parnassus, Mr. Sumarokov began to flourish."[56] On the whole it can be said that in judging Sumarokov, the next literary genera-

tion was much more indulgent with him than with Trediakovsky, but more critical of him than of Lomonosov. As Karamzin
wrote:

Sumarokov, having chosen for himself a vaster sphere, influenced the
public even more strongly than Lomonosov. Like Voltaire, he wanted
to be brilliant in many genres—and contemporaries called him our
Racine, Molière, La Fontaine, Boileau. Posterity does not think so; but
knowing the difficulty of first attempts and the impossibility of achieving perfection at once, it with pleasure finds many beauties in Sumarokov's works and does not want to judge his shortcomings severely.[57]

Sumarokov was given a modest but revered place in the history
of Russian literature, and his name was rarely mentioned out of
historical context.

His comical image was not completely forgotten either and
became secondary, like his lofty image. In his comical role Sumarokov usually appeared in anecdotes not alone but as Trediakovsky's sidekick. Trediakovsky and Sumarokov formed a comical
pair, "Trissotin and Vadius," as Belinsky called them on several
occasions. Together they were frequently juxtaposed to the great
Lomonosov. Ironically, in his comedy *Tresotinius* Sumarokov intended the role of Vadius for Lomonosov. Tradition, however,
reserved this role for the author of the comedy himself.

Lomonosov's heroic image as the first and best Russian
writer gradually acquired mythological characteristics. He became the recognized founder of the "new" Russian literature,
the father of all its accomplishments. The features typical of a
mythological culture hero were stressed (and in some cases
added) in biographies written at the end of the eighteenth and
the beginning of the nineteenth centuries.[58]

In myths the benefactor of humankind was supposed to be
of obscure origin, and Lomonosov's low social station, once a
negative trait, became a sign and a precondition of his extraordinary destiny. Karamzin, in his *Pantheon of Russian Authors*, mentioned Lomonosov's origin as giving his achievements more
value: "Born with a fiery imagination under the cold sky of
northern Russia, the son of a poor fisherman became the father
of Russian eloquence and inspired poetry." Later Belinsky put it
even more straightforwardly: "And was not Lomonosov a genius precisely because he was a fisherman from Kholmogory?"[59]

Accordingly, Lomonosov's native village became a place of worship: It was fashionable for travelers to visit it and write accounts about the place where the genius spent his early years. Murav'ev, who visited Arkhangelsk and Kholmogory in 1770–71, left the following report: "Across from Kholmogory a village, Kerostrov, Lomonosov's birthplace, is noteworthy. In one of its country huts this shining spirit originated." [60] I. I. Lepekhin, a member of the Saint Petersburg Academy of Sciences, also visited Lomonosov's native village in his travels across Russia in 1771 and left an account about it in his diary. Radishchev's friend Petr Chelishchev, who visited the place in 1791, erected a monument in Lomonosov's native village with his own poem inscribed on one of the sides. These pilgrimages continued well into the nineteenth century. The writer and journalist P. P. Svin'in visited Arkhangelsk in 1828 and there met and interviewed Lomonosov's niece.

Like every culture hero, Lomonosov was supposed to have displayed extraordinary abilities even as a young boy. His biographers stressed the giftedness and love of knowledge he showed at a tender age, which, despite numerous alleged obstacles, resulted in his receiving a primary education and eventually led him to leave his native village for Moscow and more schooling. In some accounts this passion for education acquired the significance of a divine vocation: "He hears the voice: 'Quench not the Spirit!' 'Here there is nothing more for you to know,' he is told. He abandons everything—his father's house, his old father; he goes where 'the Latin language' will open the mysteries of wisdom for him, 'where there are many books,' according to the deacon, his reading and writing teacher." [61] Similarly, Pushkin compared Lomonosov to the apostles Peter and Andrew:

> Невод рыбак расстилал по брегу студеного моря;
> Мальчик отцу помогал. Отрок, оставь рыбака!
> Мрежи иные тебя ожидают, иные заботы:
> Будешь умы уловлять, будешь помощник царям. [62]

A fisherman spread a seine on the shore of the cold sea; a boy helped his father. Youth, leave the fisherman! Different nets and different worries await you: You will catch minds, you will be the tsars' helper.

Consequently, Lomonosov's flight from home was emphasized and dramatized: "What a brilliant madness there is in this sixteen-year-old boy when, dressed only in a sheepskin coat, he flees in the cruel frost, catches up on the 70th mile with a string of sledges carrying frozen fish, and implores the head of it to take him along!"[63] Not entirely in conformity with the known facts, this flight was widely believed to have been secret.[64] Although it is well known that Lomonosov arrived in Moscow with a party of his fellow countrymen carrying frozen fish on sledges, biographers sometimes suggested that he traveled on foot: "'Lomonosov came to Moscow from Arkhangelsk on foot.' 'On foot?' some people asked. 'Yes, gentlemen, on foot.'"[65] Some sources (Novikov, Metropolitan Evgenii, Bantysh-Kamensky), in order to picture the dangers the hero encountered on his way to his goal, stressed the mythological motive of forced marriage, supposedly planned for Lomonosov by his father.

Upon his arrival in Moscow Lomonosov met a miraculous helper who was sent to him by God himself:

In Moscow, where he did not know a soul, he spent the first night in a sledge. Waking at dawn, he started to think about his situation and, weeping bitterly, fell on his knees and begged God earnestly to send him help and protection. On the very same morning the butler of a certain master came to the market to buy some fish. He was from the same place by birth and recognized Lomonosov upon getting into a conversation with him. He sheltered him at his master's house among the servants.

One of the butler's friends, a monk, allegedly helped Lomonosov to enter the Slavo-Greco-Latin Academy in Moscow.[66] Lomonosov's trip abroad for schooling took on features of a quest, a hero's adventure, in which he acquired knowledge beneficial for his native community. Certain facts that had a potential mythological meaning were emphasized by his biographers: the obstacles on the way back to Russia (the major among them occurring when, fleeing from financial difficulties in Marburg, Lomonosov was made drunk and recruited into the Prussian army and had to make a perilous escape) and especially the prophetic dream about his father's death on a desert island.[67]

Even more important for the construction of the myth were

the exaggerated accounts of the reaction to the "Ode on the Taking of Khotin" and the essay on Russian versification that Lomonosov sent to the Academy of Sciences in 1739. These works had little effect on the Academy professors and caused only minor irritation on Trediakovsky's and Sumarokov's part: Sumarokov wrote an epigram that has not survived, and Trediakovsky produced an answer to Lomonosov's criticism of his versification reform, which did not reach Lomonosov and eventually also disappeared. However, in later reports the ode was presented as a "boon" that immediately changed the course of Russian literature. Staehlin wrote in "Traits and Anecdotes for Lomonosov's Biography" about the profound impression that the ode made on the Academy professors and on the Russian public: "It was published at the Academy, presented to Empress Anna, distributed at the court, and everybody read it, admiring this new meter." Actually the ode was first published in 1751—and then in its revised form—and the essay in 1778. Nevertheless, Verevkin and Kheraskov painted the same triumphant picture. The nineteenth century took up the tradition and developed and embellished it. It can be found in Metropolitan Evgenii's and Bantysh-Kamensky's accounts of Lomonosov's life. Even Aleksei Merzliakov, whose opinions on Lomonosov in general were not favorable, wrote of the significance of the ode in strong terms, stressing the fact that it offered the Russian reader "new language, new words, new sounds." Ksenofont Polevoy, in his book *Mikhailo Vasil'evich Lomonosov*, unfolded an elaborate scene in which Empress Anna enthusiastically recommended the ode to her court. On the whole, everyone acknowledged that, as Belinsky formulated it in 1840, Russian literature began in 1739 with the "Ode on the Taking of Khotin":

Yes, last year it was precisely 100 years since the birth of Russian literature—since that time when Lomonosov's first solemn song, the "Ode on the Taking of Khotin," written in 1739, sounded—since the day when for the first time correct, pure Russian speech was heard in a literary work and the beginning was marked for the further development of the Russian language, Russian scholarship, and Russian art.[68]

Belinsky put into words an opinion that was well established by 1840: that Lomonosov was the father of Russian literature. The exaggerated claims by Lomonosov's admirers that he was the first and the best in the domain of literature were thus consolidated and approved.

In the eyes of his literary descendants, Lomonosov's personality itself acquired mythological features. Even his weaknesses were accorded heroic value in the context of the myth. Lomonosov's passionate disposition—a cause of many clashes with his colleagues and opponents—ceased to be a negative characteristic: Like Achilles and Cuchulain, he was allowed to go berserk. In the conclusion of Staehlin's "Traits and Anecdotes for Lomonosov's Biography," the poet appears as a warrior who heroically fights and defeats three mighty robbers:

I will give one example of Lomonosov's extraordinary presence of mind and strength. . . . One fine autumn evening he went on a walk all by himself to the sea along Bolshoi Prospect on Vasilevskii Island. On the way back, as dusk was falling and he was walking through the woods along the prospect, which cut through the woods, three seamen suddenly jumped out from the bushes and attacked him. There was not a soul to be seen. He defended himself from these three robbers with the greatest courage. He struck one of them with such force that he not only could not get up but for a long time could not even come to his senses; he struck another so hard in his face that he ran, all covered with blood, into the bushes; and it was not hard for him to overpower the third one; he knocked him down (meanwhile the first one came to his senses and ran into the woods) and, holding him down with his feet, threatened that he would immediately kill him if he did not reveal the names of the other two robbers and what they had wanted to do with him. This one confessed that they had wanted only to rob him and then let him go. "Ah! You riffraff," Lomonosov said, "then I will rob you." And the thief immediately had to take off his jacket, a canvas coat, and his trousers and to tie everything into a bundle with his own belt. Then Lomonosov struck the half-naked seaman once again on the legs so that he fell down and could hardly move, and he himself, placing the bundle on his shoulders, went home with his booty as with spoils of war and directly, while his memory was fresh, wrote down the names of both robbers. The next day he made an announcement about them at the Admiralty; they were immediately caught, put into shackles, and several days later were made to run a gauntlet.[69]

In conformity with gentler mores, Lomonosov's loud and unseemly quarrels and fights with fellow academicians were played down, but the episodes in which he displayed rebelliousness as well as dignified fortitude were remembered as typical of his behavior. Pushkin quoted with admiration Lomonosov's letter to Shuvalov in which, in connection with Shuvalov's attempt to reconcile him with Sumarokov, the poet wrote: "I do not want to be a fool either at the tables of high-born gentry or for other earthly rulers or even for the Lord God, who has given me my mind, unless He takes it away." [70] Right after this passage Pushkin recorded yet another example of Lomonosov's boldness and firmness, this time of obviously legendary character:

Another time, while arguing with the same grandee, Lomonosov made him so angry that Shuvalov shouted: "I will dismiss you from the Academy!" "No," Lomonosov proudly replied, "rather the Academy will be dismissed from me." Such was this humble composer of laudatory odes and courtly idylls! [71]

The probable source of this legend, Lomonosov's letter to Shuvalov of December 30, 1754, presents a much less heroic picture:

From Your Excellency's gracious conversation yesterday I have observed that malice overcomes benevolence, undermining the sanctity of the imperial command. So, if it is impossible that I, according to my meek request, be promoted in the Academy in order to curb the insidious undertakings, then I most humbly ask Your Excellency that through your fatherly interference I be transferred into another department, but best of all into the Foreign Collegium. . . . I ask Almighty God that . . . after my departure from the Academy it might become clear what it has lost, having been deprived of such a man, who for many years adorned it and always fought with the persecutors of the sciences, regardless of the danger to himself. [72]

The myth promoted epic features of Lomonosov's portrait as the father of Russian literature without particular concern for historical documentation.

Sometimes Lomonosov's quarrels with his colleagues were interpreted as the result of a lack of understanding of, or even hostility toward, the culture hero and his efforts on the part of the inert community. This is an interpretation suggested by Nikolai Polevoy:

There were Lomonosov's comrades, insufferable in their "scrupulous" sluggishness; the "punctuality" and formality of the Academy Council of that time; and with all this, Trediakovsky, a ridiculous bureaucrat; Mueller, with his dreadful coldness; Bayer, with his learned nonsense [*Kitaiskaia gramota*], who did not speak Russian; and all those people for whom Lomonosov's fiery outbursts in all fields of knowledge seemed simply boastful madness, and for whom his passionate disposition was a source of triumph, and who, with their reasonable carefulness and partial learnedness, considered themselves above him. They could not err and lose—Lomonosov erred and lost incessantly.[73]

Lomonosov's literary descendants remembered his predilection for alcohol either as the genius's regrettable but understandable response to the misfortunes of his life (the interpretation suggested by Ksenofont Polevoy, among others) or as an unusual, heroic ability, evidence of Lomonosov's superhuman nature. This was the picture presented by Bantysh-Kamensky:

At the same time he had a weakness that was destructive of his health: He consumed intoxicating spirits to excess, because of which his face was always crimson. Once Empress Elizabeth sent Lomonosov a cartload of copper coins for one ode: Altogether there were one thousand rubles. The poet, delighted by the present, ordered the sacks to be put near his bed, did not count how much money was in them, bought a scoop, and [from time to time] scooped from the sacks and set off *for a pub!*[74]

The anecdote characterized Lomonosov as a man with remarkable physical abilities, as well as a generous soul. A weakness for alcohol could not damage Lomonosov's mythological image, which easily allowed all sorts of excesses—frenzy, quick temper, and drunken fits—as manifestations of his heroic spirit.

The life of a hero requires an extraordinary conclusion. Joseph Campbell wrote about the death of a hero: "The last act in the biography of the hero is that of the death or departure. Here the whole sense of the life is epitomized. Needless to say, the hero would be no hero if death held for him any terror; the first condition is reconciliation with the grave."[75] Lomonosov's death, caused by an illness (apparently alcohol-related), was quite ordinary and could hardly provide much material for valorization. His contemporaries reacted to it rather indifferently. His biographers, however, presented this event as having been surrounded by heroic circumstances. Staehlin again was the first to offer this interpretation. He wrote in "A Précis of Lomonosov's Eulogy":

He met his death with the spirit of a true philosopher; he said, "I only regret that I leave unfinished that which I have conceived for the benefit of the fatherland, for the increment of the sciences, and the restoration of the ruined affairs of the Academy: It will die with me."

In "Traits and Anecdotes for Lomonosov's Biography" the stoical spirit of Lomonosov's deathbed monologue is even more pronounced:

Several days before his end he said to Staehlin: "My friend, I see that I have to die, and I look upon death calmly and indifferently; I regret only that I was not able to accomplish everything that I undertook for the benefit of the fatherland, for the increment of the sciences, and for the glory of the Academy, and now at the end of my life I must see that all my useful intentions will disappear with me."[76]

Lomonosov's function as a provider of literary models did not stop with his death. As was proper for a forefather, Lomonosov continued to influence the development of Russian literature. He was an arbiter, an ultimate authority, whose support Russian writers sought to resolve their arguments or to reinforce and justify their positions. From the realm of the dead he pronounced his judgment, as in a work by Semen Bobrov, "Incident in the Realm of Shadows; or, The Fate of the Russian Language" (1805), written in the context of the linguistic polemics between the Archaists and the Innovators. In this work, Lomonosov is the one who judges the Westernizer Galloruss, a character who advocates the introduction of Gallicisms into the Russian language, and sentences him to the eternal reading of Trediakovsky's *Tilemakhida*.[77]

The unusual childhood, the difficulties surmounted on the way to the fulfillment of his vocation, the trip outside the community in order to fetch the boon, heroic personal qualities, fortitude in the face of death—all these helped to characterize Lomonosov as a hero in the eyes of his literary descendants and served to promote his mythological image as the father of the "new" Russian literature, the author of all its achievements, and the highest authority for future generations.

Unlike the culture hero, the mythological fool does not have a biography; he has behavior, which is always wrong. Accounts of his life consist mostly of anecdotes about his stupid, harmful, or treacherous actions. Therefore, despite obvious similarities to Lomonosov's life, the potentially heroic circumstances of Trediakovsky's biography—his passion for knowledge, which spurred him to flee to the centers of education, first Moscow and then Paris; his devotion to his vocation; his firmness in the face of misfortune; his persistence in his work for the glory of Russian literature—did not find their way into the myth of the "new" Russian literature. On the contrary, many of these circumstances were interpreted in a comical way, providing material for the anecdotes about Trediakovsky the fool.

Trediakovsky's most important feature as a mythological antihero was his ability to create bad and harmful rules and models for the newly emerging Russian literature—bad, that is, in the opinion of his contemporaries and literary descendants. The whole range of phenomena that lay outside the path shown to Russian literature by Lomonosov (such as ternary meters, unrhymed verse, and a heavy Slavonic style) was associated with his name. Authors who chose to stray from the path risked being scorned for their affinity to Trediakovsky. Anticipating mockery, Radishchev excluded his poem *Creation of the World* from the final version of *A Journey from Petersburg to Moscow* because of its metrical similarity to Trediakovsky's *Tilemakhida*. He chose to publish instead the ode "Liberty," written in Lomonosovian iambic tetrameter. Mikhail Murav'ev, the author of the poem "Grove" (1777), the first Russian work, after *Tilemakhida*, written in hexameters, also felt uneasy because of the similarity of his work to Trediakovsky's epic poem. He wrote to Dmitrii Khvostov in the late 1770's:

I do not know yet whether you will approve of my bias toward the latter ["Grove"]. I chose for it a seldom-used meter that, nevertheless, has the right to exist in our language, as Lomonosov and Trediakovsky, the archons of the art, have decided. The latter has disgraced it by using it in *Tilemakhida*. But this learned man—who was remarkable proof that talents are allocated by nature—disfigured every kind of poetry that he touched. Maybe I have used it in vain. This is what is called the willfulness of an artist, if I may be supposed to have it.[78]

Murav'ev named both Lomonosov and Trediakovsky "archons" (*nachal'niki*) of Russian literature but stressed Trediakovsky's negative role as the author who set a bad example. Murav'ev, however, was a brave man, and soon after that he used hexameters to translate the five opening lines of the *Iliad*. It was the first—and in the eighteenth century the only—Russian translation of Homer in hexameters.

If Murav'ev (like Radishchev later) tried to overcome what was, from his point of view, the negative influence of Trediakovsky's works, other authors considered the task impossible and rejected everything that had even the slightest relation to Trediakovsky's legacy. The translator and journalist Vasilii Podshivalov, in his "Letter to a Damsel F** About Versification," published in the first issue of the magazine *A Pleasant and Useful Pastime* (1794–98), disapprovingly connected the anapestic meter with Trediakovsky's name: "It is not to be found anywhere but in Trediakovsky or other authors like him." In the same essay unrhymed verse was condemned, and, what is important here, reference was made to Trediakovsky's opinion on this matter: "I will add that rhymes are considered empty rattles by those people who do not have a talent for poetry and [do not have] that energy that . . . provides quiet and pleasant moments in life." [79] Indeed, in the 1750's and 1760's Trediakovsky consistently opposed the use of rhymes and repeatedly expressed his disapproval. Podshivalov referred to the passage in Trediakovsky's introduction to *Tilemakhida*, in which the poet called rhymes "a child's pipe" and "an adolescent's toy" and claimed that rhymed verses "jingle" with rhymes "as if to entertain infants." [80]

A special term, *tred'iakovshchina*, was even coined to label "nonaesthetic" phenomena. It occurred as early as 1789 in Nikolai L'vov's criticism of a poem by Vasilii Kapnist: "There are some awkward expressions, blunders that recall Trediakovsky [*tred'iakovshchiny*] and enjambements that the language does not allow." Stepan Zhikharev testified in his memoirs that his hexameter poem received the same epithet from an audience in 1807. [81] This caustic neologism demonstrates the mythological nature of Trediakovsky's comical image. For his contemporaries and literary descendants, the poet was an anti-demiurge, a mythological fool who, by his stupid or evil deeds, provided a paradigm for anti-poetry.

The image of Trediakovsky the anti-demiurge was endowed, in accordance with the mythological prototype, with chthonic features. His human nature was questioned. He was declared a non-Christian, and it was implied that he had relations with demons and the underworld.[82] Sumarokov clearly hinted at Trediakovsky's "nonhuman," diabolic nature in *Tresotinius*. In this comedy the character Bramarbas says about the poet's double: "He does not have human blood; he has Syrian and Chaldean blood." On the one hand, this is a reference to Trediakovsky's allegedly fruitless learning (cf. Tresotinius's remark "I have the title of teacher of Arabic, Syrian, and Chaldean languages").[83] On the other hand, however, both Syria and Chaldea (as well as Arabia, for that matter) were connected in Christian tradition with astrology and magic. In the Russian tradition Chaldeans were firmly associated with the biblical story about sending the young Hananiah, Azariah, and Mishael into the fiery furnace for their refusal to worship the golden image. Two Chaldeans were part of a miracle play, "The Furnace Act" ("Peshchnoe deistvo"), which was performed in Russia in churches during Advent in the sixteenth and seventeenth centuries. From characters in a miracle play, the Chaldeans gradually developed into the personages of popular Yuletide festivals who for twelve days ran around in jesters' dress and performed all sorts of nasty pranks. They were considered pagans at that time and had to undergo the rite of baptism on the eve of Epiphany. Thus, Sumarokov's association of Trediakovsky with Chaldeans characterized him as a repository of fruitless learning, a malicious jester, a carrier of satanic knowledge, and a pagan.[84]

Almost a hundred years after Sumarokov wrote *Tresotinius*, Lazhechnikov repeated the accusation of paganism and diabolism, calling Trediakovsky's poetry "nonhuman verse" (p. 255), meaning both "awful beyond human comprehension" and "alien to the human race, inhuman, diabolic." The two features, non-Christianity and nonhumanity, were combined in the term *nekhrest*, "non-Christian," which Lazhechnikov gave to his character: Trediakovsky acts both "nonhumanly" and "non-Christianly" when he "commits an outrage [*rugaetsia*]" upon the head of his dead enemy (p. 302).

An anonymous poem written in the late 1750's, in the context of the polemics about Lomonosov's anticlerical "Hymn to the Beard," even suggested Trediakovsky's kinship with demons:

> Кто зажег?
> Лжепророк.
> Из какого лесу?
> Он один
> Тресотин
> Сердцем сроден бесу.[85]

Who set the blaze? The false prophet. From which forest?
Tresotin is the only one who in his heart is akin to a demon.

The appellation "false prophet," which in the context of the polemics referred to Old Believers, at the same time emphasized Trediakovsky's role as a provider of bad examples.

In Khmel'nitsky's comedy *Russian Faust*, a character named Trediakovsky displays a deep interest in the supernatural. With his sidekick, Martyn Zadeka (a legendary person with a reputation as an astrologer, chiromancer, and soothsayer), he unsuccessfully tries to investigate allegations that Iakov Brius—a Russian statesman and a dilettante scientist whom tradition accused of being a black magician—engaged in sorcery and witchcraft.

Mikhail Dmitriev, in his satire "Twelve Sleepy Essays" (1839), presents Trediakovsky as the devil himself, tempting the journalist and scholar Mikhail Kachenovsky to sell his soul. Here is the portrait of Trediakovsky when he appears to collect his prey:

> Глядь! когти—каждая рука!
> Лицо—как рыло шавки!
> Из буклей—выросли рога,
> И клык—из бородавки![86]

He [Kachenovsky] sees claws on each of his [Trediakovsky's] hands! His face looks like a cur's snout! From his locks, horns have grown, and a fang has grown from a wart.

Sometimes tradition explained Trediakovsky's alleged artistic failures by the fact that he was possessed by a demon. In Iakov Kniazhnin's poem "A Battle of Poets" (1765), Trediakov-

sky is in the power of a hideous creature, Desire to Write (*pisat'
Okhota*). The monster forces the poet to write his horrid poems:

> Там Тредьяковский, сей поэзии любитель,
> Для рифмы разума, рассудка истребитель,
> На куче книг лежа, есть просит, пить в стихах,
> Пред ним чудовище о многих головах,
> Которы Аполлон сатирами считает,
> Но тщетно погубить урода он желает:
> Где была голова, там сто голов растет,
> Не кровь—чернил поток в груди его течет.
> Оно, сто книг держа рукой сухою,
> Жмет Тредьяковского нос колкою ногою
> И нудит преложить во рифмы горы книг
> И всю вселенную вместить в единый стих.[87]

There Trediakovsky, this lover of poetry, the destroyer of reason for the sake of rhyme, lying on a heap of books, asks in
verse to eat and drink. Before him there is a monster with numerous heads, which Apollo considers satires; but in vain he
wants to destroy the freak: Where a head has been, there a
hundred heads appear; not blood, but a stream of ink flows in
its chest. Holding a hundred thick books in its skinny hand, it
presses Trediakovsky's nose with a prickly foot and forces him
to put heaps of books into rhyme and to embrace the whole
universe in one line.

In other instances Trediakovsky himself was pictured as a
chthonic monster. In Pushkin's early poem "To Zhukovsky"
(1816), Trediakovsky (along with Sumarokov) appears among
the screaming monsters of the underworld, who represent the
members of the Colloquium of Lovers of the Russian Word (*Beseda liubitelei russkogo slova*), a literary group against which the
young Pushkin was engaged in a literary struggle:

> над мрачными толпами
> Во тьме два призрака склонилися главами.
> Один на груды сел и прозы и стихов—
> Тяжелые плоды полуночных трудов,
> Усопших од, поэм забвенные могилы!
> С улыбкой внемлет вой стопосложитель хилый:
> Пред ним растерзанный стенает Тилимах;

Железное перо скрыпит в его перстах
И тянет за собой гекзаметры сухие,
Спондеи жесткие и дактили тугие.[88]

Above the gloomy crowds, in darkness, two phantoms sit, bending their heads. One of them has sat on piles of prose and poems, the heavy fruits of midnight labors, the forgotten graves of deceased odes and poems! The puny versifier heeds the howl with a smile: Before him the mauled Telemachus groans; the iron pen scratches in his fingers and pulls after it dry hexameters, coarse spondees, and stiff dactyls.

As a chthonic creature, Trediakovsky appeared in stories about trips to the underworld—a genre popular in the late eighteenth and early nineteenth centuries. Unlike Lomonosov, who was presented in such works as a forefather ruling from his grave the community created by his civilizing efforts, Trediakovsky was pictured as a monster of the underworld, a demon who tortured sinners for their bad behavior during life. This was his function in Bobrov's work "Incident in the Realm of Shadows." In the conclusion of this work Lomonosov condemns a Westernizer, Galloruss, to the eternal reading and analyzing of *Tilemakhida* in the company of the Velche Furies (the Romantic equivalent of the avenging deities that was introduced by Bobrov): "Mercury takes him [Galloruss] to the cave of the Velche Furies, . . . gets a book *in quarto*, which is called *Tilemakhida*, and seats him with it between the two awful woman shades. The dismayed Galloruss, cursing the day of his new birth, his immortality, and his illusory fame, sits down on the frail turf bench and against his will opens the heavy book."[89]

Trediakovsky's alleged ties with the underworld and death were numerous and various, ranging from a mere mention of his grave, to insinuations that he had been condemned to hell for his bad poetry, to assertions that his works had deadly powers. Radishchev, in *A Journey from Petersburg to Moscow*, spoke of Trediakovsky's grave, "covered with the moss of oblivion," and suggested that someday future generations would "dig up" the poet from his grave and begin to enjoy his poetry. Nikolai Nikolev, on the contrary, did not anticipate the poet's resurrection: In his parody of Trediakovsky's poetry, "Ode 2: To the Most Wise Felitsa from the Old Russian Poet from the Realm of

the Dead" (published in 1798), Nikolev depicted Trediakovsky
as a sinner who had been condemned to hell for his writings:
"And I, a great sinner, am wasting away in hell for my unusual
passion for poetry."[90] Lazhechnikov, who in his novel faithfully
followed all the details of the myth about Trediakovsky the fool,
used every opportunity to stress the poet's alleged connection
with death. Thus, Lazhechnikov presents Trediakovsky's translation of Rollin's histories as a grave for the renowned historiographer: The volumes in Trediakovsky's bookshelves have "the
epitaph: Rollin" (p. 255). In the same passage he suggests that
Trediakovsky's translation of Fénelon's *Télémaque* is essentially a
murder of its main character: "*Ci gît* [here is buried] the son of
Odysseus, born on the island of Ithaca, cherished by Minerva
and Fénelon, and slaughtered in Saint Petersburg by the professor of eloquence" (p. 255). In another passage Trediakovsky
boasts that he can easily change an epithalamion into a poem on
death: "What is there that *we* cannot do? Oh! ho, ho! And I venture to report to you that it is necessary only to force out some
words, playful and frisky as little mountain goats, and to knock
into their place [words that are] mournful and heavy as the black
bullocks who laboriously tear the earth's womb with a plow"
(p. 257). Trediakovsky's works, as presented by Lazhechnikov,
are deadly too. Thus, Volynsky fears *Tilemakhida* "as if it were a
stone brought to kill him with its weight" (p. 55).

Sometimes, however, Trediakovsky's works, especially *Tilemakhida*, induced sleep instead of death. The magazine *All Sorts
of Odds and Ends*, published in 1769–70 under the auspices of
Catherine the Great, was the first to add this feature to Trediakovsky's mythological image. *Tilemakhida*, the magazine suggested, was the best remedy for insomnia. Radishchev, whose
purpose in the *Memorial for a Dactylo-Trochaic Knight* was to attack and, ultimately, to dissipate Trediakovsky's mythological
image, used this detail in the context of his own game. His characters also recite *Tilemakhida* to induce sleep, but a special kind
of sleep that is akin to a state of poetic inspiration.[91]

Since Hypnos and Thanatos are twins, the soporific qualities of Trediakovsky's poetry also allude to the chthonic nature
of his image as a fool. Moreover, the ability to induce death and
sleep are interchangeable in the myth, as is evident in the fol-

lowing appraisal of Trediakovsky's works by Vasilii Anastasevich in his poem "On *Tilemakhida* (1811?): "I will admit that I
often used to sleep over it [Trediakovsky's translation *A Voyage
to the Isle of Love*] like a dead man." The words used in the original, *sypal mertvetski*, "used to sleep like a dead man," imply
death as well as drunken sleep, since the word *mertvetski*, "like a
dead man," is employed almost exclusively in the expression
mertvetski p'ian, "dead drunk."[92]

This association of the mythological Trediakovsky with the
underworld explains the fact that the most widely known lines
from *Tilemakhida* were the passages that depicted the monsters
of the underworld, Death and Cerberus: "A putrid monster,
bony, deaf, dumb, and blind" and "A stout monster, wild, huge,
and with a three-throated maw."[93] Generations of Russian writers, from Radishchev to Pushkin and Nikolai Polevoy, quoted
these lines, laughed at them, referred to them as examples of the
most typical "Trediakovskian" verses, and used them to tease
their literary opponents.

By no means did Trediakovsky's supposed relations with demons, death, and the underworld, or the deadly powers of his
works, make his mythological persona frightening. These were
the features of his comical image as a mythological fool, and the
mythological fool's demonic nature in no way interferes with the
laughter he elicits. On the contrary, it promotes laughter, because laughing is the mythological way to cope with death and
chaos—which the fool represents. The fool is ridiculed not only
when he induces death but also when he himself dies or is
beaten, disfigured, or insulted and especially when he is unsuccessful in undertakings that threaten the communal order.
When lacking the mythological spirit, this laughter can be cruel,
but in the context of mythological behavior it is a perfectly justified and benevolent reaction by the community to the fool's conduct. It celebrates the victory of life over death and secures the
continuity of culture. It confirms the soundness of the rules and
norms that the fool tries to destroy by his undertakings, and ensures that the contrary behavior that the fool tries to impose on
the community will not find its way into communal practice.
The very existence of fools and their ridicule is crucial for the
preservation of the existing order and thus for the survival of the
community.

In the myth about Trediakovsky the fool, the mockery of the poet reaches truly mythological proportions. His learnedness, his persistence, the peculiarities of his literary and linguistic positions, his style and verse—everything was derided regardless of its actual merits or faults. The mere reading of his works was said to elicit irrepressible laughter. Thus, Nikolai Ostolopov wrote in his *Dictionary* (1821) about Trediakovsky's tragedy, *Deidamia* (1750): "They also say that this sovereign [Catherine the Great] wanted to see *Deidamia* on stage; but the actors were unable to perform this tragic work, because they simply could not refrain from laughter." Similarly, in the early version of the chapter "Tver" of his *A Journey from Petersburg to Moscow* Radishchev expressed concern that the use of dactyls might remind the reader of *Tilemakhida* and therefore induce laughter and interfere with his intentions.[94] Both Lazhechnikov and Nikolai Polevoy believed that the mere recitation of Trediakovsky's poetry or even mention of one of his notorious works, *Deidamia* for example, was a comical device powerful enough to elicit the reader's laughter.

In the case of Trediakovsky's works one might attempt to argue that the derision was justified by their poor quality. However, no such justification can be possibly found for the ridicule of the misfortunes that haunted Trediakovsky throughout his life. This personal aspect leaves little doubt about the mythological nature of the laughter. Outside the mythological context contemporaries and subsequent generations who laughed at Trediakovsky's ill luck would be branded extremely vicious people. However, ethical standards did not apply, since within the myth this seemingly cruel ridicule was actually directed not at Vasilii Kirillovich Trediakovsky who lived in Saint Petersburg on Vasilevskii Island and had a wife and a son, but at Trediakovsky the fool, at Tresotin, who messed up Russian literature with his ludicrous creations and thus threatened its future glory.

As I have already mentioned, Trediakovsky's literary descendants were amused by the beatings that Trediakovsky sustained from Artemii Volynsky and by "the most benevolent box on the ear" he allegedly received from Empress Anna. When discussed outside the mythological context, these events could elicit nothing but deep sympathy for Trediakovsky's sufferings. One example is Belinsky's review of *Slavic Collection* (1845),

whose editor, N. V. Savel'ev-Rostislavich, discussed the Volynsky affair. In Savel'ev's interpretation, Trediakovsky was an evil
agent of the West who partook in the destruction of Volynsky,
an ardent Russian patriot. Trying to refute another powerful cultural conception, in this case, Slavophilism, Belinsky, who nor-
mally was one of the main supporters of the myth of the beginning of the "new" Russian literature, chose to treat Trediakovsky, not as a mythological personage, but as a person, and
comical beatings immediately became torturous baiting: "Poor
Trediakovsky! Up to now the scribblers have nagged you and
could not gloat enough that in your person the dignity of a man
of letters, a scholar, and a poet was beaten with slaps and
sticks!"[95] However, compassion toward Trediakovsky's ill fortune was extremely rare. The beatings were almost universally
remembered with laughter and fiendish delight. It is noteworthy
that Lazhechnikov chose to modify the Volynsky episode in his
novel in order to reduce the chances of eliciting pity toward Trediakovsky. He replaced the beatings with a description of a
Yuletide masquerade at which Trediakovsky, like a commedia
dell'arte character, is pushed, hit, and tickled by a crowd of
maskers (pp. 61–62). In the context of the myth, upon which
Lazhechnikov relied in his interpretation of Trediakovsky's life,
beatings and masquerades were events of the same kind and
could be used interchangeably.

This laughter and delight over the poet's misfortunes was
in harmony with Trediakovsky's mythological image. From the
very emergence of this image, Trediakovsky the fool was an object of contemplated or actual thrashings. In Sumarokov's *Tresotinius*, the braggart and bully Bramarbas threatens to beat Tresotinius, and another character, Erast, forbids this. These possible
beatings are discussed at length:

Erast. No matter how Tresotinius scolds you, whether in verse or in
      prose, you will not pay him back either with a sword or with a stick.
Bramarbas. With neither.
Kimar. And with a broom or a poker?
Bramarbas. With neither.
Erast. Swear it.[96]

Tresotinius's double Krititsiondius, in the comedy *The Monsters*,
is less fortunate: The servant Arlikin beats him for his attempt to

kiss the maid Finetta. It is noteworthy that Krititsiondius himself explains the conventional nature of comical beatings. He teaches the stupid fop Diulizh about Molière's comedy *Le médecin malgré lui* (1666):

Diulizh. But is it not a misfortune when somebody is beaten?
Krititsiondius. There are special rules for that, and you should have laughed at what you were crying about.[97]

The boundary between the real Trediakovsky, who was brutally beaten by a powerful statesman, and a fictitious character with the same name, who sustained comical beatings of a clearly mythological nature, was frequently blurred, as in an anecdote published by Pushkin in 1828:

Trediakovsky once came to complain to Shuvalov about Sumarokov. "Your Excellency! Aleksandr Petrovich has hit me on my right cheek so hard that it still hurts." "How so, fellow?" Shuvalov answered. "Your right cheek hurts, and you hold your left one." "Ah, Your Excellency, you are right," Trediakovsky answered and transferred his hand to the other side.

"It often happened that Trediakovsky got beaten up," Pushkin concluded and related the story about Volynsky's attack.[98] A real-life humiliation, placed in the context of a comical theatrical brawl, lost its tragic aspect and revealed its comical potential.

Subsequent generations did not fail to ridicule Trediakovsky's less tragic misfortunes as well. Thus, it was considered extremely funny that Trediakovsky had to translate thirteen volumes of Rollin's *Histoire ancienne* and three volumes of his *Histoire romaine* twice, because the first translation was consumed in the fire that occurred in his house in 1747. Aleksandr Palitsyn attached the following note to a passage mocking Trediakovsky's diligence in his poem "An Epistle to Priveta" (1807): "Without poetic exaggeration but by precise account he wrote 100 books, including the first translation of Rollin, which burned up in a fire in his house." Likewise, Bantysh-Kamensky, immediately after mocking *Tilemakhida*, comments ironically on this event: "Besides, Trediakovsky had the patience to translate Rollin's *Ancient* and *Roman* histories *twice*, because the first translation, in manuscript, was destroyed in a fire." Belinsky referred to this event as the "barbaric twofold translation of Rollin."[99]

As in the above examples, derision for repeating the translation usually went together with mockery of Trediakovsky's diligence and prolificacy. Virtually every author who wrote about him mentioned ironically his productiveness as a writer and translator. Some of the examples have been already cited, and their number is easy to multiply: Sumarokov, Radishchev, Karamzin, Batiushkov, Palitsyn, Lazhechnikov, Bantysh-Kamensky, Pushkin, Belinsky—writers of all schools and opinions ridiculed Trediakovsky's diligence.

Sumarokov again was the first to incorporate this feature into the image of Trediakovsky the fool. His character Krititsiondius boasts: "On the song 'Farewell, My Dear,' I composed a critique in twelve volumes *in folio*. On the tragedy *Khorev* I put together six dozen epigrams, and some of them I even translated into Greek; against the gentlemen who performed Russian tragedies I wrote 99 satires in Syrian." [100] This grotesque description of the poet's exaggerated prolificacy referred the reader to Trediakovsky's extensive criticism of Sumarokov's poetry in the essay "Letter from Friend to Friend." Trediakovsky's prolificacy was also frequently described as absolutely barren, as in Palitsyn's "An Epistle to Priveta":

> Бесплодный чтитель муз, страдалец их союза,
> Пример учености, без дара и без вкуса;
> Терпенья образец, Ролленев ученик,
> Воспомнись, написав нам сотню толстых книг,
> По трудолюбию чудесный *Тредьяковский*.[101]

> The sterile admirer of the muses, who suffers in union with them, an example of learnedness devoid of gift and taste, the model of patience, Rollin's disciple, be recalled, having written for us a hundred thick books, marvelously diligent *Trediakovsky*.

One example even combines a reference to Trediakovsky's excessive productivity with a hint at his ability to cause death, in this particular case, his own. Trediakovsky, a character in Nikolai Khmel'nitsky's comedy, encouraged by praise, promises to write himself to death (*zapishus' do smerti*).[102] In these and similar characterizations Trediakovsky appears as a fool who, unable to recognize the ludicrous outcome of his actions, pursues his goal with absurd zeal until, to his audience's delight, it loses all sense.

On the other hand, his diligence and prolificacy might also refer to the inability of the mythological fool to restrain his appetite for food and sex and to his power to stimulate fertility.

Descriptions of Trediakovsky's foolish zeal frequently appeared along with ridicule of his excessive learning. Thus, in Lazhechnikov's novel Trediakovsky tortures Volynsky with a lengthy learned conversation about poetry: "Then Vasilii Kirillovich started to talk, and talked so much about Homer, Virgil, Camões, about gods and goddesses, that the patience of the mere mortals was exhausted" (p. 57). The ironic mention of "mere mortals" reminds the reader of the "nonhuman" nature of Trediakovsky's learnedness. The mockery of Trediakovsky's title professor of eloquence, especially widespread in nineteenth-century characterizations of Trediakovsky, stressed the fact that his knowledge was as meaningless as his persistence. His diligence, together with his learning and professorship, were used to support his reputation as a pedant, which was formed in the literary clashes of the mid-eighteenth century and flourished in the early nineteenth century in the atmosphere of the Romantic contempt for uninspired labor. This aspect of Trediakovsky's image as a fool also has mythological roots.

As I pointed out earlier in this chapter, Sumarokov, who introduced the image of Trediakovsky the pedant, was following European models, particularly those of Holberg and Molière. Molière's and Holberg's pedantic characters, however, had originated in a cultural tradition with definite mythological roots— folk theater. Especially important in this respect was the commedia dell'arte, which gained popularity in Europe in the end of the sixteenth and in the seventeenth centuries. One of the prominent characters in the commedia dell'arte was the pedant Dottore, a scholar from Bologna. His main characteristics were a false learnedness, a love for lengthy monologues sprinkled with Latin quotations, and illogic. He was unsuccessful in all his undertakings and was ridiculed by other characters in the play. This personage influenced the image of pedants, popular in European comedy of the seventeenth century, and found its way into Sumarokov's plays.[103]

Sumarokov, however, had the opportunity to become acquainted with commedia dell'arte directly. Beginning in 1733,

Italian troupes performed in Saint Petersburg at Empress Anna's court, and Sumarokov, as a student at the Cadet School, participated closely in court life and was most certainly admitted to the performances, perhaps even participating in them. "Sumarokov's exposure to the Italian comedy of masks is indubitable; it is known that the students of the Cadet School participated in the performances of this troupe," writes Berkov in his *History of Russian Comedy of the Eighteenth Century*.[104] The direct results of Sumarokov's familiarity with the Italian comedy are evident in *The Monsters*, where there appears a commedia dell'arte character, a servant by the name of Arlikin. But the influence of the folk theater can be detected in the comedies that Sumarokov wrote throughout his life. Sumarokov's younger contemporaries, for whom commedia dell'arte was a low folk genre, lying outside the boundaries of real art, criticized this feature of his comedic method.

Trediakovsky also noticed and ridiculed the folk background of Sumarokov's comedies. In his parody of *Tresotinius*, included in the "Letter from Friend to Friend," he emphasized the elements of farce in Sumarokov's play. He even introduced features of *skomorokh* (the itinerant comedians in medieval Russia) talk into the speech of a character, Arkhisotolash (apparently, something like "Superjerk," from French *archi-*, "supreme"; *sot*, "foolish"; and *lâche*, "mean, base"), who represented Sumarokov: "Be quiet, brutal brute, animal animal, gambler, smoker, pub goer, drunkard, mail carrier, purse snatcher, contractor of rough work!" Sumarokov's dependence on the principles of folk theater was the reason, in Trediakovsky's eyes, that *Tresotinius* deserved only "the momentary light of the marketplace, and after that eternal darkness."[105]

There is no doubt that Dottore's character was familiar to Sumarokov, since a Dottore was part of the troupe that performed at Empress Anna's court in 1733–35: Out of thirty "Italian comedies," compiled by V. N. Peretts, only three do not have this character. There are also clear indications that Sumarokov was conscious of the existing tradition of deriding pedants. In his "Epistle on Poetry" he advised the writers of comedies:

> Представь латынщика на диспуте его,
> Который не соврет без "ерго" ничего.

Present a Latinizer during the dispute, who cannot jabber
away without saying "ergo."

In his first comedies Sumarokov closely followed his own advice
and presented virtually all the comical characters recommended
in the epistle: the callous official, the incompetent judge, the
fop, and, most important, the pedant. One of his "Latinizers,"
Bobembius in *Tresotinius*, actually says "ergo."[106]

Introduced by Sumarokov and assimilated by the myth, the
image of Trediakovsky the pedant borrowed many characteristic
features from Dottore. Thus, Dottore often holds a small but
very thick book. In many portrayals Trediakovsky is pictured
with a very thick *Tilemakhida, Deidamia,* or Rollin's *History.* Such
was the description of Trediakovsky in Konstantin Batiushkov's
satirical poem "The Bard in the Colloquium of Lovers of the Russian Word" (1813):

> Се Тредьяковский в парике
> Засаленном, с кудрями,
> С Телемахидою в руке,
> С Ролленем за плечами.[107]

This is Trediakovsky in a greasy toupée with curls, with *Tilemakhida* in his hand, with Rollin behind his back.

Lazhechnikov also stresses this feature: His Trediakovsky "carried a huge volume under his arm." Nikolai Polevoy, in his comedy *The First Performance*, uses this detail to create a comical
scene in which Trediakovsky is about to torture other characters
in the play with the reading of his work: "He unbuttons his caftan and gets a huge notebook from under the skirt of his coat."
In a review of Polevoy's comedy, Belinsky dwells on this detail in
order to stress the comical nature of Trediakovsky's persona in
the play: "Exasperated, Trediakovsky leaves, having forgotten
to take his dear five-pood [180-pound] child, the manuscript of
Tilemakhida. . . . Trediakovsky comes and says that he left his
little notebook [*tetradka*]."[108] Belinsky quotes Polevoy inaccurately
here: In the play Trediakovsky forgets *Deidamia* and asks for his
"small manuscript" (*malen'kaia rukopis'*). However, Belinsky's
mistake was justified, since *Tilemakhida* is the true attribute of
Trediakovsky the fool, whereas *Deidamia* appears in this function only occasionally.

A counterfeit scholar, the pedant Dottore is, nevertheless, a "member of all the Academies." Similarly, Belinsky calls Trediakovsky a "professor of eloquence" and a "professor of poetical ingenuities," and Lazhechnikov calls him an "employee of the Saint Petersburg Academy *de science.*" [109]

Dottore's speech is abstruse, incomprehensible, and filled with garbled Latin quotations. I have already quoted references to Syrian, Chaldean, and Arabic, the languages that characterized Trediakovsky's fruitless learning and his association with the underworld. Numerous references to the inanity and incomprehensibility of his poetry add to this impression. The foolish pedant even seems to be proud of the fact that nobody can understand him. Thus, Tresotinius suggests that the unintelligibility of his song is its chief merit: "Not everyone will understand this song and its contents; here are such subtleties that they are concealed even from many learned men." Nikolev makes his Trediakovsky characterize *Tilemakhida* as a work "that will not be understood by the wisdom of the vast world." Lazhechnikov several times stresses the obscurity of Trediakovsky's works. He includes some Latin words and expressions in his speech and ascribes to him an unreasonable love of Greek and Latin. In Khmel'nitsky's comedy other characters are unable to comprehend Trediakovsky's speech, which is full of heavy Slavonicisms. Unintelligibility is one of Trediakovsky's inherent characteristics in the comedy: It is even evident from his horoscope, which predicts that the person born under the sign of Pisces (as Trediakovsky allegedly was) will be "cold, watery, and unintelligible" (*studen, vodian i temnosloven*). [110]

Even Dottore's appearance seems to influence portrayals of Trediakovsky the pedant. Both Lazhechnikov and Mikhail Dmitriev mention a wart on Trediakovsky's left cheek, Lazhechnikov five times and Dmitriev twice. We do not know if Trediakovsky really had a wart (his portraits, however, do not show any blemishes on his skin); but whether Lazhechnikov and Dmitriev singled out this trait or invented it, they did so under the influence (conscious or unconscious) of the pedant's mask in commedia dell'arte. In addition, Lazhechnikov gave Trediakovsky a round plump face ("like a map of hemispheres"), whereas in portraits his face seems to be oval. A round face is a characteris-

Vasilii Trediakovsky. Portrait by F. S. Rokotov(?). (Trediakovsky, *Izbrannye proizvedeniia*, frontispiece)

tic of fools. Dottore, although his cheeks are flaccid rather than plump, is obese as well.[111]

In Lazhechnikov's novel, the very principle of construction of Trediakovsky's image is similar to that in commedia dell'arte. As the spectator at a commedia dell'arte performance had to recognize personages by their established distinctive features, so too was the reader of the novel supposed to recognize Trediakovsky by his pedantic attributes: "smugness," a wart, and *Tilemakhida*. The author appeals to the reader to use the clues and partake in the construction of the image: "Oh! by his self-satisfaction . . . by the wart on his cheek you would recognize immediately the future professor of eloquence Vasilii Kirillovich Trediakovsky" (p. 55). The reader does not even need the name to identify the familiar pedant: "Seeing the wart on the cheek, the stupid and ingratiating mug, and slavish manner, one could think that this fiend was . . ." (p. 302). The answer was clear to everyone: This fiend was Trediakovsky.

The mythological origin of Dottore's mask easily allowed its incorporation into the emerging image of Trediakovsky the fool. Dottore's immoderate talkativeness (corresponding to Trediakovsky's literary and scholarly prolificacy) paralleled certain characteristics of the mythological fool, such as greediness and immoderation in food and sex. His false learning, stupidity, and misapplied zeal (corresponding to Trediakovsky's alleged talentlessness, lack of real knowledge, and barren diligence) paralleled the fool's poor judgment and his inability to achieve his goals despite great effort. His love for incomprehensible expressions (corresponding to Trediakovsky's alleged proficiency in Latin, Arabic, and Chaldean, as well as to the incomprehensibility of his poetry) echoed the glossolalia characteristic of fools.

Trediakovsky's mythological persona borrowed from other traditions besides commedia dell'arte. The image of Trediakovsky the fool received attributes of the jester along with those of the pedant. Trediakovsky's "Chaldean" nature, ridiculed by Sumarokov in *Tresotinius*, characterized him not only as a servant of the devil but also as a jester, a *skomorokh*. In the late 1750's the anonymous poem known as "Satire of Trediakovsky by Mr. Lomonosov" pictured him in the company of two of Empress Anna's famous jesters, Balakirev and the Italian Pedrillo (Petril):

Как Петрил тебя катал
И Балакирев гонял.
Все ревут тебе: "Кураж,
Тресотин, угодник наш!" [112]

How Petril rolled you and Balakirev chased you. Everybody
roars at you: "Go ahead, Tresotin, our pleaser!"

In Nikolev's parody of Trediakovsky, the poet, like a jester, expects laughter as a reward for his ode:

Екатерина!
Вот мне награда! . . . чтя, улыбнись.

Catherine! Here is my reward! Smile while reading it.

Similarly, Nikolai Polevoy calls him the "hilarious" (*umoritel'nyi*)
Trediakovsky, stressing his ability to amuse (as well as to kill,
umorit') the reader with his poor poetry. Belinsky calls Trediakovsky a jester directly in his review of Nikolai Polevoy's comedy. He elaborates upon this subject in his review of another
play by Nikolai Polevoy, "a dramatic tale," *Lomonosov; or, Life and
Poetry*. He writes: "At a grandees' ball, pictured by Mr. Polevoy's
marvelous brush, Trediakovsky dances to the tune of his own
stupid poems. It is a fact that even the grandees of old liked
sometimes to amuse themselves with learned folk, who were
usually hopeless drunkards and voluntary jesters." [113] Because of
the mythological spirit surviving in jesters and clowns, the jester's characteristics easily permeated the image of Trediakovsky
the fool. Trediakovsky's association with Empress Anna's epoch
(which was generally considered the epoch of jesters) and particularly his participation, although reluctant, in the famous
wedding of jesters, facilitated this permeation.

Finally, Trediakovsky's mythological image could include
characteristics of a folktale fool. In this role Trediakovsky appears in Pushkin's epigram, aimed at Mikhail Kachenovsky, the
editor of the magazine *Messenger of Europe* (1802–30) and the alleged proponent of antiquated orthography:

Там, где древний Кочерговский
Над Ролленем опочил,
Дней новейших Тредьяковский
Колдовал и ворожил:
Дурень, к солнцу став спиною,

Под холодный Вестник свой
Прыскал мертвою водою,
Прыскал Ужицу живой.[114]

Where the ancient Kochergovsky had expired over Rollin, the
Trediakovsky of modern days was engaged in sorcery and
wizardry: The fool, turning his back to the sun, sprinkled dead
water under his cold *Messenger* and sprinkled living water on
the letter *izhitsa*.

Kachenovsky (the Trediakovsky of modern days) displays contrary behavior, typical of fools: Performing a magical act on the
grave of his ancestor, he turns his back to the sun and sprinkles
his barely living *Messenger* with dead water and the hopelessly
dead and outdated letter *izhitsa* with living water, whereas the
correct actions in folktales are to sprinkle a dead person with the
dead water in order to repair all damage and then to sprinkle
this person with the living water in order to bring him or her to
life. As I have already shown, contrary behavior (which led to
the production of bad examples and antirules) was typical of the
mythological Trediakovsky, hence his association with the folktale personage.

Such was Trediakovsky's mythological image. The mythologizing consciousness of the epoch used the features of antiheroic mythological personages of different cultural traditions
for constructing and maintaining the image. With its negative
force this image helped to preserve and purify the emerging cosmos of the "new" Russian literature. It is important to remember, however, that just as there is always a trickster, a fool, or a
scapegoat in a culture hero, the opposite is also true, and a trickster, a fool, or a scapegoat can reveal his heroic nature at any
moment. Trediakovsky's image displays the features of a fool, a
scapegoat, and even a trickster. But it always retains, however
subtly, its heroic nature, which prevents the image from losing
its mythological ambivalence and from deteriorating into total
negativity and thus being obliterated from cultural memory.
Positive appraisals of Trediakovsky's activities, while rare, persisted throughout the last decades of the eighteenth and the beginning of the nineteenth centuries and served to remind the
reading public about Trediakovsky's role as an initiator of the
"new" Russian literature.

The ambivalence of Trediakovsky's mythological image is evident in such details as Murav'ev's epithet for him, *nachal'nik* (archon), his association with Chaldea, and the appellation *ugodnik* (a pleaser, an obsequious person) applied to him in the satirical poem cited above. Murav'ev implied with his characterization that Trediakovsky initiated all the bad things in Russian literature, but he nevertheless recognized Trediakovsky's precedence, negative though it was. The Chaldean language, in Russian tradition, was ascribed not only to the devil and his servants but also to "saintly fools," *iurodivye*.[115] Russian ecclesiastical tradition used the word *ugodnik*, which literally means "the one who pleases" and has a definite negative meaning in some contexts, as an epithet for saints (*sviatye ugodniki*) in the sense that they please God with their holy life. This positive meaning of the word could not have been lost on the author of the poem about Trediakovsky the jester or on his audience. The choice of epithets (archon, Chaldean, and pleaser) demonstrates the dual, ambivalent nature (foolishness and potential heroism or holiness) of Trediakovsky's mythological image.

This ambivalence revealed itself in the fact that Lomonosov's and Trediakovsky's biographers, affected by the myth, sometimes confused the details of Trediakovsky's and Lomonosov's lives, especially details that had latent mythogenic properties. Petr Perevlessky, in his introduction to Trediakovsky's *Selected Works*, asserts that the poet, like Lomonosov, spent some time in the Academy Gymnasium in Saint Petersburg before going abroad. Even more remarkably, Bantysh-Kamensky in his *Dictionary* and Lazhechnikov in his novel erroneously indicate that Arkhangelsk, rather than Astrakhan, was Trediakovsky's place of birth. The two major cities, both situated at the outskirts (the very north and the very south) of Russia, both located near water (the White and Caspian seas), were easily mistaken one for the other, the more so in that each produced a prominent cultural figure of mythological significance.[116] The contrast between Lomonosov the hero and Trediakovsky the fool was by no means absolute, and they were similar enough for the exponents of the myth to mix them up occasionally.

With the two main slots in the myth of the beginning of the "new" Russian literature filled, Sumarokov was left with a sec-

ondary role as Lomonosov's disciple or, more frequently, as Trediakovsky's ally. Sumarokov's image as Lomonosov's enemy was
also endowed with certain mythological features. Thus, Pushkin, in the poem "To Zhukovsky," presented him along with
Trediakovsky as a monster of the underworld, and Nikolai Polevoy in his comedy depicted the two as a pair of jesters. But these
features occurred only sporadically and did not form a consistent and stable image.

The distribution of roles among the writers depended upon
their personalities, certain circumstances of their lives, and the
peculiarities of their literary positions. The promotion of Lomonosov and Trediakovsky to the leading roles in the myth was facilitated by their close association with the Petrine epoch and its
mythological spirit. In many respects they were products of this
epoch, in which, thanks to the Table of Ranks introduced by
Peter I in 1722 and his encouragement of education, it was possible for a commoner to receive an education and achieve higher
social status by means of his abilities. Their lives would have sat-
isfied Peter's most idealistic dreams: Young men, aspiring to
knowledge, go to school, then go abroad to complete their education, and return to work for the benefit of their fatherland. In
this respect their lives resembled the plots of so-called tales of
the Petrine epoch, such as "The Story of the Russian Seaman
Vasilii Koriotsky," "The Story of Aleksandr, a Russian Gentleman," and "The Story of the Russian Merchant Ioan," in which
the main characters leave for foreign countries in search of,
among other things, education. The stories themselves, on the
one hand, reflected the reality of Peter's reign, when many young
people went abroad for schooling as Trediakovsky and Lomonosov would do later, and, on the other hand, made use of an ancient plot based on the primordial notion that to become an adult,
a young man has to depart temporarily from his community.

The ideas of Peter's reform inspired Trediakovsky and Lomonosov, and they saw themselves as carrying on Peter's deeds.
For their contemporaries and for subsequent generations both
Lomonosov and Trediakovsky were closely associated with Peter. As the author of the poem *Peter the Great*, Lomonosov was
Peter's apologist, and as the author of laudatory odes, he was a
panegyrist of his daughter, Elizabeth. When the myth had been

established, he even became Peter's double in the realm of literature. Batiushkov wrote: "He did the same in the difficult field of
literature as Peter the Great did in the civil field. . . . Lomonosov
woke the language of a sleeping nation; he created oratory and
poetry for it, he tried its power in all genres and prepared reliable tools for success for the talented people to come." Belinsky
agreed: "Lomonosov was the Peter the Great of Russian literature." The same view was endorsed by Fedor Tiutchev in his
poem written on the occasion of the hundredth anniversary of
Lomonosov's death.[117] Trediakovsky, on the contrary, was connected with Peter in a comical way: The tsar allegedly foretold
the poet's pitiful fate as a "perpetual toiler." The fact that Trediakovsky wrote "Elegy on Peter the Great's Death" probably
helped to associate chthonic qualities with Trediakovsky's works
and personality.

Sumarokov's name was connected with the Petrine epoch
far less strongly. He was younger than Trediakovsky and Lomonosov and by birth and education did not belong to the social
classes most devoted to Peter's grandly conceived plans. As an
ideologist for the gentry, he was alien to the national spirit of the
Petrine reforms, so dear to Trediakovsky's and especially Lomonosov's hearts.

Even more important for the distribution of roles in the
myth was the fact that the years of Trediakovsky's early activities
and success fell during the reign of Empress Anna. In Russian
tradition, she has the reputation of a monarch who strayed from
the path shown by Peter the Great. The years of her reign stand
in the Russian national consciousness as a dark decade, an epoch
of merciless executions, tortures, denunciations, intrigues, and
vengeance, brought upon Russia by Anna's German favorite,
Ernst Johann Biron. Volynsky, according to this outlook, represented national opposition to Biron's regime and perished because he confronted Biron on behalf of Russian national dignity.
In this confrontation Trediakovsky sided with the dark forces,
inasmuch as he was an enemy of Volynsky and even cashed in
on Volynsky's execution, receiving compensation for the beatings that he sustained from the former cabinet minister.

The association of Trediakovsky's name with Anna's reign
was powerful. In 1856 Lazhechnikov defended his decision to

include Trediakovsky among the characters of his *The Ice House*
by the requirements of historical truth:

> This is a different question: Did I have to put Trediakovsky in my his-
> torical novel? I did. My task was to draw correctly a picture of the epoch
> that I had undertaken to depict. Trediakovsky is its precious accessory:
> Without Trediakovsky the picture would be incomplete, one necessary
> face would be missing in the group of figures. He was as necessary for
> it as the jester Kul'kovsky, the housekeeper [*barskaia barynia*], the cele-
> bration of the goat's giving birth, the fools' wedding, and so on were
> necessary.[118]

In Lazhechnikov's eyes, Trediakovsky the fool belonged to
Anna's epoch, famous for its love for jesters and masquerades,
follies and irrational behavior. This love, in turn, linked the epoch
in popular consciousness with the recession from the cultural
gains of Petrine reign and thus, with chaos and chthonic powers.

The association with Anna's reign endowed Trediakovsky's
mythological image with two opposite but—in Russian cultural
consciousness—equally harmful associations: with the foreign
evil and with anti-Petrine forces. On the one hand, his allegedly
having sided with the German party in the Volynsky affair reinforced the opinion about his affinity for the demonic West,
provoked by his translation of the lecherous and "atheistic" *Voyage à l'île d'Amour*. On the other hand, Trediakovsky's later interest in Church Slavonic, which was perceived by his contemporaries as an attribute of pre-Petrine Russia, linked him in the eyes
of his audience with the precultural chaotic world favored by the
enemies of Peter I, who temporarily triumphed during Anna's
reign. Trediakovsky's deep interest in classical and especially
Russian antiquity, which was characteristic of his literary position from the 1750's, strengthened this association. His concern
with national tradition came too early for the educated Russian
public and, unlike the Romantic exploration of antiquity, was
perceived not as a quest for national identity but as opposition
to new and progressive trends—the opposition to westernization that was exemplified for Russians by Anna and her favorites.
Trediakovsky was thus unacceptable both to the zealots of national tradition and to the enthusiasts of Russia's westernization.

Lomonosov, on the contrary, was connected with the reign

of Elizabeth. In popular opinion it was Elizabeth, Peter's daughter, who returned the country to the right course, repairing the damage caused by Anna's disorganization and restricting foreign intervention in Russia's domestic affairs. Lomonosov thus represented the powers of order, progress, and national tradition.

Sumarokov did not have a place in this cultural scheme. His attempt, in the early 1760's, to become Catherine the Great's official panegyrist was unsuccessful. For his contemporaries and literary descendants, he was more a symbol of the nobility's independence than a laudator of any of the monarchs who reigned during his lifetime.

Lomonosov's and Trediakovsky's literary positions were also relevant in that they were assigned the leading roles in the myth. Both were poets of predominantly high genres, which, according to the aesthetics of their time, were associated with the idea of rational order and contrasted to the disarray of reality—one sees a parallel to the mythological opposition of cosmos and chaos. Trediakovsky's exaggeratedly high poetic intentions could easily be understood in a comical light. His bold literary experiments made such an interpretation even easier. Sumarokov, the poet of middle genres and moderate stylistic tastes, was neutral in this respect. His "middle" position—stressed in the passage from the magazine *Infernal Mail* quoted above, "a man of mediocre rank"—did not allow him to take either of the main roles in the myth.

The fact that Lomonosov's approach to the reform of Russian versification was more radical than Trediakovsky's was also significant in that he was subsequently endowed with the role of father of the "new" Russian literature. In his "Letter on the Rules of Russian Versification" Lomonosov proposed a pure, extreme form of syllabo-tonic verse, and his maximalist approach better marked the break with syllabic tradition than the more prudent approach suggested by Trediakovsky. Furthermore, Lomonosov abandoned the count of syllables, required by syllabic versification, and relied exclusively on the count of feet. Trediakovsky perceived the foot as a complex unit, consisting of a combination of stressed and unstressed syllables. The syllable remained an important factor in his syllabo-tonic verse, while Lomonosov was free of all associations with syllabics. Finally, Lomonosov extended the reform to verses of any length, whereas Trediakovsky initially confined it to thirteen- and eleven-syllable verses. Eventually both had to compromise, but Lomonosov's early full-stressed iambs, which suggested a radical split with syllabics, seemed in retrospect to mark the beginning of a new era in Russian poetry. Trediakovsky's early syllabo-tonics, however, retained too much resemblance to syllabics to be comprehended as a complete break with the old tradition of versification.

Sumarokov again participated in this controversy in a secondary role. Having begun his literary career as a follower of Trediakovsky's, he abandoned his teacher and accepted Lomonosov's principles of versification. The fact that he himself was an original poet, and that his participation in the development of Russian syllabo-tonics was most constructive and multifaceted, did not secure him an independent place in the myth.

For the myth, it was extremely important that Lomonosov's views not only were formulated in a more orderly way than Trediakovsky's but also were more rigid. Lomonosov's poetical system, as well as his aesthetic and linguistic views, formed early, in the first half of the 1740's, and remained virtually unchanged for more than twenty years, until his death. Trediakovsky's artistic and linguistic position, on the contrary, underwent several cardinal transformations. He never stopped looking for new ideas and forms, never ceased his quest for variety and perfection. The static monumentality of Lomonosov's ideas produced an impression of confidence and integrity and thus looked more valuable to the exponents of the myth than the dynamic and evolving views of Trediakovsky.[119] These features of Trediakovsky's aesthetic and linguistic conception invited the charges of eclecticism and incompetence. They confirmed Trediakovsky's alleged connection to chaos and disorder and reinforced his image as a mythological fool. The hero always remains himself, whereas the fool constantly changes his appearance and essence.

The personal qualities of the three writers also influenced the distribution of the mythological roles among them. The "heroic" features of Lomonosov's personality—his versatile abilities, physical strength, and passionate disposition—contributed to his characterization as the creator of Russian literature. These qualities made it easy to identify him as a culture hero. Notably,

Staehlin chose to conclude his description of Lomonosov's life with the episode depicting Lomonosov's heroic fight with three seamen.

Trediakovsky's meek and humble personality, in contrast, facilitated the development of his comical image. Lomonosov beat people up; Trediakovsky received beatings. He was vulnerable to misfortunes and calamities: fires twice (in 1736 and 1747) destroyed all of his belongings, forcing him not only to retranslate thirteen volumes of Rollin's *Histoire ancienne* but also to write anew the *Conversation on Orthography*, a voluminous treatise that contained his most important linguistic views as they had been formed by the mid-1740's. Moreover, in December 1747 a fire at the Academy of Sciences destroyed part of the already published volume of *Ancient History*, and in March 1749 Trediakovsky's kitchen and stable, as well as some of his furniture, burned. His contemporaries felt the unusual cruelty of Trediakovsky's fate. On March 29, 1749, immediately after the fire in Trediakovsky's house, Schumacher, a chancellor at the Academy, wrote, with some irony, to his colleague Grigorii Teplov: "We have a German proverb: *Wer gehaengt werden, der versaufft nicht* [The one who is to be hanged will not drown]. I do not know what to say about Mr. Trediakovsky's fate, but it hounds him terribly."[120]

Sumarokov was not meek, but he was certainly no hero. He was a nervous, irritable, and vulnerable person who suffered from a stutter and a tic and amused, rather than scared, his contemporaries with his uncontrolled fits of anger. Staehlin records an anecdote that demonstrates Sumarokov's unheroic reputation among his contemporaries:

To his [Lomonosov's] splendid burial, which was attended by the Bishop of Saint Petersburg with the most eminent clergy, some senators, and other grandees, *Sumarokov* also came. Sitting near State Councilor Staehlin, who was among the escort, he pointed to the deceased lying in a coffin and said: "The fool has quieted down and cannot fuss any more!" Staehlin answered him: "I would not have advised you to tell him that when he was alive." Lomonosov scared him so much that Sumarokov did not dare to open his mouth in his presence.[121]

Unlike Lomonosov, who rarely explained his position and who often had to be forced by his patron Ivan Shuvalov to enter into literary polemics, Sumarokov liked to expound and defend his views at length. All these features were less compatible with the idea of heroism than Lomonosov's brawling and drinking. They hardly qualified Sumarokov for the exalted role of the father of the "new" Russian literature.

Lomonosov himself was inclined to present his own deeds in heroic colors and to stress the features in his life proper for the biography of a hero. He compared himself to Hercules in the margins of Trediakovsky's *A New and Brief Method for Composing Russian Verse*. Objecting to Trediakovsky's prohibition on the alternation of masculine and feminine rhymes, Lomonosov wrote, "*Herculeum argumentum ex Arcadiae stabulo*," implying he had proved (or was about to prove) that the alternation was possible, exactly as Hercules had shown that it was feasible to cleanse the Augean stables, simply by doing it. On another occasion Lomonosov seized an opportunity to emphasize a feature in his biography typical of a hero: an unhappy childhood. This included cold and hunger, an unsupportive father, and an evil stepmother who allegedly interfered with the hero's vocation:

I . . . [had] a father who was of a kindly disposition but brought me up in utter ignorance, and an evil and envious stepmother who in every way tried to arouse my father's ire, pointing out to him that I always sat idly with a book. Therefore on many occasions I had to read and study what I could in secluded and empty places and endure cold and hunger, until I went away to the Spasskie schools.[122]

At school he was no better off. His father reproached him for his departure, he suffered from extreme poverty, and on top of everything else, "small kids [his fellow students] shouted and pointed their fingers: 'Look what a blockhead came at twenty years of age to study Latin!'"[123] This last feature—his late blooming—Lomonosov shared with many folk heroes, Ilia of Murom, a Russian folk hero, among others. Like Ilia, who remained paralyzed for the first thirty years of his life and then miraculously received health and strength, rose from his sickbed, and began a life of exploits, Lomonosov started late but swiftly overtook and surpassed his fellow students. I do not suggest that Lomonosov consciously ascribed to himself the role of a folk hero. He rather used for his accounts the patterns conveniently supplied to him by the heroic canon, familiar to him from folktales and bylinas, to which he was certainly exposed as a child.[124]

Finally, Lomonosov's early death contributed to his valorization. The formation of a myth rarely takes place before the death of its main hero. Sumarokov lived another twelve years after Lomonosov's death, sincerely trying to convince contemporaries of the injustice of their views on his own and Lomonosov's place in the history of Russian literature. This activity dramatically diminished his chances of becoming the hero of a myth.

Once the mythological images of Lomonosov and Trediakovsky had been formed, they took on a life of their own and soon overshadowed the factual knowledge about them. These images became more true than the historical truth, more convincing than facts, and more stable than memories of actual past events. They continued to function in newly developing literary contexts, adapting to the needs of each new literary generation. Their mythological nature made them useful for the construction of new authorial identities, as well as for the condemnation of opponents. These images represented literary history but helped mold the literary present. The myth of the past determined the future of literature.

Chapter 4

Archaists and Innovators: The Fool in Their Polemics

Russian literary life in the first quarter of the nineteenth century was colored by the vigorous polemics between two literary groups known in Russian literary history variously as Shishkovists and Karamzinists, Classics and Romantics, and—Tynianov's label—Archaists and Innovators.[1] The true picture of early nineteenth-century literary life is certainly more complex than Tynianov's dichotomy suggests. Many factors and issues influenced the literary confrontations of that time, and the participants in the polemics grouped and confronted each other according to various (and changeable) principles. Tynianov distinguished the "older Archaists" (Aleksandr Shishkov above all) and the "young Archaists" (Wilhelm Kuechelbecker, Aleksandr Griboedov, Pavel Katenin, et al.). The same division can be seen among the Innovators (Nikolai Karamzin and Ivan Dmitriev versus Vasilii Zhukovsky, Konstantin Batiushkov, Petr Viazemsky, the young Aleksandr Pushkin). Inside the groups, as well as between them, unanimity was relative, and it was frequently disturbed by differences of opinion. Finally, some writers cannot easily be classified, and some changed their affiliation over time. Nevertheless, Tynianov's classification is generally correct. It reflects the self-consciousness of the participants in the literary life of the period and defines well the main issue of the polemics: the Russian literary language.

The eighteenth century bequeathed to nineteenth-century Russian literature the unresolved question of literary language. Still under the spell of normative aesthetics, Russian literati of the early nineteenth century struggled to work out the principles a writer of Russian should follow. The main question was whether a writer should turn to the parlance of educated contemporaries for models or revive—often artificially—the traditional forms of the literary language of medieval Russia, Church Slavonic. The issue was made even more complicated by the fact that, in the eyes of the participants in the polemics, Church Slavonic (which its proponents did not always distinguish from Old Russian) was associated with national tradition and patriotism, whereas the orientation of the literary language toward modern Russian easily allowed—and even encouraged—the penetration of Western elements. The language arguments translated into the question of the national character (*narodnost'*) of literature. Thus, the significance of the controversy went far beyond the technical question of aesthetics, having to do also with the issues of national identity that Russia confronted, once again, in the face of its own internal problems and the great European events of the late eighteenth and early nineteenth centuries, above all, the French Revolution and the Napoleonic campaigns.[2]

The polemics focused primarily on questions of language, but many other problems vital for Russian literature, which was entering the stage of Romanticism, were also discussed in the course of the heated clashes between various groups, parties, and circles. Among them were such issues as the validity of the previously defined system of genres and the introduction of greater metrical variety, as well as more general questions of taste, goals and methods of criticism, and the professional status of literary production.

Many of the questions, especially those concerning literary language and metrics, were historically connected with Trediakovsky's activities. It was impossible to discuss these problems without mentioning Trediakovsky's name. By virtue of his mythological image as a provider of bad examples, these references, with rare exceptions, were unflattering. For the participants in the discussions, he was the one who had spoiled good ideas by implementing them awkwardly in his writings. Or, even more frequently, he was the author of the stupid ideas that one's literary opponents were trying to implement. If Lomonosov was a desirable precursor for all the groups in the dispute, Trediakovsky was a precursor whom rivals attributed to each other.

Both the Archaists and the Innovators were liable to be compared to Trediakovsky. However, the Archaists' linguistic orientation toward Church Slavonic and their interest in high literary genres made their position similar to Trediakovsky's in the later period of his life and left them especially vulnerable to mockery as Trediakovsky's descendants.[3] The Archaists' alleged affinity to Trediakovsky was ridiculed throughout the entire period of the polemics, but the derision reached its climax in the attacks against the Archaists by Arzamas, a literary association that united the opponents of the Archaists' organization, the Colloquium of Lovers of the Russian Word.[4]

The Colloquium, or Beseda, was founded in 1811. It grew out of informal literary soirées, but affiliation turned it into a serious enterprise, with bylaws, regular meetings, and a publication. Its opponents joked that its formal structure—it was divided into four departments, each headed by a chairman and a trustee—resembled that of the State Council, the supreme legislative organ established in Russia in 1810. The structure, however, served to emphasize the society's serious intentions and ceremonial significance. The society's leader was Aleksandr Shishkov, the chairman of the first department. Admiral Shishkov—a brave seaman in the past, the author of famous patriotic manifestos that he wrote in his capacity as secretary of state during the War of 1812, a conservative member in the governments of Alexander I and Nicholas I—at the time of the formation of Beseda was famous in literary circles as a poet and a scholar and as the author of the book *A Discourse on the Old and New Styles of the Russian Language* (1803). In this book Shishkov assaulted the linguistic theories of Karamzin and urged Russian writers to return to their roots, purge the Russian language of foreign influence, and make use of the national tradition available to them in the Church Slavonic translation of the Bible and in Russian folklore. Along with Shishkov, Beseda included such members as

Gavrila Derzhavin, at that time a venerable but somewhat antiquated poet; Aleksei Olenin, a scholar, a patron of the arts, and
the director of the Public Library in Saint Petersburg; Ivan Krylov, the best-known Russian fabulist; Count Dmitrii Khvostov, a
poet whose bad reputation could rival only Trediakovsky's; and
Stepan Zhikharev, a future memoirist. The literary works read
at the society's monthly meetings were published in the magazine *Readings in the Colloquium of Lovers of the Russian Word*, which
was issued irregularly in 1811–15. Beseda ceased to exist with
the death of Derzhavin, in 1816.

Unlike Beseda, Arzamas was an emphatically informal association, based on the idea of privacy, esprit de corps, and friendly
intimacy. Its members ridiculed the bureaucratic air of Beseda,
its alleged officialism and rigidity. Their own meetings—the first
took place in 1815—were designed to be friendly feasts, full of
jokes, pranks, and laughter. Their ceremonies were a concatena-
tion of jokes comprehensible only to insiders. The society's very
name was a private joke, as were the special names, picked from
Zhukovsky's ballads, that members used among themselves.
The society's hero was Karamzin, but its true inspiration was
Vasilii Zhukovsky, a poet and translator in public life and a brilliant parodist and jester in his capacity as Arzamas secretary.
The spirit of laughter and joy, of pure galimatias (as the Arzamasians called their private talk at the meetings) could not tolerate
any serious business, and the society fell victim, in 1818, not
only to Beseda's disbandment but also to the attempts by the future Decembrists Mikhail Orlov and Nikolai Turgenev to introduce politics into Arzamas activities.

Although Arzamas as a literary society existed for less than
three years (1815–18), the principles that united its participants
began to form much earlier and survived far beyond the society's last meeting. For roughly fifteen years, between the early
1810's and the Decembrist uprising in 1825, the participants
formed what the late Pushkinist Maksim Gillel'son called the
"Arzamas brotherhood"—an informal friendly circle united by
common literary interests, personal affinity, and similar literary
tastes.[5]

From the beginning the battle against the Archaists was
among the permanent items on the group's agenda. The first at-

tack by a future Arzamasian against the Archaists occurred as early as 1809, when Batiushkov wrote a poem, "A Vision on the Banks of Lethe," which soon became known to everyone interested in literary matters and made the young poet famous. In the poem, the narrator, fatigued by the works of Semen Bobrov, a poet of Archaic orientation, falls asleep and dreams of a terrible catastrophe: For some reason Apollo has killed all Russian poets, who, upon their death, appear before Minos for the last judgment. Minos spares nobody but Shishkov (by the doubtful virtue of "the bulk of his works, his firm reason, and deeds") and Ivan Krylov, who is actually saved by his fables, which are so good that they do not sink in Lethe.[6]

Trediakovsky's name appears in this first attack by an Innovator against the Archaists. Batiushkov promptly makes use of Trediakovsky's reputation as a mythological fool, declaring him the patron and precursor of the Archaists. As such, Trediakovsky enthusiastically welcomes Shishkov's arrival in the underworld:

> Певец любовныя езды
> Осклабил взор *усмешкой блудной*
> И рек: "О, муж умом не скудный!
> Обретший редки красоты
> И смысл в моей Деидамии,
> Се ты, се ты!.."[7]

The singer of the voyage of love grinned a lickerish grin and spake: "O man of mind not meager who has discovered rare beauties and sense in my *Deidamia*, here thou art, here thou art!"

In Batiushkov's interpretation, Trediakovsky and his literary descendants, the Archaists, enjoy mutual understanding: Trediakovsky greets Shishkov as a sympathizer who is capable of appreciating his much-derided tragedy. Trediakovsky, in turn, is the only one capable of understanding Semen Bobrov's poetry, famous among the Innovators for its overwrought diction and high-flown complexity:

> Один отец "Тилемахиды"
> Слова сии умел понять.
> (p. 179)

Only the singer of *Tilemakhida* could understand these words.

In Batiushkov's poem, Trediakovsky and the Archaists literally speak the same language, a comical derivative of Church Slavonic. Trediakovsky's speech is a parody of the Archaists' linguistic principles and usage as Batiushkov presents them. It is filled with Slavonicisms: *muzh* (Church Slavonic for "man"), *egda* (when), *se* (this), and so forth. In addition, Batiushkov uses the Church Slavonic verb *rek* (spake) to characterize Trediakovsky's speech. The lofty Church Slavonic expression *osklabil vzor*, "grinned," was also perceived as profoundly archaic in Batiushkov's time.[8]

Batiushkov's launching of the battle against the Archaists was later recognized and jokingly glorified in Arzamas. In May 1816 one of the society's founders, Dmitrii Dashkov, addressed Batiushkov, whose nickname in Arzamas was Achilles: "O fearless Achilles, who inflicted on them [the Archaists] the first strike and the first wound!"[9] But he did not remain a lone warrior for long, and in 1811 was joined by his friend Nikolai Gnedich, the future translator of the *Iliad*. Gnedich's position in the dispute between the Archaists and Innovators and his attitude toward Trediakovsky were not straightforward. Gnedich shared many of the Archaists' literary principles but did not join Beseda, probably more because of personal feelings than because of literary disagreements: He was invited to join Beseda as a "collaborator," rather than as a regular member, and took offense.[10] At the same time, he was friendly with many Arzamasians and took part in some of their mockery of Beseda. Gnedich was the first enthusiastic reader of "A Vision on the Banks of Lethe" and the one who started to distribute it in manuscript copies. Later on, members of Arzamas considered Gnedich a member of the Archaists' party and ridiculed him with the same expressions they used to deride the Besedists. Batiushkov, however, maintained friendly relations with him. At any rate, in 1811 Gnedich shared the Arzamasian notion of the Archaists as successors to Trediakovsky the fool and greeted the emergence of Beseda with a blasphemous parody of the Credo, in which Trediakovsky was proclaimed a prophet of the Shishkovists (pp. 23–24).[11]

Batiushkov continued his attacks against Beseda in the poem "The Bard in the Colloquium of Lovers of the Russian Word," a parody of Zhukovsky's patriotic "The Bard in the Camp of Russian Warriors" (1812).[12] The poem describes an orgy, or perhaps a wake, after a Beseda meeting, when all the visitors have gone and the regular members have stayed behind to drink and praise each other in drunken songs. Trediakovsky again appears as the Archaists' leader and inspirer, their spiritual "father":

> Но дух отцов воскрес в сынах,
> Мы все для славы дышим,
> Давно здесь в прозе и в стихах
> Как Тредьяковский пишем.
> (pp. 255–56)

But the fathers' spirit has revived in the sons; we all breathe for fame; here we have long written like Trediakovsky in prose and in verse.

Moreover, the Archaists worship the notorious fool:

> Мы все клялись, клялись тобой
> С утра до полуночи
> Писать как ты, тебе служить:
> Мы все с рассудком в споре,
> Для славы будем жить и пить;
> Нам по колено море!
> (p. 256)

We all vowed upon your name to write like you from morning to midnight and serve you; we have all quarreled with reason; we will live and drink for fame; we could not care less.[13]

In Batiushkov's interpretation, the Archaists, like Trediakovsky, use Church Slavonic (*se, muzh, ochi* [eyes]). Like him, they are fools ("have quarreled with reason"), write terrible poetry, and drink heavily. The last feature is noteworthy. As I pointed out in my discussion of Trediakovsky's mythological image, in real life he, unlike Lomonosov, did not drink. Nevertheless, Lomonosov tried to pass this characteristic on to him. Batiushkov's poem demonstrates that he succeeded, at least partially. In "The Bard," the Archaists and their ancestor, Trediakovsky, share with Lomonosov only one feature, his drunkenness:

> Пусть Ломоносов был умен
> И нас еще умнее,

> За пьянство стал бессмертен он,
>   А мы его пьянее.   (p. 256)

Lomonosov may be clever, and even cleverer than we; for his drunkenness, he became immortal, and we are even drunker.

This common feature is the one that most clearly betrays the trickster side of Lomonosov's heroic image and its intrinsic affinity with Trediakovsky's mythological image as a fool.

In 1814 the future Arzamasian Aleksandr Voeikov wrote the first version of his *Madhouse* (its last, fourth version was written in 1837–39). This work, extremely popular in the first half of the nineteenth century, reinforced the emerging connection of Trediakovsky's name with Beseda. In the poem, the author visits writers confined to a madhouse. He recognizes the lover of Church Slavonic letters, Shishkov, by the volume of Trediakovsky's poems in his hands:

> Том, в сафьян переплетенный,
> Тредьяковского стихов
> Я увидел, изумленный,—
> И узнал, что то Ш[ишк]ов.[14]

Amazed, I saw the volume of Trediakovsky's poems, bound in morocco, and realized that it was Shishkov.

Shishkov here not only reads Trediakovsky's works—which is sufficient proof of his insanity, as well as of his affinity with Trediakovsky—but also borrows Trediakovsky's most usual attribute, a book, an attribute that had been the mark of the notorious pedant since Sumarokov introduced the image more than half a century earlier. Shishkov turns out to be Trediakovsky's double, whom people recognize exactly as they did his ancestor: by the book in his hands.

The tradition of insulting comparisons between the Archaists and Trediakovsky, started by Batiushkov and developed by Gnedich and Voeikov, was continued by the Arzamasians in their mock rituals and speeches at the society's meetings in 1815–18. In March 1816 Vasilii Pushkin, an uncle of the great poet and a minor poet himself, was admitted to Arzamas with the nickname Vot (here, here you go). One of the exploits that Vasilii Pushkin had to perform during the elaborate mock admission ritual was to pierce an effigy of Shishkov with an arrow. The notorious line from Trediakovsky's *Tilemakhida* about a terrible creature of the underworld was placed on the chest of the effigy. Dashkov gave a speech, explaining the meaning of this mock symbol and saying that it represented the monstrous Beseda, whose emergence was allegedly prophesied by the "Slavophiles' patriarch," Trediakovsky: "Dear brother, . . . you will courageously fight *unguibus et rostro* [talons and beak] the Hydra of Beseda, this ludicrous monster that was prophesied so eloquently in the well-known verse of the Slavophiles' patriarch: 'A stout monster, wild, huge, three-throated, and barking'" (p. 146).[15] Like Gnedich in his "Credo," Dashkov assigned Trediakovsky the role of the prophet who foretells the emergence of Beseda. But unlike his predecessor, who played upon Christian symbolism, Dashkov emphasized the chthonic nature of Trediakovsky and his literary descendants. In the speech, Trediakovsky, with his depiction of a monster of the underworld, foretold the emergence of another chthonic monster, the Hydra of Beseda.

Trediakovsky's name and his *Tilemakhida* also represented the Besedists in Dmitrii Bludov's speech of March 15, 1816. Bludov, whose nickname in Arzamas was Cassandra, described "her" prophetic vision: "She saw in her mystical vision the ancient ungainly castle of Beseda; in front of this castle's moat Gromoboi-Trediakovsky moans in a grave; on the grave Popov lies crosswise with *Tilemakhida*" (p. 157). Vasilii Popov was one of the honorary members of Beseda. For this reason Bludov gave him *Tilemakhida* instead of the Holy Scriptures. Gromoboi was a nickname of Stepan Zhikharev. Bludov apparently called him Trediakovsky because of his former association with the Archaists and his membership in Beseda, as well as because of his poetic experiments with hexameters. For these sins, in addition to receiving the appellation Trediakovsky, Zhikharev was obliged during his initiation into Arzamas to read a mock funeral oration for himself, rather than for the Beseda member of his choice, as all other incoming members were required to do. He was called Trediakovsky yet another time in Cassandra's speech (p. 158).

Two other Arzamasians, Dmitrii Kavelin, in his speech of November 1816, and Dmitrii Severin, in his speech of April

1817, described Trediakovsky as a forefather, an Abraham, to whose bosom the deceased Archaists departed. Kavelin called the Besedist Semen Filatov a "living corpse, who has fallen asleep forever in Trediakovsky's bosom" (p. 178). Severin said about the Archaists: "Some of them, the leaders among the Chaldeans, have long since joined with Trediakovsky and are conspicuous in the dwelling of the shades for the corpulence of their mental fibers" (p. 213).

The Archaists appear in these jokes as descendants of Trediakovsky the fool. As is appropriate for the spiritual children of the inane versifier, they share many of his characteristics, first of all, stupidity. Batiushkov, in his "A Vision on the Banks of Lethe," characterized the Archaists' works as "absurd [*bezrassudny*] prose and poems." Gnedich called Shikhmatov "galimatias from galimatias, nonsense from nonsense begotten, not made, of one substance with the Father [Shishkov], through whom everything is written" (p. 23).[16] In Batiushkov's "The Bard," the drunken Archaists proclaimed "death to reason" (p. 256). The records of Arzamas meetings preserve countless jokes about the Archaists' stupidity, illogic, and madness. Dashkov claimed in his speech of December 16, 1815, that "Beseda was created in order to keep saying and writing nonsense" (p. 131). The Arzamasians called their enemies "the half-witted Chaldeans" and "the Beseda madmen" (pp. 104, 163) and laughed at their "innate stupidity," "folly," and "childishness of mind" (pp. 189, 138, 150). The society's very motto was the line from Jean Baptiste Louis Gresset's comedy *Le Méchant* (1747): "Fools are here for our little pleasures" (*Les sots sont ici-bas pour nos menus plaisirs*). For being such a foe of foolishness, the members of Arzamas admitted Gresset to their society and declared him "a deceased Arzamasian." The Arzamasians made fun of Beseda's location: Derzhavin's house, where their meetings took place, was situated near a madhouse. Zhukovsky played upon this fact, unfortunate for the Besedists, in his speech of November 11, 1815, in which he suggests to his audience that they, "mentally crossing the Obukhov Bridge and passing the yellow house of insanity, drop in at the notorious Beseda of madness" (p. 103; cf. p. 213). Viazemsky also took advantage of this fact in his epigram written in connection with Derzhavin's death:

Когда беседчикам Державин пред концом
Жилища своего не завещал в наследство,
Он знал их твердые права на желтый дом,
И прочил им соседство.[17]

When before his death Derzhavin did not bequeath his residence to Beseda members, he knew of their firm rights to the
yellow house and foretold that they would be his neighbors.

In the Arzamas interpretation the Archaists' folly acquired
distinct mythological traits, worthy of their ancestor, Trediakovsky. The Arzamasians used every opportunity to point out their
opponents' affinity with fools and jesters. They endowed the
Besedists with the traditional attributes of fools—donkeys' ears
and fools' caps. Count Aleksandr Shakhovskoy, a prominent Besedist and the author of many satirical works about the Innovators, received the nickname Shutovskoy (from the word *shut*,
"jester"). Viazemsky devoted a cycle of poems, "Shutovskoy's
Poetical Crown Presented to Him Once and for All for His Many
Exploits" (1815), to developing Shakhovskoy's image as a jester.
In this cycle, Shutovskoy, a "complete fool" who "has quarreled
with reason," displays the contrary behavior characteristic of
fools and jesters: His comedies force the audience to cry, and his
tragedies make them laugh.[18] An honorary member of Beseda,
the Moscow University curator Pavel Golenishchev-Kutuzov
gave the Arzamasians another chance to have a good laugh
when he was imprudent enough to be arrested in a Harlequin
costume. The Arzamasians seized this opportunity to emphasize the Besedists' jester nature (pp. 138, 159). The tradition of
commedia dell'arte, which Sumarokov employed for the construction of Trediakovsky's mythological image, remained essential in the new polemical context as well.

The same was true with respect to the Russian folk theater
tradition that had allowed Sumarokov to create the image of Trediakovsky the Chaldean. The Arzamasians made good use of
this tradition in their own ridicule of the Besedists. The appellation Chaldeans was the one the Arzamasians used most frequently for the Archaists. As I pointed out in my analysis of Trediakovsky's mythological image, this appellation evoked many
associations: with magic, astrology, and other fruitless and un-

holy knowledge; with the anti-Christian tradition and Satanism; but above all with the Old Russian personages of Yuletide folk festivals, the unholy malicious jesters, who for twelve days were allowed to run around in the streets and tease and even torture people. The Arzamasians reinforced the alleged affinity of the Besedists with jesters by the appellation *ded*, "grandfather," which they regularly applied to Shishkov. The word *ded* in Russian also has several connotations. In addition to the usual "father of one's mother or father" and the obvious "ancestor," it is also used in reference to some demonic creatures popular in Russian folklore, such as water and house spirits. But even more important than this association of Shishkov's name with chthonic creatures is the fact that the word *ded* can also mean a jester, a participant in Yuletide and Mardi Gras folk festivals, who makes the crowd laugh with his nonsensical rhymed talk and silly tricks.[19] Thus, the Besedists were presented by their enemies as a host of professional jesters led by the "grey-haired grandfather" Shishkov and inspired by the Chaldean Trediakovsky.

In the Arzamasians' opinion, the inane descendants of Trediakovsky, like all fools and jesters, certainly deserved beatings. Actually, the Arzamas members made it a rule "to beat the Chaldeans at every opportunity and with everything handy" (p. 103). The Arzamasians even suggested that Shakhovskoy "was created to endure the blows of sticks and to be despised by everyone" (p. 131).

In their opponents' characterizations, the Archaists also shared with their "father" Trediakovsky the features of his pedantic image. The Innovators mocked the Archaists' productiveness, their diligence, and the incomprehensibility of their works. In Batiushkov's "A Vision," Aleksei Merzliakov, a professor at Moscow University and, in the Arzamasians' view, a member of the "Moscow Beseda," the Society of Lovers of Russian Literature (*Obshchestvo liubitelei rossiiskoi slovesnosti*, 1811–37), says about himself that he is "fortunately very prolific" (p. 176). In the same poem, Dmitrii Iazykov brags about his writings: "Look, here are thousands of pages, covered with sacred dust, filled with fine print" (ibid.). Bobrov, in turn, reports that he has written three long poems and a hundred odes, which Batiushkov describes as so obscure that they can be understood only by Trediakovsky (p. 179). Viazemsky also derided the incomprehensibility of Bobrov's poetry, in two malicious epigrams written in 1810, right after Bobrov's death. In one of them Bobrov complains that his poetry could not be understood even in hell:

> Ага! Здесь, видно, так, как и на той стране,—
> Покойник говорит,—меня не понимают![20]

"Aha! here apparently it is as in the other world," says the deceased. "I am not understood!"

In Arzamas, the tradition of deriding the Archaists' alleged prolificacy and incomprehensibility continued. Dashkov mentioned "a huge notebook, covered with fine writing, in the hands of a Beseda reader" (p. 145). For Zhukovsky, the language of the Archaists' works rivals Estonian (*chukhonskii*) in incomprehensibility: "The Estonian language was for me as incomprehensible as the language of our loquacious deceased" (p. 185).

Another prominent feature of the Archaists' collective image that revealed their affinity to their chthonic ancestor, Trediakovsky, was their connection with chaos and death. The Archaists' alleged relation to death can already be seen in Batiushkov's poem devoted to their mockery. In "A Vision," the action takes place in the underworld, and most of the characters are deceased Archaists. In "The Bard," the theme of death is also prominent. The singing Archaists glorify their dead ancestors, Trediakovsky among them, and regret that the ancestors cannot join them in Beseda:

> Сей кубок чадам древних лет!
>   Вам слава, наши деды!
> Друзья! Почто покойных нет
>   Певцов среди Беседы?
>
> (p. 255)

This goblet [we drink] for the children of ancient times! Glory to you, our grandfathers! Friends! Wherefore are the deceased singers not in Beseda?

In addition, Batiushkov depicts the Archaists' poems as so much dead material lying in a bookstore:

Кладбище милое стихов—
Бумажные могилы!
Там царство тленья и мышей.

(p. 257)

A beloved cemetery of poems, paper graves! There is the realm
of decay and mice.

In Gnedich's "Credo," Shakhovskoy is "buried with writings"
and Shishkov's followers await a "resurrection" of their "dead
poems" (p. 23).

The motif of death became dominant in Arzamas jokes about
the Archaists. The Arzamasians' mock rituals and word games
were full of references to death, metaphors of death, and jokes
about Beseda as a realm of death and the Archaists as the dead.
The ritual of admission to Arzamas required a funeral oration to
one of the Beseda members:

Following the example of all other societies, every newly accepted
member of the *New Arzamas* would have to read a eulogy for his deceased predecessor. But all members of the *New Arzamas* are immortal.
Therefore, for lack of their own deceased, the *new Arzamasians* (as a
proof of their noble impartiality and even more as a proof that their hatred does not extend beyond the grave) proposed that the deceased be
borrowed from among the Chaldeans of Beseda and the Academy, in
order to reward them according to their deeds without waiting for posterity to do so. (p. 84)

This ritual was jokingly called the murder and burial of Archaists. During Arzamas meetings at least twelve Besedists and
Academy members were "buried."[21]

The motif of death, as in Trediakovsky's mythological image, was intertwined with the motif of sleep. The Arzamasians
called Beseda "a realm of darkness and sleep" (p. 157; cf. p. 92).
They endowed the society with the telling attribute of a "wreath
of poppies" (p. 97). The Innovators insinuated that the Archaists' writings induced sleep in their readers and listeners, and
called the Archaists "the poets lullers" (*poety-usypiteli*; p. 179; cf.
pp. 177, 179–180). Likewise, in Viazemsky's satirical Christmas
carol (1814), Shakhovskoy lulls Jesus to sleep with a poem:

При первых двух стихах дитя прилег головкой.
"Спасибо! дева говорит,

Читай, читай, смотри, как спит,
Баюкаешь ты ловко."[22]

After the first two verses the child lay down his head. "Thank you," the Virgin says. "Go on reading. Look how he sleeps. You lull skillfully."

The Besedists' association with death and sleep suggested their further association with chaos. Batiushkov was already emphasizing this link even before the formation of Arzamas. In his "The Bard," the Besedists hail Confusion (*Sumbur*) and profess their filial love for it:

Сумбур! Здесь сонм твоих сынов:
К тебе горим любовью!

(p. 258)

Confusion! Here is a host of your sons: We burn with love for you.

Later, in Arzamasian speeches and rituals, this characteristic became regularly attributed to the Archaists.

Association with death and chaos revealed the Archaists' alleged chthonic nature. The Arzamasians emphasized this characteristic by comparing Beseda to various chthonic creatures. The image of the monstrous Beseda, created upon Vasilii Pushkin's admission to Arzamas, was typical in this respect. In the speeches during this mock admission ceremony, Beseda was called Python, Scylla and Charybdis, Hydra, and Cerberus (pp. 143, 144, 146). On at least one other occasion the Arzamasians called their enemies Chaldean serpents (p. 221). Count Dmitrii Khvostov was called "Immortal Kashchei" (*Kashchei Bessmertnyi*; p. 107), a monstrous character from Russian folklore. He was also termed a "reptile" (*gadina*) and a "petty devil" (*bes*; pp. 115, 217). Shakhovskoy was presented as a variegated dragon (p. 168) and Gnedich, as a sorcerer (*volkhv*) and a Cyclops (p. 203; the last nickname was a nasty joke, inasmuch as Gnedich was blind in one eye). The Arzamasians depicted meetings of Beseda as witches' sabbaths:

I saw the meeting of all the sorcerers of Beseda. They were preparing to fly to the midnight gathering and with unheard-of incantations were taking off their clothes, which were, alas! as decrepit as the taste of their

Grey-haired Grandfather. . . . The new enchanters rub themselves with a mysterious ointment and cover their nakedness with the covers of Beseda books; and suddenly, like a black flock of crows and jackdaws, evoking a tempest, they leave the ground with screams and shrieks and fly to the midnight gathering (p. 128).[23]

On the whole, the members of Arzamas jokingly pictured their literary fight with Beseda as a mythological struggle between a hero and a dragon, light and darkness, cosmos and chaos. The symbolic slaying of a monster ("Hydra of Beseda") in the ceremony that took place during Vasilii Pushkin's admission to Arzamas was not an isolated example of such a fight with chthonic forces. On another occasion Vasilii Pushkin's poems were said to have "destroyed the spell of the black magicians [*chernoknizniki*] and sorcerers [*chernopistsy*] of Beseda" (p. 172). The Arzamasians compared their society to Hercules, who "in the crib strangled all the Chaldean snakes" (p. 221). Dashkov proposed fighting against the Archaists' proto-Slavophile ideology with the means proper for vampires and promised "to hammer an aspen stake into the old witch Slovena's back to prevent her from causing trouble after her death" (p. 202). Finally, Cassandra (Bludov) foretold the last decisive clash between the Innovators and the Archaists in terms of a primordial duel between the powers of light and darkness:

"O Beseda!" I exclaimed, "where are you?" Hardly had I pronounced the magic incantation when my eyes misted, the candles faded without a crackle, and a terrible darkness reigned, similar to the darkness of chaos and Labzin's works. . . . And suddenly in my garden Liudmila's rooster started to sing, and some voice rushed by with this singing, and the voice, it seems, was proclaiming above the stars, "Let there be Arzamas," and in place of the gloom of night there appeared a weak but pleasant shimmering, similar to the dawn heralding the sun. (p. 114)

Bludov included the name of Aleksandr Labzin, a writer and prominent Freemason, as a synonym for obscure irrationalism. "Liudmila's rooster" refers to Zhukovsky's first ballad, "Liudmila" (1808). In Bludov's allegory, the sounds of the ballad end the literary night as a rooster's song ends the activity of diabolic night creatures. Bludov repeated the light/darkness dichotomy in another of his speeches, "A Sleepy Opinion of the Aeolian

Harp": "No, Arzamas! Renounce darkness; you have bound yourself to serve the light" (p. 222). The young Pushkin used the same Apollonian imagery in his poem "To Zhukovsky," written in the context of the polemics with the Archaists:

> Лиющая с небес и жизнь и вечный свет,
> Стрелою гибели десница Аполлона
> Сражает наконец, ужасного Пифона.[24]

Apollo's right hand, pouring both life and eternal light from the skies, at last strikes the terrible Python down with the arrow of death.

The Arzamasians' mocking presentation of their polemics with the Archaists as a cosmic struggle between good and evil was overlaid with a patina of Christian terminology. Thus, the Innovators' society was called the New Arzamas, in contrast to the "old" (*vetkhii*) town of Arzamas and the Babylon of Beseda. The Arzamasians depicted the formation of Arzamas as the "transfiguration" of its members, who were "cleansed" by the "Lipetsk deluge" (*Lipetskii potop*, an allusion to Shakhovskoy's comedy *The Lipetsk Spa*, 1815), and received new names as upon being baptized or entering a monastery (pp. 82–83). The Arzamasians introduced a new calendar, which started in the year of the "Lipetsk deluge," 1815.

Correspondingly, the Arzamasians depicted the Besedists as foes of Christianity. They called the members pagans, and Beseda, a "Chaldean synagogue" (pp. 242, 103). Shishkov's nickname, *Sedoi Ded*, "Grey-haired Grandfather," introduced by Batiushkov and frequently used in Arzamas, possibly referred not only to his image as chief among Chaldeans but to the pagan cult of ancestors as well. On the other hand, as I have already had a chance to point out, the nickname Chaldeans by itself had strong anti-Christian connotations in the Russian tradition. Moreover, the itinerant jesters who impersonated Chaldeans in Yuletide performances were considered unholy and were even denied Christian burial. This humorous notion of the Archaists as foes of Christ found its way into one of the copies of Viazemsky's carol, quoted above. In this copy, Shakhovskoy was presented not only as Christ's "luller" but also as his crucifier: The words "the child lay down his head" read as "the child hung his head" (*ditia povis golovkoi*), an image that inevitably recalls Christ's posture in Crucifixion paintings.[25] The Besedists' chthonic nature was comprehended as infernal, and the Innovators' literary fight with them took on the significance of an apocalyptic destruction of evil.

This blasphemous game easily allowed the incorporation of the image of the "Chaldean" Trediakovsky. The potentially infernal traits of his image as a fool made him particularly suitable for the role of prophet and precursor of the "evil" Archaists. Using Trediakovsky's image in an apocalyptic context, the Innovators reinforced its infernal features and prepared the way for the emergence of the "non-Christian" Trediakovsky in Lazhechnikov's novel and Trediakovsky the devil in Mikhail Dmitriev's satire "Twelve Sleepy Essays."

The mythological spirit of the Innovators' struggle with the Archaists revealed itself in laughter, which was the central element in their attacks against Shishkov and his associates. Especially significant in this respect were jokes about death. When, by unfortunate coincidence, one of the funeral orations for a Besedist became prophetic—Ivan Zakharov died soon after Bludov read a funeral speech for him—the members of Arzamas were not in the least embarrassed. They continued to joke about him as a bad poet (pp. 206, 208), and Pushkin even registered this macabre coincidence in a line: "Where Cassandra prophesied death for Zakharov . . ."[26] Similarly, Bobrov's death did not prevent—indeed it encouraged—Viazemsky's ridicule of his poetry, as later Derzhavin's death did not stop the satirist from using his name in the epigram against Beseda. As with the derision of Trediakovsky the fool, such laughter would be cruel and improper (even in such an entirely private setting as the Arzamas meetings) but for its mythological nature.

The members of Arzamas felt the creative power of laughter and cultivated it. They distinguished between the Archaists' uncreative and, in their opinion, dull galimatias and their own "witty galimatias" (p. 221). As Dashkov pointed out in his speech in honor of Karamzin on May 6, 1816, "A galimatias is not always born from madness and does not always talk nonsense" (p. 159). Moreover, for them, laughter was an attribute of reason, and the Archaists' madness was remarkable precisely for its absence of mirth. In Beseda, the Arzamasians insisted, there reigned a "terrible silence, which has never been interrupted by the merry sound of sane reasoning" (p. 104). The Arzamasians' love for galimatias revealed the members' association with the potentially creative powers of primordial chaos, as opposed to the Archaists' dull and destructive chthonism. Hence Zhukovsky's description of Arzamas nonsense as "sacred confusion" (*sviashchennyi sumbur*; p. 229). Hence the usage of the otherworldly element of Zhukovsky's ballads in Arzamas rituals, and the occasional presentation of Arzamas meetings as gatherings of monsters.

The image of Beseda as a chthonic monster was, of course, suggested by the Archaists' literary and linguistic stance, by their orientation toward archaic elements of language, and by their keen interest in folklore. Many elements of this complex collective image emerged independently of the myth about Trediakovsky the fool, simply by virtue of the rules of the Arzamasian game. This game, full of tomfoolery and burlesque, encouraged the spontaneous emergence of mythological patterns. But it was crucial that in the Innovators' eyes the Archaists' literary position was connected with the image of Trediakovsky the fool. The Innovators were able to use elements of his mythological image, which were readily available in the literary consciousness of the epoch, for an effective condemnation of the literary activities of their opponents, which were, from the Innovators' point of view, no less harmful than those of their alleged predecessor. For the Innovators, Trediakovsky's name served as a key to understanding and labeling the phenomena that they sought to criticize. It revealed the Archaists' alleged relation to chaos and exposed them as a threat to the present order, as well as to the future of Russian literature. Trediakovsky's mythological image consequently helped to compose the collective portrait of his "descendants" as the enemies of reason and Russian literature. On the other hand, the Innovators' active use of Trediakovsky's mythological image in these new literary clashes reinforced its seeming validity and ensured its survival in the Russian literary consciousness.

The Innovators, however, were themselves susceptible to comparison with Trediakovsky. The linguistic and literary positions of their leader, Karamzin, who maintained that the literary language should be oriented toward the usage of refined society and who, in his early years, cultivated light poetry and the love theme, provided a clear parallel to the ideas of the young Trediakovsky. This similarity was hardly coincidental, since Karamzin probably knew Trediakovsky's translation of *Voyage à l'île d'Amour* and its introduction, which propagated linguistic views so similar to his own.[27] Karamzin's friend Aleksandr Petrov recommended this book to Karamzin, albeit ironically, in a letter of June 11, 1785, as a model for the "Russo-Slavonic" language (*russko-slavianskii*), which he jokingly urged Karamzin to use in his writings:

> Please make good use of this friendly criticism; you had better write your entire composition in Russo-Slavonic, in long-lingering, soaring compound words. To supplement your skill in writing in such a style, I advise you to read the compositions and translations in verse and prose of Vas[ilii] Trediakovsky, *whose little book about a voyage to the isle of love in translation from the French language I now use and read very much.*[28]

The last clause (*koego o v liubvi ezde ostrov knizhnitseiu pol'zuius', perevodnoiu, nyne, s Frantsuzskogo iazyka, i ves'ma tu chitaiu*), full of impossible inversions, is a parody of Trediakovsky's syntax. The letter suggests that the friends were familiar with at least three of Trediakovsky's works: his translation of *Voyage à l'île d'Amour*, his *Compositions and Translations in Verse and Prose*, and *Tilemakhida*. Petrov introduced the last work by a reference to "long-lingering, soaring compound words" (*dolgo-slozhno-protiazhno-pariashchie slova*), a mockery of Trediakovsky's imitations of Greek compound adjectives in *Tilemakhida* and such expressions in the introduction to the poem as "long-lingering" and "longest-lingering" (*dolgoprotiazhnyi* and *dolgoprotiazhneishii*).[29] The friends probably read the second edition of *A Voyage to the Isle of Love*, which appeared in 1778, since Trediakovsky destroyed virtually all copies of the first edition. Characteristically, Petrov chose to ignore Trediakovsky's linguistic declarations in the introduction to *A Voyage* and simply ascribed to his style those features suggested by his mythological image: bizarre inversions (which, in fact, Trediakovsky rarely employed in prose) and the Slavonic element (which the young Trediakovsky, at the time of *A Voyage*, avoided in prose and restricted in poetry). Karamzin and his advisor did not want to expose (and perhaps did not even realize) the similarity of their own linguistic position to the views of the despicable fool.

In 1822 Nikolai Bakhtin, a "young Archaist" and a critic of the Innovators' language program, pointed out this embarrassing parallel between Karamzin and his followers on the one hand and Trediakovsky on the other. He wrote:

The discovery of the secret of writing the way we speak does not belong to our age. Even before Karamzin exhorted would-be authors in this, Professor of Eloquence Trediakovsky had been propagating it for a long time. Take the trouble to read the preface to this great man's translation, *A Voyage to the Isle of Love.* . . . From this brief speech you can clearly see that some people without reason posit Trediakovsky

> With Tilemakhida in his hand,
> With Rollin behind his back,

as the leader of the Slavophiles; on the contrary, he is the true leader of those

> Who write as they speak,
> Who are read by ladies.[30]

Bakhtin rejected the traditional image of Trediakovsky the pedant, Trediakovsky the ancestor of the Archaists, and pointed out a different aspect of his artistic platform, the one that connected him with the Innovators. Quotations from Batiushkov's "The Bard" made it clear at whom Bakhtin directed his mockery. The former Arzamasian Viazemsky took it upon himself to answer Bakhtin's insinuation. He positively refused to accept Trediakovsky as a predecessor of the Innovators:

In Mr. M. I.'s words, "Trediakovsky propagated long ago the secret of writing the way one speaks." Let us assume that this is correct; but secrets in literature, as in many other fields, give honor and benefit not to Sphinxes, who keep them to themselves, but to Oedipuses, who know how to solve them. In the field of literary activity, more than in any other, intentions without execution remain futile and disappear without a trace. Trediakovsky, as an intelligent man educated in the European manner (these qualities nobody denies him), could know what was desirable for the language in his time; but as a writer without talent and skill, he could do nothing useful for it. Trediakovsky wanted to blaze a new trail; but having neither taste nor authorial talent to guide him, he became confused in his quest, perished, and did not even have the miserable honor of ruining a single follower with him.[31]

Viazemsky acknowledged Trediakovsky's effort to introduce spoken forms into the literary language, but refused to give this effort any value and, especially, refused to admit the Innovators' dependence on these experiments. Moreover, Viazemsky even declined to acknowledge that an affinity to Trediakovsky might be dangerous for one's reputation—a significant deviation from his views at the time of the Arzamasians' polemics with the Besedists, when the shoe was on the other foot and when he shared the Arzamasian opinion that a mere hint at an opponent's kinship with the notorious fool could effectively condemn that opponent in the eyes of the reading public. Notably, sometime in 1822 Viazemsky himself read Trediakovsky: "I am returning to Sergei Ivanovich his Trediakovsky," he wrote to Aleksandr Turgenev in a letter of June 20, 1822. Later, in 1830, Viazemsky came to recognize Trediakovsky's services to the field: "But, really, poor Trediakovsky has been so smeared with mud without good reason. His rules about versification are not at all bad. His idea that our language has to be formed by usage, that *we will be taught* (that is, *should be*) *to speak it skillfully by the most reasonable ministers*, etc., is quite justified. He felt that the written language alone is dead."[32] By that time the passion of the polemics with the Archaists had calmed down, and both groups had realized the necessity of a compromise between the utter archaization and the reckless modernization of the literary language. The connection with Trediakovsky consequently lost for the former participants in the stylistic dispute at least some of its insulting implications, and his legacy could be discussed more impartially.

Both Bakhtin's assault and Viazemsky's retort occurred in the 1820's, whereas in the 1810's, during the most heated polemics between Arzamas and Beseda, this possible connection with Trediakovsky was neither acknowledged by the Innovators (which is understandable, given their interpretation of the poet's legacy) nor pointed out by the Archaists. It seems that the mesmerizing effect of Trediakovsky's mythological image, with its strong archaic overtones, interfered with the memory of his early views and prevented their admission into the pool of issues. I believe, however, that at least one Innovator was aware of the danger of being compared to Trediakovsky and tried to prevent such an attack. This Innovator was Batiushkov.

Batiushkov was one of the few people in the early nineteenth century who remembered and ridiculed not only Trediakovsky "with Rollin behind his back" but also the young Trediakovsky who attempted to write *vers de société* and translated *Voyage à l'île d'Amour*. He parodied Trediakovsky's poem "Laudatory Verses to Paris" (1728) in his letter to Gnedich of August 19, 1809: "'Play, Neva muses, / Play pipes and flutes,' I will say with Trediakovsky and will embrace you with all my heart, soul, and thoughts" (p. 387). In "A Vision on the Banks of Lethe," Batiushkov twice ridicules Trediakovsky as the translator of Tallemant's novel. The mockery is intertwined with traditional jokes about Trediakovsky the diligent author of *Tilemakhida* and propagator of Slavonicisms, but the invectives contain one noteworthy detail. Batiushkov presents Trediakovsky as "the puny rider of the maidens' obstinate saddle" (*naezdnik khilyi stroptiva devstvennits sedla*; p. 174) and "a singer of the voyage of love," (*pevets liubovnyia ezdy*; p. 180). These were not just ribald references to *A Voyage—Ezda*, in Trediakovsky's translation (*ezda* can also be understood to mean "riding")—or insulting allusions to Trediakovsky's unhappy relations with the muses. I suggest that there is an additional element in Batiushkov's sarcastic remarks, and this element amounts to an attempt to discredit Trediakovsky by comparing him to Jean Chapelain, the author of a notoriously bad poem, *La Pucelle*.

As I pointed out in the previous chapter, Sumarokov was the first to compare Trediakovsky to Chapelain and thus to transplant the French literary situation of the second half of the seventeenth century to Russia. The Innovators, in turn, attempted to perform a similar maneuver: to present their polemics with the Archaists in terms of the struggle of Boileau's party against the older literary generation, the Académie française, and its organizer, Chapelain. In this travesty, Viazemsky received the roles of Claude Emmanuel Chapelle and Boileau. Thus, Pushkin called Viazemsky "Shapel' Andreevich" in his letter to Vasilii Pushkin of December 1816.[33] On the other hand, the Innovators sarcastically compared Beseda to the Académie in Arzamas protocols:

Upon hearing the name of Beseda my weak senses grow heavy, my eyelids close, my head inclines to my breast, and wonderful dreams shade me with their light wings. I see a huge temple, whose sanctity is rarely desecrated by the presence of foreigners; I read a mysterious inscription on its gate—*Sleep, death, and nonexistence*—an inscription that exposes the madness of those who have chosen immortality for their motto. (p. 92)

An explanatory note to these words was given in the margin: "Motto of the French Academy: *A l'immortalité!*"

The name of Chapelain came up naturally in the context of these jokes. Pushkin mentioned Chapelain twice in the years of the Arzamasians' clashes with the Besedists. In the fragment "Bova" (1814) he wrote:

> Часто, часто я беседовал
> С болтуном страны Эллинския
> И не смел осиплым голосом
> С Шапеленом и Рифматовым
> Воспевать героев севера.[34]

I conversed often with a prattler of Hellas and dared not hymn in hoarse voice the heroes of the North with Chapelain and Rifmatov.

Chapelain appears here as the partner of an Archaist, Sergei Shirinsky-Shikhmatov (*Rifmatov*, or "Rhymester," as Pushkin disrespectfully calls him), the author of two epic poems, *Pozharsky, Minin, Germogen; or, Russia Saved* (1807) and *Peter the Great* (1810), both of which were ridiculed by the Innovators. Chapelain, in Pushkin's interpretation, shares with Shikhmatov an important negative characteristic: a hoarse voice. The contrast between the allegedly "tender" and "pleasant" style of the Karamzinists and the "coarse" and "harsh" style of the Shishkovists was central to the Innovators' view of their linguistic quarrel with the Archaists.[35] In the poem "To Zhukovsky," Pushkin again compares the Archaists to Chapelain and the Innovators to Boileau. After severely criticizing the Archaists and mocking Trediakovsky, Pushkin proclaims: "Despréaux will emerge, and Chapelain will disappear."[36]

In 1825 Pushkin once again returned to the old arguments and derided Chapelain in his translation of a fragment of Voltaire's *La Pucelle d'Orléans* (1755). In this fragment, Pushkin's characterization of Chapelain is, again, very close to the Innovators' characterizations of the Archaists:

> О ты, певец сей чудотворной девы,
> Седой певец, чьи хриплые напевы,
> Нестройный ум и бестолковый вкус
> В былые дни бесили нежных муз,
> Хотел бы ты, о стихотворец хилый,
> Почтить меня скрыпицею своей.
> Да не хочу. Отдай ее, мой милый,
> Кому-нибудь из модных рифмачей.[37]

O you, singer of this miraculous maiden, grey-haired singer whose hoarse tunes, disorderly mind, and muddled taste in the old days enraged the tender muses; you would like, O puny poet, to honor me with your fiddle. But I do not want it. Give it, my dear, to some fashionable rhymester.

Here is the corresponding passage in Voltaire:

> O Chapelain, toi dont le violon
> De discordante et gothique mémoire,
> Sous un archet maudit par Apollon
> D'un ton si dur a raclé son histoire,
> Vieux Chapelain, pour l'honneur de ton art
> Tu voudrais bien me prêter ton génie.
> Je n'en veux point; c'est pour la Motte-Houdart
> Quant l'*Iliade* est par lui travestie.

O Chapelain, you whose violin, of discordant and gothic memory, with its bow accursed by Apollo, rasped your story in a tone so hoarse—old Chapelain, for the glory of your art you would like to lend me your genius. I do not want it at all. This was for La Motte-Houdart when he travestied the *Iliad*.

As we see, Pushkin translated some of Voltaire's epithets about Chapelain's poetry: *discordante* (*nestroinyi um* in Pushkin's fragment), *ton si dur*, (*khriplye napevy*), and *raclé* (the idea of this sound is reflected in the word *skrypitsa*, which preserves the notion of "squeaking" and which Pushkin chose over the more traditional and less expressive *skripka* or *skrypka*). But he also added several characteristics of his own from the polemical vocabulary of his youth. Grey hair, a hoarse voice, foolishness, and incoherence—all these features repeat the Innovators' mockery of "Grey-haired Grandfather" Shishkov and his supporters. Pushkin did not merely repeat Voltaire's mockery of Chapelain; he readdressed it to the Russian Chapelains whom he had fought ten years before. It was precisely for this purpose that he omitted all names from his translation, making his invective more general and hence applicable to the Russian situation.

The expression "puny poet" (*stikhotvorets khilyi*) is especially important for my analysis, for it echoes Pushkin's characterization of Trediakovsky in the poem "To Zhukovsky" as a "puny versifier" (*stoposlozhitel' khilyi*) and Batiushkov's epithet for him in "A Vision on the Banks of Lethe," "puny rider." The fact that Chapelain and Trediakovsky shared an epithet, and a rather unusual one, supports my suggestion that the two poets were connected in the minds of the Innovators and that in the portrait of "the puny rider of the maidens' obstinate saddle"—the poet rejected by the muses—Batiushkov was combining both Trediakovsky, the translator of *Voyage à l'île d'Amour*, and Chapelain, the author of *La Pucelle*. Like Sumarokov 60 years before him, Batiushkov equated Trediakovsky and Chapelain, the two "puny writers" of failed epics, and enlisted them both among the Archaists' ancestors. This move might have served to obscure the crucial difference in the views of Trediakovsky the translator of *A Voyage* and Trediakovsky the author of *Tilemakhida* and thus to prevent undesirable comparisons between the Innovators' views and those of the young Trediakovsky.

If the Innovators rejected energetically (and, in Batiushkov's case, even preventively) the accusation that they shared an affinity with Trediakovsky, the Archaists' response to similar charges was subdued. They seldom refuted or even discussed the issue. Their silence was not incidental: Their own attitude toward Trediakovsky was, at best, ambivalent. A scholar who has studied Beseda, Mark Altshuller, has correctly pointed out that the Archaists' views of Trediakovsky and his works in general were more favorable than those of the Innovators.[38] In my analysis of these views I would like to emphasize that despite the Archaists' obvious interest in Trediakovsky and their dependence on some of his principles and ideas, they, like the Innovators, were influenced by Trediakovsky's mythological image, which made it difficult for them to admit this dependence and, to a certain degree, interfered with their assimilation of the ideas that they had inherited from Trediakovsky.

Some writers in the Archaists' camp completely accepted the negative aspects of Trediakovsky's mythological image. This attitude was characteristic of Aleksandr Palitsyn, a provincial poet and a firm supporter of Shishkov's ideas. His "An Epistle to Priveta" (1807), a survey of Russian literature in verse written from the viewpoint of a foe of Karamzin, was heavily affected by the myth of the "new" Russian literature. He called Lomonosov "Pindar," "the immortal Lomonosov," and "the creator of his native language." Trediakovsky's portrait, on the other hand, included the typical features of his mythological image: talentlessness, diligence, and prolificacy. Palitsyn stressed Trediakovsky's role as a provider of bad examples, claiming that Bobrov's poem *Tavrida* (1798) took after *Tilemakhida*:

> Бобров,
> Но вкус *Хераскова* забыв в своей "Тавриде,"
> И в страсти к новому игрой трескучих слов,
> Шероховатостью и мыслей и стихов
> Подходит там в иных местах к "Телемахиде."

Bobrov, having forgotten *Kheraskov's* taste in his *Tavrida*, in his passion for novelty, in his play with grating words, in the roughness of his thoughts and verses, approaches *Tilemakhida* in certain passages.

Palitsyn included in his "An Epistle" a standard anecdote about Catherine the Great, who allegedly punished the use of foreign words in her intimate circle by having the offender recite *Tilemakhida*. In the notes to "An Epistle," Palitsyn placed a humorous reference to the fire in Trediakovsky's house that destroyed his translation of Rollin's *Histoire ancienne*—a typical anecdote about Trediakovsky the unfortunate and diligent fool.[39]

Bobrov, whom Palitsyn maliciously compared to Trediakovsky, in fact shared Palitsyn's negative opinion of the poet. As I have mentioned, in his work "Incident in the Realm of Shadows" he reserved for Trediakovsky the role of a mythological monster whose creation, *Tilemakhida*, served to punish the Innovator Galloruss. Bobrov did not recognize the similarity of some of his own poetical principles (such as his interest in high genres, metrical variety, unrhymed verse, and laborious diction) to those of Trediakovsky, and quite traditionally used the poet's name as a polemical tool. On the other hand, Bobrov, unlike Nikolai Bakhtin in 1822, did not point out, and most probably did not even notice, that the real Trediakovsky had as much in common with Galloruss as with his own mythological image. His inattentiveness to the linguistic views of the young Trediakovsky is the more noteworthy in that in the same work he emphasizes the similarity between the language situations of the eighteenth and the early nineteenth centuries. The two epigraphs to "Incident," which come from Vasilii Tatishchev's *Russian History*, condemn the introduction of foreign words into the Russian language. In case some reader might miss the similarity of the present situation to the one in Tatishchev's time, Bobrov added his own commentary: "These words were said as early as the first half of the last century to lament the damage to the language." [40] Bobrov did not burden himself with an analysis of Trediakovsky's views, but used the elements of his mythological image, readily available in the pool of polemical devices, to condemn his opponents.

Likewise, Aleksandr Vostokov, a literary scholar and a poet of Archaist orientation, refused to acknowledge Trediakovsky as his predecessor, despite the fact that many of his experiments with meter—especially his imitations of classical Greek and Roman meters—continued Trediakovsky's attempts in this field. [41] His opinion of the poet was utterly scornful. In his *Essay on Russian Versification* (1812) he presented Trediakovsky exclusively as a provider of bad examples that prevented the development of new poetical forms:

Unfortunately, from the very beginning, dactylo-trochaic hexameter fell into the hands of Trediakovsky, who also had the courage to undertake new things but who totally lacked the talent and taste to make his new undertakings attractive; and therefore with his infamous *Tilemakhida* he also made infamous the meter in which it was written, causing the public to feel an aversion toward it for a long time.

Vostokov depreciated Trediakovsky's achievements in the field of versification and rejected the idea that Lomonosov and Sumarokov had benefited from his *A New and Brief Method for Composing Russian Verse* and from his first syllabo-tonic experiments. He disputed a positive appraisal of Trediakovsky's role in the reform given in the book *An Introduction to the Science of Poetry* (1811) by the literary historian Nikolai Iazvitsky:

To this we will say: Trediakovsky is praised exclusively for his diligence and patience, and he is ridiculed for his hilarious poems; he is scorned as a bad poet who had neither genius nor taste. Perhaps he was the first to write poetry with metric feet, but certainly Lomonosov and Sumarokov did not require his guidance in this and could find the same path very easily themselves, having before them the German and French models that Trediakovsky followed. And therefore it seems quite doubtful to us whether the latter could be named *the beginning* and *the foundation* of the new Russian poetry.[42]

In his attitude toward Trediakovsky, Vostokov never overcame the influence of the myth about Trediakovsky the fool. In his metrical experiments and theoretical studies he pointedly devalued Trediakovsky's early explorations in the field of metrics.

Trediakovsky's contribution to the development of Russian hexameter was difficult to ignore completely, however, for he was the only poet who had intensively used this meter in the eighteenth century. His name inevitably emerged in the polemics that arose in connection with Gnedich's translation of the *Iliad*.[43] The issue was what meter should be employed for the translation: an imitation of the Greek hexameter, the meters used for epics in the modern tradition, or a reproduction of Russian folk meters. In a sense, the polemics were a late echo of the dispute of *les Anciens et les Modernes*, albeit in the context of the new Romantic ideas about classical antiquity and national tradition. Until then, all attempts to translate the *Iliad* into Russian, except a small experimental fragment by Mikhail Murav'ev, avoided hexameter. Gnedich himself initially started to translate the *Iliad* in alexandrines. Fear of a perceived connection with Trediakovsky was to a large extent responsible for this avoidance. But finally it became clear that for the successful reconstruction of the Greek epic in Russian it was impossible to use either alexandrines or any of the existing imitations of the "ancient Russian meter." Hexameter seemed the only solution, even if it meant having to deal with Trediakovsky's preemption.

In the dispute about hexameter, some of the Archaists took a much more hostile attitude toward Trediakovsky than the Innovators did. When Sergei Uvarov (a future Arzamasian who later abandoned the beliefs of his youth and, in the 1830's, as minister of education, formulated the notorious doctrine "Autocracy, Orthodoxy, and Nationalism") suggested in 1813 that the *Iliad* be translated in hexameters, it was Vasilii Kapnist, an honorary member of Beseda, who sharply disagreed, on the grounds that hexameters had been compromised by Trediakovsky: "Suddenly, with your slyly woven vain reasoning, you turned him [Gnedich] onto the road tramped by the author of *Tilemakhida*, he who will be eternally remembered for heavy versification. That was a very malevolent act toward me as well as toward Mr. Gnedich—and most of all toward his readers." Uvarov answered with a reference to Lomonosov, who had included one model hexameter couplet in his "Letter on the Rules of Russian Versification"; and, following Radishchev, whose evaluation of Trediakovsky in the chapter "Tver" of *A Journey from Petersburg to Moscow* he had quoted in his essay, Uvarov claimed that Trediakovsky's harmful influence could be overcome.[44]

In this discussion Gnedich was evasive with respect to Trediakovsky and hexameters. On the one hand, he closely studied his predecessor's work. His friend Zhikharev, in his *Memoirs of a Contemporary*, wrote in an entry dated February 26, 1806: "Gnedich, who had a passion for everything out of the ordinary, who had read *Tilemakhida* three times from cover to cover and even found unrivaled verses in it . . . ." On the other hand, Gnedich avoided discussing Trediakovsky in this context, apparently in order not to emphasize the embarrassing connection. Eventually, in 1829, when the translation was completed, Gnedich ascribed to himself, in the introduction to the first edition, the honor of freeing hexameter from associations with Trediakov-

sky's name and asserted that he had had "the courage to untie
Homer's and Virgil's verse from the pillory [*pozornyi stolb*] to
which Trediakovsky had chained it.[45] The negative force of Trediakovsky's image as a fool, still alive in the literary consciousness of the second quarter of the nineteenth century, prevented
Gnedich from acknowledging his debt to him.

Other Archaists, however, had a more tolerant opinion of
Trediakovsky. They not only quietly developed his ideas but
also admitted the validity of his services to Russian literature.
However, they did so with many reservations and many references to Trediakovsky the fool. Shishkov's and Derzhavin's appraisals of Trediakovsky were typical in this respect. Shishkov,
the leader of the Archaists, respected Trediakovsky as a scholar.
Trediakovsky's linguistic studies, especially his *Three Discourses
on Three Most Important Russian Antiquities*, apparently influenced Shishkov's ideas about language—in particular his concept of Church Slavonic as an early stage of Russian.[46] Nevertheless, Shishkov's attitude toward Trediakovsky was by no means
free of the dominant mythological view. Shishkov shared the
general opinion of Trediakovsky as a man devoid of poetic gift.
He wrote in his *Discourse on the Old and New Styles of the Russian
Language*: "If you write without talent, you will be considered a
Trediakovsky." Right after this comment, he hastened to rehabilitate—albeit in a footnote—Trediakovsky's translation of
Rollin's histories and his other prose works, but Trediakovsky
the fool had already shown his face. The same ambiguity can be
observed in a lengthy footnote devoted to a comparison of Trediakovsky and Kantemir. Shishkov praised Trediakovsky's linguistic knowledge and his diligence (which feature, as we know,
was incorporated into his mythological image), stressed his priority in the introduction of syllabo-tonic versification, as well as
anapests and dactyls, but refused to admit his talent as a writer:
"Trediakovsky was a diligent translator, a mediocre writer, rather
knowledgeable about the words of his language, but he did not
know what constituted the propriety, power, and beauty of
style. As regards poetry, although he was a very bad poet, he
was the one who introduced metric feet into Russian poetry and
was the first to write in anapests and dactyls." Shishkov supplemented this characterization with the traditional mockery of

Deidamia and concluded it with the inference that Trediakovsky's poetry, unlike Kantemir's, had been forgotten deservedly. Moreover, if Shishkov's linguistic theories had indeed been influenced by Trediakovsky's works, he never admitted it and always referred to Lomonosov as his model. Lomonosov remained for him the highest authority in poetry, as well as in linguistics: "There is no need to discuss Lomonosov at length: Whoever wants to be strong in language ought to know all his poetry and almost all his prose by heart." [47]

Unlike Shishkov, Beseda's other leader, Derzhavin, appreciated Trediakovsky as both a poet and a literary scholar. He was not afraid to name Trediakovsky, in his *Memoir*, as his first teacher in versification: "I derived the rules of poetry from Trediakovsky's works." [48] He incorporated the first stanza of Trediakovsky's "Paraphrase of Moses' Second Song" into his own translation of this psalm (1811). [49] He opened his *Discourse on Lyrics or on the Ode in General* (1811–13, unfinished) with a reference to Trediakovsky's pioneering effort in this direction: "Although the late Professor Trediakovsky wrote about this topic as early as 1752, he did so very briefly and showed only to a slight extent the quality, purpose, and main features of the ode; but about its beauties or its direct value, and about the opposite, he did not explain in detail." [50] This last passage, however, is not quite laudatory. First of all, Derzhavin's reference to Trediakovsky as his predecessor in the theory of lyrics is inaccurate. Metropolitan Evgenii, a literary scholar and an honorary member of Beseda, pointed out in a letter to Derzhavin the poet's mistake as to the date of Trediakovsky's *Discourse on the Ode in General*. It was actually published for the first time in 1734, as a supplement to the "Ode on the Surrender of the City of Gdansk." [51] But even more important than this mistake is the fact that although Derzhavin names Trediakovsky as his predecessor, at the same time he tries to diminish the significance of his contribution to the field.

Derzhavin's other references to Trediakovsky reveal the same ambivalence: Derzhavin acknowledges his services but limits their significance. Thus, although he praises Trediakovsky's effort to introduce "ancient tonic versification," represented, according to Derzhavin, by Russian folk songs, he points out that the effort was unsuccessful and did not produce followers. Simi-

larly, Derzhavin's mention that Trediakovsky was the first to introduce love songs into Russian poetry is also ambiguous:

If we do not take their [the songs'] appearance from Trediakovsky's
time, when he translated several French [songs] and a small poem entitled *A Voyage to the Isle of Love* and also composed several original
songs, while still in Hamburg in 1730, as, for example,

> Spring rolls,
> Throws winter down;
> Birds sing
> With titmice;
> Even foxes swish their tails,

then it is impossible, it seems, to date the origin of our new songs earlier than Peter the Great's time, when he brought us closer to Europe.[52]

Derzhavin is again mistaken, claiming that Trediakovsky's translation of Tallemant's novel was a poem. Moreover, Derzhavin
calls Trediakovsky's precedence in the genre of song into question, and on top of everything he quotes Trediakovsky's poem
"A Song That I Composed While Still in the Moscow School,
Upon My Departure to Foreign Countries" (1726), which had
already been subjected to derision by both Sumarokov, in his
essay "Response to Criticism," and Lomonosov, in his poem
"To Zubnitsky." By the time Derzhavin ridiculed it, this poem
had acquired a reputation as a perfect proof of Trediakovsky's
inability as a poet and was perceived as almost a parody of Trediakovsky's poetry in general. To quote it was certainly to reinforce the myth about Trediakovsky. In addition, it is important
to remember that Derzhavin himself wrote parodies of Trediakovsky's works, and these parodies contributed greatly to the
formation of Trediakovsky's image as a fool.

Metropolitan Evgenii, an honorary member of Beseda and
the author of the famous *Dictionary of Russian Secular Writers*
(partial publication in 1805–6, 1821–22, 1838; full publication in
1845), is usually presented by students of the subject as a supporter of Trediakovsky.[53] Indeed, his evaluations of Trediakovsky were generally benign and balanced. He acknowledged Trediakovsky's priority in the development of the Russian language
and in the introduction of syllabo-tonics, stressed the pioneering role of Trediakovsky's poetical experiments, praised his ef-

forts to introduce new genres into modern Russian literature, and found kind words for *Tilemakhida,* emphasizing Trediakovsky's success in imitating Greek antiquity: "If one were to translate Trediakovsky's *Tilemakhida* into the Greek language (because it is impossible to translate it into any other language), it would appear to be [written by] Homer. For it contains many expressive beauties, but in an attire already ancient for us, as is Homer himself." Evgenii was not even afraid to admit, albeit in impersonal form, the Archaists' dependence on Trediakovsky's linguistic principles: "So it is correct that they have now begun [*nyne nachali*] from Trediakovsky's beginning." [54]

Despite all his benevolence toward the mistreated poet, Evgenii could not escape the influence of the myth about Trediakovsky the fool, and it is easy to find traces of it in Evgenii's testimonials about him. For Evgenii, Trediakovsky retained his mythological nature, as is evident in his letter to Khvostov of September 13, 1807: "On the contrary, translate Trediakovsky: Even foreigners will laugh at him. For in him there is neither a writer nor a creator." In his *Dictionary* he writes that *Tilemakhida,* "although it has many very expressive lines," is still a work that "was read almost exclusively for fun [*dlia smekha*]." Characteristically, Evgenii attached a footnote to this observation, in which he related an anecdote about how reciting and memorizing *Tilemakhida* was a punishment in Catherine the Great's intimate circle. [55]

On the whole, Evgenii was aware of the existence of an unjust attitude toward Trediakovsky and disapproved of it, but at the same time, he accepted some of the aspects of Trediakovsky's traditional image as a fool. This explains the ambivalence in his characterizations of Trediakovsky, especially evident in the following passage:

I wish somebody among our poets would write an apology for him, for example in the form of an epistle to the realm of the dead, but not like Nikolev's caricature. In comparing Trediakovsky to our present scribes, it is possible to criticize the latter even more, regardless of the fact that they jeer at his *Tilemakhida* or at the verses *Birds sing with titmice; even foxes swish their tails.* He should be judged neither by the one nor by the other. In *Tilemakhida* we see an overripe old man, who is past his prime in writing; and in the little poem, an immature child who chases only rhymed sound. One must regard a writer between the years of thirty and fifty. In those years even Trediakovsky wrote better. Without him we would perhaps have seen neither Lomonosov nor Sumarokov, who became famous only at the time when he [Trediakovsky] had already started to fade. However, they did not imitate him, and blazed a new trail for themselves. But Petrov, it seems, sometimes looked back to him and was not fastidious about invented expressions similar to Trediakovsky's. This is what fastidious critics called inflated Slavonicisms. But Slavonicisms will always remain for us a touchstone of our eloquence.[56]

Trediakovsky, in Evgenii's opinion, deserves an apology, but it should be addressed to him in the realm of the dead, where he, as a chthonic creature, belongs. He contributed to Lomonosov's and Sumarokov's success, but they did not follow his examples. Evgenii acknowledges Trediakovsky's merits but limits their significance and questions their value. These equivocal appraisals demonstrate Evgenii's acceptance, albeit partial, of the myth about Trediakovsky the fool. He felt the injustice of the traditional opinions of Trediakovsky but did not know how to overcome their negative inertia.

In his attitude toward Trediakovsky, Evgenii stood halfway between Derzhavin and Shishkov, who hesitantly acknowledged the poet's merits, and the group of Archaists who openly declared themselves Trediakovsky's defenders. To this group belonged, among others, Iakov Galinkovsky, Vasilii Anastasevich, Nikolai Iazvitsky, whose book *An Introduction to the Science of Poetry* I mentioned in connection with Vostokov's views on Trediakovsky, and Aleksei Merzliakov.

By the beginning of the new century Galinkovsky, who in the early years of his literary career was a follower of Karamzin, had grown critical of the dilettantism and sentimentality of the literary movement inspired by Karamzin and soon after became a member of Derzhavin's literary circle. He helped Derzhavin with his work on the *Discourse on Lyrics or on the Ode in General* and, when Beseda was organized, joined as a member. Later he became the society's secretary. Thus, despite certain disagreements with the Archaists, Galinkovsky chose to affiliate himself with Beseda, personally as well as formally.[57]

Galinkovsky undertook an especially significant effort in Trediakovsky's defense. He started to propagandize in favor of

Trediakovsky in his magazine *The Chorus Leader; or, A Key to Literature* (1802–7). In the very first issue he published a passionate apology for Trediakovsky:

Our honorable Trediakovsky, by virtue of his diligence, translated it [Rollin's *Histoire ancienne*] twice; but posterity paid him badly for such tireless, exemplary industry. *Tilemakhida* alone drowned all his merits: We forgot that he himself was Rollin's disciple, first professor of our eloquence, first connoisseur of ancient authors, a man of unusual, profound scholarly knowledge, a man of broad learning such as has hardly appeared since; we forgot that he alone wrote more useful books than ten of his contemporaries, and we defamed his memory only because of his bold idea of introducing *Greek meters* into the Russian language. At the very same time Lomonosov was introducing *German* feet and rhymes, which were not any better in themselves but were championed by his great and special personal giftedness alone. He [Trediakovsky] had to walk against the current: He fell under the burden of this great undertaking; the powers of language were still weak and unformed in the early years of our literature. His rival was stronger, he triumphed, and we forgot his [Trediakovsky's] memory! I testify by his immortal spirit, by his works, that this is ignoble. Time will someday avenge this offense, and someday felicitous talents will be born who, following the road he paved, will venture to rise to the beauties of Homer's enunciation (*diction*), to introduce the majestic flow of heroic ancient verse, which is so characteristic of our native poetry.[58]

Galinkovsky, in this passage, reveals a deep understanding of the myth about Trediakovsky the fool. He shrewdly notes that Trediakovsky's reputation as a notoriously bad poet could be understood only in conjunction with the myth about Lomonosov as the father of the "new" Russian literature. Like Radishchev in the chapter "Tver" of *A Journey from Petersburg to Moscow*, he foretold a brilliant future for the poetic principles introduced by Trediakovsky once the spell of the traditional view of him was lifted.

Galinkovsky expressed the same high opinion of Trediakovsky in the introduction to his translation of the first eclogue by Horace (1804). Not only was the eclogue itself translated in hexameters ("in ancient meter," *drevnim razmerom*, in Galinkovsky's definition), which in itself was a clear reference to Trediakovsky, but the translator pointed directly to Trediakovsky as his predecessor. If Lomonosov was the father of Russian literature in its present unsatisfactory state, Trediakovsky was the first to propose the return to ancient meters—an idea that "at any rate, . . . did not cease to be great, beautiful, and deserving of the attention of our poets." [59]

Nikolai Iazvitsky was not less favorably disposed toward Trediakovsky in his book on poetry: "Trediakovsky, immortal for his diligence, perhaps did more [than Kantemir] to acquaint Russians with poetry. His mind, great for its patience, awoke man from his natural laziness, and aroused a desire to read. Trediakovsky revived in his translations ancient and modern writers of poetry and prose." Iazvitsky valued Trediakovsky's theoretical achievements, as well as the applications of his theories: "Trediakovsky prescribed the rules of poetry with one hand and with his other hand fulfilled them in reality." [60] To illustrate Trediakovsky's achievements as a poet, Iazvitsky quoted not only Trediakovsky's "Paraphrase of Moses' Second Song" but also his "Ode on the Surrender of the City of Gdansk," which had been derided by Sumarokov and Lomonosov.

Aleksei Merzliakov was more cautious in his praise for Trediakovsky, but he nevertheless assigned the poet a significant position in the history of Russian literature. In his article "A Discourse on Russian Literature in Its Present State" (1812), he rated him on a level with Lomonosov: "Lomonosov's and Trediakovsky's works are immortal." He acknowledged his services in the field of literary theory, such as his introduction of poetical rules, and his priority in the syllabo-tonic reform: "The invention of a regular cadence in verse is indisputably his." He was even inclined to excuse Trediakovsky's style: "In my opinion, Trediakovsky deserves to be excused for his style as well: The roughness of language belongs not so much to him as to his time. Compare the verses of *Tilemakhida*, which was, perhaps, excessively censured, to the other [poetry] of his age and say who wrote beter." He defended not only *Tilemakhida* but *Deidamia* as well: "There is initiating action and a denouement even in *Deidamia*." [61]

Like Galinkovsky, Vasilii Anastasevich, a poet whom the Innovators listed among the Archaists, was aware that Trediakovsky's negative reputation was more than a mere misjudgment on the part of the literary establishment. In his poem "On *Tilema-khida*," he emphasized the irrational character of general opinions about Trediakovsky and claimed that Trediakovsky's critics, the Innovators, had not even read the poet's works, which fact did not prevent these "smart alecs" from laughing at him:

> Кричат наслышкою: "Ты глупый человек!"
> И слов пяти собой сказать не зная сами,
> Живут чужим умом, вовек слывя скворцами.
> Не гневайся, мой друг, не слушай ты их врак,
> Пусть попугаи все твердят: "Дурак, дурак!"
> Кто сердится на то, сполу был кстати так.
> Чрез века три тебе хвалу воздаст потомство,
> Что первый с музами ты россов ввел в
> знакомство.[62]

[They] cry out, having gotten their knowledge from hearsay: "You are a foolish man!" And unable to say five words on their own, they depend on other people's wisdom and forever have the reputation of starlings [i.e., imitators]. Do not be angry with them, do not listen to their nonsense, let the parrots repeat, "A fool, a fool!" Whoever is angry at this deserves to be. In three centuries posterity will praise you for being the first to introduce the Russians to the Muses.

The testimonials of Trediakovsky's defenders, although laudatory, were themselves not absolutely free of mythological notions. Their very awareness of the stereotype influenced them. Trediakovsky's defenders knew that they went against the current when they challenged the general opinion of Trediakovsky as an exceptionally bad writer, hence the reservation and hesitation in their appraisals of Trediakovsky, as in Merzliakov's guarded defense of *Tilemakhida* ("perhaps excessively censured") and *Deidamia* ("even in *Deidamia* . . ."), Iazvitsky's "perhaps," and Galinkovsky's "at any rate" in the above quotations. Moreover, mythological features appeared in their statements in a straightforward form. For example, Anastasevich admits in his laudatory poem quoted above that he "used to sleep" (*sypál*) over his works and that he regrets that Trediakovsky ever wrote *A Voyage to the Isle of Love* and *Tilemakhida* because they contributed to his negative reputation. Notions about Trediakovsky's lack of talent and taste also found their way into Merzliakov's appraisal: "*Trediakovsky's* odes and fragments serve as proof that he was a learned man but could not maintain the proprieties of taste, that he knew the sources of embellishments but did not know how to use them." Galinkovsky's "Letter to the Publishers of the Academy Magazine *Compositions and Translations*" contains a similar characterization of Trediakovsky: "Unfortunately, this learned professor did not have a drop of poetic talent and in his bad poems has left us only a perfect example of a mere mechanism." Even Iazvitsky, apparently the most devoted to Trediakovsky's rehabilitation, showed signs of accepting the myth: "Of course, this ode is very far from the ones written by Lomonosov, Derzhavin, and others, because it still bears the imprint of the first experiments . . . but it contains many verses in which Trediakovsky cannot be seen." [63] That is, Trediakovsky's ode is good because his own manner, the manner of a talentless and tasteless poet, of Trediakovsky the fool, is not apparent in it. It is possible to question the extent to which these writers valued taste and talent, but it is nevertheless characteristic that they used formulas describing Trediakovsky's talentlessness, readily available from the myth about Trediakovsky the fool, to express their ambivalence with respect to Trediakovsky.

Trediakovsky's defenders valued many of his ideas as tools in their fight for the renovation of literary forms, acknowledged his services to Russian literature, developed his poetical and linguistic principles, but, unlike Radishchev before them and Pushkin after them, never challenged the myth itself. They saw only the negative side of the myth: It smeared the poet whom they respected and whose ideas they valued. They did not feel the creative power contained in the mythological notions about the unfortunate poet and therefore could not effectively use the myth to undermine the literary status quo, against which they protested, and to introduce fresh literary modes, which they propagated along with their ideas about Trediakovsky. In this respect, the lessons of Radishchev's interpretation of the myth about Trediakovsky (which the nineteenth-century defenders of Trediakovsky certainly knew)—his discovery of its creative potential and its ability to foster the growth of the new literary ideas—were lost on them. Galinkovsky and his colleagues still conceded to the myth and, to a certain extent, tried to distance themselves from Trediakovsky, anticipating the inevitable comparisons to the notorious fool, which could be damaging to their own reputations.

But why were these writers attracted to Trediakovsky at all? What allowed them to appreciate his works despite the stigma attached to them by the general opinion, which they themselves shared? Trediakovsky's admirers were not unanimous in their literary views, and the reasons for their appreciation of Trediakovsky differed. Merzliakov stressed his services in the introduction of syllabo-tonics; Galinkovsky emphasized the value of Greek versification and "ancient meter," that is, the imitation of the classical hexameter proposed by Trediakovsky; and Iazvitsky appreciated his efforts in the cause of education. But there was an important common feature in their attitude toward Trediakovsky: They valued his professionalism. They appreciated his erudition, his aspiration for the dissemination of knowledge, and his devotion to scholarship. This attitude can easily be seen in both Galinkovsky's and Iazvitsky's testimonials to Trediakovsky. It provided the basis for the following characterizations by Merzliakov as well:

Trediakovsky, a disciple of the famous Rollin, the first Russian professor, was the first to turn to this new field [literature]. Upon returning from foreign countries, having been enriched by various kinds of knowledge, having long observed French literature at the time when it was already at a high degree of perfection, he found Russian scholars still using a rude Slavonic Polish language; and in the public [he found] an unreadiness to help writers with their discrimination. He decided to give rules and examples and at court had the title of court poet. While the style of his works is coarse, in them there can be seen the previously *unknown* art of adapting oneself to subjects, place, and time; he speaks about unity, about actions, about character; he translates the *Poetics* of Boileau-Despréaux; in short, if he was not a man of great talent, he was an enlightened teacher of literature.[64]

The writers of this group appreciated Trediakovsky's professionalism because they were professional literati themselves. Anastasevich was a bibliographer, publisher, and translator. Merzliakov was a professor of literature at Moscow University and the author of manuals on literary theory. Galinkovsky turned his magazine *The Chorus Leader* into a scholarly treatise for the benefit of the reading public. Iazvitsky taught the Russian language to the empress, published several manuals on literary theory, and translated *The Lay of Igor's Campaign*. Their professionalism was not just a matter of occupation but a principle, opposed to the Innovators' interest in light poetry, their idea of literature "for ladies," and their emphatic dilettantism. The cause of serious literature, intended for the educated reader, was espoused by the members of the Friendly Learned Society (*Druzheskoe uchenoe obshchestvo*, 1801), including Merzliakov, and was upheld by Galinkovsky, who became close to this group after the society ended its existence. Anastasevich's views were of a similar nature: He defended Galinkovsky's magazine *The Chorus Leader* against the Innovators' attacks on its scholarly character.[65] His ironical attitude toward the "nonseriousness" of the Innovators' literary views can also be seen in the poem he wrote in Trediakovsky's defense: In his characterization they are "smart alecs" (*umniki*), uneducated and thoughtless.[66]

Trediakovsky the pedant met their standards of a writer. Unlike Lomonosov, who considered himself a scientist above all else and only then a linguist and a poet, and even Sumarokov, who, albeit nominally, spent more than twenty years in the service, Trediakovsky was a professional man of letters. He earned his bread with his work as a poet, literary scholar, and translator. For Trediakovsky's defenders, the titles "court poet" and "first Russian professor of eloquence" lost their comical character and became the signs of his professional status, the qualities that made him their colleague. His continuous and untiring efforts in the field of literature could elicit only sympathy on the part of this group. His diligence and seriousness, as well as his methodical, scholarly approach to belle lettres, could not dismay them, because their own approach was similar. Taste and talent thus became secondary qualities for them when compared to learning and devotion, and the absence of such qualities could not undermine the merits of an otherwise exemplary literary figure. Trediakovsky's professionalism was why Merzliakov and Galinkovsky did not allow his lack of talent and taste to interfere with their high appraisals of his achievements and why Anastasevich did not allow the boredom produced by Trediakovsky's books to prevent him from respecting and valuing Trediakovsky in his poem.

This rehabilitation of Trediakovsky the pedant by the professional literati of the early nineteenth century by no means obliterated the laughable character of this image in the literary consciousness of the epoch. The influence of this group was still minimal, and the authority of the myth at its peak. The image of Trediakovsky the fool survived among the Innovators, as well as the Archaists, and later flourished in different cultural contexts. However, the attempt at his rehabilitation was not undertaken in vain. As the idea of professionalism entered the mainstream of literature, Trediakovsky the pedant was given a chance to be evaluated as a fellow writer, and not only as a mythological fool. Such was apparently the case with Viazemsky, who, by 1830 a literary scholar himself, came to appreciate Trediakovsky's wisdom as a linguist. Similarly, Trediakovsky's professionalism became an important factor in Pushkin's reevaluation of his mythological image. The defenders of Trediakovsky from the Archaist camp missed the opportunity to employ fully the creative potential of the myth about the unfortunate poet, but their defense of Trediakovsky the pedant was the necessary foundation for the balanced interpretation of Trediakovsky's personality and his works that was later provided by Pushkin. The prerequisite for such an interpretation was the exposition of the creative powers of the myth, which task was first carried out by Aleksandr Radishchev in his analyses of Trediakovsky and his fate in the history of Russian literature.

Chapter 5

Radishchev and Pushkin: Accepting
Kinship with the Fool

The Uncle of the "New" Russian Literature

An analysis of the positive responses to Trediakovsky's legacy in
the early nineteenth century demonstrates the extraordinary vitality of the myth about Trediakovsky the fool. The myth could
not be destroyed by passionate denials, vigorous protestations,
or even the appropriation and successful development of Trediakovsky's ideas. Despite the efforts on the part of his admirers
from the Archaists' camp, Trediakovsky remained a ridiculous
pedant and a wretched poetaster to most of the literary establishment. An effort of a different kind was needed to deal with
the myth, an effort that would make use of its creative potential
and would employ its ambivalent nature to overcome the flatly
negative power of Trediakovsky's image as a fool and make it
work against stability and stagnation in literature and for change
and growth.

Aleksandr Radishchev was the first Russian writer to make
such an effort. He was suited to such a thankless task: He never
shied away from dangerous or unpopular decisions either in his
personal life or in his literary activities. A brilliant man, educated at Leipzig University, Radishchev was well versed in law,
philosophy, history, the sciences, medicine, economics, lan-

guages, and literature and very familiar with the ideas of the European Enlightenment. In his philosophy of life he was a follower of Claude Adrien Helvétius, and many of his most heroic and self-sacrificial actions, including the writing and publication of his famous *A Journey from Petersburg to Moscow*, for which he was initially sentenced to death and then pardoned by Catherine the Great and exiled to Siberia, and his suicide, committed, apparently, to protest the failure of Alexander I's attempts to introduce law and justice to Russia, were governed, paradoxically, by the consistent application of the ideas of rational hedonism. In literature, Radishchev was definitely an experimenter. He explored the persuasive powers of literature and experimented with meter and style as the means to achieve persuasiveness. This quest for new tools of expressivity was the reason why Radishchev became disappointed with humdrum and monotonous iambs, turning to nontraditional meters instead, and why he favored heavy Church Slavonicisms, making them a main component of his style. Both approaches—the search for variety in versification and the introduction of Slavonicisms to increase the persuasive power of a literary work—were connected with the name Trediakovsky. Radishchev never acknowledged the latter connection but eventually accepted the former. It took him many years to do so, and in the process he was forced not only to restore Trediakovsky's status in the history of Russian versification, undermined by the myth about the "new" Russian literature, but to reevaluate the myth itself.

Radishchev was never completely free from the myth about Trediakovsky the fool. His views of Trediakovsky's personality and works remained largely in conformity with the Pre-Romantic notions of his epoch, its ideas about poetic genius, inspiration, and taste. In some sense, Trediakovsky the pedant was no less alien to him than to the writers of Karamzin's camp. Trediakovsky remained for Radishchev "a versifier, but not a poet," and his *Tilemakhida* was "the work of a man knowledgeable in versification who, however, did not have the slightest notion of taste."[1] The mythological core of this Pre-Romantic portrait of Trediakovsky is easy to see. Moreover, Radishchev was aware that the myth ascribed Trediakovsky the role of a jester, and he agreed with this interpretation. A character in his *Memorial for a*

Dactylo-Trochaic Knight (1801; first published in 1811), Trediakovsky's proponent, B., tries to justify his own leniency toward
the poet in the following way: "One must judge him only as a
man who fell in love with Fénelon's Telemachus and wanted to
dress him in a Russian caftan, but being a bad cutter, he could
not give it a stylish look and hung bells all over it for embellish-
ment" (2: 202).

Even when Radishchev tried to refute the traditional notions about Trediakovsky, he could not free himself from the
laughter that the poet's name elicited in him and his contemporaries. In fact, he himself accepted this laughter, ridiculed
Trediakovsky, and even chose the form of parody for his major
work in Trediakovsky's defense, *Memorial for a Dactylo-Trochaic
Knight*. Although Radishchev's views of Trediakovsky and his
literary legacy underwent significant changes and he eventually
moved toward greater acceptance and even appreciation of the
oddity of his ideas, at every stage his attitude remained ambivalent. Radishchev finally came to terms with this ambivalence
when he reevaluated the myth itself, which he was able to do
only after important changes in his theoretical and literary position had taken place and he became capable of appreciating the
positive aspect of laughter.

The first time Radishchev addressed the problem of Trediakovsky and his legacy was in *A Journey from Petersburg to Moscow*. He gave the book the epigraph "A stout monster, wild,
huge, hundred-throated, and barking." The line came from the
eighteenth book of *Tilemakhida*, where it was phrased somewhat
differently: "A stout monster, wild, huge, and with a three-
throated maw."[2] Radishchev did not agree with Trediakovsky's
usage of the noun *laia* (maw) and suggested a participle *laiai*
(barking) instead. Radishchev also multiplied the number of
throats, apparently to emphasize the hideousness of the phenomena he was going to describe in his book.

Radishchev's ambiguous attitude toward Trediakovsky and
his poem is immediately apparent here. On the one hand, his
attitude was favorable. It was obviously no accident that Radishchev chose his epigraph from a book whose political ideas criticized despotism and therefore, in Radishchev's eyes, criticized
Catherine the Great's rule. Even more suitable for Radishchev's

purposes was the fact that the line came from the passage in which tyrants were condemned. Radishchev could not have failed to notice Catherine's annoyance over Trediakovsky's book, and it was unlikely that he believed the annoyance was purely literary. Radishchev saw, then, a chance to take up an argument with Catherine and the political ideas that she represented—an argument that Trediakovsky had started twenty years earlier in his *Tilemakhida*. Trediakovsky, in this context, was Radishchev's ideological predecessor, whose contribution Radishchev by no means rejected.[3] The line could have attracted Radishchev for two literary reasons as well. First, he praised its meter, albeit with reservations, in the rough draft of the chapter "Tver": "*A stout monster, huge, three-throated, and barking* is not such a bad line" (1: 431). In this quotation Radishchev also did some editing. He omitted the word *ozornyi* (wild) and retained the participle in place of the noun. The omission of the word changed the meter: Hexameter became dactylic pentameter, a meter much less provocative to eighteenth-century poetic taste than Trediakovsky's dactylo-trochees. But, given the overwhelming dominance of iambs in the poetry of that time, dactyls sounded innovative enough to Radishchev. Although he was not yet ready to accept the hexameters suggested by Trediakovsky, *Tilemakhida* attracted him as a reservoir of fresh versificational ideas. Another reason for Radishchev to choose Trediakovsky's line as an epigraph was his interest in the expressivity of formal elements in a literary work. He saw a connection between the subject matter of a work and such aspects of its form as meter and sound. Form, in Radishchev's opinion, ought to be meaningful. The difficult process of human liberation should be represented by difficult diction, and ugly social phenomena, by ugly words and imagery. Trediakovsky's line filled the bill.[4]

On the other hand, although attracted to the line, Radishchev showed much disrespect for it too. He quoted it inaccurately, correcting what he thought to be Trediakovsky's mistakes or poor judgment and editing the line for his own purposes. His praise for the line in the rough draft of the chapter "Tver" was accompanied by a comment about the laughable character of *Tilemakhida*: "You already start to smile; it seems to you that you are reading *Tilemakhida*. But laugh as you will, *a stout monster, huge, three-throated, and barking* is not such a bad line. But this is not to the point here; go ahead and laugh" (1: 431). In a later comment on this line in *Memorial*, Radishchev's judgment was even more severe:

P. His [Trediakovsky's] Death and his Cerberus are laughable:

> A putrid monster, bony, and deaf, and dumb, and
> blind;
> A stout monster, wild, huge, and with a three-
> throated maw.

B. It is certainly so, but why? Not because of the dactyl or the hexameter, but because of the ludicrous words. (2: 217)

Radishchev criticized the "ludicrous words" of his favorite line and approved of its meter. But paradoxically, the ludicrous words appeared as the epigraph to *A Journey*, and the positive appraisal of the meter did not find its way into the final version of the chapter "Tver." At the same time, Radishchev gave up the idea of including in the text of *A Journey* the poem *Creation of the World*, which was written in a nontraditional meter. For this poem Radishchev used a complicated polyrhythmic structure: He employed different meters for different parts. The variety of meters included dactylic pentameters and tetrameters, very similar to Trediakovsky's hexameters, and trochaic and iambic tetrameters. In addition, one part of the poem employed iambic lines of different lengths—two-, three-, and four-foot verses. Though the poem's genre, oratorio (*pesnoslovie*), could justify the unusual metric structure, Radishchev chose not to publish it.[5] I do not believe, as one of the editors of *A Journey*, Ia. L. Barskov, suggests, that Radishchev decided not to publish the poem for political reasons, because of its too bold philosophy (1: 448). For *Creation of the World*, in comparison with the radical ode "Liberty" and other passages in *A Journey*, this consideration would certainly be of minor significance. I think the crucial argument against the publication of the poem was its unconventional meter, which could have invited unwanted comparisons to Trediakovsky's metrical experiments. Radishchev could not risk being ridiculed for *A Journey*, which he considered the book of his life. He published instead the iambic ode "Liberty," the meter of which was traditional.

These hesitations reflected Radishchev's doubts as to the acceptability of the literary innovations he was about to introduce. It was already apparent to him that the tradition of iambic rhymed verse prevailing at the end of the eighteenth century—a tradition established, in Radishchev's understanding, by Lomonosov and Sumarokov—interfered with the development of new literary forms: "Poetry was just about to awaken, but now it is slumbering again, and versification took one step and stalled [*stalo v pen'*]" (1: 352). However, he could not yet bring himself to follow a path that in the minds of his contemporaries was clearly associated with the name of Trediakovsky the fool. The myth of the "new" Russian literature still had too much value for him and continued to interfere with his attempts to reevaluate Trediakovsky's ideas.

Radishchev's dependence on the myth is evident from the brief history of Russian poetry that he inserted in the chapter "Tver," and especially from the last chapter of *A Journey*, "Eulogy for Lomonosov." In these passages, Lomonosov appears in his established role as the father of Russian literature: "On the path of Russian literature, Lomonosov is the first" (1: 392; cf. 1: 380). He remained for Radishchev the only author of the syllabotonic reform: "Lomonosov, having understood the ridiculousness of the Polish attire of our verses, took off their inappropriate semi-caftan [*polukaftan'e*]" (1: 352; cf. 1: 385). Accordingly, Radishchev ignored Trediakovsky's role in the reform and gave him his traditional characterization as the diligent but tasteless author of *Tilemakhida*, who with his ridiculous poetry inhibited the development of Russian versification:

The indefatigable toiler Trediakovsky contributed considerably to it [the setback in the development of Russian versification] with his *Tilemakhida*. Now it is very difficult to give an example of the new versification, because examples of good and bad poetry have taken deep root. Parnassus is surrounded by iambs, and rhymes are everywhere on guard. Everyone who might conceive of using dactyls will immediately be assigned Trediakovsky as his uncle [*Trediiakovskago pristaviat diad'koiu*], and for a long time the finest child will seem a freak, until a Milton, Shakespeare, or Voltaire is born. Then Trediakovsky will be dug up from the grave, [now] covered with the moss of oblivion; good verses will be found in *Tilemakhida* and will be held up as exemplary. (1: 352–53)

Here Radishchev presents Trediakovsky as the familiar ungifted and ludicrous pedant, an author of bad examples. The epithet *vozovik* (a toiler, somebody who drags a cart, *voz*) echoes the characterization allegedly given to Trediakovsky by Peter the Great: "a perpetual toiler." *Tilemakhida*, in accordance with the spirit of the myth, served as a classic example of a bad work.

Nevertheless, even in this passage Radishchev's opinion of Trediakovsky differed from the mythological picture. The praise for Trediakovsky's metrical experiments, expressed in the rough draft of the chapter "Tver," was present, albeit less obviously, in the published version as well. Although Radishchev found it impossible to approve of Trediakovsky's poetic practice, he found his experiments to be valuable for the further development of Russian poetry. He was sure that its future depended on Trediakovsky's experiments with ternary meters, rather than on the tradition of iambic verse, established by Lomonosov. Radishchev's scenario for overcoming Trediakovsky's negative influence later became popular among the early nineteenth-century literati. They viewed the prospects for this difficult task with differing degrees of optimism, from Vostokov's skepticism, to Uvarov's confidence in future success, to Gnedich's claim that he had actually performed this task in his translation of the *Iliad*.

This innovative and extremely important idea, introduced by Radishchev in "Tver," that change was necessary for the healthy existence of literature, was totally alien to the myth of the beginning of the "new" Russian literature, as well as to the normative literary consciousness that generated it. Both the myth and normative aesthetics depended on eternal and unchangeable models that would determine literary norms for generations to come and that were not supposed to undergo any changes or corrections. In Radishchev's eyes, however, both Lomonosov, the father of Russian literature, and Trediakovsky, the mythological fool, were equally harmful to Russian literature, inasmuch as both interfered with the development of new literary forms. But Trediakovsky's fault, in Radishchev's opinion, was somewhat lighter, since his negative influence was easier to overcome and his nontraditional ideas possessed creative potential. In the 1780's, however, Radishchev was still not ready to play the role of a Milton, Shakespeare, or Voltaire and employ openly the poetical principles compromised by Trediakovsky. He had already used nontraditional meters in his poem *Creation of the World*, but did not risk publishing it. Trediakovsky's works and person were still too ridiculous for Radishchev to declare himself his disciple.

Radishchev's approval of Trediakovsky's literary ideas became more pronounced in *Memorial for a Dactylo-Trochaic Knight*. This work was written in the form of a dialogue between two characters, B., who defends Trediakovsky, and P., who criticizes him. V. P. Semennikov, a student of Radishchev and his works, suggests that by B. Radishchev meant Semen Bobrov, whose poetic position in some aspects was similar to Radishchev's, and that P. stood for Vasilii Podshivalov, a journalist and translator, the author of the "Letter to Damsel F** About Versification," which I quoted in my analysis of Trediakovsky's image as a fool.[6] Into the discussion of Trediakovsky's literary merits by B. and P. Radishchev inserted a long passage constructed according to the principles of a literary game, which idea he claimed to have borrowed from a novel by August von Kotzebue, *Geschichte meines Vaters* (1788). The themes developed in the passage, the author maintained, were randomly selected from *Tilemakhida* and then were used to generate an absurd and jocular narrative. Radishchev concluded the work with the "Apology of *Tilemakhida* and the Six-Footers," in which B. and P. return to their discussion of the meter employed in the poem and of the work's phonetic structure.

In *Memorial*, Radishchev arrived at a much more favorable judgment of Trediakovsky's services to Russian literature. Unlike ten years previously in "Tver," in his new work about Trediakovsky he acknowledged the poet's role as the initiator of the syllabo-tonic reform: "Trediakovsky understood very well what versification is and, having realized the discordancy in Simeon Polotsky's and Kantemir's verse, wrote in meters that had been used by the Greeks and Romans, i.e., those that were totally new to the Russian ear" (2: 215). Radishchev had also changed his interpretation of Trediakovsky's hexameter. In *A Journey* he did not distinguish it from the six-foot dactyl. This was precisely the approach that allowed him to omit one foot of Trediakovsky's verse while quoting it in the rough draft of "Tver." He did not see the essential difference between a dactylic pentameter and Trediakovsky's hexameter. At that time, the verse of *Tilemakhida* was just dactyls to him, and as dactyls he found it far from perfect. In *Memorial*, however, he strongly objected to the reading of the hexameters in *Tilemakhida* as dactyls: "When reading *Tilemakhida*, everybody is looking for dactyls and reads it as dactylic. Klopstock forbids precisely this." (2: 217). Radishchev points here to the source of his new understanding of Trediakovsky's metrical innovation: Friedrich Gottlieb Klopstock, the author of *Messias* (the first three cantos published in 1748, the last five in 1773), an epic written in hexameters, and of a theoretical essay, "Vom deutschen Hexameter" (1769; expanded version, 1779), in which he discusses the problems of modern imitations of classical hexameters. Following Klopstock's advice, Radishchev suggested an "accentual" reading of Trediakovsky's hexameters, counting accents, rather than feet: "If you read these verses according to the provided division and marked stresses, they will seem much more harmonious" (2: 217). Radishchev came to understand the accentual nature of Trediakovsky's verse in *Tilemakhida* and to think that the poet had produced a good Russian equivalent of the ancient Greek and Roman hexameters, the "Russian six-footer" (*shestistop Rossiiskoi*).[7]

In *Memorial*, Radishchev also praised the phonetic organization of the verse attempted by Trediakovsky in *Tilemakhida*. As I mentioned above, phonetics as a means of expressivity had already attracted Radishchev's attention when he was writing "Liberty" and *A Journey*. He was not interested in harmony per se, but used phonetics to achieve "representational expression" (*izobrazitel'noe vyrazhenie*; 1: 354), in order to express ideas through form. Analyzing the examples of the "expressive harmony" (*izrazitel'naia garmoniia*; 2: 219) in *Tilemakhida*, Radishchev discovered that Trediakovsky's approach was similar to his own, namely, that Trediakovsky had also tried to use phonetics to express meaning and was also not afraid to use harsh sounds and discordant clusters of phonemes to convey the necessary content. To support his discovery, Radishchev cited four lines from the second book of Trediakovsky's poem:

Слышимо было везде одно щебетание Птичек,
Иль благовонный дух от Зефиров веющих тихо,
С ветвиж на-ветвь Древес прелетающих в шуме
  прохладном,
Иль журчание чиста Ручья упадающа с Камня.[8]

Only birds' twittering to be sensed everywhere, or a fragrant scent from zephyrs softly blowing, flying from branch to branch in a cool rustle of trees, or the murmur of a clear brook falling from a stone.

"These are four good lines," declares B., Trediakovsky's apologist in *Memorial*, and he goes on to explain what particularly attracts him in the phonetic structure of the passage:

With the help of the *o* repeated in the beginning and the *ia*, *i*, and *e* at the end, it seems that you hear the song—not of a nightingale, not of a bullfinch, and not of a robin or a chiffchaff, but of a linnet, a crossbill, or maybe a wild siskin or a young goldfinch. Break the second line, and you will find that its beauty results from the long first part, in which the vowels *a*, *o*, *o*, *yi* flow through, so to speak, in the word *blagovonnyi* [fragrant] and are interrupted only by soft consonants and stumble smoothly only on the word *dukh* [here: scent]; then, passing slowly through the vibration of the second part [of the line], they finish exactly in accordance with the things they express. In the third line, look at how expressive the first three parts are; and in the fourth line, the first two parts, in which—with the help of the syllables *zhurch*, *chis*, *ruch* [parts of the words *zhurchanie chista ruch'ia*, "the murmur of a clear brook"], which come one after another—can it not be heard what the author is depicting? And, in the last part, the syllables, which have a similar sound and have the same vowel—*pa*, *da*, *shcha*, *mnia* [parts of the words *upadaiushcha s kamnia*, "falling from a stone"]—represent the waters falling on the rock. (2: 219–20)

Working on *Memorial*, Radishchev obviously regarded Trediakovsky as a much more significant literary figure than the Trediakovsky he had portrayed in *A Journey*. According to Radishchev's new opinion, Trediakovsky had not only declared certain promising literary principles but also employed many of them successfully. However, Radishchev's dependence on the myth of the beginning of the "new" Russian literature had not completely disappeared. As before, Lomonosov remained for Radishchev the greatest literary authority, and he "measured"

Trediakovsky against the norms proposed by the father of Russian literature: "What a line! I am sure that Lomonosov himself would praise it" (2: 219). As before, Radishchev ignored Trediakovsky's stylistic experiments with Church Slavonic and considered Lomonosov the creator of the literary Russian language, the one who successfully incorporated Slavonic elements into it:

> To his misfortune he [Trediakovsky] wrote in the Russian language before Lomonosov, by his own example, impressed taste and discrimination in expression upon Russians and, in the way he [Trediakovsky] combined words and phrases, rushed down an unexplored path on which wit was his guide—in a word, before he [Lomonosov] demonstrated the true quality of the Russian language, having found it, forgotten, in sacred books; therefore, it was impossible for Trediakovsky to learn all over again. (2: 215)

In short, Trediakovsky's image, to a large extent, retained its mythological characteristics for Radishchev. The poet, despite his proficiency in versification, which Radishchev now approved and promoted, remained, in Radishchev's eyes, a tasteless scribbler, notorious for his terrible style. What makes Radishchev's reference to Lomonosov, as well as his criticism of Trediakovsky's style, especially noteworthy is the fact that in his own quest for stylistic effects Radishchev was by no means a follower of Lomonosov's stylistic principles. In search of expressivity Radishchev turned to Church Slavonicisms so profoundly archaic that they certainly fell into the group of "uncommon and quite antiquated" (*neupotrebitel'nye i ves'ma obvetshalye*) Slavonicisms that Lomonosov had forbidden in the Russian literary language in his "Preface on the Usefulness of Church Books in the Russian Tongue."[9] Moreover, many of Radishchev's archaisms were artificial, created to increase the archaic tone of his style. This attention to the stylistic expressivity of Slavonicisms certainly bears a greater resemblance to the embellished, ornate style (*bakharskoe slovo*) developed by the mature Trediakovsky to influence the reader than to Lomonosov's stylistic moderation. Radishchev, however, did not want to acknowledge the affinity between his own stylistic principles and those of Trediakovsky—or, most probably, blinded by the opinions supplied to him by the myth of the "new" Russian literature, he was unaware that this affinity even existed.

The best evidence of Radishchev's continuing dependence on the myth is the motif of the "uncle," *diad'ka*, which was developed in the greatest detail in *Memorial for a Dactylo-Trochaic Knight* but which had appeared in Radishchev's earlier works.[10] Trediakovsky was called *diad'ka* for the first time in the chapter "Tver" of *A Journey from Petersburg to Moscow*: "Everyone who might conceive of using dactyls will immediately be assigned Trediakovsky as his *diad'ka*" (1: 353). *Diad'ka* appears in this passage as a comical double of the mythological ancestor, the parodical father: Since Trediakovsky's name and his dactyls were inseparable, everybody who used nontraditional ternary meters would be considered the literary heir of this ridiculous pedant. In a mythological context, the title *diad'ka* was ambivalent. Uncles appear in myths and epics as substitutes for fathers, and they frequently are negative personages who secretly harm their nephews. But since an uncle's charge is a future hero, the charge's potential heroism necessarily casts a heroic gleam on the *diad'ka* himself. A Milton or a Shakespeare was needed to rehabilitate the ternary meters compromised by Trediakovsky, but Trediakovsky was nonetheless the first to introduce them into Russian literature. This subtle heroic side of the *diad'ka's* image in "Tver" became even more prominent in Radishchev's later works.

The *diad'ka* motif reemerged in the poem *Bova*. The poem, which was written at the very end of the eighteenth century (probably in 1799), was based upon a popular folktale about Bova the king's son. The folktale itself used the plot of a chivalric romance that circulated in Europe beginning in the twelfth or thirteenth century. The plot appeared in Russia in the sixteenth century and soon took the shape of a folktale. In the eighteenth century the story was popular in lower social circles: It circulated in manuscripts, was published in chapbooks, and appeared in the oral tradition. As a folktale it drew Radishchev's attention. Radishchev never finished the poem, although, according to its first publishers, he wrote eleven cantos and began the twelfth. Only the introduction and the first canto have survived. In 1814 Pushkin attempted to develop the same plot, but he never finished his poem either.[11]

Two *diad'kas* were mentioned in Radishchev's *Bova*: Petr Suma, Radishchev's own serf tutor, and Bova's *diad'ka* Tsymbalda. Petr Suma is especially important for my analysis. Rather shockingly in terms of the eighteenth-century literary convention, he is presented in the poem as Radishchev's first literary teacher:

> Я вам сказку лет тех древних
> Расскажу, котору слышал
> От старинного я дядьки
> Моего, Сумы любезна.
>
> Петр Сума, приди на помощь
> И струею речи сладкой
> Оживи мою ты повесть.
>
> (1: 29)

I will tell you a tale of those ancient times, which I heard from my old *diad'ka*, dear Suma. Petr Suma, come to my aid, and with your stream of sweet speech animate my tale.

Suma's role as Radishchev's literature teacher is stressed by the fact that the address to him occupies the place in the poem traditionally reserved for a formal address to a precursor whom the author of a poem named as the literary model for his work. Moreover, the address to Suma is immediately followed by an address to a literary model more acceptable from the conventional point of view—Semen Bobrov, the author of the poem *Tavrida* (1798):

> Оживи мою ты повесть.
> Без складов она, без рифмы
> В след пойдет творцу Тавриды;
> Но с ним может ли сравниться![12]

Animate my tale. Without feet and rhyme, it will follow the creator of *Tavrida*, but how can it compete!

This discussion of meter was of primary importance to Radishchev. As I mentioned in my analysis of the chapter "Tver," in the late 1780's, when Radishchev was writing *A Journey from Petersburg to Moscow*, he was already dissatisfied with the domination of rhymed iambic verse in Russian poetry. Toward the turn of the century, this dissatisfaction increased and prompted Radishchev to experiment with metrics and unrhymed verse. Around 1799 he wrote *Bova*, using trochaic meter to create a styl-

ization of accentual folk verse. Between 1800 and his death in
1802 Radishchev started writing two poems: *Songs Sung at the
Competition in Honor of the Ancient Slavic Divinities* and *Historical
Song*. The former was an attempt to imitate the just-published
Lay of Igor's Campaign by using a complex polyrhythmic structure. The latter poem employed a meter similar to that in *Bova*.
Radishchev also tried classical meters—hexameters and Sapphic
strophes—in his shorter poems. *Bova* thus opened a series of experiments with nontraditional meters. The authorities mentioned in the introduction to the poem, Suma and Bobrov,
pointed out the directions in which Radishchev's quest for new
poetic forms was to go.

One of his models was folk poetry. The choice of a folktale
plot and the emphatic respect for Suma, the teller of folktales,
made this reference obvious for the reader. Bobrov gave Radishchev another model: unrhymed verse. The traditional iambic
tetrameters of Bobrov's *Tavrida* could not have served as an example for Radishchev's modified trochaic tetrameters in *Bova*.
Trediakovsky's metric experiments, as well as folk poetry, must
have suggested its meter. The very choice of trochees as a basis
for his new meter showed that Radishchev wanted to break with
tradition. From the beginning of syllabo-tonic versification in
Russia, trochees were much less popular than iambs and were
associated with the name of Trediakovsky, who introduced them
in his *A New and Brief Method for Composing Russian Verse* in 1735
and defended them against iambs in the famous competition
with Lomonosov and Sumarokov in 1743. In choosing trochees,
Radishchev accepted probable association with Trediakovsky.
However, he did not consider the meter of *Bova* to consist of
ordinary trochees. He defined it as verse "without feet and
rhyme," thus stressing its accentual nature. There are in fact too
many spondees in *Bova* to accept its verse as trochaic. For accentual verse of the folk type, however, this distribution of stresses
is normal. The interest in folk poetry and the belief in the accentual nature of folk verse, as well as the rejection of rhyme, again
suggest Trediakovsky's influence. Indeed, Trediakovsky had already made his famous reference to folk poetry as one of the
sources of his reform of versification in *A New and Brief Method
for Composing Russian Verse*.[13] Later he repeatedly commented

on the accentual nature of Russian folk verse. Trediakovsky's philippics against rhymes—"Gothic toys" and "child's rattles"— also were well remembered at the end of the eighteenth century. There is little doubt that Radishchev fully realized whose traditions he was developing in *Bova*: Only two years later, in *Memorial*, Radishchev would propagate his interpretation of Trediakovsky's hexameter as an accentual meter. However, he never mentions Trediakovsky by name, but instead praises Suma, Bobrov, and, later in the poem, Voltaire.

After extolling his literature teacher Suma, Radishchev suddenly switches into a comical key and derides him:

> Зане дядька мой любезной
> Человек был просвещенной,
> Чесал волосы гребенкой
> В голове он не искался,
> Он ходил в полукафтанье;
> Борода, усы обриты,
> Табак нюхал, и в картишки
> Играть мастер; еще в чем же
> Недостаток, чтобы в свете
> Прослыть славным стихотворцем
> Ироической поэмы
> Или оды или драмы?   (1: 30)

For my dear *diad'ka* was an enlightened man: He combed his hair, he did not look for lice on his head, he wore a semi-caftan, he shaved his beard and moustache and snuffed tobacco, he was a master at cards. What else do you need in order to be known in the world as a renowned poet, the author of a heroic poem or an ode or a play?

This passage may contain yet another hidden reference to Trediakovsky: A "heroic poem" (*iroicheskaia poema*) is not just mentioned but emphasized by an enjambement. Most likely the reference is to *Tilemakhida*, the ill-famed Russian heroic poem of the eighteenth century. This supposition is even more probable if M. P. Alekseev's reconstruction of the *Bova* plot as a journey is correct.[14] This would provide an additional link between Radishchev's *Bova* and Trediakovsky's *Tilemakhida* (which was subtitled *The Wandering of Telemachus, the Son of Odysseus*) and support my assumption that Radishchev in some sense dared to model his poem after the works of the notorious fool and wanted to inform his reader discreetly about the connection in his introduction.

Although Radishchev declines to identify his infamous predecessor directly, he constructs Suma in *Bova* as Trediakovsky's double. In Radishchev's interpretation, Suma and Trediakovsky have many features in common. Both have the title *diad'ka*. Both are the authors of heroic poems—Trediakovsky of *Tilemakhida* and Suma of a hypothetical one. Both inspire Radishchev in his quest for new literary forms, and both suggest folk poetry as a model. Finally, both are characterized in an ambivalent way—Radishchev respects them for what they have done and at the same time ridicules them. But now, despite the ridiculousness of his models, Radishchev does not reject literary kinship with them.

Radishchev's Suma, and consequently Suma's double, Trediakovsky, share some characteristics with Gavrila Derzhavin. This poet had once been so respected by Radishchev that in 1790, upon the publication of *A Journey to Petersburg from Moscow*, Radishchev sent one copy of the book directly to him, although they did not know each other personally. It was a gesture of trust and respect, since Radishchev attached great importance to his book and expected it either to cause an instant transfiguration of Russian society or to bring swift prosecution and death upon himself. According to a legend, which Radishchev himself apparently believed, the frightened Derzhavin marked the most dangerous passages and sent the book to the empress and later wrote a malicious epigram on its author. The legend slanders Derzhavin: His copy of the book was confiscated during the investigation of Radishchev's case. Nevertheless, the rumors of Derzhavin's betrayal undermined Radishchev's admiration for him, as Radishchev's son Pavel testified in his account of the writer's years in Siberian exile. According to Pavel, his father still continued to value Derzhavin's poetry, "Felitsa" (1782) in particular. Judging from *Bova*, however, Radishchev's esteem for the poem was no less ambivalent than his admiration for Suma and Trediakovsky, since he included a parody of "Felitsa" in his ironical praise for Suma. The phrases "he did not look for lice on his head" and "he was a master at cards" refer to the following lines in "Felitsa":

> Иль сидя дома я прокажу,
> Играю в дураки с женой;
> · · ·
> То ею в голове ищюся.[15]

> Or, sitting at home, I have fun and play cards with my wife; . . .
> or let her look for lice on my head.

The allusion to "Felitsa," ironical as it was, constituted in the literary consciousness of the late eighteenth century a reference to the idea of innovation, renewal of literary forms. Derzhavin's portrayal of himself in "Felitsa" as a half-wit whose favorite occupation, in addition to playing cards and being deloused, was reading chapbooks, particularly *Bova*, provided Radishchev with an excellent background for the legalization of such dubious models as Suma and Trediakovsky.

There was supposed to be another *diad'ka* in *Bova*: the tutor of the main hero, named Tsymbalda. The name came from the folktale that served Radishchev as a model for his poem. Tsymbalda was mentioned in the outline for the poem, but did not have a chance to act in the first canto, and we do not know what Radishchev's intentions were with regard to him. The name Tsymbalda (the name "of the most famous of all *diad'kas*"; 2: 203) was given, however, to the main character in *Memorial for a Dactylo-Trochaic Knight*.

As I have mentioned, *Memorial* consists of two parts: the first part, which starts with a discussion of *Tilemakhida* by the characters B. and P. and then switches to a fictional discourse, and the second part, called "Apology of *Tilemakhida* and the Six-Footers," in which B. defends Trediakovsky and his poem. The fictional part is written as a parody, a parody of *Tilemakhida* in the first place, but also of a whole number of other texts—the Bible, *The Minor* (1782) by Denis Fonvizin, Jean Jacques Rousseau's *Emile*, and Cervantes's *Don Quixote*. The parodical device in *Memorial* can be described essentially as follows: Radishchev took one of the main situations in Trediakovsky's (and Fénelon's) work—the mentor Fermosirid instructing Tilemakh—

and transplanted it into the family of an eighteenth-century Russian landowner, Prostiakov (Simpleton). Fermosirid became "*diad'ka* and professor" Tsymbalda (2: 204), and Tilemakh turned into the minor Falelei, a younger brother of Fonvizin's Mitrofan Prostakov.

Tsymbalda, a parodical double of Telemachus's mentor, relates to both the *diad'ka* Suma and the "*diad'ka* of Russian literature," Trediakovsky. Like Suma, Tsymbalda entertains Falelei with tales, albeit not with *Bova*, which he pointedly refuses to tell. Instead, he recites Trediakovsky's *Tilemakhida*, which he happens to know by heart. Like Trediakovsky, he is a father-substitute, a parodical father: "He soon became fond of Falelei and called him his child, and he [Falelei] used to say to him, 'My dear father!'" (2: 211). Stylistically, these words, which paraphrase Telemachus's words about Fermosirid in Trediakovsky's *Tilemakhida*, are out of place.[16] Tsymbalda was Falelei's father in the same absurd sense that Trediakovsky the fool was the "father" of Russian literature. Actually, they both were *diad'kas*, not real fathers.

Although Radishchev was still laughing at Trediakovsky, his attitude toward the comical features of Trediakovsky's image as a fool had changed substantially. Radishchev began to apply his irony not only to Trediakovsky but to the myth of Trediakovsky the fool. This attitude can already be detected in *Bova*, in which Radishchev, stressing the comical characteristics of his literary teacher Suma—and hence of Trediakovsky—nevertheless proclaims himself his disciple. In *Memorial* this attitude is even more pronounced: Radishchev parodies *Tilemakhida*, he parodies Trediakovsky, and at the same time he parodies the common opinions about Trediakovsky and his poem.

Radishchev frequently mocks the myth about Trediakovsky the fool in *Memorial*. For example, the passages about Tsymbalda reciting *Tilemakhida* clearly parallel a popular anecdote about an alleged punishment in Catherine the Great's intimate circle: memorizing or reciting excerpts from *Tilemakhida*. The anecdote was very widespread, and versions of it can be found in many nineteenth-century sources: Karamzin's *Pantheon of Russian Authors*, Metropolitan Evgenii's and Bantysh-Kamensky's dictionaries, Belinsky's essays, and other sources. In a modified form

it entered Bobrov's "Incident in the Realm of Shadows," in
which Galloruss is sentenced to read *Tilemakhida* for eternity.
Lazhechnikov used the anecdote to create a comical situation in
his novel: The main hero orders the young heroine to memorize
passages from the poem, and she complains bitterly.[17]

In his *Memorial*, Radishchev parodies yet another feature of
the myth about Trediakovsky the fool: the power of *Tilemakhida*
to induce sleep. Discussing the merits of *Tilemakhida*, B., Trediakovsky's defender, asks: "Can *Tilemakhida* not serve as Syden-
ham's liquid laudanum?" P. replies: "Of course not. It is utterly
worthless, even to fight insomnia" (2: 202). The most direct parallel to this exchange is the ridicule of *Tilemakhida* in the magazine *All Sorts of Odds and Ends*, in which *Tilemakhida* is recommended to a fictitious correspondent as a cure for insomnia. P.'s
protestations are, thus, ironical: They deny not only the merits
of *Tilemakhida* but also an opinion of the poem sanctioned by
Catherine the Great herself, who was widely believed to be
the sponsor of the magazine. At the same time, the ability of
Tilemakhida to induce sleep is an essential motif in the fictional
part of *Memorial*. The soporific qualities of *Tilemakhida* propel
the plot: Tsymbalda lulls Falelei to sleep with recitations of
Tilemakhida, and the poem induces dreams in both characters.
These dreams, as I plan to demonstrate later in this chapter, are
quite different from the dull and uncreative "dead sleep" allegedly induced by *Tilemakhida* in the traditional accounts of
Trediakovsky the fool.

The reevaluation of the myth did not altogether eliminate
Radishchev's ironical attitude toward Trediakovsky, but the nature of his irony changed dramatically. The parody in *Memorial*
lost its satirical, destructive power, and the laughter became
creative and revitalizing. The very choice of objects for parody in
Memorial demonstrates the ambivalent (in Mikhail Bakhtin's
sense of the word) character of Radishchev's laughter: "It is
gay, triumphant, and at the same time mocking, deriding. It asserts and denies, it buries and revives."[18] Radishchev valued the
overwhelming majority of the parodied works and authors (the
Bible, Fonvizin, Rousseau, Cervantes), and in serious contexts
he treated them with respect. The only work toward which
Radishchev's attitude was probably purely negative is Kotzebue's

Geschichte meines Vaters. Radishchev borrowed from Kotzebue the method for his work—excerpting random passages from *Tilemakhida* to parody. In parodying all other works in *Memorial*, Radishchev did not intend to reduce their literary value. His mockery had a different end: to undermine the scornful opinions about the hero of his work, Trediakovsky. The parody of *Don Quixote* in *Memorial* is an apt example of this kind of rehabilitating mockery.

The name Don Kishot appears in the introduction to *Memorial* in the list of topics that, as the author claims, were randomly selected from *Tilemakhida* for chapter 4 (2: 201). In the list of topics before chapter 4 this name is missing, but it emerges in the course of the chapter. Don Quixote's name plays an important role in this chapter: It betokens the transformation of an everyday reality into a fictitious one as a consequence of the reading of a literary work. This is precisely the device that Cervantes himself used in his book. After reading knightly romances, Don Quixote saw giants instead of windmills and a beautiful castle instead of an inn. Similarly, Tsymbalda and Falelei, influenced by *Tilemakhida*, imagine a smithy to be the entrance to Tartarus, a blacksmith to become the ruler of the underworld, and the fire in a forge to be the flames of hell:

Having read many of these books that fell to his share after his master's death—although he was not exactly like Don Quixote, whose head was full of knightly romances, and what was only in his imagination did not happen before his eyes—Tsymbalda, every time he found the smallest similarity between what was before his eyes and what he had read about, used to recite that similar passage from the book, having rather a sharp memory in his old age. So, having noticed the smithy still far off, he exclaimed: "The most terrible cave was there." (2: 213)

Tsymbalda is quoting from *Tilemakhida*, book 18.[19] Later he creates a potpourri of lines from the same book. Gradually Falelei responds to Tsymbalda's recitations and comes to believe that he really is in Tartarus. Tsymbalda turns an everyday reality into a fictitious one on two other occasions, albeit not so vividly. A barn becomes a cave, and the serf girl Luker'ia, or Lushka, like Cervantes's heroine, receives a lofty Greek name equivalent to her commonplace one (2: 211, 212).

Tsymbalda shares with Don Quixote this quality of transforming reality into fiction. For Radishchev, the ability to transfigure ugliness into beauty and the ordinary into the enchanted was the quintessence of Don Quixote's personality. He cites it in *Bova*:

> Были рыцари не хуже
> Славна в свете Дон Кишота.
> В рог охотничей, в волторну
> Всем трубили громко в уши:
> "Дульцинея Тобозийска
> Всех прекраснее на свете."
> А как возришься в красотку,
> То увидишь под личиной
> Всех белил, румян и мушек
> Обезьяну или кошку,
> Иль Московску щеголиху.

> (1: 43)

There were knights no worse than the famous Don Quixote. They would trumpet a hunter's horn, a French horn, into everybody's ears: "Dulcinea del Toboso is the fairest on earth." But if you peer at a beauty, you will see a monkey, a cat, or a Moscow coquette under the mask of all the ceruse, rouge, and beauty spots.

In Radishchev's eyes, this was the quality by which a Don Quixote could be recognized. Tsymbalda certainly was not a Don Quixote (he "was not exactly like Don Quixote") but constituted his parodical double. At the same time, Tsymbalda and Trediakovsky are correlated, and Trediakovsky is consequently akin to the Knight of the Dolorous Countenance. This kinship is reinforced by the sobriquet given to Trediakovsky in the title of the work: "Dactylo-Trochaic *Knight*" (*vitiaz'*).

This correspondence to Don Quixote shows that the essence of Trediakovsky's comical image had radically changed for Radishchev. In *Memorial*, Trediakovsky is funny in the same way Don Quixote is funny: He is laughable but at the same time deserves respect. It had been inconceivable for Radishchev to be the disciple of a fool, even if this fool developed sensible ideas. But to be a follower of Don Quixote was acceptable, since his path was the path of an original, albeit somewhat idiosyncratic, talent.

Radishchev's initial interest in Trediakovsky was determined to a large extent by his own dissatisfaction with the rigid metrical system used by Russian poets at the end of the eighteenth century. Unlike the majority of his contemporaries, Radishchev very early realized the validity of the metrical decisions suggested by Trediakovsky. Nevertheless, it took him more than ten years to free himself (and even then not completely) from his dependence on the myth of Trediakovsky the fool.

Radishchev's interest in Trediakovsky, however, went far beyond attention to his metrical innovations. Radishchev's studies of Trediakovsky and his mythological image related, Radishchev thought, to the problem of literary development. Even while working on *A Journey*, he was convinced that the renewal of poetic forms was essential if literature was to flourish. Radishchev understood the negative qualities of Lomonosov's role as an invincible literary authority who prevented the introduction of nontraditional literary forms. At the same time, interested as he was in the artistic decisions proposed by Trediakovsky, he was dismayed by the laughter that the mere mention of Trediakovsky's name almost inevitably elicited. Radishchev was able to overcome his reservations about Trediakovsky only after he had changed his attitude toward laughter itself.

Around the turn of the century Radishchev ceased to see laughter as incompatible with serious literature. For him, the comical entered the realm of aesthetics. He wrote two works at this time, *Bova* and *Memorial*, in which comicality is not subordinate to the purposes of satire—in which laughter is valuable in itself. Radishchev even proposed the same criterion, laughter, for the evaluation of his own work and Trediakovsky's. He writes in the introduction to *Memorial*: "Reader! If you smile only once, then I have reached my goal" (2: 201). On the next page he says the same about Trediakovsky: "If the creator of *Tilemakhida* forces you to smile, then a crown is prepared for him."

With the help of laughter Radishchev undermined the myth of the beginning of a "new" Russian literature and destroyed the notions about unshakable authority that this myth supported.

Laughter became a tool for chipping away petrified literary forms and clearing the way for innovation. For the development of Radishchev's literary consciousness, Trediakovsky's image as a fool was no less important than his poetic theory and works. Trying to comprehend and then to reevaluate this image, Radishchev became convinced that change in literary forms was essential for the healthy development of literature. Along the way, he discovered the myth about Trediakovsky the fool to be instrumental in this renewal of form.

Trediakovsky and Pushkin: Myth and History

Radishchev's apology for Trediakovsky, first printed in the last volume of the *Collection of Works Left After the Deceased A. N. Radishchev*, published by his sons in 1806–11, at the peak of the polemical squabbles between the Archaists and the Innovators, did not have a visible impact upon the dispute. Radishchev's prediction, in *A Journey from Petersburg to Moscow*, that the harm inflicted by Trediakovsky upon Russian literature could be eventually overcome, found its way into the polemical exchanges (although the book was banned) and was supported by some polemicists concerned with the renovation of the Russian metrical system, but his suggestion, in *Memorial*, that Trediakovsky's ideas were not harmful but beneficial for the development of Russian literature was apparently not taken seriously. The extraordinary stability of the mythological image of Trediakovsky and its usefulness as a polemical tool account for this inattention to Radishchev's attempt at rehabilitating the unfortunate poet.

Pushkin already knew Radishchev's works, including the banned *Journey* and the ode "Liberty," as a very young man. Radishchev's radical ideas influenced Pushkin's political thinking, but he also appreciated Radishchev's poetry, particularly his poem *Bova*, which Pushkin attempted to imitate in 1814. In the unfinished fragment with the same title Pushkin named Radishchev his highly valued predecessor:

> Петь я тоже вознамерился,
> Но сравняюсь ли с Радищевым?[20]

I also intend to sing, but could I ever be equal to Radishchev?

The view of Trediakovsky that Radishchev expressed in *A Journey* would have been known to Pushkin even in his student years, since it emerged in the polemics about hexameter in the early 1810's, of which Pushkin certainly was aware. Pushkin most probably read *Memorial* as well, since it was published in the same collection of Radishchev's works as *Bova*, although in a different volume. However, at that time Pushkin chose to ignore the appraisal of Trediakovsky's views on versification promoted by Radishchev. Only twenty years later did Pushkin grow to appreciate both Trediakovsky's skill as a poet and Radishchev's view of his metrical experiments. Even less appealing for the young Pushkin should have been Radishchev's attempt to rehabilitate Trediakovsky the fool. In the 1810's Pushkin was fascinated by the merry game of ridiculing the Archaists in which his older friends, the members of Arzamas, were engaged. He shared their view that Trediakovsky was the laughable ancestor of the preposterous Archaists, a chthonic monster, and a "puny versifier." Only gradually, as he became more independent in his views on literature and could examine Trediakovsky's works and ideas by himself, did Pushkin's opinion of the poet begin to change. Eventually, like Radishchev, Pushkin arrived at an understanding of the mythological nature of Trediakovsky's traditional image. This understanding allowed Pushkin to appreciate the creative potential of the myth and to enjoy it as an aesthetic entity. As an example of the artistic interpretation of reality, the myth of Trediakovsky the fool became for Pushkin a source of poetic inspiration. Also contributing to Pushkin's change of heart, in addition to Radishchev's interpretation of Trediakovsky, which Pushkin embraced in the early 1830's, were the Archaists' opinions of the poet, especially the view of him as a professional man of letters formulated by Trediakovsky's sympathizers. Pushkin's own interest in history and the ways it is formed, particularly his attention to the historical anecdote, contributed to his new understanding of Trediakovsky's fate. Pushkin's historicism became for him a way to deal with the myth of Trediakovsky the fool. His new conceptions of historical fact and historical truth helped to reveal the falsehood of the traditional notions about Trediakovsky and to condemn their cruelty and unfairness. Pushkin destroyed the myth by confronting it with historical facts—and its destruction allowed him to evaluate Trediakovsky and his contributions in historical perspective.[21]

In the 1810's only the comical side of Trediakovsky's mythological image existed for Pushkin. At that time, he not only supported the image of Trediakovsky the fool but participated in its construction. He first tried his hand at this as a student at the Lyceum, a school that he attended from 1811 to 1816, in the literary disputes that took place among his classmates who were interested in literature. In 1813 he included Trediakovsky's name in an epigram attacking his friend at the Lyceum, Wilhelm Kuechelbecker:

> Внук Тредьяковского Клит гексаметром песенки
>   пишет,
> Противу ямба, хорея злобой ужасною дышит.
>
> (1: 21)

Cletus, Trediakovsky's grandson, writes songs in hexameters
and breathes a terrible rage against iambs and trochees.

In this poem, Pushkin uses Trediakovsky's name to condemn literary phenomena that were alien to his emerging taste as an Innovator. Trediakovsky appears in his mythological role as the ancestor of a worthless poet and the provider of harmful examples, in this case, hexameter. It is noteworthy that by the 1810's trochees had lost their association with Trediakovsky. The popularity of trochaic imitations of folk poetry, as well as the intensive employment of the trochee in love poems around the turn of the century, apparently destroyed this link, which Radishchev had still perceived fifteen years before.

About a year after writing the epigram, in 1814, Pushkin compared Kuechelbecker to Trediakovsky once more, this time in print. In "To a Poet Friend," which was the first of Pushkin's poems ever to be published, he called Kuechelbecker "another father of a second *Tilemakhida*" (1: 25). Again Trediakovsky appeared in his traditional role as the author of the notorious epic, and Kuechelbecker was presented as a poet following his predecessor's bad example.

For Pushkin at that time, the comparison to Trediakovsky characterized Kuechelbecker as an Archaist, and Pushkin derided him as such. Pushkin's squabble with Kuechelbecker was a rehearsal of his future clashes with the Besedists, in which he longed to, but did not yet, participate. Pushkin joined the attacks in 1816. In the poem "To Zhukovsky," he depicted the Besedists' "ancestor" Trediakovsky as a chthonic monster who gives his blessing to the wild and insane Besedists: "The puny versifier heeds the howl with a smile" (1: 195). Later in the poem Trediakovsky appears as a prophet or apostle of the Besedists. They swear on Trediakovsky's *Tilemakhida* as on the Bible:

> Все, руку положив на том "Тилимахиды,"
> Клянутся отомстить сотрудников обиды.
>
> (1: 196)

Everyone, having placed his hand on the volume of *Tilemakhida*, swears to avenge the insults to his colleagues.

In Pushkin's poem, Trediakovsky has passed on to his literary descendants the main characteristics of his mythological image: the laughable character of his poetry, his archaic style, the soporific effect of his works, insanity, and the association with the underworld.

The only deviation on Pushkin's part from the Innovators' interpretation of Trediakovsky in those early years occurred in the poem "To Batiushkov" (1814), in which Pushkin appeals to Batiushkov, referring to his mockery of Trediakovsky in "A Vision on the Banks of Lethe" and "The Bard in the Colloquium of Lovers of the Russian Word": "But leave Trediakovsky in his so often disturbed peace" (1: 74). The defense, however, turns out to be ambiguous, because Pushkin immediately enrolls Trediakovsky among the "absurd poets": "Alas! We will find enough absurd poets besides him" (1: 74). Trediakovsky, despite Pushkin's advice to Batiushkov not to laugh at him, remained the familiar fool.

With the demise of Arzamas and gradual disintegration of the Arzamasian brotherhood, jokes about Trediakovsky subsided. In the early 1820's Pushkin rarely recalled the notorious pedant by name. Apart from the disappearance of a proper context for ridiculing him, Pushkin could have had another reason for not mentioning Trediakovsky's name: He was in the process of revising the principles upon which the Innovators' mockery of Trediakovsky and the Archaists had been based. He was reassessing the value of tradition and innovation in literature and especially in language. In this connection, the reevaluation of Trediakovsky's place in Russian literary history was unavoidable. Yet, at that time, Pushkin still did not acknowledge Trediakovsky's contributions to Russian literature, and his rare remarks about Trediakovsky remained ambiguous at best. In 1822, in the fragment "On French Literature," Pushkin discussed the harmful consequences of the French influence upon Russian literature and commented in parentheses on Trediakovsky's reform of versification: "Trediakovsky reluctantly [or "unwittingly," *nekhotia*] separated by means of versification [*otdelil stikhslozheniem*]" (12: 191). It is true that in this (not quite intelligible) fragment Pushkin seems to present Trediakovsky as the only eighteenth-century Russian writer who resisted the harmful—that is, from Pushkin's point of view—custom of imitating French models: He introduced syllabo-tonic verse, which was not connected to French tradition, in place of syllabic verse, which was similar to the French system of versification. Pushkin might have had in mind Trediakovsky's famous assertion in the 1735 version of *A New and Brief Method for Composing Russian Verse* that he used Russian folk poetry as a model in his reform:

Certainly these gentlemen apparently thought that I took this new versification from the French, but in that they are as far from the truth as French versification is from this new one of mine. . . . It is true that almost all the terms that are used in respect of verse I borrowed from French versification, but the essence itself [I borrowed] from our own native, most ancient poetry of the simple folk.[22]

Whether Pushkin knew the 1735 version of *A New and Brief Method* at the time is not clear. The revised version of the treatise, published in 1752 in the first volume of Trediakovsky's *Compositions and Translations in Verse and Prose* without the quoted passage, was much better known in the nineteenth century. It was the 1752 edition that Pushkin bought for himself in the 1830's. However, Pushkin's remark about Trediakovsky quoted below suggests that some of Trediakovsky's early works were familiar to Pushkin in the 1820's, although it is not clear which ones. In any case, regardless of the source of his information in the parenthetical remark about Trediakovsky, Pushkin drastically depreciated the significance of his achievement with the comment that he restricted French influence on Russian literature "reluctantly" or even "unwittingly." The traditional negative attitude toward Trediakovsky still prevailed.

Pushkin judged Trediakovsky even more harshly in the essay "On Mr. Lémontey's Preface to the Translation of I. A. Krylov's Fables" (1825). In a footnote to some favorable remarks on Lomonosov's usage of Slavonic elements in the literary language, Pushkin derided Trediakovsky's view of the matter: "It is interesting to see how daintily Trediakovsky ridicules Lomonosov's Slavonicisms, how seriously he advises him to adopt the *lightness* and *elegance of expressions of refined company* [*shchegolevatost' rechenii izriadnoi kompanii*]" (11: 33). Boris Uspensky holds that Pushkin, in this comment, joins Trediakovsky in criticizing Lomonosov's linguistic position.[23] I disagree with him on this point. Although in this essay Pushkin disapproves of many aspects of Lomonosov's poetical legacy, the footnote in question is attached to the passage in which Pushkin praises the Slavonicisms in Lomonosov's style. In *The Language of Pushkin*, Viktor Vinogradov correctly argues that in this characterization Pushkin "accepts Shishkov's formula in evaluating Lomonosov"— that is, sides with the Archaists in the question of language.[24] Indeed, this passage and the work in general have a clear anti-Karamzin tendency. Compare, in this respect, Pushkin's rejection, in the same essay, of literature "for ladies," the pivotal point of the Karamzinists' literary platform. Pushkin says: "Milton and Dante wrote not for the *condescending smile of the fair sex*" (11: 33). The emphasized words sound like an ironical quotation from Karamzin. The source of Pushkin's quotation from Trediakovsky is unknown (Uspensky, in his book on the history of Russian literary language suggests the oral tradition), but it obviously reflects Trediakovsky's early linguistic position, which, as Nikolai Bakhtin pointed out in 1822, resembled the Innovators' position on the language of literature.[25] Trediakovsky appears in Pushkin's comment in his traditional role as the generator of wrongheaded literary ideas, but the exponents of these ideas are not the Archaists any more but Pushkin's former allies, the Innovators. Pushkin presents Trediakovsky as an awkward predecessor of the Karamzinists, whose principles Pushkin no longer shared. In this remark, he deviates from the view of Trediakovsky as a propagator of Slavonicisms and the father of the Archaists, a view that he and his former circle used to espouse, but does not abandon the standard view of Trediakovsky as a foolish and ridiculous opponent of the great Lomonosov and a provider of bad models.

At the end of the 1820's Pushkin still accepted the traditional opinions about Trediakovsky as a fool, but his attitude toward these opinions began to show some important signs of change as he started to reevaluate the myth. In "Fragments from Letters, Thoughts, and Notes" (1827), he included an anecdote relating the story of Trediakovsky's complaint to Shuvalov about the slap in the face that he had allegedly received from Sumarokov, and Shuvalov's witty reply. Trediakovsky appears in this anecdote in his traditional role, that of a fool who gets beaten up, but the fool unexpectedly manifests features of a Christian martyr. In the fragment, Trediakovsky enacts a commandment given in the Sermon on the Mount, albeit in a comical way: "'How so, fellow?' Shuvalov answered. 'Your right cheek hurts, and you hold your left one.' 'Ah, Your Excellency, you are right,' Trediakovsky answered and transferred his hand to the other side" (11: 53). Although placed in a comical context, the allusion to the Scriptures marked the emergence of Pushkin's awareness of the dual (foolish and heroic) nature of Trediakovsky's mythological image and signified the beginning of its reevaluation, which he would undertake in earnest in the 1830's. Trediakovsky remained a fool in Pushkin's eyes (he was still funny, he still deserved beatings, and he still displayed contrary behavior in that left and right were reversed for him), but Pushkin became conscious of the tragic aspect of his image as a fool (however subtle) and thus acquired the ability to sympathize with him as a human being.

This new attitude toward Trediakovsky the fool, more favorable than before, manifested itself in a remark about Trediakovsky in a letter of February 19, 1828, addressed to Mikhail Pogodin, the editor of the magazine *Moscow Herald* (1827–31) and Pushkin's friend. Pushkin wrote, in connection with Pogodin's frictions with the pro-government journalist Faddei Bulgarin and his gazette *The Northern Bee* (1825–59): "And you, dear Mikhailo Petrovich, console yourself and, as Trediakovsky says, spit at [i.e., shrug off] that bitch *The Northern Bee*" (14: 5). Pushkin is quoting from Trediakovsky's poem "A Song That I Composed While Still in the Moscow School, Upon My Departure to Foreign Countries":

Плюнь на суку
Морску скуку.[26]

Spit at the bitch seasickness.

On the one hand, Pushkin is quoting an early syllabic poem by Trediakovsky that everyone had ridiculed for quite some time: the notorious poem with the birdies and little foxes that was assaulted by Sumarokov in 1750, by Lomonosov in 1757, and by Derzhavin in the 1810's. Moreover, Pushkin creates the deliberately absurd construction *suka pchela*, "bitch of a bee," as if referring to the traditional notion of Trediakovsky as a ludicrously helpless stylist. On the other hand, Pushkin humorously advises Pogodin to follow Trediakovsky's example in his relations with his literary enemy. The advice might suggest that Pushkin saw a certain parallel between the merciless eighteenth-century literary polemics, in which Trediakovsky's image as a fool originated, and contemporary clashes with the journalists of Bulgarin's camp. In any case, he took Pogodin and Trediakovsky's side, enrolling himself, Pogodin, and Trediakovsky against Bulgarin.

I believe that this sympathetic view of Trediakovsky reflected Pushkin's concept of literary professionalism, which began to take shape in the second half of the 1820's. Pushkin's new ideas about the essence of literary work and the writer's place in society allowed him to see Trediakovsky's fate in a different light and to put it into the context of such problems (urgent for Pushkin at this time) as the writer's professional independence and dignity. Trediakovsky the battered and humiliated man of letters certainly served as a model to avoid rather than imitate, but simply paying attention to the abuse of Trediakovsky by his contemporaries and literary descendants signified a totally new approach to the myth about Trediakovsky the fool. Pushkin's subsequent reevaluation of the myth was closely connected with the development of his views on literary professionalism.[27]

However, despite some changes in Pushkin's view of Trediakovsky, the mythological image was by no means dead in Pushkin's consciousness in the late 1820's. Along with sympathetic or partly sympathetic remarks, the poet continued to use the image of Trediakovsky the fool for polemical purposes. In 1828–31 Pushkin employed Trediakovsky's image as a fool in his attacks against Mikhail Kachenovsky, his magazine *Messenger of Europe*, and the magazine's chief critic at the time, Nikolai Nadezhdin.

Messenger of Europe was founded by Karamzin in 1802. It was the first so-called thick journal, which combined political news with literary works and critical surveys. In the almost thirty years of its existence, the magazine saw a succession of publishers, and since 1815 it had irrevocably fallen into the hands of Mikhail Kachenovsky. By the end of the 1820's the magazine was stagnating. Between 1828 and 1830 it underwent a temporary revival, which was primarily connected with the name of Nikolai Nadezhdin, a young and insolent critic who made his debut in *Messenger of Europe* in November 1828 and who formulated the program of the journal for the late 1820's. Nadezhdin's disrespectful statements, which were published in the magazine, his lamentations over the "hopeless state" of Russian literature, which insulted virtually all parties involved in contemporary literary life, and his calls for a return to the eternal ideals of art and an abandonment of the modern decadent Romantic forms were the reason for the intense irritation with the magazine that the literati felt. Pushkin, annoyed by Kachenovsky and Nadezhdin's program in general and directly offended by Nadezhdin's sharp criticism of his works, including *Count Nulin* (1828) and *Poltava* (1829), was among the bitterest enemies of the magazine. In 1829 alone, Pushkin wrote nine epigrams and a number of satirical prose pieces aimed at the magazine's publisher and its new chief critic.

The magazine's publisher, Kachenovsky, was an old enemy of Pushkin's. The poet's attacks against the journalist went back to the 1810's and early 1820's. M. A. Tsiavlovsky, in his analysis of their relations, suggests that Pushkin first took offense at Kachenovsky in 1816, when he refused to publish Pushkin's poetry in his magazine.[28] Certain features of Kachenovsky's image as it emerged in Pushkin's early attacks on him anticipated the connection of Trediakovsky's and Kachenovsky's names in the epigrams written in the late 1820's. In these early assailments, Pushkin endowed Kachenovsky with the distinct characteristics of a mythological fool. In an epigram of 1821, Pushkin characterized Kachenovsky as someone who deserved and received beatings: "He seeks the rod by instinct" (2: 223). In an epigram written in 1824, Pushkin stressed the soporific qualities of Kachenovsky's writings:

> Охотник до журнальной драки
> Сей усыпительный Зоил
> Разводит опиум чернил
> Слюною бешеной собаки.
>
> (2: 346)

A lover of journalistic brawls, this sleep-inducing Zoilus dilutes the opium of his ink with the saliva of a rabid dog.

Moreover, Pushkin included Kachenovsky among the "puny," along with Chapelain and Trediakovsky. He wrote to Viazemsky in a letter of January 2, 1822, in connection with Viazemsky's poem attacking Kachenovsky, "An Epistle to M. T. Kachenovsky" (1820): "I quarrel with you only about your epistle to Kachenovsky: How could you enter the arena with this puny fistfighter . . . ?" (13: 34). There was even an indication that Pushkin might actually join Trediakovsky's and Kachenovsky's names as early as 1825. The poet Ivan Kozlov wrote in his letter to Pushkin of May 31, 1825: "Our journalists become more trivial every day. Your two epigrams about the one in Moscow [i.e., Kachenovsky] make one die of laughter, especially [the parts about] *Basil* and *Michel*."[29] The epigram about "Basil and Michel" did not survive, but it is likely that the names referred to Vasilii Trediakovsky and Mikhail Kachenovsky, who would become doubles in Pushkin's epigrams four years later.

In a way, Pushkin's attacks on Kachenovsky continued the Arzamasian struggle with the "foes of reason," Trediakovsky's descendants from the Archaists' camp. Indeed, Kachenovsky had stormy relations with the Innovators and in the late 1810's was one of the routinely attacked figures in their polemics against the Archaists. As early as 1815, his name was ironically mentioned along with Shishkov's in Arzamasian speeches.[30] The attacks intensified in 1818, after Kachenovsky's sharp criticism of Karamzin's *History of the Russian State*. Viazemsky considered it the Arzamasians' duty to rebuff Kachenovsky and wrote several epigrams on this occasion. Pushkin, urged on by Viazemsky, also entered the polemics and condemned the criticizer of Karamzin in an insulting epigram (2: 61). When Pushkin resumed his assaults on Kachenovsky and his *Messenger of Europe* at the end of the 1820's, Trediakovsky's name appeared in these attacks quite naturally, along with Arzamasian stylistics. Pushkin himself referred readers to the vocabulary of his youth, signing one of the epigrams "Arz[amasian]."

Trediakovsky's name emerged in two of Pushkin's epigrams attacking Kachenovsky written in 1829. Playing upon the consonance of Trediakovsky's and Kachenovsky's last names, Pushkin created the image of "a modern Trediakovsky" who shared the traditional attributes of Trediakovsky the fool, such as stupidity, pedantry, contrary behavior, and a connection to the underworld. Trediakovsky appeared in Pushkin's epigrams as Kachenovsky's double, ancestor, or accomplice. In the epigram "Literary News," which mocked Kachenovsky's plans for the revival of his magazine, Trediakovsky awaited Kachenovsky in the other world in order to start a magazine:

В Элизии Василий Тредьяковский
(Преострый муж, достойный много хвал)
С усердием принялся за журнал.
. . .
И только ждет Василий Тредьяковский,
Чтоб подоспел [Михайло Каченовский].
(3: 153)[31]

In Elysium, Vasilii Trediakovsky (a sharp man, deserving of much praise) has zealously set to work on a magazine. . . . And Vasilii Trediakovsky waits only for [Mikhailo Kachenovsky] to arrive.

In this poem, Pushkin pictures the two as collaborators and implies that Trediakovsky's wretched literary enterprise was impossible without his follower Kachenovsky. In the other poem,

"Epigram" (3: 156), the subject of which is also the attempt by the *Messenger of Europe* to reestablish itself, Pushkin makes Kachenovsky Trediakovsky's double, "the Trediakovsky of modern days." He calls Trediakovsky "the ancient Kochergovsky"—a malicious distortion of Kachenovsky's surname, derived from the word *kocherga*, "a poker." Both are pictured with a bad, voluminous book, a traditional attribute of Trediakovsky the pedant: "The ancient Kochergovsky" dies translating Rollin's histories ("expired over Rollin"), and "the Trediakovsky of modern days" tries to revive his dead magazine. The fact that Kachenovsky was a professional historian probably reinforced Pushkin's choice of Rollin's works over *Tilemakhida*. Attempting to revive his magazine and the archaic letter upsilon, Kachenovsky the fool employs incorrect (reversed) magic actions. The efforts on Kachenovsky's part to revive upsilon paralleled Trediakovsky's interest in questions of orthography, which the myth about Trediakovsky the fool interpreted as an attempt to preserve ancient letters in the modern Russian alphabet and attributed to his pedantry. Kachenovsky, in Pushkin's portrayal, is indistinguishable from Trediakovsky as the myth presented him. Like his counterpart, he is a pedant interested in outdated elements of language and a fool who does everything the wrong way around.

Certain features of Kachenovsky's literary and linguistic position—especially the "Greek" orthography accepted in his magazine—invited comparisons to Trediakovsky the fool. Kachenovsky's critics at the end of the 1820's were well aware of the similarities, and Pushkin was not the only one to take advantage of them. In the magazine *Son of the Fatherland* (1812–44) we find the following ridicule of Kachenovsky's idiosyncratic spelling habits:

"Почему для большего сходства" с "приснопоминаемым профессором елоквенции," "не пишут они, подобно ему: піима, піита, велікій, стіх, хореіческій, Делфіческй Аполлін, мусікія и пр.?"[32]

"Why, for the sake of a closer resemblance" to "the oft-recalled professor of eloquence," "do they not write, like him: *poem, poet, great, verse, trochaic, Apollo at Delphi, music*, etc.?"

This passage ridicules Kachenovsky's overuse of the letter iota (*i*) and compares his preference for this letter to Trediakovsky's suggestion, in his *Conversation on Orthography*, that eta (и) be eliminated from the Russian alphabet and that the letter iota (*i*) be retained and used for the sound [i] in all positions. Kachenovsky's archaic spelling also became the object of parody in the "Historical Epigram" (1829) of Evgenii Baratynsky. Baratynsky mockingly spelled the title of the poem with an upsilon at the beginning of the first word and iotas as the sixth letter of the first word and the third letter of the second. Pushkin himself parodied Kachenovsky's orthography in a similar way. In the essay "A Fragment from Literary Chronicles" (1829), he wrote Kachenovsky's first name and patronymic, Mikhail Trofimovich, with iotas, and in one of the epigrams quoted above he spelled the word *izhitsa* with an upsilon as the first letter of the word (11: 79–81, 3: 156).

This mockery of Kachenovsky's orthography demonstrates how indifferent the users of the myth, including Pushkin in the late 1820's, were toward Trediakovsky's actual views. In fact, in his treatise on orthography, Trediakovsky advocated the elimination of the upsilon, inasmuch as it duplicated the letter в, beta—used in Cyrillic for the sound [v] or, in other positions, for eta and iota. As for the letters iota and eta, he held them equally suitable for the sound [i] and preferred iota to eta because it made the Russian alphabet closer to the Latin alphabet used by modern Western languages.[33] Contrary to the belief popular among his literary descendants, Trediakovsky did not try to enforce traditional spelling rules in his proposed reform of orthography but sought to introduce an innovative spelling system based on phonetics rather than grammar. By no means was he an irrational traditionalist in his views on orthography at that time. Actually, he tried to reorganize Russian spelling according to the laws of reason and the nature of the Russian language as he understood them. He called, among other things, for the elimination from the Russian alphabet of letters that, in Trediakovsky's opinion, unnecessarily duplicated each other. It is true that Trediakovsky often sought in antiquity the answer to the question, What is natural for the Russian language? but venerability was not his only, and at that time not even his main, criterion in his choice of spelling rules. Trediakovsky's contemporaries regarded many ideas expressed in his treatise as far too innovative, rather than too conservative. His literary descendants, however, assumed that Trediakovsky the pedant was by definition an aficionado of outdated letters and, therefore, the ancestor of Kachenovsky. To compromise Kachenovsky's linguistic ideas it was sufficient to compare them to Trediakovsky's; that the resemblance was superficial at best was of minor significance to the polemicists. The image of Trediakovsky the fool fulfilled its polemical function regardless of how little it corresponded to the original man.

In 1836, when Pushkin's views of the literary Russian language, as well as his attitude toward Trediakovsky, had changed, he rehabilitated Kachenovsky's experiments with spelling. Nikolai Gogol, in his essay "On the Development of Journalistic Literature in the Years 1834 and 1835" (1836), attacked Osip Senkovsky, a writer and a critic, the founder and editor of the commercially successful magazine *Library for Reading* (1834–65). Among other things, Gogol ridiculed Senkovsky's criticism of the words *sei* (this) and *onyi* (that), somewhat bookish equivalents of *etot* and *tot*, and compared Senkovsky's assault on these words to "old Trediakovsky's case for the letter *izhitsa* and the decimal *i*, which later, not so long ago, a certain professor supported."[34] Gogol used both Trediakovsky's and Kachenovsky's names in the traditional way, to condemn his literary enemy. The actual content of their views was irrelevant to him, and he ignored it completely. His comparison did not even hold from the point of view of logic: Gogol said Senkovsky criticized archaic forms, whereas Trediakovsky and Kachenovsky supported them. But illogic did not bother Gogol, for, in his opinion, a comparison to Trediakovsky the fool could in itself damage Senkovsky's position.

Pushkin disagreed with Gogol on all points. In his "Letter to the Editor" (1836) he wrote:

But you unjustly compared the persecution of *sei* and *onyi* to the introduction of *i* [iota] and *v* [upsilon] into the spelling of Russian words, and in vain disturbed the remains of Trediakovsky, who never argued with anybody about these letters. The learned professor, who wanted to transform our orthography, acted by himself, without a previous example. I would note in passing that Mr. Kachenovsky's orthography is not a difficult novelty, but has existed for a long time in our sacred books. Every man of letters who has received a classical education is obliged to know its rules, even if he does not follow them. (12: 96)

In this passage, Pushkin refuses to replace Trediakovsky's actual views with the opinions that the myth had ascribed to him: Pushkin had already ceased to regard Trediakovsky as just a mythological fool whose name was useful in literary polemics. Consequently, he rejects the use of the myth about Trediakovsky for crude polemical purposes and declines to consider Kachenovsky a descendant of Trediakovsky. Kachenovsky's model, in Pushkin's interpretation, is not Trediakovsky the fool, not Trediakovsky the historical personality, but the Bible.

In the late 1820's Pushkin still valued the polemical potency of the myth about Trediakovsky, and he used its versatile resources to condemn yet another literary enemy, the chief critic on the staff of Kachenovsky's magazine, Nikolai Nadezhdin. In his attacks on Nadezhdin, Pushkin expressed his irritation with the newly emerging group of plebeian intellectuals, the *raznochintsy*, of whom Nadezhdin was the self-chosen representative. The age of the dominance of the nobility over Russian culture was coming to an end, in the late 1820's, and a new group of writers and journalists, who were children of merchants, priests, and petty bureaucrats, was coming to the fore as a distinct cultural force. The differences of opinion on both sides easily translated into the language of social hostilities. Nadezhdin introduced social overtones into the literary polemics by his objections to what he considered to be dilettantism and conceptual emptiness in the Romantic works of the "literary aristocracy," Pushkin first of all. Iurii Mann, in his essay on Nadezhdin, plays down the social motives for Nadezhdin's polemical attacks on Pushkin, claiming that they would be a "too straightforward explanation" of his severe criticism of Pushkin's works.[35] But there is little doubt that social antagonism was present in Nadezhdin's criticism, as well as in Pushkin's retaliatory attacks. Nadezhdin's severe animadversions against Pushkin as "a young master" (*barich*), a representative of the "literary aristocracy," called forth Pushkin's reciprocal accusations of vulgarity and his spiteful censure of the plebeian spirit he found to be inherent in Nadezhdin's literary opinions. Mockery of Nadezhdin's low origin was a permanent element of Pushkin's attacks on the critic. In the fragment "The Society of Moscow Literati" (1829), Pushkin calls Nadezhdin "a young man from the honest estate of servants" (11: 85). In one of his epigrams from the same year he pictures him as Kachenovsky's flunky. Even Nadezhdin's writings, in Pushkin's presentation, bore signs of his low origin and mean occupation. Pushkin repeatedly describes his works as the productions of a flunky or a seminarian.

In Pushkin's portrayals, Nadezhdin, as a plebeian, had plebeians for his spiritual forebears. In "The Society of Moscow Literati"—in which Pushkin parodies plans for the revival of the *Messenger of Europe*, announced by Kachenovsky and Nadezhdin in 1828—Pushkin names those ancestors: Trediakovsky and Nikolai Kurganov.

Several Moscow literati, who bring true honor to our age with their works, as well as with their morals, seeing the helpless state of our literature and being bored by the sounds of ringing cymbals, decided to organize a society for the dissemination of Kurganov's and Trediakovsky's sound critical rules, and for the restraint of apostates and scoffers within the bounds of obedience and decency. (11: 85)

The name of Kurganov directly refers the reader to plebeian literature. Nikolai Kurganov was the author of a famous eighteenth-century book called the *Primer* (the first edition was published in 1769 under the title *Russian Universal Grammar*). It contained a popular version of Lomonosov's *Russian Grammar* (1755) and a collection of proverbs, anecdotes, aphorisms, poetry, and the like. It was addressed to the general reader and was so popular among the undereducated public at the end of the eighteenth century and even during the first third of the nineteenth century that in 1837 it appeared in its eleventh edition. Pushkin himself regarded this book as reading for ordinary people. In his "History of the Village of Goriukhino" (1829–30), he mentions the *Primer* as one of two or three books owned by the family of "respectable, but simple," provincial landlords (8: 127).

To Pushkin, Kurganov's name was a familiar polemic tool, for the Innovators used it in their attacks against the Archaists to symbolize the outdated, casting Kurganov in the role of Shishkov's antiquated inspirer. In Batiushkov's "The Vision," Shish-

kov said about himself: "I was taught to write by Kurganov."
Dashkov, in one of his speechs to Arzamas, also implied that
Kurganov impelled Shishkov to compose his *Discourse on the Old
and New Style*.[36] Pushkin himself used Kurganov's name, along
with Trediakovsky's, in one of his poems criticizing Kachenovsky, the epigram "Literary News" (3: 156).

Trediakovsky, the son of a priest and a former student at the
Slavo-Greco-Latin Academy, the humble recipient of beatings
and mockery, the author of allegedly outdated poetry and pedantic prose, seemed to be a natural ally of Kurganov's. Certain
features of Trediakovsky's mythological image, such as his diligence, his learnedness, and, above all, his status as a professional man of letters, made it possible to picture him as a spiritual forefather of the plebeians. As I pointed out in the previous
chapter, in the 1800's and 1810's Trediakovsky's defenders from
the Archaist camp (Galinkovsky, Anastasevich, Merzliakov et
al.), who were mostly plebeian intellectuals themselves, hailed
his professionalism and contrasted it to what they claimed to be
the dilettantism of the Karamzinists. For them Trediakovsky's
professionalism was a valuable quality, which made the poet
worthy of their attention and respect. Pushkin himself probably
contemplated the irony of Trediakovsky's fate as a professional
man of letters in the years just before the polemics with the *Messenger of Europe*. Pushkin's conclusions, as we remember, were
ambiguous, and in the context of his clashes with Nadezhdin,
the positive aspects of Trediakovsky's professionalism apparently were overshadowed for Pushkin by such negative consequences of his professional status as lack of independence and
the necessity of satisfying his patrons. The dull diligence and
pedantry that the myth about the beginning of the "new" Russian literature ascribed to Trediakovsky, as well as the servility
he supposedly displayed at Empress Anna's court, easily translated into plebeianism, and the poet became in Pushkin's eyes
the spiritual father of the "drunken seminarian" and "flunky"
Nadezhdin and his associates.

This was precisely the role that Pushkin ascribed to Trediakovsky in yet another polemical piece against Nadezhdin. In a
letter, written in 1831, to the publisher of the literary supplement to the newspaper *Russian Invalid* (1813–1917) about the

first part of Gogol's *Evenings on a Farm near Dikanka* (1831), Pushkin expresses his concern about the criticism of the book expected from certain journalists, Nadezhdin above all, and pleads with other critics not to follow their example:

> For God's sake, take his [Gogol's] side, if journalists, as usual, attack the *indecency* of his expressions, the *bad tone*, etc. It is time indeed for us to deride *les précieuses ridicules* of our literature, the people who always speak about the fair lady readers whom they have never had, about the high society to which they are not invited, and all this in the style of Professor *Trediakovsky's* valet. (11: 216)

Pushkin did not name Nadezhdin in this letter, but his readers certainly remembered his earlier mockery of Nadezhdin as "a young man from the honest estate of servants" and Kachenovsky's flunky and recognized the quotations from Nadezhdin's criticism of *Count Nulin*. They easily identified in Trediakovsky's valet (*kamerdiner*) the former contributor to the *Messenger of Europe*. It was clear to Pushkin, as well as to his readers, that Trediakovsky, by virtue of his low social station, could not possibly have had a real valet. If he could have, the servant would undoubtedly have been a particularly base sort of a person. The style of this imaginary valet of the pedant "Professor" Trediakovsky would certainly have been especially tasteless. *Les précieuses ridicules* would remind Pushkin's readers of the young Trediakovsky and his translation of Tallemant's novel. In combination with the professorship, this reference stressed the low mixture of pedantry and preciosity that Pushkin wanted to emphasize and ridicule in Nadezhdin's literary position.[37]

The versatility of Trediakovsky's image as a fool allowed Pushkin to employ it in clashes over topical literary matters, be they the traditional mockery of literary enemies or the new arguments over the professionalization and plebeianization of literature. However, if the plebeian character of the emerging journalism annoyed him, in the late 1820's Pushkin was not completely against literary professionalism itself. By that time, he had long outgrown the emphatically dilettantish attitude toward literary work inherited in the 1810's from his friends the Innovators. For the mature Pushkin, knowledge and hard work were a necessity for successful literary production. In 1829 he put his conviction into words:

Many are displeased with our journalistic polemics for their bad style, their ignorance of decorum, etc. This displeasure is quite unjustified. A learned man, engaged in his work, immersed in thought, might have no time to appear in society and acquire the skills of its vain refinement, like an idle inhabitant of *le grand monde*. We have to be indulgent toward his naive coarseness—the pledge of his conscientiousness and love of truth. Pedantry has its good side. It is ridiculous and disgusting only when light-headedness and ignorance are expressed in the language of a drunken seminarian. (17: 65)[38]

In this fragment, Pushkin still defends professionalism from plebeians, especially the "drunken seminarian" Nadezhdin. But he was already willing to sacrifice decorum and elegance, qualities that Pushkin did not take lightly, to the need for serious commitment to literary activities.

Pushkin did not publish this fragment. He returned to it in the middle of the 1830's, when he revised it for his collection of notes *Table-talk*. By that time his belief that a writer should be a professional, equipped with knowledge and skills, had become even stronger. By the beginning of the 1830's, plebeianism had ceased to disturb Pushkin, and in 1831 he became a contributor to Nadezhdin's *Telescope* (1831–36). He completely rehabilitated pedantry, plebeianism, and *mauvais ton* in the new version of the fragment included in *Table-talk*: "Pedantry has its good side. It is ridiculous and disgusting only when petty-mindedness and ignorance express themselves in its language" (12: 164). The target of Pushkin's attack here is ignorance in a writer, not plebeianism and the pedantry frequently ascribed to plebeian literati.

Pushkin's regard for Trediakovsky increased along with his growing respect for professionalism. In 1833 he acquired Trediakovsky's books *Oration on Eloquence* (1745) and the two-volume *Compositions and Translations in Verse and Prose*, in which the revised version of Trediakovsky's *A New and Brief Method for Composing Russian Verse* was published.[39] Pushkin thoroughly studied Trediakovsky's theoretical works, and the results of these studies can be seen in Pushkin's statements about him in the 1830's. Those statements reflect Pushkin's new—serious and respectful—opinion about the commonly ridiculed writer. In the essay "A Journey from Moscow to Petersburg," which was a sort of dialogue with Radishchev's *A Journey from Petersburg to Mos-*

cow, he devotes a long passage to a favorable appraisal of Trediakovsky's scholarly and literary services to Russian literature:

Trediakovsky was certainly a respectable and decent man. His philological and grammatical studies are very remarkable. He had a broader conception of Russian versification than Lomonosov and Sumarokov did. His love for Fénelon's epic does him credit, and the idea of translating it into verse, and the very choice of meter, prove his extraordinary sense of elegance. In *Tilemakhida* there are many good verses and felicitous turns of phrase. . . . Delvig often cited the following line as an example of a fine hexameter:

> Odysseus's ship,
> Dividing the waves as it ran, left her sight and
> vanished.

In general the study of Trediakovsky does more good than the study of our other old writers. Sumarokov and Kheraskov certainly are not worthy of Trediakovsky; but *habent sua fata libelli*. (11: 227)

In his praise for Trediakovsky, Pushkin refers to the expert opinion of his late classmate the poet Anton Delvig. Delvig's high opinion of Trediakovsky's imitation of the Greek epics was characteristic, since in the late 1820's he himself had experimented with ancient Greek meters. The quotation comes from the first book of *Tilemakhida*, the section in which Calypso mourns Odysseus's departure:

> Корабль Одиссеев,
> Бегом волны деля, из-очей ушел, и-сокрылся.[40]

Praise for Trediakovsky the scholar, as I attempted to demonstrate in the previous chapter, was common in the first quarter of the nineteenth century. What was new in Pushkin's characterization was that he absolutely preferred Trediakovsky's studies in the theory of verse to those of Lomonosov and Sumarokov.[41] Even more amazing was Pushkin's acknowledgment of Trediakovsky's "sense of elegance" (*chuvstvo iziashchnogo*) as revealed in the notorious *Tilemakhida*. It is significant that although Pushkin realized that his characterization contradicted the general opinion of Trediakovsky, he did not resort to the reservations so usual in praising Trediakovsky's merits. Moreover, Pushkin even identified with Trediakovsky to some degree, since he applied to both Trediakovsky and himself a remark by Terentianus, a Latin grammarian and the author of a treatise on prosody: "*Habent sua fata libelli*," "Books have their fates." He had used it in 1830 to describe what he thought was the critics' unfair treatment of his own poem *Poltava*. Then, in the unfinished essay "Refutation of the Critiques," he wrote: "*Habent sua fata libelli. Poltava* did not enjoy success. Probably it did not even deserve it, but I was spoiled by the reception given to my earlier and much weaker works; besides, this work is completely original, and this is what we sweat for" (11: 164). The fragment was published in 1831. Pushkin's attitude toward Trediakovsky had changed so much that he was not afraid to acknowledge, albeit indirectly, his own similarity to the notorious fool.

The eulogy for Trediakovsky was appropriate in "A Journey from Moscow to Petersburg." In this essay Pushkin expresses his view of Russian versification, and some of his own ideas coincide with those proposed by Trediakovsky. Thus, he approves Radishchev's attempts to reform Russian versification and his experiments with "ancient lyrical meters." As was clear to Pushkin, Radishchev was inspired in these experiments by Trediakovsky: "Radishchev, being an innovator at heart, tried to change Russian versification as well. His studies of *Tilemakhida* are remarkable. He was the first among our writers to write in ancient lyrical meters" (11: 262). Although his reasons were different from Trediakovsky's, Pushkin also shared with Trediakovsky the conviction that Russian poetry should use unrhymed verse: "I think that in time we will turn to unrhymed verse. There are too few rhymes in the Russian language. One [rhyme] induces another" (11: 263).

In 1834 Pushkin worked on an essay that he titled "On the Insignificance of Russian Literature." In the essay itself and in the outlines and rough drafts for it he commented again on Trediakovsky and his role in the history of Russian literature. These comments are remarkable. While overall they are somewhat less favorable than the appraisal in "A Journey from Moscow to Petersburg" and more along the lines of the myth about Trediakovsky the fool, they reflect some new aspects in Pushkin's understanding of the fate that Trediakovsky and his ideas suffered in the course of Russian literary development.

In the outlines and rough drafts Pushkin wrote, rather traditionally, about Trediakovsky's talentlessness, "respectable insignificance" (*pochtennaia nichtozhnost'*), impotence, and diligence
(11: 498 n. 11) and did not mention his role as a reformer of versification, ascribing it to Lomonosov: "Kantemir. Lomonosov.
Trediakovsky. Kantemir's influence is destroyed by Lomonosov;
Trediakovsky's, by his talentlessness. Trediakovsky's respectable struggle. He is defeated" (11: 494–95).[42] In the most pol-
ished version of this essay Pushkin includes the famous anecdote about Peter the Great's foretelling Trediakovsky's sad lot as
a diligent and ungifted pedant: "He [Peter] glanced upon literature absentmindedly but shrewdly. He . . . foresaw in a poor
schoolboy *the eternal toiler* Trediakovsky" (11: 269).

However, despite the characterizations inspired by the myth
about Trediakovsky the fool, the image of the poet that Pushkin
provides in this essay is far from flatly negative. In citing the anecdote about Peter the Great, Pushkin excludes from it the second, degrading part of Peter's prediction—that Trediakovsky
would never become a master writer. He leaves only the remark
about his diligence, a characteristic that was by no means derog-
atory in Pushkin's eyes at that time. Trediakovsky's unfortunate
fate, predicted by Peter, elicited no delight on Pushkin's part—
the reaction so characteristic of all other narrators of the anecdote. For Pushkin, Trediakovsky the toiler deserved compassion. In the rough version of this passage, he wrote that Peter
"predicted ~~for Trediakovsky the perpetual toiler~~ his sad lot"
(11: 498). Moreover, Pushkin repeatedly stressed his respect for
Trediakovsky. Even Trediakovsky's insignificance turned out to
be "respectable." Notably, Pushkin described Trediakovsky and
Russian literature with the same epithet: "insignificant."

It is impossible to guess what Pushkin's final characterization of Trediakovsky in this essay would have been, since its
most complete version stopped right before what was supposed
to be the exposition of Russian literary history, and the anecdote
about Peter remained the only comment on Trediakovsky. But it
seems likely that Trediakovsky's portrait would hardly have
been a conventional one. The drafts and outlines testify that instead of picturing him as a ridiculous fool, ignorant and smug,
Pushkin attempted to portray a competent, albeit not brilliant,

professional man of letters who alone among his contemporaries was a real expert in literary matters. As Pushkin put it in
one of the rough drafts for the essay: "At this time Trediakovsky
[was] the only one who knew his job" (11: 495). Pushkin admitted Trediakovsky's talentlessness but still respected the poet. He
admired the fact that in a hopeless situation, against all odds,
the poet still continued to work and struggle to fulfill his professional duties. Pushkin even used the lofty word *borenie* (struggle)
instead of the neutral *bor'ba* to describe Trediakovsky's devotion
to his profession.

The ideas of labor, diligence, and devotion to one's vocation
became, for Pushkin, the quintessence of Trediakovsky's merits.
In *Table-talk* he wrote again about Peter the Great's characterization of Trediakovsky: "Everybody knows the words of Peter the
Great when the twelve-year-old student Vasilii Trediakovsky
was introduced to him: *a perpetual toiler*! What a view! what pre-
cision in definition! Indeed, what was Trediakovsky, if not a perpetual toiler?" (12: 169). Again Pushkin chose to omit the punch
line of the anecdote: that it would be impossible for Trediakovsky to become a master. In the full version of the anecdote
Trediakovsky's diligence is incompatible with mastery, but for
Pushkin, in the 1830's, it had become a necessary part of mastery, a condition for becoming a real writer. In one of his last references to Trediakovsky, in the essay about *The Lay of Igor's Campaign*, titled "The Song of Igor's Campaign" (1836), Pushkin,
discussing the meaning of the particle *li*, appealed to his authority as a professional philologist: "In songs it sometimes has no
meaning and is inserted for meter, as are the particles *i, chto, a,
kak uzh, uzh kak* (*Trediakovsky's observation*)" (12: 148). Pushkin is
probably referring to Trediakovsky's footnote in the essay "On
Ancient, Middle, and New Russian Poetry" (1755), in which Trediakovsky describes the usage of particles (*ai, nenai, nu,* etc.) for
the sake of meter in folk songs and in church singing.[43] Pushkin, in his essay, cites Trediakovsky's opinion in support of his
own point of view—reversing completely his stand in his early
poems, where he remembered Trediakovsky only as a provider
of bad models.

As soon as Pushkin acknowledged Trediakovsky's services
to Russian literature and accepted him as an authority on liter-

ary matters, it became clear to him that Trediakovsky's reputation as a fool was validated only by tradition. In 1836, in the essay "Aleksandr Radishchev," he revealed his awareness of this tradition, mentioning that Radishchev "loved" Trediakovsky "because of the very same feeling that forced him to scold Lomonosov: his disgust for common opinions" (12: 35). Conscious of the fictional character of traditional notions about Trediakovsky, Pushkin nevertheless enjoyed the aesthetic opportunities that the myth provided and took advantage of them. In *The Captain's Daughter* (1836), Pushkin playfully reproduced the common notions about Trediakovsky at the early stage of their formation, in the 1770's. In chapter 4 of the novel the villain, Shvabrin, ridicules the poetry of the hero, Grinev. Shvabrin compares Grinev's love song to Trediakovsky's: "But, to my great vexation, Shvabrin, usually indulgent, firmly declared that my song was not good. 'Why so?' I asked him, hiding my vexation. 'Because,' he said, 'such verses are worthy of my teacher, Vasilii Kirilych Trediakovsky, and remind me very much of his love couplets" (8: 300). In this passage, Pushkin presents Trediakovsky in his usual role as the provider of bad models. However, Trediakovsky appears in Shvabrin's comments as a writer of love poetry rather than in his more prevalent role as the pedantic author of *Tilemakhida* or the translator of Rollin's histories. The mention, albeit unfavorable, of Trediakovsky's love poetry could reflect Pushkin's intention to undermine the validity of the poet's image as a pedant and thereby to challenge the myth of Trediakovsky the fool.

Pushkin played with the traditional notions about Trediakovsky the fool on several other occasions. In *Table-talk* he stressed the anecdotal nature of the story about Peter the Great and Trediakovsky, placing it right after an identical anecdote about Peter and a certain seaman whom the tsar predicted would never rise beyond the rank of petty officer (*michman*) (12: 168–69). Again, Pushkin pointedly omitted the pessimistic part of the prediction from the anecdote about Trediakovsky, but he retained it in the anecdote about the seaman. Pushkin also parodied the anecdotes about Trediakovsky in his "A Journey from Moscow to Petersburg." The serious and laudatory characterization of Trediakovsky in this essay was preceded by a typical anecdote, probably of Pushkin's own invention. In this anecdote, Lomonosov's and Trediakovsky's traditional roles were jokingly reversed:

The widow of an old professor, having heard that the talk was about Lomonosov, asked: "Which Lomonosov are you speaking about? not about Mikhailo Vasil'evich, are you? Wasn't he a shallow person! They [members of his household] would always drop in on us to borrow a coffeepot. Trediakovsky, Vasilii Kirilovich—now, he was a respectable and decent man." Trediakovsky certainly was a respectable and decent man.[44]

Trediakovsky's decency, in Pushkin's presentation, has a dual nature: *Poriadochnyi* (decent) can also mean "orderly." The word comically stresses the pedantry of Trediakovsky's approach to the chores of running his household as opposed to Lomonosov's supposed levity. As if to corroborate the myth, Pushkin invents the anecdote about Trediakovsky the pedant, but he ironically pictures this pedantry as a "good" pedantry, as thoroughness in housekeeping. This pedantry amuses Pushkin, but does not interfere with Pushkin's respect for Trediakovsky as a poet and scholar.

While Pushkin appreciated the aesthetic potential offered by the myth about Trediakovsky the fool, he refused to accept the myth as a historically correct picture of the past. Moreover, challenged by historical evidence, the myth began to lose its aesthetic appeal for Pushkin and eventually disintegrated. The features of the legend about Trediakovsky, which had been justified by its mythological spirit, acquired, in Pushkin's eyes, their direct meaning. Mythological laughter became cruel gloating, and mythological beatings, brutal torments.

In Pushkin's fragment of 1827 about Trediakovsky's and Sumarokov's alleged fight, the mythological laughter was still alive. The theme of martyrdom was only alluded to and did not prevent Pushkin from seeing the funny side, not only in the anecdote about an obviously fictional event, the poets' fray, but in the episode with Volynsky as well. The tragic outcome of the conflict with Volynsky did not prevent Pushkin from concluding the fragment with a humorous and even slighting description of the incident: "It often happened that Trediakovsky got beaten up. In the Volynsky case, it is said that once, on the occasion of some sort of celebration, he requested an ode from the court poet Vasilii Trediakovsky, but the ode was not ready, and the hot-tempered state secretary punished the careless versifier with a walking stick" (11: 53). Pushkin does not offer a single word of compassion for Trediakovsky in this passage, and, moreover, uses the word *piita* (versifier), which in the nineteenth century began to acquire a scornful overtone, instead of the neutral *poet* or the lofty *piit*. At this point, the story about Trediakovsky, beaten by everybody, easily accommodates a historical document (the record of the Volynsky case). Moreover, the mythological spirit of the story compelled Pushkin to recast the document in terms suggested by the myth about Trediakovsky the fool rather than by the document itself (probably one of Trediakovsky's complaints).

However, when Pushkin returned to this topic in his letter to Lazhechnikov of November 3, 1835, his tone was quite different, and the theme of martyrdom had developed from a humorous reference into a serious and compassionate characterization of Trediakovsky as a martyr: "In defense of Vasilii Trediakovsky, I must say I am ready to argue with you. You insult a man who in many respects deserves our regard and gratitude. In the Volynsky case, indeed, he plays the role of a martyr. His report to the Academy is extremely touching. It is impossible to read it without feeling indignant toward his tormentor" (16: 62). By this time Pushkin's opinion about Trediakovsky as a "respectable" man of letters had been firmly established. Pushkin recognized his fate as "sad" and acknowledged his services to Russian literature. Trediakovsky's lack of success no longer interfered with Pushkin's scholarly investigation of his legacy. I would suggest that Pushkin could even have identified with Trediakovsky's misfortunes to some degree. I believe that in the 1830's he felt that the humiliating role he was forced to play at the court of Nicholas I was similar to the one that Trediakovsky had played at the court of Empress Anna. In his diary entry of May 10, 1834, Pushkin discusses once again his appointment as a gentleman of the chamber, so mortifying to his pride: "But I can be a subject, even a slave, but a flunky and a jester I will not be even for the heavenly ruler [*tsar' nebesnyi*]" (12: 329). Pushkin was, of course, paraphrasing Lomonosov's words to Shuvalov, which he also quoted in "A Journey from Moscow to Petersburg." It is Lomonosov whose proud stance Pushkin wanted to imitate, but the vocabulary of his paraphrase, the appellations of "flunky" and "jester" in particular, evoke Trediakovsky as he was presented by the myth. Pushkin's helpless remark indicates that he was not sure whether he himself had not already been forced into Trediakovsky's position; therefore, he was not inclined to join Lazhechnikov in gloating over the poet's tragic fate.

In addition to personal considerations, Pushkin's new views on history, historical fact, and the proper use of historical documents were a strong incentive for Pushkin to reject Trediakovsky's traditional image as Lazhechnikov had presented it. From the late 1820's history became a focal point of Pushkin's attention as a writer. In the 1830's he became absorbed in scholarly studies of history and developed a professional attitude toward the subject.[45] The question of historical fact and historical truth, in their connection with the problem of verisimilitude in literature, was of extreme importance to Pushkin as a historian and writer. Lazhechnikov's novel compelled Pushkin to evaluate the myth about Trediakovsky the fool in the light of his new approach to these problems.

Pushkin realized that the traditional judgments about Trediakovsky, reflected in Lazhechnikov's novel, were based on rumor, hearsay, and anecdotes. Pushkin valued historical anecdotes, wrote them down, and planned to publish them in a collection known under the title *Table-talk*. Anecdotes were living history to him, preserving the spirit of the past, the personalities of participants in historical events, and their unique point of view. Moreover, as Toibin, in his study of Pushkin's interest in history in the 1830's, remarks, "The legend, folktale, and myth are constantly present in Pushkin's works, not only as a source of topics but also as a source of style and the principles of artistic thinking."[46] But, in Pushkin's opinion, in order to become part of a literary work, an anecdote had to be judged against historical fact: An artistic approach to history required conformity with historical truth in the broad sense of the word and called for a respect for historical evidence. Pushkin's own historical research in the late 1820's and 1830's took him to archives and taught him

to evaluate sources critically. In the 1830's oral tradition still retained for Pushkin its psychological and aesthetic value, but as a
source of historical information, it required verification by documents. Revealing in this respect are the results of the investigation, by the late Pushkin scholar Ilia Feinberg, of the sources of
the anecdote "Someone by the Name of Prince Kh.," which
Pushkin included in *Table-talk* (12: 169). In his essay "Pushkin's
Historical Anecdote," Feinberg convincingly demonstrates that
what Pushkin tried to present as a typical anecdote, seemingly
unreliable, proved to be based on a document, a personal letter
of Catherine the Great's, extracted by Pushkin from the archive
of his friend the poet Ivan Miatlev.[47] Common opinions about
historical events and figures did not persuade Pushkin any more,
unless they were supported by historical evidence. He included
the anecdote about Peter the Great and Trediakovsky in *Table-
talk* because his own studies of Trediakovsky demonstrated the
validity of Peter's characterization. He did not accept Lazhechnikov's interpretation of Trediakovsky's personality because it contradicted the historical documents with which he was familiar.
The verification of Lazhechnikov's presentation of historical
events with documents would, in Pushkin's opinion, undermine
the novel as a whole and expose its aesthetic weakness: "Maybe
with respect to artistry *The Ice House* is better than *The Last Page*
[Lazhechnikov's first novel], but historical truth is not observed
in it, and in time, when the Volynsky case is published, this certainly will harm your creation" (16: 62). For Pushkin, the confrontation with historical evidence destroyed the myth about
Trediakovsky the fool, which had provided material for the Trediakovsky in Lazhechnikov's novel, and the mythological beatings acquired tragic overtones. The writer's humiliation, exposed in its cruel reality, could not amuse Pushkin any more.

Pushkin apparently planned further assaults on the myth by
means of historical documents. That he wanted to publish some
material on Trediakovsky in his magazine *The Contemporary*
(1836) we know because he placed Trediakovsky's name on the
list of essays that he intended to publish in 1837.[48] Exactly what
Pushkin had in mind is not known, but the Pushkin scholar
N. N. Petrunina, in her analysis of this list, suggests that Pushkin was preparing to publish Trediakovsky's February 1740 re-

port to the Academy of Sciences about the beatings inflicted on him by Volynsky.[49] If her supposition is correct, the publication would have indicated a further development of Pushkin's new approach to the myth about Trediakovsky the fool: its refutation with a historical document.

In his confrontation with the myth about Trediakovsky the fool, Pushkin initially concentrated on the rehabilitation of the pedantic side of Trediakovsky's mythological image. He arrived at the conclusion that pedantry and excessive diligence in a writer do not deserve to be ridiculed but should elicit respect, regardless of the aesthetic results they yielded. Pushkin's understanding of literary work as requiring serious study and hard labor led him to an appreciation of Trediakovsky the pedant. In defending Trediakovsky, Pushkin was fully aware that his views contradicted the general notions about the poet as a mythological fool. He understood the legendary nature of these notions, enjoyed the aesthetic opportunities they offered to his artistic imagination, but rejected their value as historical evidence. Unlike Radishchev, who, in dealing with the myth about Trediakovsky, did not reject traditional notions about him, but reevaluated them, Pushkin destroyed the myth by confronting it with historical facts as he understood them. Radishchev did not assault the essence of the established views about Trediakovsky—the ridicule of the mythological fool—but proved that the ridiculous was not necessarily bad and, moreover, often possessed creative powers. Pushkin stripped the anecdotes about Trediakovsky of their mythological spirit and refused to laugh at Trediakovsky's fate.

Pushkin's opinion of Trediakovsky followed the main stages of his literary development and to a large extent reflected the problems that concerned him as an artist. As a young Innovator, he played with Trediakovsky's image as a chthonic monster who threatened the well-being of Russian literature, and used it in polemics with his literary opponents, the Archaists. After Pushkin abandoned the Innovators' position, Trediakovsky became, in his portrayal, a Karamzinist of the old days who bothered Lomonosov with his critiques. In Pushkin's polemics with the "seminarian" and "flunky" Nadezhdin, Trediakovsky was a plebeian who had provided models for what Pushkin considered to be Nadezhdin's tasteless plebeian critical statements. In the 1830's Trediakovsky's name entered Pushkin's meditations on the essence of literary work, and the diligent pedant became a respectable expert on literary matters. This reevaluation of traditional notions about Trediakovsky reflected the changes in Pushkin's understanding of creativity and the changes in his thinking about the position of a writer in society, as well as the changes in his approach to historical truth and historical fact, which took shape during his studies of Russian history. Pushkin realized the mythological nature of the notions about Trediakovsky supplied by contemporary culture, rejected them, and began to treat Trediakovsky as a fellow writer who had worked diligently and fruitfully for the benefit of Russian literature, was undeservedly slandered by his literary descendants, and was in need of rehabilitation by historical evidence.

Chapter 6

The Afterlife of the Myth About Trediakovsky

Pushkin's handling of the myth about Trediakovsky the fool should have killed it, for he stripped the myth of its mythological ambivalence and, therefore, of its resistance to reason and its indifference to moral judgment. However, a study of the circulation of the myth in the nineteenth and twentieth centuries suggests that the outcome of Pushkin's attempt to destroy the myth was uncertain at best. On the one hand, Pushkin's interpretation reached at least some of his contemporaries and induced them to reexamine Trediakovsky's standing in the history of Russian literature. In addition, the surge of interest in history and historical documents in the late 1840's and 1850's, which emerged independently of Pushkin's effort, once again drew attention to the inadequacy of Trediakovsky's image as a mythological fool. On the other hand, the impact of Pushkin's interpretation of Trediakovsky's legacy was diminished by the fact that the works in which he attempted to reevaluate it did not become accessible to the general public during his lifetime. "A Journey from Moscow to Petersburg" was partially published only in 1841; the fragments of the essay "On the Insignificance of Russian Literature" appeared in 1855; and "Aleksandr Radishchev," in 1857. Nor did Lazhechnikov make public his controversy with Pushkin

about Trediakovsky's image in *The Ice House* until 1856. Consequently, Pushkin's views on Trediakovsky could not have had an
immediate effect on popular opinion about the poet as a mythological fool. Furthermore, some of the eighteenth-century materials published in the 1840's and 1850's actually reinforced the
myth, because they presented the views of Trediakovsky's eighteenth-century opponents, who were by definition critical of the
unfortunate poet. The myth about Trediakovsky the fool thus
showed two opposite tendencies. Challenged by its critics and
made somewhat obsolete by the passage of time, it tended to
fade, but it retained its attractiveness as a tool in literary polemics. Its usefulness as a polemical device, in turn, perpetuated its
existence.

Among the people who paid attention to Pushkin's reevaluation of Trediakovsky's legacy was Mikhail Pogodin, the man
whom, in 1828, Pushkin humorously advised to follow Trediakovsky's example and shrug off the trouble that Bulgarin had
caused "and spit at that bitch *The Northern Bee*."[1] Pogodin became interested in Trediakovsky and his works in the 1840's.
His biographer, N. P. Barsukov, published a letter from Mikhail
Dmitriev, from which it is evident that, in 1840, Pogodin was
planning to print Trediakovsky's poetry in his magazine *The
Muscovite* (1841–55). Dmitriev urged Pogodin not to do so, arguing that Trediakovsky's poetry was a mere "curiosity" and was
"in addition very silly," which proved to Dmitriev that Trediakovsky himself was also silly.[2] Dmitriev's arguments did not im-
press Pogodin, and around 1845, while contemplating an essay
called "Russian Literature at the Beginning of Its Career [*poprish-
che*]" (never written), he wrote with sympathy about Trediakovsky: "Poor Trediakovsky. They should erect a monument to
him."[3] Pogodin further developed the ideas, promoted by Pushkin, about posterity's ingratitude toward Trediakovsky and the
necessity of confronting the myth about Trediakovsky the fool
with historical documents. He wrote in one of his later notes
concerning the poet's fate:

About Trediakovsky . . . I have now accumulated much material—
enough for a whole book—which will await a conscientious person
[*deiatel'*]. It is time to restore this character, distorted by ignorance,

thoughtlessness, and hastiness. Trediakovsky was strange indeed, ri-diculous in some ways, but in others, which are completely disre-garded, he is worthy of our respect and gratitude as the first toiler and martyr of Russian literature.[4]

Pushkin's influence can be suspected not only in the main idea about rehabilitating Trediakovsky with the help of historical evi-dence but also in the very choice of words: "respect and grati-tude," "toiler and martyr." Pogodin eventually published Tre-diakovsky's report to the Academy of Sciences about the beatings by Volynsky, which Pushkin had apparently been preparing for publication in his magazine *The Contemporary*.[5]

Pushkin's interpretation of Trediakovsky as a professional man of letters who was treated unjustly by his contemporaries and literary descendants probably inspired yet another defender of Trediakovsky: Irinarkh Vvedensky, the author of an essay that appeared in the periodical *Northern Review* (1848–50) in 1849. In this essay, Vvedensky protested against the scornful treat-ment of Trediakovsky's life and works in the introduction to his *Selected Works*, edited by Petr Perevlessky. Perevlessky, whose chief goal apparently was, as Pekarsky notes in his biography of Trediakovsky, "to maintain merriment in his readers," commit-ted, among other inaccuracies and to the advantage of his own point of view, a distortion of Pushkin's words about Trediakov-sky in "A Journey from Moscow to Petersburg." His interpreta-tion implied that Delvig had found only one good verse in all of *Tilemakhida*. Vvedensky corrected Perevlessky and, although he did not approve of Russian hexameters in principle, quoted at random from *Tilemakhida*, citing hexameter verses that, in his opinion, were "not better, but at the same time not worse, than many of the latest hexameters" of the nineteenth century. How-ever, the question of hexameters was of secondary importance to Vvedensky. For him Perevlessky's ridicule of Trediakovsky's versification symbolized the injustice the poet had received at the hands of both contemporaries and literary descendants. As a historian of literature, Vvedensky was fascinated by the ques-tion of what caused this harsh treatment, which, in his eyes, was completely uncalled for: "Yes, once again: *habent sua fata viri eruditi* [learned men have their fates]! Reading and rereading

Trediakovsky's works and looking deeply into the circumstances of his life, one asks oneself willy-nilly: what for and why has unfathomable fate haunted Trediakovsky with such relentless cruelty during his lifetime and after his death?"[6] In characterizing Trediakovsky, Vvedensky promoted Pushkin's interpretation of the poet as a diligent and learned man of letters mistreated by his opponents and literary progeny. His paraphrase of Pushkin's Latin sentence about Trediakovsky, *habent sua fata libelli*, emphasized Trediakovsky's erudition and professionalism. Like Pushkin, Vvedensky confronted the myth about Trediakovsky the fool with historical evidence—Trediakovsky's works and the facts of his life.

Even without Pushkin's direct influence, the verification of the myth about Trediakovsky through historical documents seemed imminent in the mid-nineteenth century. For Russian historians in general, and historians of literature in particular, this was a time of avid interest in historical documents and a time of numerous publications of all kinds of materials. The active publication of eighteenth-century documents by and about Trediakovsky began in the late 1840's. Some of those documents, such as archival materials regarding Trediakovsky's schooling abroad and his career at the Academy of Sciences, as well as his writings themselves, worked to destroy the myth. Other material served to reinforce it. Especially influential in this respect was the poetry written in the course of the literary polemics of the mid-eighteenth century, whose publication reintroduced the image of Trediakovsky as he had appeared in epigrams and parodies by his literary rivals—the very same image that had served as a starting point for the formation of the mythological image of Trediakovsky the fool.[7] The inability of literary historians to distinguish between the end products of past events and contemporary accounts of the same events led to the further confusion between Trediakovsky's mythological image and the historically reliable reconstruction of his personality. This confusion perpetuated Trediakovsky's reputation as a mythological fool and helped to preserve it in Russian cultural consciousness.

The archival publications and the attempts at a scholarly evaluation of Trediakovsky's legacy displeased the proponents of the myth. Lazhechnikov, whose novel, as Pushkin had pre-dicted, could be harmed by the publication of historical docu-ments, wrote with irritation in his memoir on Pushkin:

I expatiated on Trediakovsky, because since the appearance of *The Ice House*, he has become a hobbyhorse on which our reviewers gallop—to the point and not to the point. Not a few spears have been broken for the restoration of his memory. In one magazine article, written at the end of the great year of 1855, this exploit [i.e., the restoration of Tredia-kovsky's memory] was even presented as all but the most important service of our modern criticism—as if it were a matter of restoring the offended memory of, say, Karamzin or Derzhavin![8]

Lazhechnikov was not alone in his disagreement with Tre-diakovsky's defenders. The myth about Trediakovsky the fool continued to enjoy broad support in the 1840's and 1850's. One of the nineteenth-century critics who chose to ignore Pushkin's attempt to undermine traditional opinions about Trediakovsky was Vissarion Belinsky. Belinsky's view of Trediakovsky as a mean and talentless pedant took shape at the beginning of his career as a reviewer, and it remained virtually unchanged over the course of his life. Belinsky did not pay attention to the char-acterization given to Trediakovsky in Pushkin's "A Journey from Moscow to Petersburg" when the essay was published in 1841. He continued to develop instead the image of Trediakovsky that Pushkin first introduced in his polemics with Nadezhdin. Tre-diakovsky appeared in Belinsky's critical essays as a plebeian whose barren pedantry ruined all of his undertakings:

Trediakovsky, with his fruitless learning, with his talentless diligence, with his scholastic pedantry, with his unsuccessful attempts to intro-duce regular tonic meters and ancient hexameters into Russian ver-sification, with his barbaric poems and barbaric twofold translation of Rollin . . . all that was done by Trediakovsky turned out to be unsuc-cessful—even his attempts to introduce regular tonic meters into Rus-sian poetry.[9]

Belinsky translated Trediakovsky's alleged talentlessness di-rectly into baseness. He wrote with astonishing spite in support of Lazhechnikov's treatment of Trediakovsky: "Undoubtedly Trediakovsky was a low little creature: Model mediocrity with monstrous pretensions to genius necessarily presupposes a man to be either a fool or a scoundrel."[10] Belinsky seems to have hated Trediakovsky precisely for the trait that united him with the wretched poet—for his plebeian professionalism—and he hastened to dissociate himself from the notorious "professor of eloquence."

The image of Trediakovsky as a mythological fool continued to be relevant in new polemical contexts. In the 1840's it was actively used in the polemics between the Westernizers and the Slavophiles. As usual, Trediakovsky's mythological image was used to condemn literary opponents: The Westernizers accused the Slavophiles of an affinity to Trediakovsky. Stepan Shevyrev was very often compared to the notorious fool: Aleksandr Herzen called him the first professor of eloquence since Trediakovsky's time, and at least three times, Belinsky compared Shevyrev's attempts to create a Russian equivalent of Italian octaves to Trediakovsky's experiments with hexameter.[11] Literary opponents also compared Shevyrev's style to Trediakovsky's. Barsukov, in his work on Pogodin, cites the words about Belinsky that Shevyrev uttered shortly after the critic's death: "Lomonosov disliked Trediakovsky merely for his distortion of the Russian language... Belinsky does not think like Lomonosov... He even compares me with Trediakovsky because I attack Iskander's style, and I do not know how many times he has done so."[12] Shevyrev is referring to the controversy over his essay "The Dictionary of Solecisms, Barbarisms, and All Sorts of Isms in Modern Russian Literature," in which he criticized Herzen's style and which Belinsky ridiculed in 1848, in his "View of Russian Literature in 1847."[13] Shevyrev modeled the expression "to compare with Trediakovsky," *podnosit' sravnenie s Trediakovskim*, after the idiom *podnosit' duraka*, "to call someone a fool." In the spirit of the myth, Shevyrev uses Trediakovsky's name as a synonym for the word *fool*.

Naturally, the Slavophiles refused to accept Trediakovsky as their predecessor. As is evident from Shevyrev's words, they tried to present Trediakovsky as a Westernizer who distorted the Russian language with principles borrowed from Western languages. Moreover, the Slavophiles attempted to picture him as a despicable collaborator, in league with Biron, Empress Anna's German favorite, and as a foe of the Russian nation in general

and of the national genius Lomonosov in particular. Lazhechnikov, in *The Ice House*, was the first to suggest this interpretation,
and N. V. Savel'ev-Rostislavich, in his essay on the origins of
Russian statehood, developed and embellished it.[14] In the essay
"A Critical Survey, in All Respects, of the Theory of the Scan-
dinavian Origin of Russ, from 1735 to 1845," Savel'ev scolded
Trediakovsky for supporting the so-called Norman theory of the
origins of the Kievan state. In 1749–50, in the dispute over G. F.
Mueller's dissertation "The Origin of the Russian Name and Nation," Trediakovsky had indeed agreed with Mueller on the Scan-
dinavian origin of the first Kievan princes. However, Savel'ev
chose to ignore the fact that in his mature years, in the treatise
Three Discourses on Three Most Important Russian Antiquities, Trediakovsky advocated the idea of the native origins of Russian
statehood. Thus, the mythological image of Trediakovsky the
fool continued to interfere with the objective evaluation of his
views.

The review of Savel'ev's essay was the only occasion that it
occurred to Belinsky to question the validity of Trediakovsky's
mythological image and to acknowledge his own kinship with
him as a professional man of letters:

Was not it indeed a nice time when the grandee Volynsky, who is pronounced a patriot, amused himself by feeding the poor scribbler with
boxes on the ear from his own hands? Regardless of what sort of a man
Trediakovsky was, he still was a *scribbler* [*pisaka*], a *writer's* [*pisatel'*]
brother in craft, if not in talent. And the writers of our time take Volynsky's side in this shameful incident![15]

In the heat of the debate Belinsky apparently forgot that ten
years before, he himself had greeted a similar interpretation of
Trediakovsky by Lazhechnikov with the passage about Trediakovsky as a "low little creature" and "model mediocrity."

By the 1860's Trediakovsky's reputation as an exemplary bad
poet had faded somewhat. The publication of mid-eighteenth-
century polemics, the research into details of eighteenth-century
literary life, and simply the remoteness in time of the literary
clashes in which his image as a fool took shape all contributed
to the attenuation of Trediakovsky's mythological persona. For
Nikolai Chernyshevsky and Nikolai Dobroliubov, the leading

critics of the 1850's and 1860's, eighteenth-century Russian literature was more of academic interest than of any immediate aesthetic value. The struggle between Lomonosov and Trediakovsky was no longer relevant, and the names of the two rivals frequently appeared together on lists of outdated writers of the past epoch.

Nevertheless, the memory of Trediakovsky as a wretched versifier did not vanish completely, and his mythological image refused to go away. Dobroliubov remembered the formula "our poor toiler Trediakovsky." He discussed the Volynsky episode, and although he "forgave" Trediakovsky for his unseemly behavior, he called his actions "fawning" (*presmykanie*). Trediakovsky was also cited as a provider of harmful examples and an ancestor of all bad writers. Chernyshevsky mentioned Derzhavin's tastelessness, which "strongly resembled Trediakovsky's." Dobroliubov named Trediakovsky an ancestor of the Slavophiles and of all bad poets. The image of Trediakovsky the fool, although removed from the context of the myth of the "new" Russian literature, continued its existence in the Russian cultural consciousness.[16]

The myth about Trediakovsky remained a challenge to scholars of eighteenth-century Russian literature in the nineteenth and twentieth centuries. It resisted exposure by historical documents, continued to interfere with the impartial evaluation of Trediakovsky's works, and made it difficult to determine how literary ideas were transmitted. Moreover, the myth of the "new" Russian literature experienced a sudden revival among Soviet scholars of the late 1940's and early 1950's. The atmosphere of Russian nationalism, characteristic of that epoch, made the image of Lomonosov as the father of Russian literature (and Russian science, linguistics, historiography, etc.) extremely attractive. His primary enemies were the German members of the Academy of Sciences in Saint Petersburg, but the mythological images of Trediakovsky and his sidekick Sumarokov, who maliciously interfered with Lomonosov's glorious deeds, came conveniently into the picture of Lomonosov's heroic struggle for the triumph of Russian literature and science. The commentary to Lomonosov's *Complete Works*, published by the Academy of Sciences in 1950–59, demonstrates this approach.

The long and active life of the myth about the "new" Russian literature in the Russian cultural consciousness made Trediakovsky's name a synonym for failure. In this capacity it has entered the vocabulary of Russian cultural idioms. Even when the myth was still active, both Trediakovsky's defenders and his attackers tended to use his name as a common noun. Shishkov, despite his respect for Trediakovsky as a scholar, took advantage of this usage to stress Trediakovsky's exemplary talentlessness: "If you write without talent, you will be considered a Trediakovsky [or: 'will be a Trediakovsky,' *budesh' Tred'iakovsky*]." Batiushkov employed Trediakovsky's name in the plural: "O barbarians! O Krasheninnikovs! O Trediakovskys!" Viazemsky formed an adverb out of the poet's name, *po-Trediakovski*, "Trediakovsky-style." The usage did not disappear under the effort to destroy the myth. Pogodin, who proposed erecting a monument to commemorate Trediakovsky's sufferings, nevertheless remarked several years later: "It is possible to make such a fool of yourself that you'll be enlisted among the Trediakovskys [*zapishut v Tred'iakovskie*]." Perevlessky, in his introduction to Trediakovsky's *Selected Works*, claimed that Trediakovsky's name "was made into a swear word." Eventually, this usage spread beyond the sphere of literature and entered common parlance. N. V. Vol'sky, an economist and the author of memoirs about Lenin, observed about Chernyshevsky: "Chernyshevsky seemed to me some sort of Trediakovsky trying to make a career in political economy [*podvizaiushchiisia v politicheskoi ekonomii*]." [17]

Mikhail Zoshchenko, in his *Blue Book* (1935), epitomized Trediakovsky as a symbol of failure. In the section of the book that contains stories about failures, he describes Trediakovsky's conflict with Volynsky in terms borrowed from the myth about Trediakovsky, peppering the description with elements of Soviet speech. Trediakovsky, in Zoshchenko's portrayal, appears in his usual role of battered fool and provider of bad models. To stress the latter feature, Zoshchenko says that the poem Trediakovsky wrote for the wedding of jesters had become "historical" and "had entered, so to speak, the iron repository of Russian literature," as opposed to the golden repository of positive models. Zoshchenko even suggests that the poor quality of Trediakovsky's verses retrospectively justified Volynsky's ire: "Actually, for fairness' sake, it would have been better to have beaten the poet's mug after the writing of this poem. But the minister was in a hurry. And he took the trouble before it was written. And thereby, so to speak, acted, to some extent, correctly from the standpoint of pedagogics."[18]

Zoshchenko's view of Trediakovsky as an exemplary failure is not, however, straightforward, for Zoshchenko deliberately does not make clear who failed whom—Trediakovsky Russian poetry, or Russia Trediakovsky. He opens his passage on Trediakovsky's misfortune with an announcement whose wording was purposely ambiguous: "Among big failures it is possible also to register an attitude toward poetry that failed in its day" (*Iz bol'shikh neudach mozhno takzhe soschitat' v svoe vremia neudachnoe otnoshenie k poezii*). From this sentence it is not clear whether Trediakovsky failed in his aspirations to become a decent poet or whether Russian society failed to recognize Trediakovsky's poetic contributions to Russian literature and to defend him from Volynsky's assault. Moreover, Zoshchenko's reader was bound to recognize the modern Soviet notion of "social order" (*sotsial'nyi zakaz*) in Volynsky's demand that Trediakovsky write poetry to order: "And so we need you to write a little poem [*stishki*] on the occasion of this amusing wedding. And inasmuch as you are a poet, we expect of you a blossoming of your creativity in this respect." I believe that Zoshchenko, who once himself refused to fulfill the social order presented to him by the new socialist era, should have identified with the reply he ascribes to Trediakovsky: "I do not intend to squander my poetical gift on such affairs. Find yourself another poet."[19] In Zoshchenko's interpretation, the image of Trediakovsky as a failure retained its mythological ambivalence and ability to function in new cultural contexts.

In addition to converting Trediakovsky's name into a synonym for failure and talentlessness, the Russian literary consciousness has ascribed to Trediakovsky the fool the role of guardian of phenomena that lie outside the boundaries approved by traditional taste. The mythological nature of Trediakovsky's image as a fool ensured the survival of the literary principles advocated by Trediakovsky but rejected by common opinion. The memory of Trediakovsky the fool kept the memory of his "blunders" alive and made them available for further development whenever a need for alternative literary forms arose. If the Russian Formalist Viktor Shklovsky was right and the thread of evolution in art goes, not from fathers to sons, but from uncles to nephews, this explains why the works of Trediakovsky, the eternal "uncle" of Russian literature, continue to be a reservoir of unconventional ideas and stimuli for changing the status quo in literature and why his name continues to be used as a declaration of one's artistic independence.[20]

From the very beginning of the existence of the myth, the image of Trediakovsky the fool served to promote unconventional metrics. To be sure, the comical nature of his mythological persona repelled prospective followers, but once the reformers felt the real need for innovation in metrics, they turned to Trediakovsky's legacy for guidance. I might mention Radishchev, Gnedich, and Pushkin, all of whom arrived at the understanding that Trediakovsky's ideas about versification were indispensable for them in their own quest for metrical innovations.

Trediakovsky's role as a supplier of stylistic ideas was less prominent, for his reputation as an exceptionally bad stylist constituted the core of his mythological image and thus made the thought of dependence on his stylistic concepts especially repulsive. Even Radishchev, despite all his regard for Trediakovsky and despite the obvious similarities in their stylistic experiments, could not bring himself to acknowledge Trediakovsky's merits as a stylist. Nevertheless, Trediakovsky's literary descendants turned to his legacy, albeit secretly, for stylistic innovations. Radishchev was not alone in his unacknowledged indebtedness to Trediakovsky. Karamzin and his friend and colleague Aleksandr Petrov were familiar with Trediakovsky's works, notably with his translation *A Voyage to the Isle of Love* and its "proto-Karamzinist" introduction. Shishkov apparently looked for inspiration in Trediakovsky's *Three Discourses on Three Most Important Russian Antiquities*, as probably did the Slavophiles, at least in their attempts at etymology. Trediakovsky the fool, the provider of bad models rejected by everyone, remained the source of creative ideas for writers who sought to change stylistic norms.

Trediakovsky's mythological image maintained its significance as a supplier of unconventional literary ideas well into the twentieth century. Moreover, the twentieth century, with its love of extravagance and shocking effects, even savored the taste of scandal that remained attached to the name of Trediakovsky. It was not only out of a desire to restore justice to the unfortunate poet by introducing the reader to his smooth compositions in French that Mikhail Kuzmin translated the early French poems by Trediakovsky. Surely he enjoyed the discrepancy that he created by juxtaposing his elegant imitations of French love poetry of the Regency period with the image of the rude and ugly fool, beaten and despised by everyone, but still ceaselessly writing his barbaric poems in Russian.

Invoking Trediakovsky's name was the way to declare one's artistic independence or, rather, unconventionality. The Russian Futurists, particularly Vadim Shershenevich, who quoted Trediakovsky in his critical essays, and Dmitrii Kriuchkov, who wrote a sonnet about the poet claiming that those who do not appreciate him do not deserve the title of poet themselves, as well as the Imagists, used Trediakovsky's name with precisely this function.[21] Trediakovsky's reputation as a difficult, obscure poet, concerned not so much with euphony but with the expressivity of formal elements, even at the expense of smoothness, and unafraid of risky experimentation, fascinated the Futurists and the Imagists no less than it had attracted Radishchev more than a hundred years earlier. Even more captivating for them was the image of Trediakovsky the fool itself. For the twentieth-century modernists, it became a symbol of provocative creativity, of revolutionary disregard for tradition, and of contempt for conventional success.

It was in this function that the Imagist Anatolii Mariengof employed Trediakovsky's image in *A Conspiracy of Fools* (1921).[22] In this play (a tragedy by—or of—Mariengof, *tragediia Mariengofa*, as the author defined its genre), Trediakovsky, having received a box on the ear from Empress Anna, decides that such an insult can be cleansed only with blood and becomes the head of a conspiracy against the autocrat. The conspirators, who include the empress's jesters and dwarfs, plan to assassinate her. Despite Trediakovsky's ingenuity, the conspiracy fails, and the jesters face torture and death.

The Trediakovsky portrayed by Mariengof is far removed

from the historical Trediakovsky. The playwright worked instead with the traditional image of Trediakovsky as a bad poet. He was apparently familiar with the myth of Trediakovsky the fool, especially with Lazhechnikov's version. He knew precisely which details gave the legend its mythological character and stressed them in his portrayal of the poet. Thus, he apprehended the connection of Trediakovsky's mythological image with commedia dell'arte. At one point in the play, when the fools think that the conspiracy has been exposed, Trediakovsky suggests that they imitate a commedia dell'arte performance in order to confuse the secret police (pp. 59–60).

Mariengof was conscious of the ambivalence of Trediakovsky's image in the myth, its lofty and low aspects. His Trediakovsky displays the features of a jester, of a saintly fool, and of a poet inspired by the muses. It is no accident that Trediakovsky, in Mariengof's interpretation, becomes the head of the conspiracy of fools. Mariengof presents the coalition as eternal and natural: "Let the poet's association with fools be glorified in the centuries to come!" (p. 49). Notably, the coalition includes not only jesters but also saintly fools (*iurodivye*) and martyrs who sacrifice their lives for the conspiracy. At the same time, Mariengof endows Trediakovsky with such attributes of genius as an extraordinary childhood under the patronage of the muses:

> Так учит нас с издетства вдохновенье,
> Такую песнь поет нам муза, качая колыбель.
> О, Муза. Муза.
> Единственная мать, кормилица и повитуха…
>
> (pp. 45–46)

Inspiration teaches us thus from childhood, the muse sings us such a song while rocking the cradle. O Muse, Muse. The only mother, nurturer, and midwife.

In his portrayal of Trediakovsky, Mariengof even refuses to distinguish clearly between the notorious fool and the father of Russian literature, Lomonosov. Trediakovsky's poem in the play pictures Empress Anna as the incarnation of Russia and does so in explicitly sensual terms:

> Широко, как врата, раздвинуты у монархини
> ноги,

На двух материках ступни стоят,
России царственную тогу
Покорно лижет Балтика и Каспий.

(pp. 40–41)

The monarch's legs are parted widely like the gates, the feet
stand on two continents, the Baltic and Caspian seas humbly
lap at Russia's regal toga.

This image in fact very much resembles Lomonosov's famous
ode of 1748 "On the Anniversary of Empress Elizabeth's Ascending the Throne," which presents the empress as an embodiment of Russia and also has distinct sexual overtones:

Седит и ноги простирает
На степь, где Хину отделяет
Пространная стена от нас;
Веселый взор свой обращает
И вкруг довольства исчисляет,
Возлегши лактем на Кавказ.[23]

[Russia] sits and spreads her legs upon the steppe where
China is separated from us by the extended wall; she turns her
lively eyes and takes stock of the prosperity around her, lean-
ing with her elbow upon the Caucasus.

Mariengof, in his play, was interested not so much in the Tredia-
kovsky-Lomonosov controversy as in emphasizing the lofty aspect of Trediakovsky's mythological image. For this purpose,
Trediakovsky's image could easily borrow features from the
image of Lomonosov, the father of Russian literature—or, if we
take into account the parodical nature of Mariengof's imitation
of Lomonosov's ode, lend its foolish elements to the lofty image
of Lomonosov.

As a true poet, Mariengof's Trediakovsky was bound to remain alone: "Only the son of the muse is not in the herd: He
himself pastures winds and seas" (p. 46). Mariengof thus interprets Trediakovsky's infamy in future centuries as the fatal consequence of his vocation, a sign of his belonging to the guild of
poets:

О, судьба, острей точи
Железные мечи

Всенародной неблагодарности
И золотые тернии
На венце славы.   (p. 18)

O fate, sharpen the iron swords of the national ingratitude and
the golden thorns in the crown of glory.

Mariengof endows this lonely and tragic Christ-like character with autobiographical features. As T. L. Nikol'skaia notes in
an article on Mariengof and Trediakovsky, the characterization
that one of the fools gives of Trediakovsky, "the one who gets
intoxicated with poetry," *stikhami p'ianstvuet*, refers to the title
of Mariengof's collection, *I Vaunt of My Poetry, Stikhami chvan-
stvuiu*.[24] It is important to remember, however, that the allusion
to drinking reflects an aspect of Trediakovsky's mythological image introduced by Lomonosov, namely, his alleged alcoholism.
It also is reminiscent of the opening line of his "Ode on the Surrender of the City of Gdansk," *Koe trezvoe mne pianstvo* (What a
sober intoxication). In any case, Mariengof proclaimed his kinship with the notorious fool and his pride in having Trediakovsky for his alter ego. He used Trediakovsky's mythological image to declare his contempt for conventional literary values, for
the winners in the realm of art, and for the mob who despise
poets and beat them up. Trediakovsky's tragedy became Mariengof's tragedy. The image of Trediakovsky the fool once again
demonstrated its versatility and adaptability to a new literary
situation.

In recent times three prominent Soviet writers have been attracted to Trediakovsky and the story of his life: Vadim Shefner,
who, in 1967, wrote a cycle of poems dedicated to the poet; Vera
Panova, who, in 1968, devoted a play to the Volynsky episode;
and Iurii Nagibin, who, in the 1970's, wrote two novellas about
Trediakovsky's early years in Astrakhan, Moscow, and Europe
and his conflict with Volynsky. All three writers were influenced
by the myth about Trediakovsky the fool, although each in a different manner. Each retains some features of his mythological
image, his talentlessness perhaps, or his faintheartedness in the
face of ordeals, the beatings, the ambivalent creativity, the kinship with jesters, or the connection with the realm of death, but
all three reveal the positive, heroic potential of his mythological

image as well. Even while portraying Trediakovsky as a humble and pitiful jester, they emphasize his role as a provider of positive examples for future Russian writers. Shefner, Panova, and Nagibin seem to be fascinated by the fact that abjectness and pride, wretchedness and awareness of one's vocation, technical helplessness and richness of aesthetic ideas—all the features that the ambiguous image of Trediakovsky as a mythological fool allow one to explore—can evidently coexist in a poet.

Of the three writers, Shefner uses the myth about Trediakovsky in the most constructive way. He savors the mythological spirit of the traditional notions about Trediakovsky and makes them part of his interpretation of the poet's role in the history of Russian literature. Shefner portrays Trediakovsky as a creator of Russian poetry but stresses "chthonic" features of his image, his connections with the "pre-cultured" period of Russian belles lettres. Thus, he calls Trediakovsky "the poet of the zero cycle" (*poet nulevogo tsikla*), that is, a poet working before the beginning of literary history.[25] Trediakovsky is the one who is destined to lead Russian literature "from the darkness of the hollows to the mountain heights" (p. 59). He guides the still blind Russian muse, and the tragedy of his fate is that the muse will "send him to humiliation [*poruganie*]" upon gaining her sight. Unlike the eighteenth- and nineteenth-century interpreters of Trediakovsky's mythological image, Shefner presents Trediakovsky's alleged connections with primordial chaos in a positive light, but these connections still distinguish the poet as a chthonic creature and reveal his links to death and the underworld. Thus, in Shefner's characterization, Trediakovsky "conducts his work" underground, "at the level of grave worms, at the line of subsoil waters" (p. 62). His cruel fate will lead him to disgrace (*opala*), which is depicted as "basement darkness" (*podval'nyi mrak*). The theme of Trediakovsky's death is for Shefner such an important point in his biography that two poems out of eleven are entirely dedicated to this event.

The mythological nature of Trediakovsky's portrayal in Shefner's poems also reveals itself in the ambiguity of his image as the initiator of Russian literature. His very gift is in doubt. Shefner depicts Trediakovsky as a true poet who chose his occupation because he was destined for, and could not escape, his vocation (pp. 59, 60, 63). At the same time, the muse that inspires him is still blind and voiceless and wanders in darkness (p. 59). Trediakovsky's poetic work is rough, unskilled (*chernaia*; p. 62). In addition, his dignity as a poet and a creator of Russian literature is compromised by his obsequiousness and fawning. However, the negative features of his image do not disqualify him as a poet and the creator of Russian literature:

> В своей угодливости вязкой
> Порою жалок ты, пиит.
> Но за одическою маской
> Взор прорицателя горит.
>
> (p. 63)

Poet, in your sticky obsequiousness you are sometimes piteous. But behind your odic mask there blaze the eyes of a prophesier.

Shefner gives Trediakovsky Lomonosov's most usual attribute: the title of odic poet. This blurs the differences between the recognized father of the "new" Russian literature and his antagonist. The usual formula (Trediakovsky might have his merits, but . . .") is reversed here, and the primary importance of Trediakovsky's poetic gift is asserted over his weaknesses as a human being living in a certain historical period. Those weaknesses even serve to his advantage. In Shefner's interpretation, it is precisely the negative traits of Trediakovsky's image and his cruel fate that ensure his eternal fame:

> Но чем торопливей хоронят,
> Тем дольше их помнят потом.
>
> (p. 66)

And the more hastily they bury them [the poets], the longer they remember them.

The plural pronoun "them," *ikh*, emphasizes that the portrait of Trediakovsky created by Shefner has a general meaning, that in the poet's image as a mythological fool he sees the eternal features of all poets—first and foremost himself. Indeed, the author, like Mariengof before him, identifies with Trediakovsky:

> И, словно будущим рожденный,
> Из прошлого—навстречу мне—

Гонец шагает, отраженный
В зеркально–зыбкой глубине.

Он из былого, из былого
Спешит, бесхитростный связной,
Неся неведомое слово,
Еще не сказанное мной.   (p. 67)

And, as if born of the future, toward me from the past comes a messenger, reflected in the shifting depths of the mirror. He hurries from the past, from the past, a naive messenger who carries the unknown word that I have yet not said.

Shefner names Trediakovsky the forefather of all Russian poets—a move made possible by the myth about Trediakovsky the fool, which preserved for us, along with Trediakovsky's negative image, his potential to assume the lofty role of the creator of Russian literature.

Panova's play, *Trediakovsky and Volynsky*, also reveals its author's familiarity with the details of the myth about Trediakovsky the fool, although this familiarity seems to come mostly from Lazhechnikov's novel, on which the play heavily depends for both historical facts and their interpretation. For example, as in Lazhechnikov's novel, Panova describes Volynsky's encounter with Trediakovsky as not particularly violent—almost a joke. When Trediakovsky is beaten with sticks, he comically screams: "I am a Russian poet! I gave life and law to tonic versification! I am a professor of eloquence!"[26] The poet's indignation, however, is not justified in the play: The servants beat him halfheartedly. To emphasize the comical aspect of the beating, a jester arrives immediately afterward and mocks the poet's cries. Panova borrows from Lazhechnikov the very method of depicting Trediakovsky the fool, and like Lazhechnikov, she is not concerned with historical truth: In the quoted passage, Trediakovsky's assertion that he is a professor of eloquence is an obvious anachronism, since he became a professor in 1745, five years after Volynsky was executed. The author notifies the reader in her introductory remarks (p. 294) that she does not feel bound by historical facts in her play, but the important point is that she allows the same inaccuracies in her description of Trediakovsky that can be found in Lazhechnikov's novel. Her reason for including those inaccuracies is similar to Lazhechnikov's: She too works with the mythological image of Trediakovsky (of which the professorship is a prominent feature) rather than with his real biography, and the image does not require fidelity to facts. Since she derives her portrait of Trediakovsky from the myth, Panova, like Lazhechnikov, uses commedia dell'arte devices. Thus, she twice refers to the wart that supposedly decorated Trediakovsky's face, presenting it as a sign by which the notorious fool can be easily recognized: "Perhaps I should call that one, with a wart?" Volynsky's servant suggests. Volynsky immediately understands whom he means: "Trediakovsky? Call him" (p. 299; cf. p. 302).

However, Panova's interpretation of mythological notions about Trediakovsky differs from Lazhechnikov's in many important ways. She emphasizes positive features of his image as a fool. Laughable and beaten up, he is still a poet. His muse is an old maiden—"not a very young person, but rather an elderly one in a Greek tunic" (p. 303)—but she is a real muse, inspiring and exacting. Trediakovsky, in Panova's interpretation, is akin to jesters (pp. 296, 305, 327), but his firm belief in his own vocation is presented in such a manner that the reader feels obliged to take it seriously. Finally, the way his role in the Volynsky affair is depicted differs sharply from Lazhechnikov's presentation. Unlike the malicious character in *The Ice House*, Trediakovsky forgives his tormentor and, after he is executed, laments the cruelties of this world, asks for safety for himself, and prays for Volynsky's soul (pp. 342–43). This monologue, full of tragic and pathetic overtones, effectively destroys the mythological image of Trediakovsky, with which Panova works in her play, and reveals—rather unexpectedly—the human side of Trediakovsky the fool. The reader is suddenly compelled to perceive this character as a personage in a historical drama rather than in commedia dell'arte. The reader is, however, perplexed by the change and fails to uncover the moment when the transformation of genres takes place or its justification. Panova pays dearly for her indebtedness to Lazhechnikov and her failure to recognize a mythological fool in Lazhechnikov's character. Placed in the context of a historical drama, the myth compromises conventions of the genre and undermines the play's verisimilitude.

Nagibin, in his stories "A Runaway" and "The Isle of Love," clearly sets out to destroy the myth about Trediakovsky the fool and to create instead a realistic account of the poet's life. In fulfilling this task, he finds himself writing about episodes for which there is insufficient historical evidence. In his search for details he is compelled to turn to the very notions about Trediakovsky that he is trying to destroy. Among other things, he depends on the myth for the description of Trediakovsky's appearance and borrows from it the features of Trediakovsky's image as a fool, warts, round face, and all.[27] The myth supplies Nagibin with material for the depiction of the young Trediakovsky's conflict with his father: The old priest is upset with the oddities that his son displays from childhood. These oddities clearly indicate the boy's unusual destiny, whatever it may be—to become a poet or a mythological fool. The myth helps Nagibin to interpret Trediakovsky's devotion to his vocation: The traditional anecdote about the meeting of the future poet and Peter the Great and its significance for Trediakovsky's destiny is analyzed twice (pp. 52–53, 122–23). The myth even offers an insight into Trediakovsky's unconscious: Nagibin's Trediakovsky, as if in anticipation of his cruel fate, is afraid of fires (p. 74).

In the spirit of the myth, Nagibin's Trediakovsky, although a true poet, is nevertheless eccentric and akin to jesters (pp. 52, 92, 128, 132, etc.). Despite the heroism that he displays in pursuing his destiny, despite his commendable devotion to his vocation, for which he bravely sacrifices his personal happiness, despite his setting positive models for Russian literature (the system of syllabo-tonic versification and the compassion for human suffering that, in Nagibin's view, is characteristic of Russian literature), despite even the lofty Romantic elements in Nagibin's portrayal of Trediakovsky as a lonely and tormented human being, but a happy one because he is chosen—despite all these heroic traits Trediakovsky still remains a familiar laughable fool in many episodes in Nagibin's stories. The ambiguity of his image as the true poet and the creator of Russian literature is reflected in the epithet "Forerunner" (*Predtecha*; p. 155)—the other name for John the Baptist—that is, somebody who comes before a true hero. Moreover, in the first novella Trediakovsky actually misinterprets his vocation, abandoning his first wife Fedos'ia (called in the story a lofty variant of this name, Feodosiia) and running away from her to Moscow and then to Paris in order to fulfill his destiny as he understands it:

Trediakovsky was not as good in respect of poetic talent and just the skill of composing poetry as Lomonosov and Sumarokov, but he was the only one among all of his contemporaries to have a heartbreaking lyrical note in his poetry. And this note broke through all the awkwardness of his heavy verses—[it was] pure, resonant, and cordial—here in the poem about Paris, here in a song about a little boat that sails away to sea, here in a dirge about the faraway fatherland, here, completely unexpectedly, in some sort of absurd and ugly rhymed nonsense. . . . He did not recognize his muse and passed it by. And she was near his heart—poetry herself, love herself. Ah, if he had abandoned . . . all of gallant, literary, theatrical, scholarly Paris, which had already given him everything that it could, and returned to Astrakhan, clung to Feodosiia's tormented bosom, laved it at least with a last tear, Russian poetry would have received its first lyrical poet.

Apparently, it was not to be! (p. 113)

Nagibin obviously wanted to rehabilitate his hero. Even deficiencies that he perceived in Trediakovsky's skill as a poet did not divert Nagibin from this task. But he could not shake off the influence of the myth about Trediakovsky the fool and was overwhelmed by it. He was forced to make the myth part of his historical novellas, which he apparently saw as an attempt to replace a historically incorrect and unjust portrayal of Trediakovsky as the worst Russian poet with an adequate description of him as a human being—neither especially good nor very bad, gifted, but limited by his disposition and by the epoch in which he lived. The myth about Trediakovsky the fool proved to be more powerful than Nagibin could withstand, despite his skill as a writer of historical novellas.

Efforts by several generations of Trediakovsky's defenders to the contrary, the image of the mythological fool, the "uncle" of Russian literature, has ultimately proved indestructible. It has maintained its existence in the Russian cultural consciousness for more than two centuries, serving as a tool in polemics, a reservoir of fresh ideas, a means of declaring one's refusal to accept conventional aesthetic values. It has prompted Russian writers

to ponder the writer's place in society and the writer's responsibility to follow his or her vocation. The myth about Trediakovsky continues to regenerate itself. It may still prove productive
for future generations of Russian writers.

Conclusion

Several factors determined the appearance and content of the myth of the beginning of the "new" Russian literature. The spirit of eighteenth-century Russian culture in general, prone to mythologizing, made its emergence possible. The literary polemics of the middle of the century, inspired partly by the mythological spirit of the epoch and partly by the idiosyncrasies of contemporary aesthetics, suggested the images of the heroes of the myth, while personal and biographical factors played an important role in the selection of its main heroes. The development of these primal images into full-scale mythological characters was shaped by the requirements of the myth itself and by the cultural context in which the myth circulated.

Once the myth of the beginning of the "new" Russian literature formed, it began to play an active part in the literary life of the late eighteenth and early nineteenth centuries. The images of its main characters retained their mythological vitality, but acquired fresh meaning in the context of the new literary ideas and served as effective critical tools in the new literary discussions. Trediakovsky's image as a mythological fool was even more useful than Lomonosov's in this respect. Its double nature, heroic and comical, made Trediakovsky's name particularly suitable for the condemnation of alien literary notions, as well as for the introduction of fresh literary ideas by authors who were not repelled by its comical features.

In its first function, the mythological image of Trediakovsky was used in the polemics between the Archaists and the Innovators. Playing upon the notions about Trediakovsky as a proponent of outdated language and a foe of reason and progress, the Innovators, especially the members of Arzamas, employed the image of Trediakovsky the fool in their criticism of the Archaists in general and the Besedists in particular. Some of the Archaists tried to repulse these attacks and rehabilitate Trediakovsky, but their own ambiguous attitude toward him did not allow these attempts to succeed.

Radishchev was among the literary figures of the late eighteenth and early nineteenth centuries who accepted the comicality of Trediakovsky's image and converted its negative power into a creative force. Pushkin, in turn, having initially used Trediakovsky's name in the traditional way as a symbol of talentlessness and stylistic clumsiness, eventually refused to take Trediakovsky's mythological image as the correct reflection of its historical prototype. He tried to destroy the myth by confronting it with historical documents and exposing its cruelty and injustice.

The myth about Trediakovsky the fool refused to die, however. Despite Pushkin's attempts to undermine its validity and the efforts of historians of literature, who in the late 1840's started to publish historical materials damaging to the myth, it continued to serve as a tool in literary polemics well into the twentieth century. Moreover, Russian writers persisted in using it to announce their artistic independence and adherence to idiosyncratic literary principles.

The fate that Vasilii Trediakovsky and his legacy have suffered in the course of Russian cultural history presents an important lesson to a historian of literature. This lesson is manifold. First of all, the story of Trediakovsky forces students of literature to reexamine once again the criteria they use to assign ratings to literary figures of the past. It stresses the fact that we cannot rely on the testimonials of contemporaries alone, even if they seem impartial and reasonable. It demonstrates that the testimonials of contemporaries might be influenced not only by their own individual biases and idiosyncrasies but also by generally accepted legends concerning the reputation of the writer in question. The prevalence of a legend could assure us of its faithfulness to the reality it represents, but all it proves is the attractiveness of the legend to a large number of people. For several generations of Russian writers the myth of the beginning of the "new" Russian literature was a convenient and convincing way to describe the history of eighteenth-century Russian literature. This myth supported Trediakovsky's reputation as the most wretched poet of all time and prevented the impartial evaluation of his legacy.

In certain cases we cannot rely on our own criteria for evaluation either. These criteria might be inapplicable to the phenomena that we seek to evaluate, because the phenomena lie outside the path of development approved by tradition. Our criteria, be they conventions of taste or modern methods of evaluation based on statistics or psychology, depend on the tradition in which we have been brought up, and are irrelevant with regard to works that deviate from this tradition. The key to Trediakovsky's poetics is lost, and modern Russian readers cannot appreciate his works. Instead, even the most sophisticated of these readers substitute the image of a comical pedant, extracted from cultural memory, for the historical Trediakovsky, and parodies of his works for his actual poems. They laugh at the result, sure that they are laughing at the real Trediakovsky. The myth, together with the powerful literary tradition fostered by Trediakovsky's opponent Lomonosov, stands between us and Trediakovsky; it interferes with our ability to evaluate his works and forces us to deal with his reputation rather than with his works per se.

Putting aside the question of whether it pays to assign ratings to the writers of the past, I would like to emphasize that Trediakovsky's case convincingly demonstrates that it certainly pays to investigate why particular ratings were assigned by contemporaries or immediate literary descendants. Research into the ways in which reputations are formed introduces us to the workings of literary life and allows us to examine its idiosyncrasies in great detail. In comparison with the study of what we consider to be the real facts about literary figures, the study of reputations tells us important things about the general principles governing the emergence of historical accounts of the past.

Specifically, the myth about Trediakovsky the fool illustrates the vitality of the ancient patterns of thinking that still underlie the formation of collective notions and that interfere with modern, logical thinking far more often than we would care to acknowledge. As Ernst Cassirer, who saw the mythmaking ability as a manifestation of dangerous irrational forces at work in modern mass consciousness, wrote in his book *The Myth of the State*: "For myth has not been really vanquished and subjugated. It is always there, lurking in the dark and waiting for its hour and opportunity. This hour comes as soon as the other binding forces of man's social life, for one reason or another, lose their strength and are no longer able to combat the demonic mythical powers."[1] Whether dangerous, as Cassirer and Roland Barthes believe, or beneficial, as some of Joseph Campbell's and Mircea Eliade's assertions suggest, the ability to create myths manifests itself in modern societies in more ways than one. For my analysis, however, the most important is the part that mythopoetic forces take in the formation of historical accounts of the past. Rafael Patai, a Hebrew scholar and the author of a book on the role of myths in modern societies, observes with reference to the mythopoetic tendencies in modern communal consciousness: "We can see the same [mythopoetic] forces at work in transforming the historical facts of individual lives into mythical accounts and the real figures of men who played certain roles in modern history into mythical images, as soon as their deaths enable such metamorphoses to set in."[2] My material suggests that the last condition, although it certainly speeds the formation of the myth, does not necessarily hold, but the gist of Patai's statement agrees with what the fate of Trediakovsky the fool teaches us.

This last lesson could be especially useful for a student of Russia. Mythmaking can be observed in all cultures, and literary histories of various nations include figures similar to Trediakovsky the fool or Lomonosov the father of Russian literature. One good example is the excessively harsh evaluation of Jean Chapelain, whose reputation was established by Boileau and his allies in the course of bitter polemical exchanges with their literary predecessors and developed by following generations of French writers into a full-scale portrait of a model failure. Although Chapelain's image as the worst French poet of all time never reached the mythological proportions of Trediakovsky's image as a fool, it is a fair enough parallel to Trediakovsky's parodical persona. To point to candidates for the role of father of a national literature, such as Dante or Adam Mickiewicz, is equally apt.

However, it seems safe to suggest that, compared to other ethnic groups, Russians have been especially prone to myth-making in the course of constructing their cultural history. In addition to the myths about Trediakovsky and Lomonosov, one might mention the extraordinary place assigned to Pushkin. His reputation as the best Russian poet, dear to the soul of every Russian, sometimes puzzles the non-Russian reader. The emotional affinity that Russians feel toward Pushkin is amazing. In February 1987, a century and a half after the poet's death, crowds of his admirers wept outside his last residence in Leningrad. Their grief was still fresh in their hearts. The quality of Pushkin's works alone certainly cannot account for such devotion to his memory, but the distinct mythological overtones of his image in Russian cultural memory can probably help to explain it. Indeed, Pushkin not only has a reputation as the best Russian poet, but he is also the one who, in the words of Sergei Fomichev, a Pushkin scholar, "comes to earth and says, 'This thing is called such-and-such, that thing so-and-so.'"[3] Giving names to things is a typical function of a culture hero. At the same time, Pushkin is frequently evoked by Russians as a comical figure. Thus, he is the hero of numerous anecdotes, most of them obscene. These anecdotes apparently served as a model for the Russian absurdist Daniil Kharms, who, in a series of sketches, portrayed Pushkin as a laughable fool and a total failure.[4] It is noteworthy that Pushkin, like Trediakovsky, can appear in the role of an uncle. His name frequently serves as a substitute for a word *uncle* in expressions of the type "Who will do that, someone's uncle?"—meaning that there is no one but the addressee to take up some burdensome task—and "Who did that, perhaps someone's uncle?"—meaning that one's guilt is clear beyond any doubt so there is no point in denying it. This usage has found its way into Russian fiction. Mikhail Bulgakov parodies it in his novel *The Master and Margarita* (1928–40). One character in this novel, a building superintendent, has a habit of asking his tenants: "And who will pay the rent, Pushkin?" or "So, Pushkin has stolen a light bulb from the stairwell?" or "So, Pushkin will buy heating oil?"[5] A modern Russian prose writer, Venedikt Erofeev, has also taken advantage of this usage. Dasha, a character in his book *Moscow to the End of the Line* (1969), haunts her lover with a question about their—yet unborn and even unconceived—children: "And who will raise the kids for you? Pushkin, perhaps?"[6] Pushkin's image in Russian culture has, thus, two distinct hypostases, that of a culture hero, an ancestor of the community in its present state ("a blood relative," as Fomichev put it in his interview with Felicity Barringer), and that of a fool. This combination suggests a classic mythological personage with a dual line of behavior, both lofty and low—namely, a trickster.[7] It seems ironical that Pushkin, who worked so hard to destroy the myth about Trediakovsky the fool, has himself received in Russian cultural memory the role of a mythological ancestor.

Writers in general are far more charismatic figures in Russian culture than in modern Western cultures. The huge crowds that gather for a poetry reading or for the funeral of a popular poet—as for that of the poet and singer Vladimir Vysotsky—bear testimony to their charisma. The natural parallel with popular cult figures in the West does not work too well. Russians require much more from their heroes—first of all, they expect them to resolve social and existential problems. The confidence in the writer's power to influence the world manifests itself in every Russian writer's belief that he or she is indeed destined to change things for the better, as well as in the audience's conviction that the writer really is capable of doing just that and the authorities' fear of the writer's spiritual power over people— hence the file of martyrs persecuted by the authorities in the history of Russian literature, from Archpriest Avvakum, to Radishchev, to Nikolai Gumilev, to Osip Mandelstam, to Anna Akhmatova, to Boris Pasternak, to Joseph Brodsky, and hence the self-destructive behavior of writers who believe they have failed to fulfill their destiny: Nikolai Gogol, Mikhail Lermontov, Sergei Esenin, Vladimir Maiakovsky, Marina Tsvetaeva, Mikhail Zoshchenko, and many others. The unrealistic expectations that Russians have of their writers recall the ancient belief in the poet's magic powers. This belief seems to survive somehow in the Russian cultural consciousness and to contribute to the affinity for mythmaking so prominent in Russian culture.

Outside the realm of literature, I would like to recall such manifestations of mythological thinking in the Russian cultural consciousness as its fascination with power figures, such as Ivan the Terrible, Peter the Great, and Stalin, the self-proclaimed "father of nations." I would like to call attention to the idolization of Lenin, which has evolved into a typical ancestor cult. The Russians' sensitivity to cultural and political change, pointed out by Lotman and Uspensky, their tendency to comprehend change either as the ultimate destruction of the existing order or as the beginning of an absolutely new phase of national development, echoes the ancient need for the periodic renewal of community life that manifested itself in the symbolic destruction of the existing social structure and its reconstruction on new grounds.

Reference Matter

Notes

For full authors' names, titles, and publication data see the Works Cited, pp. 287–300.

Introduction

1. See Zoshchenko, *Izbrannoe*, 1: 317–19, for the written version of the legend. Cf. a variant of the same plot circulating in oral tradition: Little Volodia passed gas, blamed it on a cat, repented, and would never fart again.

2. Wellek, p. 49; see also p. 52.

3. For recent discussions of this set of problems see Fish; B. H. Smith; and Tompkins, esp. chap. 7.

4. Kunik, ed., 1: 205; originally in French.

5. I quote the eulogy from *M. V. Lomonosov v vospominaniiakh sovremennikov*, p. 38.

6. Empress Elizabeth, in 1750, ordered Lomonosov and Trediakovsky to write a tragedy apiece. The former wrote *Tamira and Selim* and *Demofont* and the latter, *Deidamia*. See Vissarion Belinsky's opinion of Lomonosov as a historian: "In respect to history he was as much of an ass as Trediakovsky" (a Feb. 17, 1847, letter to V. P. Botkin, in Belinsky, 12: 331).

7. The epitaph, whose author was I. K. Golenevsky, was published in Russian and Latin by N. I. Novikov in his *An Attempt at a Historical Dictionary of Russian Writers* (1772). The words about Lomonosov

as the initiator of syllabo-tonics and as a playwright are presented only in the Latin version.

8. Originally in German; I translate from the Russian translation published in Kunik, ed., 2: 401–2. I will frequently refer to Jacob von Staehlin's accounts of Lomonosov's life given in "A Précis of Lomonosov's Eulogy" (1765; Kunik, ed., 2: 383–87) and "Traits and Anecdotes for Lomonosov's Biography" (Kunik, ed., 2: 390–405). Staehlin, contrary to his claims, was never Lomonosov's friend, but rather his enemy, which makes his praises of Lomonosov's talents and achievements especially precious for the purposes of my analysis. Staehlin's pet idea, that Lomonosov borrowed his revolutionary versification from J. C. Guenther, did not interfere with the formation of an idealized image of Lomonosov as long as Lomonosov retained the title of the first poet to introduce German principles of versification to Russia.

9. Elagin, *Opyt povestvovaniia o Rossii* (first published in 1803); I quote from *M. V. Lomonosov v vospominaniiakh sovremennikov*, pp. 86, 88.

10. Karamzin, *Sochineniia*, 1: 590.

11. Sumarokov, "Predislovie k 'Nekotorym strofam dvukh avtorov,'" in his *Polnoe sobranie sochinenii*, 9: 247–48. Sumarokov is referring to the epitaph quoted above from the monument erected on Lomonosov's tomb by Lomonosov's admirer Chancellor M. I. Vorontsov.

12. Kunik, ed., 2: 394.

13. *Adskaia pochta*, November 1769, letter 80, p. 276. The Lyricist was, of course, Lomonosov.

14. Because of the syncretism of primitive thinking, such mythological personages as creative beings, demiurges, and culture heroes can share and exchange their characteristics and functions. Ideally, the creator makes the universe, the demiurge manufactures cosmic and cultural objects, as well as people, and the culture hero fetches objects that already exist but are hidden or removed and brings them to the people to be used. In real myths it is difficult to distinguish between these personages and their functions. In addition, the terms are used inconsistently; sometimes *demiurge* is used for the mythological personage who creates natural objects; *culture hero*, for the one who makes culture. See Alfred Métraux, "Culture Hero," in *Funk and Wagnalls Standard Dictionary of Folklore, Mythology, and Legend*; E. M. Meletinsky, "Demiurg," in *Mify narodov mira*.

15. On the ancient elements in the legends about a poet's vocation see Zhirmunsky.

16. For examples see Radishchev, 1: 380; Pushkin, *Sochineniia v shestnadtsati tomakh*, 12: 302; Belinsky, 7: 107, 9: 673.

17. Pelton, p. 15. On the trickster as the original culture hero ("trickster-fixer") see Ricketts, esp. pp. 334, 343.

18. See Erminie W. Voegelin, "Twins," in *Funk and Wagnalls Standard Dictionary of Folklore, Mythology, and Legend*; Ricketts, pp. 341–43; Campbell, pp. 292–95; Meletinsky, *Poetika mifa*, p. 183, and "Kul'turnyi geroi," in *Mify narodov mira*. Claude Lévi-Strauss, who sees the trickster's double nature as essential for the fulfillment of his role as a mediator, considers this split into two personages a weakening of this function; see his *Structural Anthropology*, p. 166.

19. Pelton, p. 15.

20. Norman, p. 151 and n. 1 on the same page.

21. Lotman and Uspensky, "Rol' dual'nykh modelei," p. 6; Berdiaev, p. 7 et passim.

22. On the eschatological tradition in seventeenth- and early eighteenth-century Russia see Chistov; Pliukhanova, "O lichnostnom soznanii," and "O narodnoi eskhatologii."

23. For a useful summary of discussions on Russia's break with the Middle Ages see Likhachev. For a collection of different interpretations of Peter's reign see Raeff, ed.

24. Garrard, p. 10. On the mythogenic spirit of the epoch see Lotman and Uspensky, "Mif-imia-kul'tura," pp. 296–99; "Rol' dual'nykh modelei," pp. 24–25; and "Otzvuki kontseptsii 'Moskva—tretii Rim,'" p. 236. On the mythological nature of Peter's image in Russian culture see Pliukhanova, "'Istoricheskoe' i 'mifologicheskoe'" and "Izobrazhenie istoricheskogo litsa." For an exhaustive examination of Peter the Great's image in Russian culture see Riasanovsky.

25. Prokopovich, pp. 126, 128; Trediakovsky, *Izbrannye proizvedeniia*, p. 58 (see the revised version in Trediakovsky, *Sochineniia*, 1: 574); Kantemir, p. 75; Lomonosov, *Polnoe sobranie sochinenii*, 8: 109. On the deification of Peter the Great in Lomonosov's poetry see Serman, *Poeticheskii stil' Lomonosova*, pp. 67–70.

26. For the quotations see Radishchev, 1: 150; Karamzin, *Pis'ma*, p. 198; Pushkin, *Sochineniia v shestnadtsati tomakh*, 5: 56.

27. Ilya Serman draws attention to this trait in Trediakovsky's and Lomonosov's literary consciousness in his book *Poeticheskii stil' Lomonosova*, pp. 90–91, 96–97.

28. Trediakovsky, *Izbrannye proizvedeniia*, pp. 390–91.

29. Trediakovsky, *Sochineniia*, 3: 647, 1: 257–68.

30. Lomonosov, *Polnoe sobranie sochinenii*, 7: 10, 7: 592, 10: 399. An English translation of Lomonosov's "Letter" appears in Silbajoris.

31. Sumarokov, *Stikhotvoreniia*, pp. 379, 95.

32. Karamzin, "Poeziia," in his *Polnoe sobranie stikhotvorenii*, p. 63.
33. Bestuzhev, p. 547; Nadezhdin, p. 65; Kireevsky, p. 60; Belinsky, 1: 22.
34. See Nekliudov, p. 132.

Chapter 1

1. For eighteenth- and early nineteenth-century apologies for Trediakovsky see Novikov's magazine *Drone*, sheet 20, and the entry on Trediakovsky in his *A Historical Dictionary*; Radishchev, *Memorial for a Dactylo-Trochaic Knight* (1801); Pushkin, "A Journey from Moscow to Petersburg" (1833–35). For the treatment of Trediakovsky by nineteenth-century scholars see Vvedensky; Kunik, ed., 1: xi–xxi; Pekarsky, "Zhizneopisanie V. K. Trediakovskogo," in his *Istoriia*, pp. 1–258. An ardent twentieth-century proponent of Trediakovsky was Sergei Bondi; see his "Trediakovsky, Lomonosov, Sumarokov," pp. 58–113. Important recent studies of Trediakovsky include Rice; the collection *Venok Trediakovskomu*; Rosenberg; Uspensky, *Iz istorii*, chaps. 2 and 3, and the earlier version of the book, "The Language Program," pp. 250–74.

2. For examples in several popular textbooks see Blagoy, *Istoriia*, pp. 134, 136, 137; O. V. Orlov, p. 286; Mirsky, p. 43; Brown, pp. 71–72; Čiževskij, p. 410. For a reference to Trediakovsky's "somewhat barbaric type of personality" see V. S. Baevsky, "Barokko i klassitsizm v stikhovedcheskikh traktatakh Trediakovskogo i Lomonosova," in *M. V. Lomonosov i russkaia kul'tura*, p. 28.

3. On Trediakovsky's years in his native Astrakhan and in Moscow see Pekarsky, *Istoriia*, pp. 2–7; Maikov; Samarenko. On Latin schools in Astrakhan see Florovsky, pp. 328–34, and Nakhimov, "Uchebnye zavedeniia Astrakhani v pervoi polovine XVIII veka," in *Venok Trediakovskomu*, pp. 27–35. On Trediakovsky's studies in Paris see Pekarsky, *Istoriia*, pp. 8–9.

4. On the significance of Trediakovsky's years in Holland and Paris see Serman, "Trediakovsky i prosvetitel'stvo," pp. 209–14; Serman, *Russkii klassitsizm*, pp. 113–17; Kibal'nik; Iu. M. Lotman, "'Ezda'"; and Uspensky's works on Trediakovsky as a linguist.

5. Pekarsky, *Istoriia*, p. 26 n. 2; originally in French.

6. Pekarsky, *Istoriia*, p. 28 n.

7. *Materialy*, p. 393; originally in French. For Trediakovsky's own translation of this document into Russian see Pekarsky, *Istoriia*, p. 43. For a Latin version of his employment conditions see *Materialy*, p. 380.

8. Pekarsky, *Istoriia*, p. 58. On Trediakovsky as a translator see Deriushin, *V. K. Trediakovsky—perevodchik*; Barenbaum; L. V. Petrunina,

"Trediakovsky kak perevodchik ital'ianskikh komedii," in *Venok Trediakovskomu*, pp. 64–69.

9. Trediakovsky translated ten volumes of Rollin's *Histoire ancienne* (1730–38; the translation was published in 1749–62), sixteen volumes of his *Histoire romaine* (1738–41; the translation was published in 1761–67), and four volumes by Rollin's disciple Jean Baptiste Louis Crévier, *Histoire des empereurs jusqu'a Constantine* (1750–56; the translation was published in 1767–69). Charles Rollin was among Trediakovsky's professors in Paris. His lectures significantly influenced Trediakovsky's political, literary, and linguistic views (see Kruglyi; Serman, "Trediakovsky i prosvetitel'stvo," pp. 211–13; Kibal'nik).

10. On the episode see Pekarsky, *Istoriia*, pp. 77–83; Solov'ev, *Istoriia Rossii*, pp. 529–33; Timofeev, "V. K. Trediakovsky," pp. 12–13; Trediakovsky's petition to the empress of Nov. 12, 1740, in *Pis'ma*, pp. 48–49, and A. B. Shishkin's commentary on it, pp. 63–64. On Volynsky see Roginsky, pp. 311–12.

11. Lomonosov also became a professor of chemistry in 1745. Both Lomonosov and Trediakovsky had to struggle for their appointments, but the troubles they faced were of different kinds: Trediakovsky's appointment was apparently opposed by the Academy Conference, whereas Lomonosov's was slowed down by Schumacher. See Pekarsky, *Istoriia*, pp. 106–12; "Iz dela o Trediakovskom," *Moskvitianin*, 15, part 4 (1853): 27–48; Lomonosov, *Polnoe sobranie sochinenii*, 10: 748–52.

12. For an overview of their polemics see Berkov, *Lomonosov*; Serman, *Poeticheskii stil' Lomonosova*, chap. 6, and *Mikhail Lomonosov*, chap. 7.

13. Trediakovsky, *Izbrannye proizvedeniia*, p. 366. For an English translation of Trediakovsky's treatise see Silbajoris.

14. Two scholars, V. N. Peretts and V. N. Toporov, deny both Trediakovsky and Lomonosov the authorship of the reform. They consider Ernst Glueck, a German preacher who spent two years in Russia and who attempted to write Russian syllabo-tonic poetry, to be its true author (see Peretts, "Trediakovsky kak novator v stikhoslozhenii" and "Pastor Ernst Gliuk i ego russkie stikhotvoreniia," in his *Istoriko-literaturnye materialy*, pp. 35–141; Toporov, "E. Gliuk i 'nemetskaia' poeziia pervoi treti XVIII v.," in *M. V. Lomonosov i russkaia kul'tura*, pp. 11–16).

15. On the reform see Bondi, pp. 82–113; Berkov, "Iz istorii russkoi poezii"; Timofeev, *Ocherki stikha*, chap. 6; Bucsela; Silbajoris, pp. 1–35; Gasparov, "Russkii sillabicheskii trinadtsatislozhnik" and "Lomonosov i Trediakovsky—dva istoricheskikh tipa novatorov stikha," in *M. V. Lomonosov i russkaia kul'tura*, pp. 27–28; B. P. Goncharov, "Stikhovedcheskie vzgliady Trediakovskogo i Lomonosova. Reforma russkogo

stikhoslozheniia," in *Vozniknovenie russkoi nauki o literature*, pp. 73–89; Drage; G. S. Smith; V. S. Baevsky, "'Starshaia' i 'mladshaia' linii russkikh stikhovedcheskikh idei," in *M. V. Lomonosov i russkaia kul'tura*, pp. 35–39; Serman, *Mikhail Lomonosov*, pp. 52–61.

16. On Trediakovsky's linguistic views see Vinokur; Uspensky, *Pervaia russkaia grammatika*, pp. 51–76; Uspensky, "Trediakovsky i istoriia russkogo literaturnogo iazyka," in *Venok Trediakovskomu*, pp. 40–44; Uspensky, "The Language Program"; *Iz istorii*, chaps. 2 and 3; Iu. S. Sorokin, "Stilisticheskaia teoriia i rechevaia praktika molodogo Trediakovskogo," in *Venok Trediakovskomu*, pp. 45–54; Rosenberg, chap. 1; A. A. Alekseev, "Epicheskii stil' 'Tilemakhidy'" and "Evoliutsiia."

17. See Rice; Karlinsky, "Tallemant"; A. S. Kurilov and K. V. Pigarev, "Teoretiko-literaturnaia mysl' v Rossii XVIII v.," in *Vozniknovenie russkoi nauki o literature*, pp. 44–50; G. V. Moskvicheva, "Trediakovsky i stanovlenie zhanrovoi sistemy russkogo klassitsizma," in *Venok Trediakovskomu*, pp. 55–57; L. N. Dushina, "Trediakovsky i russkaia ballada XVIII veka," in *Venok Trediakovskomu*, pp. 62–63; M. F. Grishakova, "Trediakovsky i traditsiia russkoi ody," in *M. V. Lomonosov i russkaia kul'tura*, pp. 31–35; Karlinsky, *Russian Drama*, pp. 73–75; Bochkarev, pp. 84–96.

18. Trediakovsky's letter to Schumacher of Jan. 18, 1731, in *Pis'ma*, p. 45; originally in French. On Trediakovsky as a Baroque and therefore outdated writer see Čiževskij, pp. 412–14; Brown, p. 72; Rosenberg, pp. 240–41, 369, and the conception of her work in general; Baevsky, "Barokko i klassitsizm v stikhovedcheskikh traktatakh Trediakovskogo i Lomonosova." An example of an approach with a nonjudgmental discussion of Baroque features in Trediakovsky's works is Shishkin, "V. K. Trediakovsky."

19. I attempted to demonstrate the consistency of Trediakovsky's evolution in my essay "Evoliutsiia."

20. N. N. Bulich, one of the first students of eighteenth-century literary polemics, pointed this out in his book *Sumarokov*. Uncivil polemics were not even a specifically Russian feature: We have only to recall Boileau's bluntness toward his literary enemies, or the conflict between John Dennis and Alexander Pope. For recent examples of this approach see Silbajoris, p. 8; Brown, p. 54; Rosenberg, p. 277. The latter, however, on p. 282, disputes Trediakovsky's reputation as a malicious informer.

21. See Radishchev, 1: 352–53, 2: 201–21; Karamzin, *Sochineniia*, 1: 583. For modern opinions about Trediakovsky's lack of talent see Nabokov, p. 481; Rice, pp. 275–77; Heim, pp. 60, 73; O. V. Orlov, p. 273.

22. Serman, *Poeticheskii stil' Lomonosova*, pp. 135–36.

23. For a discussion of the Russian Baroque see Panchenko, pp. 167–208.

24. Lomonosov, *Polnoe sobranie sochinenii*, 7: 93 and 284–85. Lomonosov has the reputation of being the least "rational" Russian poet of the eighteenth century (see Tynianov, "Oda kak oratorskii zhanr," in his *Poetika*; Gukovsky, *Russkaia poeziia*, pp. 14–19; Serman, *Poeticheskii stil' Lomonosova*, chap. 6).

25. Trediakovsky, "Pis'mo . . . ot priiatelia k priiateliu," in Kunik, ed., 2: 473, 463; hereafter "Letter from Friend to Friend." Cf. Trediakovsky's criticism of Sumarokov's alleged "intoxicated enthusiasm" with his own notion of "sober intoxication," introduced in his "Ode on the Surrender of the City of Gdansk" (1734).

26. Boris Meilakh, "Talant," in *Slovar' literaturovedcheskikh terminov*, p. 396. The *Princeton Encyclopedia of Poetry and Poetics* does not even have an entry on talent, and the entry "Evaluation" does not discuss how talent and literary value correlate. Wellek and Warren, in their *Theory of Literature*, also fail to address this relationship.

27. On the problem of literary value see Richards's classic *Practical Criticism*; Vodička; Markiewicz; Wellek, pp. 1–20; Segers; B. H. Smith. See Segers and Smith for a bibliography on and history of the problem.

28. For a recent assessment of the problem of changing taste see B. H. Smith, pp. 36–42.

29. Trediakovsky, *Sochineniia*, 2: xlv–xlvii. A *bakhar'* is a narrator of folktales, a storyteller, a talker, sometimes a fibber, or somebody who heals with the help of incantation. On stylistic diversity as a principal and conscious feature of Trediakovsky's style see A. A. Alekseev, "Evoliutsiia," pp. 117–19, 122, 125.

30. On Sumarokov as a follower of Trediakovsky see Berkov, *Lomonosov*, pp. 34–35; for the quoted passage see p. 34. On Trediakovsky's other followers see Berkov, "U istokov dvorianskoi literatury" and "Petr Suvorov." On Lomonosov's dependence on Trediakovsky's treatise see Berkov, *Lomonosov*, pp. 54–55; Pekarsky, *Istoriia*, p. 292; Silbajoris, p. 22. Serman, in his *Poeticheskii stil' Lomonosova*, pp. 208–18, demonstrates how Trediakovsky's "Letter from Friend to Friend" compelled Sumarokov and Lomonosov to revise some of their artistic principles. Rosenberg discusses Lomonosov's and Sumarokov's acknowledgment of Trediakovsky's expertise in her dissertation, pp. 285–86. For Derzhavin's remark see his "Zapiski," in *Sochineniia*, 6: 443n. For his parodies of Trediakovsky's poetry see *Mnimaia poeziia*, p. 135.

31. For Martynov's data see his "Trediakovsky," p. 81. See Karamzin's remark in Karamzin, *Sochineniia*, 1: 584. It is likely that Karamzin himself as a young boy (or, at least, the main character in his *Letters of a Russian Traveler*) not only read Trediakovsky's translation but ardently enjoyed it: "I was eight or nine years old when I read the Roman [history] for the first time and, imagining myself a little Scipio, kept my head

266 Notes to Pages 41-47

high" (Pis'ma, p. 271). Karamzin's biographer, M. P. Pogodin, confirms that as a young boy, Karamzin read Trediakovsky's translation of Rollin; see his Karamzin, 1: 15. For Grech's testimony see Grech, p. 206.

32. Bolotov, cols. 259, 327–28.

33. Martynov, pp. 81–83.

34. V. P. Stepanov, "Trediakovsky i Ekaterina II," in Venok Trediakovskomu, p. 92.

35. Livanova, p. 47; Speransky, p. 171; Pozdneev; Martynov, pp. 84–85.

36. For references to this anecdote see Pushkin, Sochineniia v shestnadtsati tomakh, 11: 269 and 12: 169; Lazhechnikov, Ledianoi dom, p. 60 (hereafter in this chapter and Chapter 3, references to this edition are given in the text); Khmel'nitsky, pp. 41–42; Bantysh-Kamensky, 5: 146. The last source is especially rich in anecdotes about Trediakovsky. The unreliability of Bantysh-Kamensky's information was analyzed by Pekarsky, Istoriia, p. 4 n. 2.

37. About the box on the ear and the beatings by Volynsky see Lazhechnikov, Ledianoi dom, pp. 56–57; Bantysh-Kamensky, 5: 147; Petr Perevlessky, Introduction to Trediakovsky, Izbrannye sochineniia, xvii; Nekrasov, 6: 119. Pekarsky (Istoriia, pp. 38–39) discusses the legendary nature of the story about the box on the ear. In 1828 Pushkin (Sochineniia v shestnadtsati tomakh, 11: 53) related another anecdote of the same sort.

38. See Dmitriev, pp. 5–6; Lazhechnikov, Ledianoi dom, p. 56.

39. Lazhechnikov, "Znakomstvo moe s Pushkinym," p. 178.

40. Russkaia stikhotvornaia parodiia, p. 10. The lines are from Derzhavin's parody of Trediakovsky; see it in Mnimaia poeziia, p. 135.

41. Cf. Khmel'nitsky's disregard for chronology in his comedy Russian Faust. Action in this play takes place in 1730, but Trediakovsky is portrayed as the author of Deidamia (1750), the translator of Rollin (Trediakovsky's translation was published in 1749–69), and the propagator of his own treatise on orthography (1748).

42. Bantysh-Kamensky, in his Dictionary, 5: 146, made the same mistake. I will return to this remarkable mix-up.

43. For Belinsky's remarks on Trediakovsky see 1: 203; 2: 145 n; 3: 15; 4: 415; 5: 487; 6: 601; 7: 16, 123–24; 9: 181, 299.

44. Perevlessky, Introduction to Trediakovsky, Izbrannye sochineniia, p. xi.

45. In Tynianov, Poetika, p. 308. In this essay Tynianov refers to the "parodical" (parodiinyi) and the "folkloric" (fol'klornyi) Trediakovskys. The "parodical Trediakovsky" is apparently "Trediakovsky as he was presented in parodies," and "folkloric" implies that there was a

legend about Trediakovsky, based on his portrayals in parodies, and that this legend passed for a historically correct picture. The essay was first published in 1977, and Tynianov's idea was not developed until Karen Rosenberg addressed some aspects of this problem in her dissertation (pp. 15, 27–28). Tynianov also mentions Trediakovsky's "parodical personality" (*parodicheskaia lichnost'*) in his commentary on parodies of Trediakovsky's poetry in *Mnimaia poeziia*, p. 419 n. 86.

46. Pekarsky, *Istoriia*, p. 198; Pekarsky, *Redaktor*, pp. 16–17.

Chapter 2

1. Ilya Serman, in his essay "Bova i russkaia literatura," stresses the role that *Bova* and other chivalric romances assimilated by Russian literature in the seventeenth century played in the transition from medieval literary notions to modern aesthetic ideas that occurred in Russian literary consciousness during the eighteenth century.

2. Lomonosov's exact date of birth is unknown. Different sources give various dates from 1709 to 1712, but scholars have agreed to consider it Nov. 8, 1711.

3. There were foreign grammars of the Russian language, as well as an unpublished Russian grammar, before Lomonosov's. See Uspensky, *Pervaia russkaia grammatika*.

4. Pushkin, *Sochineniia v shestnadtsati tomakh*, 11: 249.

5. At some point, however, Trediakovsky expressed a wish to dedicate the posthumous edition of his tragedy *Deidamia* to Sumarokov. It was published in 1775 with such a dedication.

6. For a description of Lomonosov's comments see Berkov, *Lomonosov*, pp. 54–67; for the comparison of Lomonosov to Cerberus see p. 55. The original is located in the Archives of the Academy of Sciences in Leningrad, *fond* 20, *opis'* 2, no. 3.

7. Quoted in Kunik, ed., 1: xli. For Lomonosov's remark on Sumarokov's epigram see Lomonosov, *Polnoe sobranie sochinenii*, 9: 634.

8. Sumarokov, *Stikhotvoreniia*, pp. 383–84.

9. For a recent discussion of this competition see Shishkin, "Poeticheskoe sostiazanie."

10. Pekarsky, *Istoriia*, pp. 130–31.

11. Kunik, ed., 2: 435–500.

12. For the analysis of this conflict see Serman, *Poeticheskii stil' Lomonosova*, pp. 192–98.

13. Sumarokov, *Polnoe sobranie sochinenii*, 10: 26.

14. Serman, *Poeticheskii stil' Lomonosova*, pp. 229–34.

15. See the playbill in Berkov, *Lomonosov*, pp. 102–3. For Elagin's satire and the polemical exchanges see *Poety XVIII veka*, 2: 372–92.

16. Lomonosov, *Polnoe sobranie sochinenii*, 8: 630.

17. Berkov, *Lomonosov*, pp. 254–65. See Andrei Shuvalov's speech in *L'année littéraire*, 5 (1760): 194–203, and in Berkov, "Neispol'zovannye materialy," pp. 356–66. See Sumarokov's laments in Lebedev., comp., *Bibliograficheskie zapiski*, 15 (1858): 453. Berkov interprets Lefevre's "blunder" as a conscious attempt to reconcile Lomonosov and Sumarokov in order to achieve certain political ends favored by his patrons, the Shuvalovs and the Vorontsovs (pp. 256–57). Indeed, around this time, in January 1761, Ivan Shuvalov directly ordered Lomonosov to reconcile with Sumarokov. In a furious letter, Lomonosov refused (Lomonosov, *Polnoe sobranie sochinenii*, 10: 545–47). While Berkov's interpretation is of no particular relevance to my present argument, it is important to remember that his book, which is extremely rich in facts, relies too heavily on the sort of straightforward sociological explanations popular in Soviet scholarship in the 1930's.

18. Published in Pekarsky, *Istoriia*, pp. 256–57.

19. Lomonosov, *Polnoe sobranie sochinenii*, 10: 545–46.

20. Sumarokov, *Polnoe sobranie sochinenii*, 9: 247.

21. Kunik, ed., 2: 404.

22. Bantysh-Kamensky, 3: 195–96, 5: 150.

23. See, for example, Bulich, pp. 61–62; Skabichevsky, pp. 10–11; Ivanov, pp. 136–58 passim; Berkov, *Lomonosov*, pp. 98–102, 285–86; Silbajoris, p. 8; Rice, p. 61; Rosenberg, pp. 241, 277.

24. Gukovsky, "O russkom klassitsizme," pp. 52–53.

25. Chernov, p. 6.

26. See Gukovsky, *Russkaia poeziia*, "K voprosu," and "O russkom klassitsizme"; for newer discussions of Classicism see Kupreianova; Jones.

27. On their different literary beliefs see, for example, Tynianov, "Oda kak oratorskii zhanr," in his *Poetika*; Gukovsky, *Russkaia poeziia*, chap. 1; Berkov, "Problema"; Gukovsky, "Trediakovskii"; Morozov; Serman, *Poeticheskii stil' Lomonosova*; Iu. V. Stennik, "Teoretiko-literaturnye vzgliady Lomonosova," in *Lomonosov i russkaia literatura*, pp. 31–47.

28. Serman, *Poeticheskii stil' Lomonosova*, p. 208.

29. See Gukovsky, "K voprosu."

30. Serman, *Poeticheskii stil' Lomonosova*, pp. 208–18, 230–31, 244–45.

31. Lomonosov's comment in the margins of Trediakovsky's *A New and Brief Method for Composing Russian Verse*, in Berkov, *Lomonosov*,

p. 57; Sumarokov, *Stikhotvoreniia*, p. 349; Trediakovsky, "Letter from Friend to Friend," pp. 447, 444–45.

32. Sumarokov, *Stikhotvoreniia*, p. 358.

Chapter 3

1. Trediakovsky, *Izbrannye proizvedeniia*, p. 383; Lomonosov, *Polnoe sobranie sochinenii*, 8: 543. Shtivelii is Trediakovsky. Lomonosov first objected to Trediakovsky's prohibition in 1739, in his "Letter on the Rules of Russian Versification" (7: 16).

2. Lomonosov, *Polnoe sobranie sochinenii*, 8: 542; "Epigramma na El[agina]," in *Poety XVIII veka*, 2: 386–87.

3. A. A. Morozov, "Russkaia stikhotvornaia parodiia," in *Russkaia stikhotvornaia parodiia*, pp. 13, 15–17.

4. Lomonosov, *Polnoe sobranie sochinenii*, 10: 493–94. This piece of criticism, disguised as a private letter, was intended for public circulation (see comments in 8: 1020 and 10: 822). Serman published excerpts from a more complete eighteenth-century copy of this letter in his essay "Iz literaturnoi polemiki," p. 101.

5. Trediakovsky, "Letter from Friend to Friend," p. 472.

6. On these features of parody see Tynianov, "O parodii," in his *Poetika*, pp. 297–98.

7. Sumarokov, *Polnoe sobranie sochinenii*, 3: 76.

8. Lomonosov, *Polnoe sobranie sochinenii*, 8: 211.

9. Trediakovsky, "Letter from Friend to Friend," pp. 476–77.

10. See *Slovar' Akademii Rossiiskoi*, 6: 784, definition 2. Interestingly, in his famous *A Discourse on the Old and New Styles of the Russian Language* (1803), the leader of the Archaist movement, Aleksandr Shishkov, chose precisely this verb to illustrate his assertion that the meanings of words in different languages cannot be absolutely identical despite the existence of an area with similar meaning (Shishkov, *Sobranie sochinenii i perevodov*, 2: 39–41). He certainly remembered the controversy, in his time revived by Karamzin's neologism *touching* (*trogatel'nyi*), since he quoted Lomonosov's epigram in a footnote on p. 123.

11. Sumarokov, *Stikhotvoreniia*, pp. 354, 350.

12. Trediakovsky, "Letter from Friend to Friend," pp. 455–56, 470–71. The second "shortcoming" was actually a misprint in the first edition of Sumarokov's "Ode to Empress Elizabeth" (1743). Trediakovsky pretended (or actually thought) that the mistake reflected Sumarokov's poor ability as a poet, and proposed nonessential morphological alterations that restored the correct meter.

13. Trediakovsky, "Letter from Friend to Friend," p. 446.

14. Kunik, ed., 2: 424.

15. Shlonsky, p. 797. The same idea can be found in Tynianov, "O parodii," in his *Poetika*, p. 301, and "Dostoevsky i Gogol' (k teorii parodii)," in his *Poetika*, p. 201. Tynianov's point of view was developed in B. Begak, "Parodiia i ee priemy," in Begak et al., pp. 51–65, esp. p. 54.

16. Tynianov, "O parodii," in his *Poetika*, p. 294.

17. Trediakovsky, "Letter from Friend to Friend," p. 473.

18. Ginzburg, pp. 32–38.

19. See Viazemsky's letter in Pushkin, *Sochineniia v shestnadtsati tomakh*, 13: 223.

20. For examples see Serman, *Poeticheskii stil' Lomonosova*, pp. 202–19.

21. Tynianov, "O parodii," in his *Poetika*, p. 302.

22. Lomonosov, *Polnoe sobranie sochinenii*, 8: 630.

23. For the quoted passage see Sumarokov, *Polnoe sobranie sochinenii*, 10: 14. On Trediakovsky and foppish culture see Uspensky, *Iz istorii*, pp. 134–55; Iu. M. Lotman, "'Ezda.'"

24. Sumarokov, *Stikhotvoreniia*, p. 307.

25. The clumsiness of the diction is emphasized by the employment of one-syllable words throughout the second line. Their use could parody Lomonosov's initial attempt to write syllabo-tonic verses without pyrrhics—an attempt abandoned soon thereafter—and at the same time, it could ridicule Trediakovsky's and Lomonosov's long-standing dispute about one-syllable words. Trediakovsky, in his *A New and Brief Method for Composing Russian Verse*, corollary 1, claimed that these words are always "long," that is, stressed. Lomonosov disputed this in his "Letter on the Rules of Russian Versification" (in his *Polnoe sobranie sochinenii*, 7: 12). Finally, Trediakovsky agreed, in his revised *Method for Composing Russian Verse* (1752), chap. 1, paragraph 15, to consider one-syllable words "common" (*obshchie*) with respect to stress and to allow them therefore to take both strong and weak positions in a syllabo-tonic verse, but only as a poetic license that makes it easier to compose verses in Russian. Sumarokov continued the argument in the essay "On Versification": "Mr. Trediakovsky, no matter how much he had heard from me about spondees, simply could not understand that a spondee in our languages is sometimes a trochee and sometimes an iamb, and believed, because of his failure to understand, that spondees become trochees and iambs solely through the writer's wish" (*Stikhotvoreniia*, p. 384).

26. Sumarokov, *Polnoe sobranie sochinenii*, 5: 358. For Trediakovsky's defense of *s* see his *Sochineniia*, 3: 88–89.

27. Lomonosov, *Polnoe sobranie sochinenii*, 8: 542. For an analysis of

another of Lomonosov's epigrams attacking Trediakovsky's orthography, "About the Doubtful Pronunciation of the Letter *G* in the Russian Language," see Uspensky, "Foneticheskaia struktura."

28. See Kholshevnikov.

29. On Trediakovsky's hexameter see Burgi, pp. 41–68; Gasparov, "Prodrom," pp. 375–77. Bondi (pp. 79–81) considered Trediakovsky's hexameter to be the best in the Russian tradition.

30. See the commentary by M. I. Sukhomlinov in Lomonosov, *Sochineniia*, 2: 391–99.

31. Trediakovsky, "Letter from Friend to Friend," p. 442; see more on this subject in Rulin, pp. 260–63; Rezanov, pp. 233–35.

32. For a typological classification of comedic plots and situations see Knutson.

33. The title "rhetorician" (Sumarokov, *Polnoe sobranie sochinenii*, 5: 343) helps identify Lomonosov, who by 1750 was the author of two manuals on rhetoric, as a prototype of Bobembius. There is a third pedant in *Tresotinius*, by the name of Ksaksoksimendius. His main attribute is a heavy Slavonic style. It is believed that in this character Sumarokov parodied the academician S. P. Krasheninnikov, who was a translator, botanist, and ethnographer.

34. In his essay "On Orthography," Sumarokov recorded Lomonosov's comment on the letters Φ and θ, which were used in Russian to represent the same sound, [f]. Lomonosov's argument resembles Bobembius's position in *Tresotinius*: "I asked Mr. Lomonosov why he had preserved Φ, but not θ; that he answered in the following way: 'This letter stands with its hands on its hips, and therefore is more vigorous.' This answer is jeering, and not serious," concluded Sumarokov (*Polnoe sobranie sochinenii*, 10: 9).

35. For an analysis of Vaugelas's influence on Trediakovsky see Uspensky, "Trediakovsky i istoriia russkogo literaturnogo iazyka," in *Venok Trediakovskomu*, p. 40; Uspensky, "The Language Program," pp. 255, 258, 269–70; Uspensky, *Iz istorii*, pp. 131–34.

36. On Chapelain and his reputation see Van Roosbroeck; Willey.

37. Sumarokov, *Polnoe sobranie sochinenii*, 5: 297; Trediakovsky, "Letter from Friend to Friend," p. 438.

38. Sumarokov, *Polnoe sobranie sochinenii*, 5: 298.

39. "At dinner pages wait on him—an honor that makes him equal to Chapelle, if not Tasso" (Lazhechnikov, *Ledianoi dom*, p. 266). Lazhechnikov compared Trediakovsky to Claude Emmanuel Chapelle, a friend and collaborator of Boileau's. I believe that Lazhechnikov made a mistake and that he meant to compare Trediakovsky the author of *Tilemakhida* to Chapelain, the author of another notoriously bad epic

poem, *La Pucelle*. The mention of Torquato Tasso, known for his *Gerusa-lemme Liberata*, supports this supposition. Chapelle never had a reputation as an epic poet. He was known as a brilliant polemicist—the reason his name was used as a nickname for Viazemsky. On the use of Chapelain's name in the polemics between the Innovators and the Archaists see Chapter 4.

40. Trediakovsky, *Sochineniia*, 1: 266.

41. Sumarokov, *Izbrannye proizvedeniia*, p. 287.

42. *Poety XVIII veka*, 2: 399–400, 401. The expression *polnymi ustami* in the conclusion of the first poem could mean both "in great gulps" and "with your full lips"—a possible reference to Lomonosov's appearance. Tsyganosov is a comical modification of Lomonosov's name.

43. "Na Teleliuia," in *Poety XVIII veka*, 2: 389 (author unknown); Trediakovsky, "Samokhval," in ibid., p. 371; "Na Teleliuia," in ibid., p. 388.

44. Sumarokov, "Osel vo l'vovoi kozhe," in his *Izbrannye proizvedeniia*, p. 208; Trediakovsky, "Ne znaiu . . . ," in *Poety XVIII veka*, 2: 393.

45. Lomonosov, *Polnoe sobranie sochinenii*, 10: 545.

46. Trediakovsky, "Letter from Friend to Friend," p. 483. For the demonstration of Trediakovsky's assertion see p. 484.

47. Trediakovsky, "Nadpis' na S[umarokova]," in Afanas'ev, p. 519n. Cf. also Lomonosov, *Polnoe sobranie sochinenii*, 8: 659, and Trediakovsky, "Letter from Friend to Friend," p. 459. On the mockery of Sumarokov's appearance and handicaps see Uspensky, "K istorii," pp. 84–86.

48. Lomonosov, *Polnoe sobranie sochinenii*, 9: 634.

49. Ibid., 8: 630. For Trediakovsky's epigram see his *Izbrannye proizvedeniia*, p. 416. Lomonosov ridiculed Trediakovsky's rhyme *krasoul' / khodul'* as early as 1739, in his "Letter on the Rules of Russian Versification" (Lomonosov, *Polnoe sobranie sochinenii*, 7: 16).

50. Sumarokov's mocking name for Lomonosov, Firs Firsovich Homer, given to him after he published the first canto of the heroic poem *Peter the Great*, appeared as a reaction to these lofty "titles" (see Sumarokov, *Izbrannye proizvedeniia*, p. 260).

51. N. Popovsky, "Nadpis' k portretu M. V. Lomonosova," in *Poety XVIII veka*, 1: 114.

52. I. Elagin, "Epistola g. Elagina k g. Sumarokovu" ["Satira na petimetra i koketok"], in *Poety XVIII veka*, 2: 372.

53. Pekarsky, *Istoriia*, p. 232. The meter of the poem is an imitation of the "heroic verse" proposed by Trediakovsky in 1735.

54. Radishchev, 1: 352; Karamzin, *Sochineniia*, 1: 584.

55. Poroshin, p. 301.

56. Radishchev, 1: 389; M. M. Kheraskov, "Rassuzhdenie o rossiiskom stikhotvorstve," in Berkov, ed., p. 293.

57. Karamzin, *Sochineniia*, 1: 592–93. Count Dmitrii Khvostov, whose literary views in general were very different from Karamzin's, expressed a very similar opinion; see *Poety 1790–1810-kh godov*, pp. 437–38 n. 2.

58. The three most influential biographies of Lomonosov that promoted his heroic image were an entry in Novikov's *A Historical Dictionary*, Staehlin's "Traits and Anecdotes for Lomonosov's Biography" (1783), and Mikhail Verevkin's "Life of the Late Mikhailo Vasilevich Lomonosov," included in the 1784 edition of Lomonosov's *Complete Works*, published by the Academy of Sciences. Although Verevkin used additional sources, he relied heavily on Staehlin's German manuscript. It was through Verevkin, then, that Staehlin's materials, unpublished until 1850, contributed to the legend about Lomonosov. Novikov's and Verevkin's biographies were reprinted in the late eighteenth and early nineteenth centuries in many collections of Lomonosov's works and in reference books. Later interpretations of Lomonosov's life to a large extent depended on these essays, supplemented by oral tradition.

59. Karamzin, *Sochineniia*, 1: 590; Belinsky, 1: 387. Compare these statements to the anonymous poem "The Disguised Beard; or, Hymn to a Drunken Head" written in the 1750's: "Ugly because of drunkenness / And always immature in mind, / You are of mean birth, / Although you are honored with titles; / But when you are stripped of all your titles / For your immeasurable drinking, / Fury, deception, and conceit, / You will be [simply] a drunken fisherman" (quoted in Berkov, *Lomonosov*, pp. 217–18).

60. Murav'ev, "Otryvki iz 'Trekh pisem,'" in *M. V. Lomonosov v vospominaniiakh sovremennikov*, p. 67.

61. N. Polevoy, "Lomonosov," p. 241. The wording of the address comes from 1 Thessalonians 5: 19. This reference helped Polevoy to stress the idea that Lomonosov's genius had divine origin.

62. Pushkin, "Otrok" (1830), in *Sochineniia v shestnadtsati tomakh*, 3: 241.

63. N. Polevoy, "Lomonosov," p. 241.

64. The information on Lomonosov's departure from home is rather contradictory. Most probably, it was semisecret, because he had papers and the authorities' permission and became a runaway only after he had failed to return a year later. Serman, in his *Mikhail Lomonosov*, defines Lomonosov's departure as "completely official" (p. 17).

However, eighteenth-century biographers (most importantly, Staehlin, Novikov, and Verevkin) presented it as totally secret.

65. K. Polevoy, 2: 5.

66. Staehlin, "Traits and Anecdotes," in Kunik, ed., 2: 391. See also Verevkin, "Zhizn' pokoinogo Lomonosova," in *M. V. Lomonosov v vospominaniiakh sovremennikov*, p. 43; Bantysh-Kamensky, 3: 187–88; N. Polevoy, "Lomonosov," p. 242.

67. See Staehlin, "Traits and Anecdotes," in Kunik, ed., 2: 395–98, 399–400; Verevkin, "Zhizn' pokoinogo Lomonosova," in *M. V. Lomonosov v vospominaniiakh sovremennikov*, pp. 45–46, 47; K. Polevoy, 1: 277–87; N. Polevoy, "Lomonosov," pp. 247–48.

68. Staehlin, "Traits and Anecdotes," in Kunik, ed., 2: 394; Merzliakov, p. 87; Belinsky, 3: 487. See also Verevkin, "Zhizn' pokoinogo Lomonosova," in *M. V. Lomonosov v vospominaniiakh sovremennikov*, p. 45; Kheraskov, "Rassuzhdenie o rossiiskom stikhotvorstve," in Berkov, ed., pp. 292–93; K. Polevoy, 2: 1–11. Serman points out in his *Mikhail Lomonosov*, p. 59, that later critics' high opinion of the ode was amplified by the fact that they knew only the 1751 version but thought it to be the original written by the young Lomonosov in 1739; they naturally were amazed at the maturity of this alleged first attempt by an inexperienced poet and ascribed the success to Lomonosov's brilliance.

69. Staehlin, "Traits and Anecdotes," in Kunik, ed., 2: 404–5.

70. Lomonosov, *Polnoe sobranie sochinenii*, 10: 546. Pushkin quoted from memory and therefore not quite accurately: "I, Your Excellency, do not want to be a fool either for the grandees or even for the Lord my God" (*Sochineniia v shestnadtsati tomakh*, 11: 254).

71. Pushkin, *Sochineniia v shestnadtsati tomakh*, 11: 254.

72. Lomonosov, *Polnoe sobranie sochinenii*, 10: 518–19.

73. N. Polevoy, "Lomonosov," pp. 251–52. G. F. Mueller was a historiographer and a member of the Academy of Sciences; Lomonosov had frequent arguments with him over various issues, important and unimportant (see Pekarsky, *Istoriia*, pp. 382–83, 574, 610–13, 685–87, 720–28). G. S. T. Bayer was a specialist in classical languages, on which he was a considerable authority, and a professor at the Academy.

74. Bantysh-Kamensky, 3: 198. In a footnote Bantysh-Kamensky cites his father as a source—an indication that the anecdote circulated in oral tradition.

75. Campbell, p. 356.

76. Kunik, ed., 2: 386, 403. Verevkin and Bantysh-Kamensky followed Staehlin's report, as did Metropolitan Evgenii in his *Dictionary of Russian Secular Writers*, 1: 29. Evgenii erroneously substituted Staehlin's name, less known among the general public, for Ivan Shuvalov's, well

known in relation to Lomonosov, revealing the legendary character of this episode. Staehlin also reported that Lomonosov's death occurred during Easter week. Although the coincidence is obviously a historical fact, it could help to support the mythological accounts of his death.

77. Bobrov, "Proizshestvie v tsarstve tenei, ili Sud'bina rossiiskogo iazyka," in Lotman and Uspensky, "Spory," p. 280.

78. From Murav'ev's letter to D. I. Khvostov, published in the commentary to the poem "Roshcha" in Murav'ev, p. 339.

79. [V. S. Podshivalov], "Pis'mo k devitse F** o rossiiskom stoposlozhenii," in *Priiatnoe i poleznoe preprovozhdenie vremeni*, 1 (1794): 95–97.

80. Trediakovsky, *Sochineniia*, 2: xlviii.

81. See L'vov's letter of Dec. 23, 1789, in *Pis'ma*, p. 388. See Zhikharev's testimony in Zhikharev, pp. 352–53.

82. For a discussion of the fool's demonic nature and his association with death see Willeford, pp. 88–91.

83. Sumarokov, *Polnoe sobranie sochinenii*, 5: 353, 344.

84. On the connotations that the Syrian language had in Orthodox Christian tradition see Uspensky, "Vopros." On Chaldeans in Russian popular tradition see Faminitsyn, pp. 100–105.

85. Lomonosov, *Polnoe sobranie sochinenii*, 8: 827. In eighteenth-century collections the anonymous poem was attributed to Lomonosov, but his authorship is unlikely.

86. M. Dmitriev, "Dvenadtsat' sonnykh statei," in *Epigramma i satira*, p. 302. The title parodies Zhukovsky's ballad "Twelve Sleeping Maidens," a popular subject for parody in the first half of the nineteenth century.

87. Kniazhnin, "Boi stikhotvortsev," in *Poety XVIII veka*, 2: 406–7.

88. Pushkin, *Sochineniia v shestnadtsati tomakh*, 1: 195.

89. Bobrov, "Proizshestvie v tsarstve tenei," in Lotman and Uspensky, "Spory," p. 280.

90. Radishchev, 1: 353; Nikolev, "Oda 2" in *Mnimaia poeziia*, p. 140.

91. See *Vsiakaia vsiachina*, sec. 3, p. 15; sec. 5, pp. 30–32; sec. 7, pp. 46–47. On Radishchev's reaction to this mockery see Chapter 5. It is noteworthy that Dmitriev's satire on Kachenovsky, in which Trediakovsky plays a major part, is called "Twelve Sleepy Essays."

92. *Poety 1790–1810-kh godov*, p. 566. On the connection between sleep and death see Hillman.

93. Trediakovsky, *Sochineniia*, 2: 567, 576.

94. Ostolopov, 3: 342; Radishchev, 1: 431. Cf. Denis Fonvizin's mockery of *Deidamia* in his letter of Dec. 14, 1763, in Fonvizin, p. 328.

95. Belinsky, 9: 189–90.

96. Sumarokov, *Polnoe sobranie sochinenii*, 5: 356.

97. Ibid., 5: 291.

98. Pushkin, *Sochineniia v shestnadtsati tomakh*, 11: 53.

99. Palitsyn, "Poslanie k Privete," in *Poety 1790–1810-kh godov*, p. 778 n. 4; Bantysh-Kamensky, 5: 148; Belinsky, 10: 8.

100. Sumarokov, *Polnoe sobranie sochinenii*, 5: 296.

101. Palitsyn, "Poslanie k Privete," in *Poety 1790–1810-kh godov*, p. 748.

102. Khmel'nitsky, *Russkii Faust*, p. 136.

103. Sometimes the pedant could constitute a character separate from Dottore, but their characteristics were very similar; see Oreglia, p. 87.

104. Berkov, *Istoriia*, p. 13. For the commedia dell'arte plays familiar to Sumarokov see Peretts, ed. Trediakovsky was the main translator of these plays (L. V. Petrunina, "Trediakovsky kak perevodchik ital'ianskikh komedii," in *Venok Trediakovskomu*, pp. 64–69).

105. Kunik, ed., 2: 499, 438.

106. Sumarokov, *Izbrannye sochineniia*, p. 121; Sumarokov, *Polnoe sobranie sochinenii*, 5: 343.

107. Batiushkov, *Sochineniia*, p. 256.

108. Lazhechnikov, *Ledianoi dom*, p. 55; N. Polevoy, *Pervoe predstavlenie Mel'nika—kolduna, obmanshchika i svata*, in his *Dramaticheskie sochineniia*, 2: 68; Belinsky, 3: 288.

109. Oreglia, p. 84; Belinsky, passim; Lazhechnikov, *Ledianoi dom*, p. 40.

110. Sumarokov, *Polnoe sobranie sochinenii*, 5: 339–40; Nikolev, "Oda 2," in *Mnimaia poeziia*, p. 143; Lazhechnikov, *Ledianoi dom*, pp. 12, 256; Khmel'nitsky, *Russkii Faust*, pp. 86–87, 125, 50.

111. Lazhechnikov, *Ledianoi dom*, pp. 41, 55, 255 (mentioned twice), 302; M. Dmitriev, "Dvenadtsat' sonnykh statei," in *Epigramma i satira*, pp. 295, 302. On the fool's and Dottore's round faces see Willeford, pp. 10–11; Oreglia, p. 86.

112. Lomonosov, *Polnoe sobranie sochinenii*, 8: 829.

113. Nikolev, "Oda 1," in *Mnimaia poeziia*, p. 139; N. Polevoy, "Lomonosov," p. 257; Belinsky, 3: 268, 7: 16.

114. Pushkin, *Sochineniia v shestnadtsati tomakh*, 3: 156. M. T. Kachenovsky (Kochergovsky, in Pushkin's poem) used a peculiar orthography in his magazine; for example, the letter *izhitsa* (upsilon) figured in words of Greek origin. This reminded Kachenovsky's contemporaries of Trediakovsky's ideas on orthography. For more on Kachenovsky and his alleged similarity to Trediakovsky see Chapter 5.

115. Likhachev and Panchenko, p. 125.

116. On the mythological meaning of water see Jung, pp. 46, 49–50.

117. Batiushkov, "Rech o vliianii legkoi poezii na iazyk," in his *Sochineniia*, p. 362; Belinsky, 9: 674. See also Belinsky, 1: 42, 1: 43, 6: 600. For the analysis of Tiutchev's poem see Ospovat.

118. Lazhechnikov, "Znakomstvo moe s Pushkinym," p. 179. Lazhechnikov lists the personages and episodes in his novel that he considers characteristic for the epoch in question.

119. Berkov shrewdly pointed out this crucial difference between Lomonosov's and Trediakovsky's views (*Lomonosov*, p. 41).

120. Pekarsky, *Istoriia*, p. 142.

121. Staehlin, "Traits and Anecdotes," in Kunik, ed., 2: 403–4.

122. Lomonosov, *Polnoe sobranie sochinenii*, 10: 481–82. In the original, Lomonosov's sentence is ungrammatical, since it uses the participle *having* (*imeiuchi*) in place of a verb. *Spasskie shkoly* was another name for the Slavo-Greco-Latin Academy.

123. Lomonosov, *Polnoe sobranie sochinenii*, 10: 479.

124. On an unhappy childhood as a typical feature in the life of a hero see Nekliudov, p. 138; on late bloomers see Nekliudov, p. 137.

Chapter 4

1. Tynianov, "Arkhaisty i Pushkin" (1926), in his *Pushkin i ego sovremenniki*, pp. 23–121.

2. For an interpretation of the polemics in the context of Russian cultural issues see Lotman and Uspensky, "Spory."

3. For a comparison of the Shishkovists' and Trediakovsky's views see Altshuller, *Predtechi slavianofil'stva*, pp. 309, 310–12, 315–17; Uspensky, "The Language Program," pp. 262–73, and *Iz istorii*, chap. 3.

4. *Beseda liubitelei russkogo slova*; hereafter: Beseda. I have chosen to use the Russian word because it combines two meanings, "conversation" and "assembly," and the second meaning gives the word an archaic overtone that no English equivalent provides.

5. See Gillel'son, "Materialy," and *Molodoi Pushkin*, pp. 141–42.

6. Ilya Serman suggests that the poem was written on behalf of Krylov; see his *Konstantin Batiushkov*, p. 36. Altshuller convincingly supports this hypothesis in his essay "Krylov," pp. 171–72. This circumstance, however, is irrelevant for my argument, since regardless of the author's original intention, the poem was widely seen as an assault on the Shishkovists.

7. Batiushkov, *Sochineniia*, p. 180; hereafter in this chapter references are given in the text. In one of the manuscript copies of "The Vision" a note was appended to the words "lickerish grin": "In *A Voyage to the Isle of Love* the *lickerish grin* is explained." The author of the note

apparently was referring ironically to Trediakovsky's explanations of allegories, such as Luxury (*Roskosh'*), Respect (*Pochtenie*), and Precaution (*Predostorozhnost'*), in his translation of Tallemant's novel. The expression *bludnaia usmeshka* does not appear in the book. The closest expression is *sladkoi usmekh* (a sweet grin), used to characterize the Zephyrs (Trediakovsky, *Sochineniia*, 3: 657). The explicit eroticism of Trediakovsky's translation probably inspired the epithet in Batiushkov's parody.

8. In modern Russian the expression *osklabil vzor* is utterly absurd, since it literally means "bared one's eyes," suggesting an analogy with *osklabil zuby*, "bared one's teeth." However, in Church Slavonic *osklabliatisia* meant "to smile," and this meaning was still alive in the beginning of the nineteenth century (see *Slovar' Akademii Rossiiskoi*, 4: 400). The word *vzor*, in addition to meaning "glance, look," also meant "look, face" (see *Slovar' Akademii Rossiiskoi*, 1: 495, definition 2, and *Slovar' russkogo iazyka*, 3: 138, definition 2). The expression was therefore supposed to mean "smiled with one's face, grinned." Batiushkov apparently parodied the lines in Trediakovsky's ode "Spring Warmth": "Everyone sat near his girlfriend / Inclining to her a smiling face" (*Osklablennyi skloniv k nei zrak*; Trediakovsky, *Izbrannye proizvedeniia*, p. 358). Batiushkov employed the fact that the Church Slavonic *zrak*, "face, image, look," was gradually acquiring the meaning "eye, pupil" in the Russian language, that is, becoming a partial synonym for the word *vzor*. Thus, Batiushkov's joke included a complex play on the archaic and modern, Church Slavonic and Russian, meanings of the words. In the late 1820's, Pushkin used the same expression ironically in chapter 6, stanza 8, of his *Eugene Onegin*.

9. *Arzamas*, p. 173; hereafter in this chapter references are given in the text.

10. Altshuller, *Predtechi slavianofil'stva*, pp. 98–100.

11. Trediakovsky is named a prophet in *Arzamas* on p. 23. For the Arzamasians' mockery of Gnedich see pp. 199, 203, 215.

12. Batiushkov used the form of Zhukovsky's poem but did not ridicule it. Tynianov insisted on distinguishing between the two kinds of parody: The first kind derides a target work, whereas the second uses the work as a model but does not degrade it (Tynianov, "O parodii," in *Poetika*, pp. 290–92). The irony or satire is directed to phenomena other than the parodied work, as it is in Batiushkov's "The Bard," as well as, for that matter, in Gnedich's "Credo." As Gnedich's work did not mean that he was a bad Christian, Batiushkov's use of Zhukovsky's poem did not mean that he was not fond of his poetry. Zhukovsky's "The Bard," probably due to its popularity, was frequently parodied in this manner (see Tynianov, "O parodii," p. 291). Aleksandr Izmailov

took part in the composing of Batiushkov's "The Bard." He wrote three stanzas, of which Batiushkov included two (see Batiushkov, *Sochineniia*, pp. 586–87).

13. Literally, "the sea reaches only to our knees"; compare the saying *P'ianomu more po koleno*, "A drunkard could not care less."

14. A. F. Voeikov, "Dom sumasshedshikh," in *Poety 1790–1810-kh godov*, p. 298.

15. The quotation suggests that members of Arzamas knew Trediakovsky's line from Radishchev's *A Journey from Petersburg to Moscow* and *Memorial for a Dactylo-Trochaic Knight*, rather than directly from *Tilemakhida*: It reflects the changes introduced by Radishchev. For a discussion of these changes see Chapter 5.

16. The word *galimat'ia* was used by Batiushkov in his "The Bard" to describe the Archaists' writings. This word, however, had a double meaning for the members of Arzamas: It was also used for their own deliberately absurd literary jokes—poems, epistles to friends, and especially Arzamas records; see Iu. M. Lotman, "Poeziia 1790–1810-kh godov," in *Poety 1790–1810-kh godov*, pp. 23–26; Lotman and Uspensky, "Spory," pp. 291–92 n. 38; Krasnokutsky; Roninson.

17. Viazemsky, *Stikhotvoreniia*, p. 103. Dashkov quoted this epigram—not quite correctly—in his speech of March 16, 1817 (*Arzamas*, p. 201). *Zheltyi dom* (yellow house) is a synonym for a madhouse, after the Saint Petersburg asylum, in the Obukhov hospital, which was painted yellow and to which the Arzamasians' mockery referred.

18. Viazemsky, *Stikhotvoreniia*, pp. 88–89.

19. Faminitsyn, pp. 100, 115.

20. Viazemsky, *Stikhotvoreniia*, p. 55. Cf. "To the Portrait of an Exalted Poem," in ibid.

21. The academy in question here is the Russian Academy, founded in 1783. Shishkov became the academy's president in 1813. For more references to death in Arzamas meetings see *Arzamas*, pp. 104, 107, 123, 136, 173, 194, 217.

22. Viazemsky, *Stikhotvoreniia*, p. 69.

23. "Beseda's books" are the issues of the Beseda publication, *Readings in the Colloquium of Lovers of the Russian Word*.

24. Pushkin, *Sochineniia v shestnadtsati tomakh*, 1: 196.

25. Viazemsky, *Izbrannye stikhotvoreniia*, p. 399.

26. A fragment from Pushkin's speech at an Arzamas meeting in autumn 1817; see it in Pushkin, *Sochineniia v shestnadtsati tomakh*, 2: 463.

27. Uspensky suggests that Karamzin was exposed to Trediakovsky's linguistic ideas by Anton Barsov, a professor at Moscow Univer-

sity, who, in turn, was Trediakovsky's student in the 1750's; see his introduction to Barsov, pp. 10–15.

28. Karamzin, *Pis'ma*, p. 503.

29. Trediakovsky, *Sochineniia*, 2: xxiv, lxiii. See the analysis of the letter in Uspensky, *Iz istorii*, p. 157 n. 165.

30. [Nikolai Bakhtin], "Spisok s pis'ma M. I. k g. Izdateliu ot 28 marta 1822 goda," *Vestnik Evropy*, 13–14 (1822): 36–37.

31. Viazemsky, *Polnoe sobranie sochinenii*, 1: 90–91. "M. I." was a pen name used by Bakhtin in his essay.

32. On Viazemsky's returning Trediakovsky's works see *Ostaf'evskii arkhiv*, 2: 265. For Viazemsky's favorable opinion of the poet see his *Zapisnye knizhki*, pp. 200–201. Viazemsky quoted from Trediakovsky's "Speech to the Russian Assembly."

33. Pushkin, *Sochineniia v shestnadtsati tomakh*, 13: 6. Cf. Pushkin's letter to Viazemsky of March 27, 1816, in ibid., p. 2. For more on this subject see Tomashevsky, "Pushkin i Bualo," and "Pushkin i frantsuzskaia literatura," in his *Pushkin i Frantsiia*, pp. 106–7.

34. Pushkin, *Sochineniia v shestnadtsati tomakh*, 1: 63.

35. Lotman and Uspensky, "Spory," pp. 224–37.

36. Pushkin, *Sochineniia v shestnadtsati tomakh*, 1: 196.

37. Ibid., 2: 451.

38. Altshuller, *Predtechi slavianofil'stva*, pp. 308–27.

39. A. Palitsyn, "Poslanie k Privete," in *Poety 1790–1810-kh godov*, pp. 747 (on Lomonosov), 748 (on Trediakovsky's lack of talent and his prolificacy), 769 (on Bobrov), 760 (on Catherine the Great), 778 (on fire).

40. S. Bobrov, "Proizshestvie v tsarstve tenei," published in Lotman and Uspensky, "Spory," p. 255.

41. See Gasparov, "Prodrom, Tsets i natsional'nye formy gekzametra," p. 377, for a comparison of Trediakovsky's and Vostokov's imitations of classical hexameters.

42. Vostokov, *Opyt o russkom stikhoslozhenii*, p. 29, and his Review of *Vvedenie v nauku stikhotvorstva*, p. 305.

43. On the polemics see Burgi, chap. 5; Egunov, pp. 174–88; Etkind, pp. 19–27.

44. Kapnist, "Pis'mo g. Kapnista g. Uvarovu ob ekzametre," in *Chtenie*, 17: 20–21. The passage contains a parody of Trediakovsky's style: inversions, complex adjectives, and Slavonicisms. For a modern edition of this letter and Kapnist's second letter to Uvarov see Kapnist, 2: 186–95, 196–224. For Uvarov's essay see *Chtenie*, 13: 56–69. For Uvarov's answer to the first of Kapnist's letters see *Chtenie*, 17: 47–66.

45. Gnedich, p. 318.

46. See Altshuller, *Predtechi slavianofil'stva*, pp. 310–12.

47. Shishkov, *Rassuzhdenie o starom i novom sloge rossiiskogo iazyka*, in his *Sobranie sochinenii*, 2: 121, 317n, 319–21n. On Lomonosov see *Rassuzhdenie o starom i novom sloge rossiiskogo iazyka*, 2: 296n. Cf. also 2: 3, 122, and "Rassuzhdenie o krasnorechii Sviashchennogo Pisaniia," in ibid., 4: 39, 61.

48. Derzhavin, 6: 443n.

49. Derzhavin's attention to this poem even sanctioned subsequent praise for it by other literary figures. Thus, its merits were acknowledged by Belinsky, who said that Trediakovsky "let it out by chance" (*obmolvilsia*; Belinsky, 5: 468), and by Shevyrev, Review of *Polnaia russkaia khrestomatiia*, 5: 243. Nikolai Iazvitsky highly praised Trediakovsky's poem in his book *Introduction to the Science of Poetry*, but since both works appeared in 1811, it is not clear whether Derzhavin influenced Iazvitsky or whether Iazvitsky's book drew Derzhavin's attention to this psalm.

50. Derzhavin, *Rassuzhdenie o liricheskoi poezii ili ob ode voobshche*, in his *Sochineniia*, 7: 516–17.

51. For this letter see Derzhavin, 7: 612.

52. Derzhavin, *Rassuzhdenie o liricheskoi poezii ili ob ode voobshche*, in his *Sochineniia*, 7: 596, 608.

53. Altshuller, *Predtechi slavianofil'stva*, pp. 314–16; Uspensky, "The Language Program," pp. 272–73; Uspensky, *Iz istorii*, pp. 196–98.

54. For Evgenii's remark on *Tilemakhida* see his letter to Dmitrii Khvostov of April 30, 1820, in Grot, ed., p. 188; cf. his letter to Khvostov of Dec. 10, 1808, in Zabelin, ed., p. 249, in which Evgenii admits that he enjoys reading *Tilemakhida*. For Evgenii's remark on Trediakovsky's merits as a linguist see his letter to Khvostov of May 7, 1822, in Grot, ed., p. 195.

55. Grot, ed., p. 140; Evgenii, 1: 221 and 221n.

56. Evgenii, a letter to Khvostov of July 24, 1813, in Grot, ed., pp. 149–50.

57. On Galinkovsky see Iu. M. Lotman, "Pisatel'"; Altshuller, *Predtechi slavianofil'stva*, pp. 312–13. On Galinkovsky's disagreements with the Archaists see Lotman, pp. 238–41.

58. Galinkovsky, "O slavneishikh istorikakh," *Korifei*, 1: 68–69.

59. Galinkovsky, "Pis'mo k izdateliu akademicheskogo zhurnala *Sochineniia i perevody*, pisannoe 26 dekabria 1804 goda," in *Chtenie*, 10: 119–26; for the quotation see p. 121.

60. I quote from Vostokov, Review of *Vvedenie v nauku stikhotvorstva*, pp. 301–2, and Altshuller, *Predtechi slavianofil'stva*, p. 316.

61. Merzliakov, pp. 68, 78, 77–78, 77.

62. Anastasevich, "O 'Tilemakhide,'" in *Poety 1790–1810-kh godov,* p. 566.

63. Merzliakov, p. 84; Galinkovsky, "Pis'mo k izdateliam," in *Chtenie,* 10: 121; Iazvitsky, quoted in Vostokov, Review of *Vvedenie v nauku stikhotvorstva,* p. 303.

64. Merzliakov, pp. 76–77.

65. Anastasevich, "S udovol'stviem chitaia . . . ," in *Severnyi vestnik* 2: 163–78.

66. I refer here not to the actual content of the Karamzinists' views but to the literary stance assumed by Karamzin and his followers. Karamzin was in fact also a professional (one of the first who, as a matter of principle, made literature a source of income) and certainly took literature seriously, but his literary program, at least until 1803, the year when he abandoned literature and turned to history, called for a literature of "pleasant trifles" (compare in this respect Karamzin's collection *My Trifles,* 1794, expanded edition 1797, and Dmitriev's, *And My Trifles,* 1795).

On Merzliakov's anti-Karamzinism see Iu. M. Lotman, *A. S. Kaisarov,* pp. 40–43. On Galinkovsky's position see Iu. M. Lotman, "Pisatel'," pp. 234–38. On Anastasevich's literary views see Iu. M. Lotman, "K kharakteristike mirovozzreniia Anastasevicha," pp. 26–27; Briskman, pp. 20–27.

Chapter 5

1. Radishchev, 2: 217, 221; hereafter in this chapter references to this collection are given in the text.

2. Trediakovsky, *Sochineniia,* 2: 576. For the interpretations of the changes introduced by Radishchev see A. S. Orlov, p. 35.

3. On the political ideas in *Tilemakhida* and their possible role in provoking Catherine's hostile remarks about Trediakovsky see A. S. Orlov, pp. 22–34. Orlov (pp. 33–34) suggests that Catherine could have been especially annoyed by the passage in book 8 that depicts a regicide in circumstances similar to those of the coup of 1762 (Trediakovsky, *Sochineniia,* 2: 223–28) and that she might have taken personally. W. E. Brown (pp. 65–66) agrees with Orlov. In a commentary on *A Journey from Petersburg to Moscow,* Ia. L. Barskov also stresses the importance of the political ideas in *Tilemakhida* for Radishchev's choice of the epigraph to his book (Radishchev, 1: 479). In the commentaries to *Memorial for a Dactylo-Trochaic Knight* L. V. Pumpiansky argues that Radishchev did not approve of the "moral and political tendency" of the books by Fénelon and Trediakovsky (2: 395). In fact, in *Memorial* Radishchev criti-

cizes the "invention [*vymysel*] of this book," "unnecessary and inappropriate [features] of the heroic poem," and "weak or tedious passages" (2: 202)—i.e., the plot and composition of the work, rather than its political ideas.

4. For Radishchev's views on form and content see Radishchev, 1: 354, 2: 219–20.

5. About the acceptability of polyrhythmic compositions in musical genres see Gasparov, *Ocherk istorii russkogo stikha*, pp. 72–74.

6. For Semennikov's opinion see his *Radishchev*, p. 304 n. 2.

7. On Radishchev's studies of Klopstock see Radishchev, 2: 397–98.

8. Trediakovsky, *Sochineniia*, 2: 50.

9. Lomonosov, *Polnoe sobranie sochinenii*, 7: 588.

10. See the Introduction on the meaning of the word in Russian. Since no translation (*custodian, tutor*, or *uncle*) fully conveys the meaning of the original, I will hereafter use the Russian term.

11. On *Bova* in the Russian tradition see Kuz'mina, *Rytsarskii roman na Rusi*; Serman, "Bova i russkaia literatura." On Radishchev's *Bova* see L. M. Lotman; Kuz'mina, "Skazka o Bove v obrabotke Radishcheva"; M. P. Alekseev.

12. Radishchev's interest in Bobrov's poetic principles (nontraditional versification, a heavy and impeded style, grandiose imagery, etc.) constitutes a separate problem that lies outside the boundaries of the present work; on this subject see Altshuller, "Poeticheskaia traditsiia Radishcheva," pp. 114–24. Radishchev also mentioned Voltaire among his models (1: 29–30, 36). The reference is significant in the light of Radishchev's new approach to the comic, which I shall discuss later in this chapter.

13. Trediakovsky, *Izbrannye proizvedeniia*, pp. 383–84. On Trediakovsky's views on folk poetry see Shtokmar, pp. 17–19; Gasparov, "Russkii sillabicheskii trinadtsatislozhnik," pp. 62–63. On trochaic imitations of folk poetry at the turn of the century see Gasparov, *Ocherk istorii russkogo stikha*, pp. 71–72, 127.

14. M. P. Alekseev, pp. 163–74.

15. Derzhavin, 1: 139. For Radishchev's opinions of Derzhavin and his "Felitsa" see *Biografiia A. N. Radishcheva*, pp. 70, 76.

16. Trediakovsky, *Sochineniia*, 2: 46.

17. Karamzin, *Sochineniia*, 1: 584; Evgenii, 1: 221 n; Bantysh-Kamensky, 5: 148; Belinsky, 1: 47; Bobrov, "Proizshestvie v tsarstve tenei," in Lotman and Uspensky, "Spory," p. 280; Lazhechnikov, *Ledianoi dom*, pp. 73, 75.

18. Bakhtin, pp. 11–12.

19. Trediakovsky, *Sochineniia*, 2: 557.

20. Pushkin, *Sochineniia v shestnadtsati tomakh*, 1: 63; hereafter in this chapter references to this collection are given in the text.

21. For studies of Pushkin's views on Trediakovsky see Blagoy, "Pushkin," pp. 106, 124–25; Ariel'-Zalesskaia, pp. 340–41; Petrunina, pp. 153–54; Altshuller, *Predtechi slavianofil'stva*, pp. 326–27.

22. Trediakovsky, *Izbrannye proizvedeniia*, pp. 383–84.

23. Uspensky, "The Language Program," p. 256, and *Iz istorii*, p. 134.

24. Vinogradov, p. 36.

25. For Uspensky's suggestion see his "The Language Program," pp. 284–85 n. 49, and *Iz istorii*, p. 134 n. 116.

26. Trediakovsky, *Izbrannye proizvedeniia*, p. 95.

27. On the question of Pushkin's professionalism see Eikhenbaum, pp. 62–70; André Meynieux, esp. pp. 298–302 and chap. 4; Todd, pp. 107–8.

28. Tsiavlovsky, pp. 359–64.

29. Originally in French. See this letter in Pushkin, *Sochineniia v shestnadtsati tomakh*, 13: 176–77.

30. *Arzamas*, p. 131.

31. In Pushkin's text Kachenovsky's name was replaced by asterisks.

32. I quote from Kozmin, p. 117. Kozmin gives a summary of materials from the magazine, rather than a precise quotation. Between 1825 and 1838 *Son of the Fatherland* was edited by Nikolai Grech and Faddei Bulgarin.

33. See Trediakovsky, *Sochineniia*, 3: 78–79, 89–93.

34. Gogol, pp. 160–61. Iota was the tenth letter of the old Russian alphabet and was used in Old Russia for the number ten, hence its name, decimal *i*, as distinct from и, the eighth letter.

35. Mann, "Fakul'tety Nadezhdina," in Nadezhdin, p. 30.

36. Batiushkov, *Sochineniia*, p. 180; *Arzamas*, p. 199.

37. In 1828–31 Nadezhdin was trying to establish his academic career. He defended his doctoral dissertation, "De Poesi Romantica," in 1830 and was appointed a professor in the Department of the Theory of Fine Arts and Archeology in Moscow University in December 1831. Nadezhdin's scholarly aspirations emphasized for Pushkin his similarity to Trediakovsky.

38. The variant of the last sentence is ". . . are expressed by the language of *Messenger of Europe* and *Athenaeum*." The magazine *Athenaeum* (1828–30) published a severe criticism of the fourth and fifth chapters of Pushkin's *Eugene Onegin* in 1828 (no. 4).

39. See Ariel'-Zalesskaia, pp. 340–43.

40. Trediakovsky, *Sochineniia*, 2: 3.

41. It remains unclear to what extent Pushkin realized that the theory of versification summarized in the second version of Trediakovsky's *A New and Brief Method for Composing Russian Verse* was the result of a collective effort on the part of Trediakovsky, Lomonosov, and Sumarokov.

42. In Pushkin, *Sochineniia v desiati tomakh*, 7: 494, the word *pochtennoe* (respectable) is given as *postoiannoe* (constant). Being unable to investigate the editorial reasons for the change, I would like to point out that the word *pochtennyi* is a recurrent epithet for Trediakovsky in Pushkin's vocabulary in the 1830's.

43. Trediakovsky, *Izbrannye proizvedeniia*, p. 427.

44. Pushkin, *Sochineniia v desiati tomakh*, 7: 195. This version differs slightly from the text in *Sochineniia v shestnadtsati tomakh*, 11: 226–27.

45. For analyses of Pushkin's interest in history see Tomashevsky, *Pushkin*, 2: 154–99; Toibin, *Pushkin. Tvorchestvo 1830-kh godov*; Toibin, *Pushkin i filosofsko-istoricheskaia mysl'*.

46. Toibin, *Pushkin. Tvorchestvo 1830-kh godov*, p. 38.

47. Feinberg, pp. 36–47.

48. Pushkin, *Sochineniia v desiati tomakh*, 7: 370.

49. Petrunina, p. 159.

Chapter 6

1. Pushkin, *Sochineniia v shestnadtsati tomakh*, 14: 5.

2. Barsukov, 5: 493–94.

3. Barsukov, 8: 142.

4. Barsukov, 11: 484.

5. *Moskvitianin*, 1, part 2 (1845): 43–46.

6. Vvedensky, pp. 54–55. For Pekarsky's comment on Perevlessky's edition see Pekarsky, *Istoriia*, p. 226.

7. See Shevyrev; Afanas'ev.

8. Lazhechnikov, "Znakomstvo moe s Pushkinym," p. 180. Lazhechnikov attacks an essay by S. M. Solov'ev, "Pisateli russkoi istorii XVIII veka (V. K. Trediakovsky)."

9. Belinsky, 10: 8.

10. Belinsky, 3: 15; cf. 7: 16.

11. Herzen, p. 118; cf. Barsukov, 7: 462; Belinsky, 2: 145n, 9: 147, 181.

12. Shevyrev, "Otvety," p. 123.

13. Belinsky, 10: 357–58.

14. Savel'ev-Rostislavich, ed., pp. clxxix–clxxxii.

15. Belinsky, 9: 189.

16. For Chernyshevsky's opinions of Trediakovsky see his *Polnoe sobranie sochinenii*, 1: 597, 7: 326. Dobroliubov mentions Trediakovsky in his *Sobranie sochinenii*, 1: 41, 269, 354, 488; 2: 253–54, 338, 346; 4: 299.

17. For these examples see Shishkov, *Sobranie sochinenii*, p. 121; Batiushkov, a letter to Gnedich of Sept. 6, 1809, in his *Nechto*, p. 210; Viazemsky, a letter to A. I. Turgenev of Dec. 29, 1835, in *Ostaf'evskii arkhiv*, 3: 281; Pogodin, quoted in Barsukov, 10: 570; Perevlessky, Introduction to Trediakovsky, *Izbrannye sochineniia*, p. xi; Vol'sky, p. 111.

18. Zoshchenko, *Izbrannoe*, 2: 195.

19. Ibid., pp. 195–96. For Zoshchenko's reaction to the idea of social order see his "O sebe."

20. Shklovsky, p. 27.

21. On the Futurists' and the Imagists' interest in Trediakovsky see Markov, pp. 99, 388 n. 11, 415 n. 106; T. L. Nikol'skaia, "V. K. Trediakovsky i russkii avangard," in *M. V. Lomonosov i russkaia kul'tura*, p. 66.

22. Hereafter references to Mariengof's play are given in the text. On Trediakovsky's image in the play see Nikol'skaia, "V. K. Trediakovsky i russkii avangard," in *M. V. Lomonosov i russkaia kul'tura*, pp. 67–68.

23. Lomonosov, *Polnoe sobranie sochinenii*, 8: 222. The unusual spellings (*sedit, laktem*) are Lomonosov's.

24. Nikol'skaia, "V. K. Trediakovsky i russkii avangard," in *M. V. Lomonosov i russkaia kul'tura*, p. 67.

25. Shefner, p. 61. Hereafter references are given in the text. For a rather shallow discussion of Shefner's poems about Trediakovsky see E. N. Kononko, "V. K. Trediakovsky v tvorchestve Vadima Shefnera," in *Venok Trediakovskomu*, pp. 100–102.

26. Panova, p. 327. Hereafter references are given in the text.

27. Nagibin, pp. 51, 55, 106, 110, 127. Hereafter references are given in the text.

Conclusion

1. Cassirer, *The Myth of the State*, p. 280.

2. Patai, p. 77.

3. Quoted in Barringer.

4. See the anecdotes in Sazhin, pp. 58–59.

5. Bulgakov, pp. 136–37.

6. Erofeev, p. 94.

7. On the dual nature of Pushkin's image in Russian culture see Siniavsky, pp. 8–10. The author discusses obscene anecdotes about Pushkin and expressions with his name on pp. 8 and 9.

Works Cited

Adskaia pochta. 1769.

Afanas'ev, A. N. "Obraztsy literaturnoi polemiki proshlogo stoletiia." *Bibliograficheskie zapiski,* 15 (1859): 449–76, 17 (1859): 513–28.

Alekseev, A. A. "Epicheskii stil' 'Tilemakhidy.'" In *Iazyk russkikh pisatelei XVIII veka.* Leningrad, 1981, pp. 68–95.

———. "Evoliutsiia iazykovoi teorii i iazykovaia praktika Trediakovskogo." In *Literaturnyi iazyk XVIII veka. Problemy stilistiki.* Leningrad, 1982, pp. 86–128.

Alekseev, M. P. "K istolkovaniiu poemy A. N. Radishcheva 'Bova.'" In *Radishchev. Stat'i i materialy.* [Leningrad], 1950, pp. 158–213.

Altshuller, M. G. "Krylov v literaturnykh ob"edineniiakh 1800–1810-kh godov." In *Ivan Andreevich Krylov. Problemy tvorchestva.* Leningrad, 1975, pp. 154–95.

———. "Poeticheskaia traditsiia Radishcheva v literaturnoi zhizni nachala XIX veka." *XVIII vek,* 12 (1977): 113–36.

———. *Predtechi slavianofil'stva v russkoi literature. (Obshchestvo "Beseda liubitelei russkogo slova").* Ann Arbor, 1984.

Ariel'-Zalesskaia, G. G. "K izucheniiu istorii biblioteki A. S. Pushkina." *Pushkin. Issledovaniia i materialy,* 2 (1958): 334–53.

Arzamas i arzamasskie protokoly. Ed. M. S. Borovkova-Maikova. Leningrad, 1933.

Bakhtin, Mikhail. *Rabelais and His World.* Trans. Helene Iswolsky. Cambridge, Mass., 1968.

Bantysh-Kamensky, D. N. *Slovar' dostopamiatnykh liudei Russkoi zemli, soderzhashchii v sebe zhizn' i deianiia znamenitykh polkovodtsev, mini-*

strov i muzhei gosudarstvennykh, velikikh ierarkhov pravoslavnoi tserkvi, otlichnykh literatorov i uchenykh, izvestnykh po uchastiiu v sobytiiakh otechestvennoi istorii. 5 vols. Moscow, 1836.

Barenbaum, I. E. "Izdanie frantsuzskoi perevodnoi knigi v Rossii vo vtoroi chetverti XVIII v." In *Kniga v Rossii do serediny XIX veka*, ed. A. A. Sidorov and S. P. Luppov. Leningrad, 1978, pp. 87–95.

Barringer, Felicity. "Soviet Vigils Held Widely for Pushkin." *New York Times*, Feb. 15, 1987, sec. 1, p. 7.

Barsov, A. A. *Rossiiskaia grammatika.* Ed. B. A. Uspensky. Moscow, 1981.

Barsukov, N. P. *Zhizn' i trudy M. P. Pogodina.* 22 vols. Saint Petersburg, 1888–1910.

Batiushkov, K. N. *Sochineniia.* Ed. D. D. Blagoy. Moscow-Leningrad, 1934; rpt. The Hague, 1967.

——. *Nechto o poete i poezii.* Moscow, 1985.

Begak, B., et al. *Russkaia literaturnaia parodiia.* Moscow-Leningrad, 1930.

Belinsky, V. G. *Polnoe sobranie sochinenii.* 13 vols. Moscow, 1953–56.

Berdiaev, Nikolai. *Russkaia ideia. Osnovnye problemy russkoi mysli XIX veka i nachala XX veka.* Paris, 1971.

Berkov, P. N. *Istoriia russkoi komedii XVIII veka.* Leningrad, 1977.

——. "Iz istorii russkoi poezii pervoi treti XVIII veka (K probleme tonicheskogo stikha)." *XVIII vek*, 1 (1935): 61–81.

——. *Lomonosov i literaturnaia polemika ego vremeni.* Moscow-Leningrad, 1936.

——. "Neispol'zovannye materialy dlia istorii russkoi literatury XVIII veka." *XVIII vek*, 1 (1935): 327–76.

——. "Petr Suvorov—zabytyi poet 1730-kh godov. (K istorii shkoly V. K. Trediakovskogo)." In *Problemy sovremennoi filologii. Sbornik statei k semidesiatiletiiu akademika V. V. Vinogradova*, ed. M. V. Khrapchenko et al. Moscow, 1965, pp. 327–34.

——. "Problema literaturnogo napravleniia Lomonosova." *XVIII vek*, 5 (1962): 5–32.

——. "U istokov dvorianskoi literatury XVIII veka (Poet Mikhail Sobakin)." *Literaturnoe nasledstvo*, 9–10 (1933): 421–32.

——, ed. "'Rassuzhdenie o rossiiskom stikhotvorstve.' (Neizvestnaia stat'ia M. M. Kheraskova)." *Literaturnoe nasledstvo*, 9–10 (1933): 287–94.

Bestuzhev, A. A. [A. Marlinsky, pseud.]. *Sochineniia v dvukh tomakh.* Vol. 2. Moscow, 1958.

Biografiia A. N. Radishcheva, napisannaia ego synov'iami. Moscow-Leningrad, 1959.

Blagoy, D. D. *Istoriia russkoi literatury XVIII veka.* 3rd ed. Moscow, 1955.

——. "Pushkin i russkaia literatura XVIII veka." In *Pushkin—rodona-*

chal'nik novoi russkoi literatury, ed. D. D. Blagoy and V. Ia. Kirpotin. Moscow-Leningrad, 1941, pp. 101–66.

Bochkarev, V. A. *Russkaia istoricheskaia dramaturgiia XVII–XVIII vv.* Moscow, 1988.

Bolotov, A. T. *Zhizn' i prikliucheniia, opisannye im samim dlia svoikh potomkov.* Supplement to *Russkaia starina*, vol. 1. Saint Petersburg, 1870.

Bondi, Sergei. "Trediakovsky, Lomonosov, Sumarokov." In Trediakovsky, *Stikhotvoreniia*, pp. 7–113.

Briskman, M. A. *V. G. Anastasevich.* Moscow, 1958.

Brown, W. E. *A History of Eighteenth Century Russian Literature.* Ann Arbor, 1980.

Bucsela, John. "The Birth of Russian Syllabo-Tonic Versification." *The Slavonic and East European Review*, 9 (1965): 281–94.

Bulgakov, Mikhail. *Master i Margarita.* In his *Izbrannoe.* Moscow, 1980, pp. 9–318. Translated into English as *The Master and Margarita* by Michael Glenny. London, 1985.

Bulich, N. N. *Sumarokov i sovremennaia emu kritika.* Saint Petersburg, 1854.

Burgi, Richard. *A History of Russian Hexameter.* Hamden, Conn., 1954.

Campbell, Joseph. *The Hero with a Thousand Faces.* Bollingen Series, no. 17. Princeton, N.J., 1972.

Cassirer, Ernst. *Das Mythische Denken.* Vol. 2 of *Die Philosophie der symbolischen Formen.* Berlin, 1925.

———. *The Myth of the State.* New Haven, Conn., 1946.

Chernov, Igor'. *Iz lektsii po teoreticheskomu literaturovedeniiu. Barokko. Literatura. Literaturovedenie. (Spetsial'nyi kurs).* Tartu, 1976.

Chernyshevsky, N. G. *Polnoe sobranie sochinenii v piatnadtsati tomakh.* 15 vols. Moscow, 1939–53.

Chistov, K. V. *Russkie narodnye sotsial'no-utopicheskie legendy. XVII–XIX vv.* Moscow, 1967.

Chtenie v Besede liubitelei russkogo slova. 19 vols. 1811–16.

Čiževskij, Dmitrij. *History of Russian Literature: From the Eleventh Century to the End of the Baroque.* The Hague, 1960.

Deriushin, A. A. *V. K. Trediakovsky—perevodchik: stanovlenie klassitsistskogo perevoda v Rossii.* Saratov, 1985.

Derzhavin, G. R. *Sochineniia.* 9 vols. Saint Petersburg, 1864–83.

Dmitriev, M. A. *Melochi iz zapasa moei pamiati.* 2nd ed. Moscow, 1869.

Dobroliubov, N. A. *Sobranie sochinenii v deviati tomakh.* 9 vols. Moscow-Leningrad, 1961–64.

Drage, C. L. "The Introduction of Russian Syllabo-Tonic Prosody." *The Slavonic and East European Review*, 54 (1976): 481–503.

Egunov, A. N. *Gomer v russkikh perevodakh XVIII–XIX vekov.* Moscow-Leningrad, 1964.

Eikhenbaum, Boris. *Moi vremennik. Slovesnost'. Nauka. Kritika. Smes'.* [Leningrad], 1929.
Epigramma i satira. Iz istorii literaturnoi bor'by XIXgo veka. Comp. V. Orlov. Vol. 1, *1800–40.* Moscow-Leningrad, 1931.
Erofeev, Venedikt. *Moskva-Petushki.* 2nd ed. Paris, 1981.
Etkind, Efim. *Russkie poety-perevodchiki ot Trediakovskogo do Pushkina.* Leningrad, 1973.
Evgenii, Metropolitan [E. A. Bolkhovitinov]. *Slovar' russkikh svetskikh pisatelei, sootechestvennikov i chuzhestrantsev, pisavshikh v Rossii.* 2 vols. Moscow, 1845.
Faminitsyn, A. S. *Skomorokhi na Rusi.* Saint Petersburg, 1889.
Feinberg, I. L. *Chitaia tetradi Pushkina.* Moscow, 1976.
Fish, Stanley. *Is There a Text in This Class? The Authority of Interpretive Communities.* Cambridge, Mass., 1980.
Florovsky, A. V. "Latinskie shkoly v Rossii v epokhu Petra Pervogo." *XVIII vek,* 5 (1962): 316–35.
Fonvizin, D. I. *Sobranie sochinenii v dvukh tomakh.* Vol. 2. Moscow-Leningrad, 1959.
Garrard, J. G. "The Emergence of Modern Russian Literature and Thought." In *The Eighteenth Century in Russia,* ed. J. G. Garrard. Oxford, 1973, pp. 1–21.
Gasparov, M. L. *Ocherk istorii russkogo stikha. Metrika. Ritmika. Rifma. Strofika.* Moscow, 1984.
———. "Prodrom, Tsets i natsional'nye formy gekzametra." In *Antichnost' i Vizantiia.* Moscow, 1975, pp. 362–85.
———. "Russkii sillabicheskii trinadtsatislozhnik." In *Metryka słowiańska,* ed. Zdzisława Kopeczyńska. Wrocław, 1971, pp. 39–63.
Gillel'son, M. I. "Materialy po istorii arzamasskogo bratstva." *Pushkin. Issledovaniia i materialy,* 4 (1962): 287–326.
———. *Molodoi Pushkin i arzamasskoe bratstvo.* Leningrad, 1974.
Ginzburg, L. Ia. *O lirike.* 2nd ed. Leningrad, 1974.
Gnedich, N. I. *Stikhotvoreniia.* Leningrad, 1956.
Gogol, N. V. *Polnoe sobranie sochinenii.* Vol. 8, *Stat'i.* N.p. 1952.
Grech, N. I. *Zapiski o moei zhizni.* Saint Petersburg, 1886.
Grot, Ia. K., ed. "Perepiska Evgeniia s Khvostovym." *Sbornik otdeleniia russkogo iazyka i slovesnosti,* 5, no. 1 (1868): 97–216.
Gukovsky, G. A. "K voprosu o russkom klassitsizme. (Sostiazaniia i perevody)." *Poetika,* 4 (1928): 126–48.
———. "O russkom klassitsizme." *Poetika,* 5 (1929): 21–65.
———. *Russkaia poeziia XVIII veka.* Leningrad, 1927.
———. "Trediakovsky kak teoretik literatury." *XVIII vek,* 6 (1964): 43–72.
Heim, M. H. [M. H. Berman]. "Trediakovskij, Sumarokov, and Lomo-

nosov as Translators of West European Literatures." Ph.D. diss.,
Harvard University, 1971.

Herzen, A. I. *Sobranie sochinenii v tridtsati tomakh.* Vol. 2. Moscow, 1954.

Hillman, James. *The Dream and the Underworld.* New York, 1979.

Ivanov, I. I. *Istoriia russkoi kritiki.* Part 1. Saint Petersburg, 1898.

"Iz dela o Trediakovskom. Dlia biografii Trediakovskogo." *Moskvitianin,* 15 (1853): 27–48.

Jones, W. G. "A Trojan Horse Within the Walls of Classicism: Russian
Classicism and the National Specific." In *Russian Literature in the Age
of Catherine the Great,* ed. A. G. Cross. Oxford, 1976, pp. 95–120.

Jung, C. G. "The Psychology of the Child Archetype." In *Essays on a
Science of Mythology: The Myths of the Divine Child and the Divine
Maiden,* by C. G. Jung and Carl Kerényi. Rev. ed. New York, 1963,
pp. 70–100.

Kantemir, Antiokh. *Sobranie stikhotvorenii.* Leningrad, 1956.

Kapnist, V. V. *Sobranie sochinenii v dvukh tomakh.* Moscow-Leningrad,
1960.

Karamzin, N. M. *Pis'ma russkogo puteshestvennika.* Leningrad, 1984.

———. *Polnoe sobranie stikhotvorenii.* Moscow-Leningrad, 1966.

———. *Sochineniia.* Ed. A. Smirdin. 3 vols. Saint Petersburg, 1848.

Karlinsky, Simon. *Russian Drama from Its Beginnings to the Age of Pushkin.*
Berkeley, Calif., 1985.

———. "Tallemant and the Beginning of the Novel in Russia." *Comparative Literature,* 15, no. 3 (1963): 226–33.

Khmel'nitsky, N. I. *Russkii Faust ili Briusov Kabinet.* In his *Sochineniia,*
ed. A. Smirdin, vol. 2. Saint Petersburg, 1849, pp. 4–137.

Kholshevnikov, V. E. "Zametki o russkom stikhe XVIII veka. 1. Pochemu Trediakovsky predpochital iambu khorei." *XVIII vek,* 13
(1981): 229–34.

Kibal'nik, S. A. "Ob odnom frantsuzskom istochnike esteticheskikh
vzgliadov Trediakovskogo." *XVIII vek,* 13 (1981): 219–28.

Kireevsky, I. V. *Izbrannye stat'i.* Moscow, 1984.

Knutson, Harold C. *Molière: An Archetypal Approach.* Toronto, 1976.

Korifei, ili Kliuch literatury. 1802.

Kozmin, N. K. *Nikolai Ivanovich Nadezhdin. Zhizn' i nauchno-literaturnaia
deiatel'nost', 1804–1836.* Zapiski istoriko-filologicheskogo fakul'teta
Imperatorskogo Sankt Peterburgskogo universiteta, no. 111. Saint
Petersburg, 1912.

Krasnokutsky, V. S. "O svoeobrazii arzamasskogo 'narechiia.'" In *Zamysel, trud, voploshchenie.* Moscow, 1977, pp. 20–41.

Kruglyi, A. "O 'Rimskoi istorii' Rollenia v perevode Trediakovskogo."
Zhurnal ministerstva narodnogo prosveshcheniia, 8 (1876): 226–33.

Kunik, A. A., ed. *Sbornik materialov dlia istorii Imperatorskoi Akademii Nauk v XVIII veke.* 2 vols. Saint Petersburg, 1865.

Kupreianova, E. N. "K voprosu o klassitsisme." *XVIII vek,* 4 (1959): 5–44.

Kuz'mina, V. D. *Rytsarskii roman na Rusi. Bova, Petr Zlatykh Kluchei.* Moscow, 1964.

———. "Skazka o Bove v obrabotke Radishcheva." In *Problemy realizma v russkoi literature XVIII veka.* Moscow-Leningrad, 1940, pp. 257–91.

Lazhechnikov, I. I. *Ledianoi dom.* In his *Sochineniia v dvukh tomakh,* vol. 2. Moscow, 1963, pp. 7–309.

———. "Znakomstvo moe s Pushkinym." In *Pushkin v vospominaniiakh sovremennikov. V dvukh tomakh,* vol. 1. Moscow, 1974, pp. 167–82.

Lebedev, P. S., comp. "Novye materialy dlia biografii Sumarokova." *Bibliograficheskie zapiski,* 15 (1858): 451–60.

Lévi-Strauss, Claude. *Structural Anthropology.* Vol. 2. Trans. Monique Layton. New York, 1976.

Likhachev, D. S. "Byla li epokha petrovskikh reform pereryvom v razvitii russkoi kul'tury?" In *Les cultures slaves à l'epoque de la formation et du developpment des nations slaves. XVIII–XIXes ss. Les matériaux de la conférence internationale de l'UNESCO.* Moscow, 1978, pp. 170–74.

Likhachev, D. S., and A. M. Panchenko. *"Smekhovoi mir" Drevnei Rusi.* Leningrad, 1976.

Livanova, T. N. *Russkaia muzykal'naia kul'tura XVII veka v ee sviaziakh s literaturoi, teatrom i bytom. Issledovaniia i materialy.* Vol. 1. Moscow, 1952.

Lomonosov, M. V. *Sochineniia.* 8 vols. Saint Petersburg-Leningrad, 1891–1948.

———. *Polnoe sobranie sochinenii.* 10 vols. Moscow-Leningrad, 1950–59.

Lomonosov i russkaia literatura. Ed. A. S. Kurilov. Moscow, 1987.

Lotman, Iu. M. *Andrei Sergeevich Kaisarov i literaturno-obshchestvennaia bor'ba ego vremeni.* Uchenye zapiski Tartuskogo universiteta, no. 63. Tartu, 1958.

———. "'Ezda v ostrov liubvi' Trediakovskogo i funktsiia perevodnoi literatury v russkoi kul'ture pervoi pol. XVIII v." In *Problemy izucheniia kul'turnogo naslediia.* Moscow, 1985, pp. 222–30.

———. "K kharakteristike mirovozzreniia Anastasevicha." *Uchenye zapiski Tartuskogo universiteta,* 56 (1958): 17–27.

———. "Pisatel', kritik i perevodchik Ia. Galinkovsky." *XVIII vek,* 4 (1959): 230–56.

Lotman, Iu. M., and B. A. Uspensky. "Mif-imia-kul'tura." *Trudy po znakovym sistemam,* 6 (1973): 282–303. Translated as "Myth—Name—Culture." In *Soviet Semiotics: An Anthology,* ed. Daniel P. Lucid. Baltimore, 1977, pp. 147–70.

————. "Otzvuki kontseptsii 'Moskva—tretii Rim' v ideologii Petra Pervogo. (K probleme srednevekovoi traditsii v kul'ture barokko)." In *Khudozhestvennyi iazyk srednevekov'ia*. Moscow, 1982, pp. 236–49.

————. "Rol' dual'nykh modelei v dinamike russkoi kul'tury." *Uchenye zapiski Tartuskogo universiteta*, 414 (1977): 3–36. Translated as "Binary Models in the Dynamics of Russian Culture (to the End of the Eighteenth Century)." In *The Semiotics of Russian Cultural History*, ed. Alexander D. Nakhimovsky and Alice Stone Nakhimovsky. Ithaca, N.Y., 1985, pp. 30–66.

————. "Spory o iazyke v nachale XIX veka kak fakt russkoi kul'tury." *Uchenye zapiski Tartuskogo universiteta*, 358 (1975): 168–322.

Lotman, L. M. "'Bova' Radishcheva i traditsiia zhanra poemy-skazki." *Uchenye zapiski Leningradskogo universiteta*, 33, no. 3 (1939): 110–40.

Maikov, L. N. "Molodost' Trediakovskogo do ego poezdki za granitsu (1703–1726)." *Zhurnal Ministerstva narodnogo prosveshcheniia*, 312 (July 1897): sec. 2, 1–22.

Mariengof, Anatolii. *Zagovor durakov. Tragediia*. N.p. 1922.

Markiewicz, Henryk. "Evaluation in the Study of Literature." In *Poetyka—Poetics—Poetika*, ed. Donald Davie et al. Warsaw, [1961], pp. 795–810.

Markov, Vladimir. *Russian Futurism: A History*. Berkeley, Calif., 1968.

Martynov, I. F. "Trediakovsky i ego chitateli-sovremenniki." In *Venok Trediakovskomu*, pp. 80–88.

Materialy dlia istorii Imperatorskoi Akademii Nauk. 2 (1886).

Meletinsky, E. M. *Poetika mifa*. Moscow, 1976.

Merzliakov, A. F. "Rassuzhdenie o Rossiiskoi slovesnosti v nyneshnem ee sostoianii." *Trudy obshchestva liubitelei rossiiskoi slovesnosti*, 1 (1812): 53–110.

Meynieux, André. *Pouchkine, homme de lettres et la littérature professionnelle en Russie*. Paris, 1966.

Mirsky, D. S. *A History of Russian Literature: From Its Beginnings to 1900*. New York, 1958.

Mnimaia poeziia. Materialy po istorii poeticheskoi parodii XVIII i XIX vv. Ed. Iu. N. Tynianov. Moscow-Leningrad, 1931.

Morozov, A. A. "Lomonosov i barokko." *Russkaia literatura*, 2 (1965): 70–96.

Murav'ev, M. N. *Stikhotvoreniia*. Leningrad, 1967.

M. V. Lomonosov i russkaia kul'tura. Tezisy dokladov konferentsii, posviashchennoi 275-letiiu so dnia rozhdeniia M. V. Lomonosova. (28–29 noiabria 1986 g.). Tartu, 1986.

M. V. Lomonosov v vospominaniiakh i kharakteristikakh sovremennikov. Comp. G. E. Pavlova. Moscow-Leningrad, 1962.

Nabokov, Vladimir. "Notes on Prosody." In his *"Eugene Onegin": A Novel by Aleksandr Pushkin*, vol. 3. Bollingen Series, no. 72. New York, 1964, pp. 448–540.

Nadezhdin, N. I. *Literaturnaia kritika. Estetika.* Ed. Iu. Mann. Moscow, 1972.

Nagibin, Iurii. *Sobranie sochinenii v chetyrekh tomakh.* Vol. 4. Moscow, 1981.

Nekliudov, S. Iu. "'Geroicheskoe detstvo' v eposakh Vostoka i Zapada." In *Istoriko-filologicheskie issledovaniia. Sbornik statei imeni akademika N. I. Konrada.* Moscow, 1974, pp. 129–40.

Nekrasov, N. A. *Polnoe sobranie sochinenii i pisem.* 12 vols. Moscow, 1948–53.

Norman, Dorothy. *The Hero: Myth, Image, Symbol.* New York, 1969.

Novikov, N. I. *Opyt istoricheskogo slovaria o rossiiskikh pisateliakh.* In his *Izbrannye sochineniia*, ed. G. P. Makogonenko. Moscow-Leningrad, 1951, pp. 277–370.

Oreglia, Giacomo. *Commedia dell'arte.* Trans. Lovett F. Edwards. New York, 1968.

Orlov, A. S. "'Tilemakhida' V. K. Trediakovskogo." *XVIII vek*, 1 (1935): 5–60.

Orlov, O. V. "Vasilii Trediakovsky." In *Istoriia russkoi literatury XVII–XVIII vekov*, by A. S. Eleonskaia et al. Moscow, 1969, pp. 273–86.

Ospovat, A. L. "Tiutchev o Lomonosove. (K stikhotvoreniiu 'On, umiraia, somnevalsia...')." *Uchenye zapiski Tartuskogo universiteta*, 781 (1987): 127–31.

Ostaf'evskii arkhiv kniazei Viazemskikh. 6 vols. Saint Petersburg, 1899–1913.

Ostolopov, Nikolai. *Slovar' drevnei i novoi poezii.* 3 vols. Saint Petersburg, 1821; rpt. Munich, 1971.

Panchenko, A. M. *Russkaia stikhotvornaia kul'tura XVII veka.* Leningrad, 1973.

Panova, Vera. *Sobranie sochinenii v piati tomakh.* Vol. 4. Leningrad, 1970.

Patai, Rafael. *Myth and Modern Man.* Englewood Cliffs, N.J., 1972.

Pekarsky, P. P. *Istoriia Imperatorskoi Akademii Nauk v Peterburge.* Vol. 2. Saint Petersburg, 1873.

———. *Redaktor, sotrudniki i tsenzura v russkom zhurnale 1755–1764 godov.* Saint Petersburg, 1867.

Pelton, Robert D. *The Trickster in West Africa: A Study of Mythic Irony and Sacred Delight.* Berkeley, Calif., 1980.

Peretts, V. N. *Istoriko-literaturnye materialy i issledovaniia.* Vol. 3. Saint Petersburg, 1902.

————, ed. *Ital'ianskie komedii i intermedii predstavlennye pri dvore Impera-tritsy Anny Ioannovny v 1733–1735 gg. Teksty.* Petrograd, 1917.

Petrunina, N. N. "Dva zamysla Pushkina dlia 'Sovremennika.'" *Russkaia literatura*, 4 (1966): 153–60.

Pis'ma russkikh pisatelei XVIII veka. Leningrad, 1980.

Pliukhanova, M. B. "'Istoricheskoe' i 'mifologicheskoe' v rannikh biografiiakh Petra Pervogo." In *Vtorichnye modeliruiushchie sistemy.* Tartu, 1979, pp. 82–88.

————. "Izobrazhenie istoricheskogo litsa v literature perekhodnoi epokhi. (Natsional'nye korni istoricheskoi biografii XVIII veka)." Avtoreferat dissertatsii na soiskanie stepeni kandidata filologicheskikh nauk. Tartu, 1982.

————. "O nekotorykh chertakh lichnostnogo samosoznaniia v Rossii XVII v." In *Khudozhestvennyi iazyk srednevekov'ia.* Moscow, 1982, pp. 184–200.

————. "O nekotorykh chertakh narodnoi eskhatologii v Rossii XVII–XVIII vekov." *Uchenye zapiski Tartuskogo universiteta*, 645 (1985): pp. 54–70.

Poety 1790–1810-kh godov. Ed. M. G. Altshuller and Iu. M. Lotman. Leningrad, 1971.

Poety XVIII veka. Ed. G. P. Makogonenko and I. Z. Serman. 2 vols. Leningrad, 1972.

Pogodin, M. P. *Nikolai Mikhailovich Karamzin, po ego sochineniiam, pis'mam i otzyvam sovremennikov. Materialy dlia biografii.* 2 vols. Moscow, 1866.

Polevoy, Ksenofont. *Mikhail Vasil'evich Lomonosov.* 2 vols. Saint Petersburg, 1887.

Polevoy, Nikolai. "Mikhailo Vasil'evich Lomonosov." In his *Ocherki russkoi literatury.* Vol. 1. Saint Petersburg, 1839, pp. 230–80.

————. *Dramaticheskie sochineniia i perevody.* Part 2. Saint Petersburg, 1842.

Poroshin, Semen. *Zapiski.* 2nd ed. Saint Petersburg, 1881.

Pozdneev, A. V. "Proizvedeniia V. Trediakovskogo v rukopisnykh pesennikakh." In *Problemy istorii literatury*, ed. M. N. Zubkova. Moscow, 1964, pp. 87–100.

Priiatnoe i poleznoe preprovozhdenie vremeni. 1794–98.

Prokopovich, Feofan. *Sochineniia.* Ed. I. P. Eremin. Moscow-Leningrad, 1961.

Pushkin, A. S. *Polnoe sobranie sochinenii v desiati tomakh.* Ed. B. V. Tomashevsky. 4th ed. 10 vols. Leningrad, 1977–79.

————. *Polnoe sobranie sochinenii v shestnadtsati tomakh.* 16 vols. Leningrad, 1937–49.

Radishchev, A. N. *Polnoe sobranie sochinenii.* 3 vols. Moscow-Leningrad, 1938–52.

Raeff, Marc, ed. *Peter the Great Changes Russia.* 2nd ed. Problems in European Civilization, ed. John Ratté. Lexington, Mass., 1972.

Reyfman, Irina [Vladimirova, I. D., pseud.]. "Evoliutsiia literaturnykh vzgliadov V. K. Trediakovskogo." *Uchenye zapiski Tartuskogo universiteta,* 604 (1982): 32–47.

Rezanov, V. I. "Iz razyskanii o komediiakh Sumarokova." In *Pamiati P. N. Sakulina.* Moscow, 1931, pp. 233–38.

Riasanovsky, Nicholas V. *The Image of Peter the Great in Russian History and Thought.* New York, 1985.

Rice, J. L. "V. K. Trediakovsky and the Russian Poetic Genres. 1730–1760: Studies in the History of Eighteenth Century Russian Literature." Ph.D. diss., University of Chicago, 1965.

Richards, I. A. *Practical Criticism: A Study of Literary Judgement.* London, 1924.

Ricketts, M. L. "The North American Indian Trickster." *History of Religion,* 6, no. 2 (1965): 327–50.

Roginsky, A. B. "'Ledianoi dom': legenda i istoriia." In *Ledianoi dom,* by I. I. Lazhechnikov. Moscow, 1988, pp. 306–14.

Roninson, O. A. "O 'grammatike' arzamasskoi 'galimat'i.'" *Uchenye zapiski Tartuskogo universiteta,* 822 (1988): 4–17.

Rosenberg, Karen. "Between Ancients and Moderns: V. K. Trediakovskij on the Theory of Language and Literature." Ph.D. diss., Yale University, 1980.

Rulin, P. I. "Pervaia komediia Sumarokova." *Izvestiia po russkomu iazyku i slovesnosti,* 2, no. 1 (1929): 237–69.

Russkaia stikhotvornaia parodiia. (XVIII–nachalo XX v.). Ed. A. A. Morozov. Leningrad, 1960.

Samarenko, V. P. "V. K. Trediakovsky v Astrakhani. (Novye materialy k biografii V. K. Trediakovskogo)." *XVIII vek,* 5 (1962): 358–63.

Savel'ev-Rostislavich, N. V., ed. *Slavianskii sbornik.* Vol. 1. Saint Petersburg, 1845.

Sazhin, V. N. "Literaturnye i fol'klornye traditsii v tvorchestve D. I. Kharmsa." In *Literaturnyi protsess i razvitie russkoi kul'tury XVIII–XIX vv.* Tallinn, 1985, pp. 57–61.

Segers, Rien T. *The Evaluation of Literary Texts: An Experimental Investigation into the Rationalization of Value Judgements with Reference to Semiotics and Esthetics of Reception.* Studies in Semiotics, no. 22, ed. Thomas A. Sebeok. Lisse, Neth., 1978.

Semennikov, V. P. *Radishchev. Ocherki i issledovaniia.* Moscow-Petrograd, 1923.

Serman, Ilya. "Bova i russkaia literatura." *Slavica Hierosolymitana*, 7 (1985): 163–70.

———. "Iz literaturnoi polemiki 1753 goda." *Russkaia literatura*, 1 (1964): 99–104.

———. *Konstantin Batiushkov*. New York, 1974.

———. *Mikhail Lomonosov: Life and Poetry*. Trans. Stephany Hoffman. Jerusalem, 1988.

———. *Poeticheskii stil' Lomonosova*. Moscow-Leningrad, 1966.

———. *Russkii klassitsizm. Poeziia. Drama. Satira*. Leningrad, 1973.

———. "Trediakovsky i prosvetitel'stvo (1730-e gody)." *XVIII vek*, 5 (1962): 205–22.

Severnyi vestnik. 1804.

Shefner, Vadim. *Vtoraia pamiat'. Stikhi*. Leningrad, 1981.

Shevyrev, S. P. "Dokumenty iz portfelia Millera. Chetyre epigrammaticheskie stikhotvoreniia Lomonosova." *Moskvitianin*, 1, no. 1 (1854): 1–4.

———. "Otvety." *Moskvitianin*, 2 (1848): 105–30.

———. Review of *Polnaia russkaia khrestomatiia*. *Moskvitianin*, 5 (1843): 218–48; 6 (1843): 501–33.

Shishkin, A. B. "Poeticheskoe sostiazanie Trediakovskogo, Lomonosova i Sumarokova." *XVIII vek*, 14 (1983): 232–46.

———. "V. K. Trediakovsky i traditsii barokko v russkoi literature XVIII veka." In *Barokko v slavianskikh kul'turakh*. Moscow, 1982, pp. 239–54.

Shishkov, A. S. *Sobranie sochinenii i perevodov*. Vols. 2, 4. Saint Petersburg, 1824, 1825.

Shklovsky, Viktor. *Literatura i kinematograf*. Berlin, 1923.

Shlonsky, Tuvia. "Literary Parody: Remarks on Its Method and Functions." *Proceedings of the Fourth Congress of the International Comparative Literature Association*, 2 (1966): 797–801.

Shtokmar, M. P. *Issledovaniia v oblasti russkogo stikhoslozheniia*. Moscow, 1952.

Silbajoris, Frank Rimvydas. *Russian Versification: The Theories of Trediakovskij, Lomonosov, and Kantemir*. New York, 1968.

Siniavsky, Andrei [Abram Terts, pseud.]. *Progulki s Pushkinym*. London, 1975.

Skabichevsky, A. M. *Ocherki istorii russkoi tsenzury (1700–1863)*. Saint Petersburg, 1892.

Slovar' Akademii Rossiiskoi. 2nd ed. 7 vols. Saint Petersburg, 1806–22.

Slovar' literaturovedcheskikh terminov. Ed. L. I. Timofeev and S. V. Turaev. Moscow, 1974.

Slovar' russkogo iazyka XVIII veka. 5 vols. to date. Leningrad, 1984–.

Smith, Barbara Herrnstein. *Contingencies of Value: Alternative Perspectives for Critical Theory*. Cambridge, Mass., 1988.

Smith, G. S. "The Reform of Russian Versification: What More Is There to Say?" *Newsletter of the Study Group on Eighteenth-Century Russia*, 5 (1977): 39–44.

Solov'ev, S. M. *Istoriia Rossii s drevneishikh vremen*. Vol. 10. Moscow, 1963.

———. "Pisateli russkoi istorii XVIII veka (V. K. Trediakovsky)." *Arkhiv istoriko-iuridicheskikh svedenii, otnosiashchikhsia do Rossii*, 2, part 1 (1855): 46–49.

Speransky, M. N. *Rukopisnye sborniki XVIII veka. Materialy dlia istorii russkoi literatury XVIII veka*. Moscow, 1963.

Sumarokov, A. P. *Izbrannye proizvedeniia*. Leningrad, 1957.

———. *Polnoe sobranie sochinenii v stikhakh i proze*. 2nd ed. 10 vols. Moscow, 1781–82.

———. *Stikhotvoreniia*. Ed. A. S. Orlov. N.p. 1935.

Timofeev, L. I. *Ocherki istorii i teorii russkogo stikha*. Moscow, 1958.

———. "Vasilii Kirillovich Trediakovsky (1703–1769)." In Trediakovsky, *Izbrannye proizvedeniia*, pp. 5–52.

Todd, William Mills. *Fiction and Society in the Age of Pushkin: Ideology, Institutions, and Narrative*. Cambridge, Mass., 1986.

Toibin, I. M. *Pushkin i filosofsko-istoricheskaia mysl' v Rossii na rubezhe 1820 i 1830 godov*. Voronezh, 1980.

———. *Pushkin. Tvorchestvo 1830-kh godov i voprosy istorizma*. Voronezh, 1976.

Tomashevsky, B. V. *Pushkin*. 2 vols. Moscow–Leningrad, 1956–61.

———. "Pushkin i Bualo." In *Pushkin v mirovoi literature*. Leningrad, 1926, pp. 13–63.

———. *Pushkin i Frantsiia*. Leningrad, 1960.

Tompkins, Jane. *Sensational Designs: The Cultural Work of American Fiction, 1790–1860*. New York, 1985.

Trediakovsky, V. K. *Izbrannye proizvedeniia*. Moscow-Leningrad, 1963.

———. *Izbrannye sochineniia*. Ed. M. P. Perevlessky. Moscow, 1849.

———. "Pis'mo, v kotorom soderzhitsia rassuzhdenie o stikhotvorenii, ponyne v svet izdannom ot avtora dvukh od, dvukh tragedii, i dvukh epistol, pisannoe ot priiatelia k priiateliu." In A. A. Kunik, ed., 2: 435–500.

———. *Sochineniia*. Ed. A. Smirdin. 3 vols. Saint Petersburg, 1849.

———. *Sochineniia i perevody kak stikhami tak i prozoiu*. 2 vols. Saint Petersburg, 1752.

———. *Stikhotvoreniia*. Ed. A. S. Orlov. N.p. 1935.

———, trans. *Argenida, povest' geroicheskaia*. By John Barclay. 2 vols. Saint Petersburg, 1751.

Truten'. 1769.

Tsiavlovsky, M. A. *Stat'i o Pushkine*. Moscow, 1962.

Tynianov, Iu. N. *Poetika. Istoriia literatury. Kino*. Moscow, 1977.

———. *Pushkin i ego sovremenniki*. Moscow, 1968.

Uspensky, B. A. "Foneticheskaia struktura odnogo stikhotvoreniia Lomonosova." In *Semiotyka i struktura tekstu. Studia poświecone VII Międzynarodowemu kongresowi slawistów, Warszawa 1973*. Wrocław, 1973, pp. 103–29.

———. *Iz istorii russkogo literaturnogo iazyka XVIII–nachala XIX veka. Iazykovaia programma Karamzina i ee istoricheskie korni*. [Moscow], 1985.

———. "K istorii odnoi epigrammy Trediakovskogo (epizod iazykovoi polemiki serediny XVIII veka). *Russian Linguistics*, 8, no. 2 (1985): 75–127.

———. "The Language Program of N. M. Karamzin and Its Historical Antecedents." In *Aspects of the Slavic Language Question*, vol. 2, *East Slavic*, ed. Riccardo Picchio and Harvey Goldblatt. Yale Russian and East European Publications, no. 4-b. New Haven, Conn., 1984, pp. 235–96.

———. *Pervaia russkaia grammatika na rodnom iazyke. Dolomonosovskii period otechestvennoi rusistiki*. Moscow, 1975.

———. "Vopros o siriiskom iazyke v slavianskoi pismennosti: pochemu d'iavol mozhet govorit' po-siriiski?" In *Vtorichnye modeliruiushchie sistemy*. Tartu, 1979, pp. 79–82.

Van Roosbroeck, G. L. "Chapelain décoiffé, a Battle of Parodies." *PMLA*, 39 (1924): 872–96.

Venok Trediakovskomu. Volgograd, 1976.

Vestnik Evropy. 1802–30.

Viazemsky, P. A. *Izbrannye stikhotvoreniia*. Moscow-Leningrad, 1935; rpt. The Hague, 1967.

———. *Polnoe sobranie sochinenii*. Ed. S. D. Sheremet'ev. 12 vols. Saint Petersburg, 1878–96.

———. *Stikhotvoreniia*. Leningrad, 1986.

———. *Zapisnye knizhki. (1813–1848)*. Moscow, 1963.

Vinogradov, V. V. *Iazyk Pushkina. Pushkin i istoriia russkogo literaturnogo iazyka*. Moscow-Leningrad, 1935.

Vinokur, G. O. "Orfograficheskaia teoriia Trediakovskogo." In his *Izbrannye raboty po russkomu iazyku*. Moscow, 1959, pp. 468–89.

Vodička, F. "The History of the Echo of Literary Works." In *A Prague School Reader on Esthetics, Literary Structure, and Style*, ed. and trans. Paul Garvin. Washington, D.C., 1964, pp. 71–81.

Vol'sky, N. V. [N. Valentinov, pseud.]. *Vstrechi s Leninym*. New York, 1953.

Vostokov, A. Kh. *Opyt o russkom stikhoslozhenii*. 2nd ed. Saint Petersburg, 1817.

―――. Review of *Vvedenie v nauku stikhotvorstva*, by N. I. Iazvitsky. *Sankt-Peterburgskii vestnik*, 2, no. 5 (1812): 229–39; no. 6 (1812): 293–306.

Vozniknovenie russkoi nauki o literature. Moscow, 1975.

Vsiakaia vsiachina. 1769–70.

Vvedensky, Irinarkh. "Trediakovsky." In *Russkaia poeziia*, ed. S. A. Vengerov, vol. 1. Saint Petersburg, 1897, pp. 50–55.

Wellek, René. *Concepts of Criticism*. Ed. Stephen G. Nichols, Jr. New Haven, Conn., 1963.

Wellek, René, and Austin Warren. *Theory of Literature*. 3rd ed. San Diego, Calif., 1977.

Willeford, William. *The Fool and His Scepter: A Study in Clowns and Jesters and Their Audience*. [Kingsport], 1969.

Willey, W. Z. "Jean Chapelain, the Oracle of Aristotle." *Studies in Philology*, 37, no. 1 (1940): 51–63.

Zabelin, I. E., ed. "Pis'ma i zapiski ot raznykh lits k gr. D. I. Khvostovu." *Bibliograficheskie zapiski*, 8 (1859): 238–51.

Zhikharev, S. P. *Zapiski sovremennika*. Moscow-Leningrad, 1955.

Zhirmunsky, V. M. "Legenda o prizvanii pevtsa." In his *Izbrannye trudy. Sravnitel'noe literaturovedenie. Vostok i Zapad*. Leningrad, 1979, pp. 397–407.

Zoshchenko, Mikhail. *Izbrannoe v dvukh tomakh*. 2 vols. Leningrad, 1978.

―――. "O sebe, o kritikakh i o svoei rabote." In *Mikhail Zoshchenko. Stat'i i materialy*. Leningrad, 1928, pp. 8–11.

Index

In this index an "f" after a number indicates a separate reference on the next page, and an "ff" indicates separate references on the next two pages. A continuous discussion over two or more pages is indicated by a span of page numbers, e.g., "57–59." *Passim* is used for a cluster of references in close but not consecutive sequence.

Library of Congress Cataloging-in-Publication Data

Reyfman, Irina.
  Vasilii Trediakovsky : the fool of the new Russian litera-
ture / Irina Reyfman.
    p.   cm.
  Includes bibliographical references.
  ISBN 0-8047-1824-5 (alk. paper)
    1. Trediakovskiĭ, V. K. (Vasiliĭ Kirillovich), 1703–1769—
Criticism and interpretation.   2. Russian literature—18th
century—History and criticism.   I. Title.
PG3319.T7Z85   1990
891.712—dc20   90-9682
                                                              CIP

⊗ This book is printed on acid-free paper